Voor Jessica en Mikis

ACKNOWLEDGEMENTS

Debts, both personal and professional, have accrued over the many years it has taken me to complete this thesis. The warmth and loyalty I have received from many quarters have buoyed me up and kept me going throughout. It would be inappropriate to single out any one person for particular mention — except in one case. I regret more than I can express that Els Verhoeff is not alive to see the work finished that her humanity, her hospitality and her excellent cooking made more bearable than it would otherwise have been. As for the others, family and friends, I consider it, as George Herbert might say, a "reasonable sacrifice" to leave them out and in doing so embrace them all.

I am deeply grateful for the professional guidance and unfailing support of Prof. Dr. A. Verhoeff (Dept. of English, Utrecht). He has taught me much at all times and no less this last year which has been such a sad and difficult one for him.

My thanks are due to Prof. E.S. de Jongh (Dept. of Art History, Utrecht) who gave generously of his time and knowledge and willingly allowed me the use of his library. His suggestions made even the final stages of the writing of this book exciting and rewarding.

The same holds true for Dr. F.G.M. Broeyer (Dept. of Theology, Utrecht) whose help was given in a most liberal and friendly spirit in areas I was unfamiliar with.

Drs. P.J. Verhoeff (Dept. of English, Utrecht) gave useful advice on medieval and philological matters. Drs. A. van Akkeren (Barlaeus Gymnasium, Amsterdam) improved my translations from Latin.

Prof. Dr. R.H. Green (University of Florida) read and commented on an early draft of my book. Prof. Dr. C.A. Patrides (University of Michigan) kindly sent me a new copy of his edition of Herbert's poetry after having noticed the state of the old one. Prof. Dr. A. Cohen (Dept. of Phonetics, Utrecht) said the right words at the right time.

I am very grateful to my colleague Drs. M. Peeck-O'Toole who was willing to take time off from her own research to read the whole manuscript and correct it in more places than I like to admit. My colleague Dr. J.W. Bertens is to be thanked for being willing to share a room at the English Department with me for a longer period than the average marriage lasts.

J.A.M. Renkers not only typed the manuscript but deciphered and incorporated without complaint my numerous last minute additions and corrections. Drs. F.M. van Oosterbosch accepted the arduous task of correcting the proofs which he did cheerfully and with great accuracy.

The Faculty of Letters of the University of Utrecht gave me the opportunity to be relieved of teaching duties by awarding me a 'Hugen-holtz'-year in 1977-78. Without this these acknowledgements would never have been written at all.

The librarians and staffs of many institutions have been helpful. I mention especially those of the British Library in London, the Bodleian Library in Oxford, the University Library in Amsterdam and the Art History Departments in Amsterdam and Utrecht who have given me the kind of support that is essential for a book of this kind. I am also grateful to the photographic departments of the British Library, the Bodleian Library and the University Library in Amsterdam for their assistance in producing the photographs.

Finally, I wish to thank my students without whom academic life would have been pointless for me.

University of Utrecht,
December 1983

CONTENTS

LIST OF ILLUSTRATIONS

LIST OF ABBREVIATIONS

B	MS. Tanner 307 in the Bodleian Library
W	MS. Jones B 62 in Dr. Williams' Library
Works	*The Works of George Herbert*, ed. F.E. Hutchinson (Oxford: Oxford Univ. Press, 1941)
BJA	*British Journal of Aesthetics*
CL	*Comparative Literature*
EA	*Etudes Anglaises*
E.E.T.S.	Early English Text Society
ELH	*ELH: A Journal of English Literary History*
ELN	*English Language Notes*
ELR	*English Literary Renaissance*
Expl	*Explicator*
HLQ	*Huntington Library Quarterly*
JAAC	*Journal of Aesthetics and Art Criticism*
JWCI	*Journal of the Warburg and Courtauld Institutes*
JWI	*Journal of the Warburg Institute*
MED	*Middle English Dictionary*
MLR	*Modern Language Review*
MP	*Modern Philology*
Neophil	*Neophilologus*
N&Q	*Notes and Queries*
OED	*Oxford English Dictionary*
PMLA	*PMLA: Publications of the Modern Language Association of America*
RenP	*Renaissance Papers*
RES	*Review of English Studies*

A NOTE ON EDITIONS USED

- All references to Herbert's writings are to Hutchinson's edition of 1941 (*Works*) unless specified otherwise.

- All references to the Book of Common Prayer are to the 1604 version as printed in William Keeling, *Liturgiae Brittanicae* (1842).

- All references to the Bible are to the King James Version (1611; modernized spelling), but earlier influential versions, in particular the Great Bible of 1539-40 and the Geneva Bible of 1560, have been consulted for textual variants (see Weigle, *The New Testament Octapla* (n.d.)).

CHAPTER ONE

INTRODUCTION

1. Preamble.

Originally this book was to be a study of Herbert's pattern poems only. As the investigation progressed the need for a wider perspective was increasingly felt. In the following paragraphs the various preliminary phases of the investigation will be touched upon. The purpose of providing this concise history of a piece of research is to make clear how and why the original plan was abandoned or rather fundamentally revised. In this way the rationale of the structure of the investigation in its present form will evolve more or less naturally.

Herbert wrote two pattern poems: "The Altar," "Easter-wings" and possibly a third, "The Church-floore." In pattern poems the typographical shape of the words on the page resembles or evokes a concrete object or a geometrical form. In successful pattern poems the typography adds significantly to the meaning of the poem as a whole. The assumption underlying the original aim of the investigation was that a general survey of the history of the pattern poem in and outside England and a classification of the various types of pattern poems could provide the framework within which Herbert's use of the form is to be understood.

The various strands of the tradition lead as far away as Greece, Alexandria, Persia and India and as far back as 300 B.C.; they yield exotic, enticing examples and occasionally interesting poetry.[1] For the

---

1. Apart from the thesis by Margaret Church (see n.2) several books by 19th century scholars contain a multitude of pattern poems. See, for example, *Curiosités Littéraires*, Bibliothèque de Poche par une société de Gens de Lettres et d'érudits (Paris, 1845); W.R. Alger, *The Poetry of the East* (Boston, 1856); I.D'Israeli, *Curiosities of Literature* (London: Routledge, 1867); Charles C. Bombaugh, *Oddities and Curiosities of Words and Literature: Gleanings for the Curious* (1890), rpt. ed. Martin Gardner (New York: Dover, 1961); William S. Walsh, *Handy-Book of Literary Curiosities* (London, 1894); Carolyn Wells, *A Whimsey Anthology* (New York: Scribner, 1906). In more recent times the titles of books and articles containing pattern poems demonstrate a more serious attitude towards the subject on the part of their authors: Charles Boultenhouse, "Poems in the Shapes of Things," *Art News Annual* (1959), 65-83; Berjouhi Bowler, *The Word as Image* (London: Studio Vista, n.d. but probably 1970); Massin, *Letter and Image* (London: Studio Vista, 1970); Milton Klonsky, ed., *Speaking Pictures* (New York: Harmony Books, 1975).

European development of the tradition Margaret Church's unpublished thesis "The Pattern Poem" (1944) is an invaluable aid.[2] Church's study contains hundreds of examples of pattern poems and poems resembling pattern poems.[3] The most important source for Herbert is the *Greek Anthology*, which was available to him in various 16th and 17th century editions. The *Greek Anthology* contains several pattern poems among which poems in the shape of an altar and wings.[4] Pattern poetry was a persistent, though minor, tradition in Roman times and throughout the Middle Ages, reaching its peak during the Renaissance.[5] In English literature the greatest number of pattern poems was written in the late sixteenth and early seventeenth centuries. Altar-shaped poems were common and the very first English pattern poem was wing-shaped.[6]

After virtually dying out towards the end of the seventeenth century the tradition came fully alive again in the work and ideas of Mallarmé and Apollinaire at the end of the nineteenth century and in the experimental poetry of movements such as Dadaism and Futurism at the beginning of our own century. Finally, the tradition produced a remarkably widespread and internationally oriented offshoot in the concrete poetry movement of the fifties and sixties. A study of the exact nature of the relation between concrete poetry and pattern poetry is still wanting.[7]

2. Margaret Church, "The Pattern Poem," Diss. Radcliffe College 1944. Dick Higgins' booklet on the subject, although totally inadequate from the theoretical, scholarly, and critical point of view, is mentioned here for completeness' sake: *George Herbert's Pattern Poems: In their Tradition* (West Glover: Unpublished Editions, 1977).
3. It is unfortunate that Church does not define the pattern poem. She includes many poems which do have a varying number of syllables in each line but are not really pattern poems because their shapes do not bear any relation to their content; in some cases it is difficult even to recognize an object or a geometrical form in the typographical shape of the poems.
4. The Greek pattern poems are available in the bilingual Loeb edition of *The Greek Anthology*, ed. & trans. W.R. Paton, V (London: Heinemann, 1918), 124-135 and, in the same series, in *The Greek Bucolic Poets*, ed. J.M. Edmonds (London: Heinemann, 1912), pp. 485-511.
5. Publius Porfirius Optatianus (4th c.) was the main link between the Alexandrians of the Greek Anthology and the Middle Ages. He imitated the pipes and altars of the Greek Anthology and added, among other things, a poem in the shape of an organ. Some of the medieval practitioners were Alcuin, Aldhelm, Boniface, and — the most extravagant of them all — Hrabanus Maurus.
6. See Margaret Church, "The First English Pattern Poems," *PMLA*, 61 (1946), 636-50.
7. A large collection of concrete poems can be found in Emmett Williams, ed., *An Anthology of Concrete Poetry* (New York: Something Else Press, 1967); see also the exhibition catalogue *Concrete Poetry* (Amsterdam: Stedelijk Museum, 1970) with useful introductions by Paul de Vree, Reinhard Döhl and Bob Cobbing. John Hollander, himself the writer of a book of pattern poems (*Types of Shape* (New York:

3

Nous ne pouvons rien trouver sur la terre
Qui soit si bon, ni si beau que le verre.
Du tendre amour berceau charmant,
C'est toi, champêtre fougère,
C'est toi qui sers à faire
L'heureux instrument
Où souvent pétille,
Mousse et brille
Le jus qui rend
Gai, riant,
Content.
Quelle douceur
Il porte au cœur!
Tôt,
Tôt,
Tôt,
Qu'on m'en donne,
Qu'on l'entonne;
Tôt,
Tôt,
Tôt,
Qu'on m'en donne,
Vite et comme il faut:
L'on y voit sur ces flots chéris
Nager l'allégresse et les ris.

A CIRCULAR GHAZAL BY SHAHÍN GIRAY
Hammer-Purgstall, *Geschichte der Chane der Krim*

4

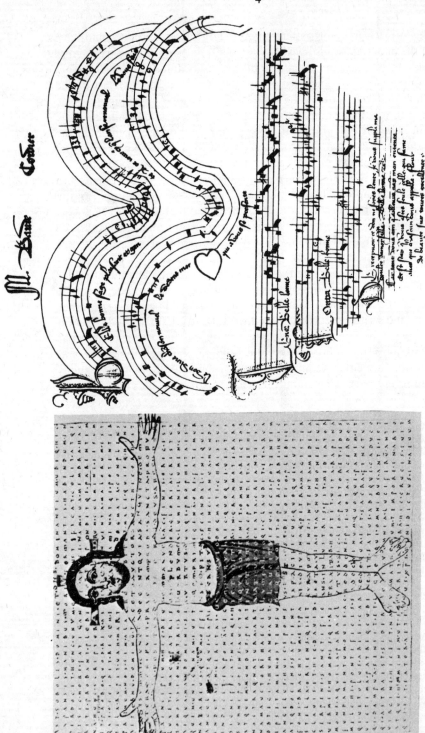

3

4

A historical survey of pattern poetry shows that Herbert could have found the material for his own pattern poems both in the classical sources available to him and in the pattern poetry of his immediate predecessors and contemporaries. Such a survey also enables one to classify the collected material, something that was not done by Church.[8] One criterion for distinguishing among different types of pattern poems is the relation between typographical pattern and the horizontal line. On the one hand there are pattern poems in which the poet sticks to the usual horizontal movement of the line. In this type of pattern poetry there is usually a close relation between the syllabic patterns of the poems and their visual shapes. The visual shape arises from variations in the number of syllables per line. On the other hand there are pattern poems in which the succession of words on the page is not made subject to the ordering principle of the line, but to other, not necessarily literary principles (see figs. 1 and 2).

Another way of classifying the material is by looking at content rather than shape. Two main lines of development of the pattern poems can be distinguished, the one profane and aiming at diversion, the other religious and written to instruct (see figs. 1-4).[9] And, finally, a distinction can be made between patterns that imitate or suggest an object that functions as a metaphor within the total meaning of the poem and patterns that are either geometrical or 'floating' and bear a more tenuous relation to the poem's meaning.[10] Herbert's pattern poems belong to the

---

Atheneum, 1969), gave a succinct account of pattern poetry in its relation with concrete poetry in *The New York Review of Books*, December 8, 1977. Unlike Hollander — and most other makers of concrete poetry — I believe the two traditions have common roots. A useful collection of essays on the visual aspect of literature is Richard Kostelanetz, ed., *Visual Literature Criticism* (Carbondale: Southern Illinois Univ. Press, 1979). For further references see Chapter Two, 3.

8. In Appendix B of her dissertation Church lists all the pattern poems, defining their shapes, such as "heart," "wings," "egg," "lozenge," "pyramid," and so on.

9. I owe the Persian ghazal to the article by A.L. Korn, "Puttenham and the Oriental Pattern-Poem," *CL*, 6 (1954), 289-303; Panard's wineglass is from *Curiosités Littéraires*, p. 22; the *carminum quadratum* by Hraban Maur from *De Laudibus Sanctae Crucis*, facs. ed. (Graz: Akademische Druck- u. Verlagsanstalt, 1972), fol. 6ᵛ; the heart-shaped "Belle bonne" in which the bars of the musical score together with the text create the pattern is from a manuscript in the Musée Condé, 1047, at Chantilly. See Donald J. Grout, *A History of Western Music*, 3rd ed. (New York: W.W. Norton, 1980), pp. 134-139; Baude Cordier's "Belle bonne" is reproduced on p. 135.

10. Advocates of concrete poetry would claim that there is a further category in which the word loses its semantic function and becomes a combination of graphic signs: "the conscious perception of the material and its structure, the material as the sum total of all the signs with which we make poetry" (Eugen Gomringer, qu. in *Concrete Poetry*, p. 9). Cf. Dick Higgins, "The Strategy of Visual Poetry: Three Aspects," in *Visual Literature Criticism*, pp. 41-50.

6

category in which the matter is religious, the purpose serious and the relation between pattern and poem that of metaphor. A specific account of the place Herbert occupies in the pattern poem tradition will be provided in Chapter Three.

More is necessary than a study of the formal-historical framework of pattern poetry, however. Simmias of Rhodes (3rd c. B.C.), who was influenced by the school of Alexandria and whose pattern poems are part of the *Greek Anthology,* wrote pattern poetry within a different cultural and philosophical context and with a different purpose from Herbert's, although the patterns of both poets share certain external characteristics. Simmias' poems stem from the pastoral tradition and the epigram. Herbert's are related not only to the Greek source but to the contemporary Renaissance tradition of the emblem, which combines word and image in a different though comparable way. That emblems exerted a pronounced influence on Herbert's work has been argued convincingly by Rosemary Freeman in *English Emblem Books* (1948).[11] Emblems and pattern poems are but two of the expressions of the symbolic mode of thinking which pervaded the cultural and philosophical climate in the Renaissance. It surfaced in many aspects of life, art and letters: in masques and pageants, tapestries and embroidery, painting and sculpture, emblem books and literature. Voluminous tomes on heraldry, seals and devices, books on the symbolism of fireworks and, most important of all, veritable encyclopaedias on the intriguing subject of hieroglyphics appeared and were avidly perused.[12] All these pheno-

11. Rosemary Freeman, *English Emblem Books* (London: Chatto & Windus, 1948), pp. 148-172.
11. Rosemary Freeman, *English Emblem Books* (London: Chatto & Windus, 1948), pp. 148-172.
12. Henry Estienne, *Exposition et explication des devises, emblèmes et figures énigmatiques du feu construit devant l'hostel de ville, par MM. le prévost des marchands et eschevins de Paris, sur l'heureuse naissance et retour du Roy* (Paris, 1649). The *Hieroglyphica* of Horapollo, a Greek manuscript, discovered in 1419 and printed in Venice in 1505, went through numerous editions in the course of the 16th century. The work led to all kinds of speculations about the symbolical and allegorical significance of the Egyptian hieroglyphs. The rise of what Panofsky called "Egyptomania and emblematism" (E. Panofsky, *Meaning in the Visual Arts* (New York, 1955; rpt. Harmondsworth: Penguin, 1970), p. 195)) originated in Horapollo's treatise and led to a profusion of emblem books in the sixteenth century, the first of which was Andrea Alciati's *Emblemata* (Augsburg, 1531). The accumulated knowledge in this field was collected in the great encyclopaedia by Pierio Valeriano, *Hieroglyphica* (Basle, 1556). The extent to which all visual and symbolical expressions were regarded as complementary to each other is shown by the title of Henry Estienne's book: *L'Art de Faire les Devises, où il est traicté des Hieroglyphiques, Symboles, Emblemes, Aenygmes, Sentences, Paraboles, Revers de Medailles, Armes, Blasons, Cimiers, Chiffres & Rebus* (Paris, 1645). It was translated into English by Thomas Blount, *The Art of Making Devises* (London, 1646). In the "Epistre," dedicated to Cardinal Mazarin, Estienne explains why these subjects appealed so much to the mind of Renaissance man:

mena manifest the extent to which the relation between word, image and object permeated the cultural life of the period.

Besides the broad relation between the emblem as a way of thinking and literature, there is also the more direct influence exerted on literature by the emblem books. It is frequently possible to point out a specific relationship between an emblem and a corresponding image in a poem. This latter relation between emblem and image also occurs in Herbert's work. For a study of Herbert's work it is particularly relevant therefore to turn to sacred emblematic material. The fact that the corpus of English emblem books is relatively small does not make such a comparison less worthwhile since the emblem movement, like the concrete poetry movement today, was an international affair. Whitney, the author of the first complete emblem book in the English language (1586), had his book printed at Leyden, deriving most of his material from continental sources and Wither, whose book of emblems was published in 1635, was so eager to use the high quality plates of a Dutch engraver that he was prepared to wait a good number of years in order to procure them.[13]

The emblem books that are most relevant for the study of Herbert's verse are the religious emblem books written, mainly by Jesuit priests, in the early decades of the seventeenth century. The Jesuits realized the great didactic potential of the emblem as a visual aid to religious instruction. Using the fashion for profane love emblems in which Cupids were shown involved in all kinds of amorous adventures, they transformed them into emblems of divine love. The place of the naked Cupids was taken by Amor Divinus and Anima — the human soul — , both decently dressed.[14] It is to this particular emblem tradition that Herbert owes most.

A recognition of the influence of emblems not only leads to a better

---

J'ay crû Monseigneur, que vostre Eminence ne desapprouveroit pas celuy-cy, qui n'est pas seulement agreable, mais necessaire, puis que antiennement les Ægyptiens cachoient & descrouvoient par leur Hieroglyphiques, qui approchent des Devises, les plus beaux secrets de leur Philosophie & de leur Religion, & que les plus grands Monarques ont laisse par les mesmes figures leurs inclinations & leurs actions les plus celebres à la posterité, où elle peut s'instruire des sciences & de l'histoire sans avoir besoin de la longue lecture des livres (pp. iv, v).

13. See Freeman, p. 142. Geoffrey Whitney, *A Choice of Emblemes* (Leyden, 1586), ed. Henry Green (1866; rpt. New York: Benjamin Blom, 1967); George Wither, *A Collection of Emblemes, Ancient and Moderne* (London, 1635), ed. John Horden (rpt. Menston: Scolar Press, 1968). In "To the Reader" (A1v) Wither explains why he was prepared to wait some twenty years for the plates.

14. See "Profane and Sacred Love," in Mario Praz, *Seventeenth Century Imagery*, 2nd ed. (Rome, 1964), pp. 83-168.

8

understanding of the visual pattern of Herbert's pattern poems but also clarifies the connection between the emblematic aspect of these poems and emblematic images and image-clusters in some of his other poems. The emblem in the broad sense of the word is a cohesive factor in Herbert's work as a whole. The pattern poems, being part of the total poetic structure of *The Temple*, should not, therefore, be studied separately from the other poetry. There is all the more reason to emphasize this since for a long time Herbert's pattern poems were seen as aberrations rather than as unities integrated within his work. Their shapes were not recognized as emblematic images but as 'pretty devices.'[15] If the pattern poems are emblems in which picture and poem are conflated, many other poems are, in a sense, emblems without pictures. Mario Praz went even further in calling *The Temple* "a conspicuous case of a mute emblem-book (i.e. wanting only the plates.)."[16]

To approach the pattern poems as integrated units of *The Temple* is defensible on other grounds as well. The unity of Herbert's work partly hinges on what has been called its architectonic structure. Walker (1962) argues that there is a relation between Herbert's poetic cycle and the temple of Solomon as it is described in the Bible.[17] Within the architectonic structure of Herbert's work as a whole "The Altar" occupies a functional position as the first poem of *The Church*, the middle section of *The Temple*.

All the aspects of Herbert's poetry mentioned above, the visual impact of the pattern poems, the emblematic nature of his poetry and the architectonic structure of his work, share one essential feature: they all have visual characteristics. In his book on Herbert Joseph Summers (1954) discusses this feature in a chapter called "The Poem as Hieroglyph."[18] It is equally possible, I believe, to call these visual elements manifestations of a concept that exerted great influence on the thinking and work of artists and poets alike in the Renaissance, Horace's *ut pictura poesis*.[19]

15. See Chapter Two for further references.
16. Praz, p. 226.
17. John David Walker, "The Architectonics of George Herbert's *The Temple*," *ELH*, 29 (1962), 289-306. Contemporary evidence can be found in Thomas Fuller, *A Pisgah-Sight of Palestine* (London, 1650), pp. 351-364 and William Chub, *Two fruitfull and godly Sermons . . . the one touching the building of Gods Temple, the other what the Temple is* (London, 1585).
18. Joseph H. Summers, *George Herbert: his Religion and Art* (London: Chatto & Windus, 1954), pp. 123-46.
19. The simile as used here is to be taken in its classical sense: 'as is painting so is poetry.' In the Renaissance its meaning was frequently reversed. See Paul Oskar Kristeller, *Renaissance Thought II* (New York: Harper & Row, 1965), pp. 182-83. The history of the concept from Horace onwards has been described extensively by several

9

The preliminaries sketched here and their implications point the way towards the definitive organisation of the investigation. Whereas in the early stages the relation of Herbert's pattern poems to pattern poetry was a central concern it soon became clear that even a generic approach towards those poems could not do without a recognition of the influence of emblems on much of Herbert's poetry. This is not a genre study but a study that concentrates on particular images occurring within particular poems. By tracing the role and the meaning of emblematic aspects of Herbert's poetry we should be better equipped to interpret that poetry.

I have selected four poems from *The Church* as the basis for the study of the emblematic aspect in Herbert's verse: "The Altar" and "Easter-wings," two pattern poems, "The Pilgrimage" and "Love(III)." The poems are taken from different parts of *The Church* and represent different aspects and phases in what could be seen as the main subject of the cycle: the life of the Christian pilgrim. The pattern poems will be studied, as I intimated before, not only as pattern poems *per se* but as integrated entities within the toal structure of *The Church*. "The Pilgrimage" is a poem the structure of which seems to be rather unlike that of most Herbert poems: it is very explicitly allegorical. The poem seems to ward off close analysis by its stark and unadorned use of stock allegorical labels. As the analysis will show, this is poetic strategy, a strategy of contrast to increase the impact of the second part of the poem. "Love(III)" is the final poem of *The Church*. The imagery of the senses in that poem will be the main subject of the analysis; the imagery is handled in a way characteristic of Herbert, that is with deceptive naturalness and simplicity, qualities that prove to be, on closer analysis, the result of intense poetic concentration and a thorough amalgamation of ideas. In many ways the poem is the culminating point of *The Church*.

Thematically, the poems studied cover three important territories in Herbert's work: the senses as instruments of perception, the pilgrimage of life and sacred love. The poems do not simply represent one of these themes but in each poem the three themes are present with varying emphasis. Sacred love is the be-all and end-all of Herbert's concern. The attitude he demonstrates in his poetry towards the senses and the pilgrimage of life derives its significance from his basic concern with the manifestation of Divine Love on earth and the attempt of the human pilgrim to come to terms with that manifestation.

The emblematic strain is strong in each of the poems. As I said before, the pattern poems are in fact emblems: both picture and text are

---

scholars so that here only its relevance for the understanding of Herbert's work needs to be taken into account. For further references see Chapter Two, 2.1. and n. 17 of that chapter.

10

presented to the reader. "The Pilgrimage" is allegorical; its imagery is
emblematic and appeals to our visual imagination. "Love(III)" is a
"mute emblem" of the Amor/Anima type; the use of sensuous imagery is
characteristic of that particular type of emblem.

The close analysis of the way the imagery works in these poems will, I
hope, yield both the framework for a valid interpretation of the poems
themselves and a refinement of our insight into Herbert's poetic method
as such.

2. Critical approaches and strategies.

2.1. Source and analogy.

In any investigation of a more or less scholarly nature much of the
literary and other material presented to help solve interpretative problems consists of source material. It is important to distinguish clearly
between those cases in which a text or picture may be regarded as a direct
source for the poem that is being analysed and those in which such a text
or picture is analogous to the text analysed.[1] In this study the main
emphasis falls on analogies, not on sources. In the process of tracing the
intended meaning of a specific text or an image in that text parallel
examples are just as useful as sources and sometimes even more helpful
than the obvious source. Source material frequently calls attention to an
individual, isolated characteristic of a text, whereas analogical examples
bring out common features of a number of texts. Source hunting means
following a single trail, collecting analogical evidence is like tracing a
spider's web — I leave it to the reader to decide who in this simile is the
spider and who the poor fly. Let me illustrate these ideas by an example.

It is well known that an old chronicle play, *The True Chronicle History
of King Leir*, was the source for several details in Shakespeare's *King
Lear*. Thus in Shakespeare's play the king, realizing the full extent of his
daughters' ingratitude, cries out in despair:

> Judicious punishment! 'twas this flesh begot
> Those pelican daughters. (III, iv, 74-5)

These lines are parallelled in *The True Chr. H. of King Leir*:

> I am as kind as is the Pellican
> That kils it selfe, to save her young ones lives. (II. 512-13)[2]

---

1. Cf. Samuel C. Chew, *The Pilgrimage of Life* (New Haven: Yale Univ. Press,
1962), p. 87, p. 175. Also Roland Mushat Frye in *Milton's Imagery and the Visual Arts*
(Princeton: Princeton Univ. Press, 1978): " . . . we must be careful not to mistake
analogues for sources" (p. 5).
2. *The True Chronicle History of King Leir* (1605), ll. 512-13, qu. in Kenneth Muir,
ed., *King Lear*, The Arden Shakespeare, 8th ed. (London: Methuen, 1952), III, iv, l.
75n.; also introd., p. xxx and Appendices, p. 226.

There are obvious correspondences and equally obvious differences between these texts. The verbal correspondences are sufficiently clear to justify the claim that the lines from the old story were the source of the quoted lines from Shakespeare's *Lear*. The source text does not, however, help much in determining the meaning of the central metaphor in the passage from *Lear*, that of the pelican. The word pelican occurs in both texts. In the *Chronicle* as a noun that is part of a simile in which a quality of the king is compared to that of the bird; in *Lear* as an adjective qualifying the characters of the king's daughters. In the former instance the metaphor is used to emphasize the king's kindness, in the latter it stresses the daughters' ingratitude. The *meaning* of the metaphor in *Lear* cannot be adequately explained by referring to the source text. It can only be understood better if the passages are analysed on the level of conventional meaning, if one is aware of the images, stories and allegories that underlie them.[3] Ferguson (1954) summarizes the symbolic significance of the pelican thus:

> According to legend, the pelican, which has the greatest love of all creatures for its offspring, pierces its breast to feed them with its own blood. It is on the basis of this legend that the pelican came to symbolize Christ's sacrifice on the Cross, because of His love for all mankind. In this sense, it also symbolizes the Eucharistic Sacrament. This interpretation is supported by Psalm 102:6, 'I am like a pelican of the wilderness,' which is an accepted allusion to Christ. The pelican is sometimes shown nesting on the top of the Cross.[4]

Traditionally, then, the pelican was regarded as an emblem of self-sacrifice. A typical example of this use of the image occurs in Whitney's *A Choice of Emblemes* (1586):

> The Pellican, for to revive her younge,
> Doth peirce her brest, and geve them of her blood.[5]

Whitney's emblem is analogous to Ferguson's gloss and the lines from the *Chronicle* and differs from the metaphor in *Lear* in two respects: a) the word "pelican" is attributed to the parent bird rather than the brood and b) it has a favourable rather than an unfavourable meaning.

There is another instance where Shakespeare uses the pelican image with connotations similar to those in *Lear*. In *Richard II*, II, i, 126-7, John of Gaunt blames Richard for having been involved in the murder of Gloucester, uncle to the King:

---

3. See section 2.2. of this chapter for an explanation of the phrase "level of conventional meaning."
4. George Ferguson, *Signs & Symbols in Christian Art* (London: Oxford Univ. Press, 1954), p. 23. See also Louis Réau, *Iconographie de l'Art Chrétien*, I (Paris: Presses Universitaires de France, 1955), pp. 94-96.
5. Whitney, *A Choice of Emblemes*, p. 87, ll. 1-2.

That blood already, like the pelican,
Hast thou tapp'd out and drunkenly carous'd.

In a note to this passage Ure writes: "When applied to the parent the story commemorates self-sacrifice . . . and became a popular emblem for Christ's sacrifice . . . when to the children, ingratitude."[6] Both sacrifice and ingratitude are elaborated in an emblem from Wither's *A Collection of Emblemes* (1635) that bears the motto:

Our Pelican, *by bleeding, thus,*
Fulfill'd the Law, *and cured* Vs. (see fig. 5)[7]

The picture shows the pelican wounding her own breast to feed her young. In the background we see the crucified Christ whose blood fills the chalices held high by the people at the foot of the Cross. On the top of the Cross we can just make out the pelican on its nest. Thus far the emblem exemplifies the gloss from Ferguson in every detail. The text, however, not only emphasizes the sacrifice of the pelican/Christ but also the ingratitude of the offspring/mankind:

For, this our *Hieroglyphick* would expresse
That *Pelican*, which in the *Wildernesse*
Of this vast *World*, was left (as all alone)
Our miserable *Nature* to bemone;
And, in whose eyes, the teares of pitty stood,
When he beheld his owne unthankfull *Brood*
His *Favours*, and his *Mercies*, then, contemne
When with his wings he would have brooded them. (ll. 7-14)

The idea of the "unthankfull Brood" that we find in Wither's emblem and in *Lear* can be traced back to that extremely popular and influential book on animals, stones and trees, the early medieval *Physiologus*.[7] The *Physiologus* consists of allegorized and Christianized legends, mostly from much older sources. "The anonymous author of *Physiologus* infused these venerable pagan tales with the spirit of Christian moral and mystical teaching, and thereafter . . . *Physiologus* became an established source of medieval sacred iconography and didactic poetry and was used in the preaching manuals and religious textbooks of the later Middle

6. Peter Ure, ed., *Richard II*, The Arden Shakespeare, 4th ed. (London: Methuen, 1966), p. 58n. Cf. *Hamlet*, ed. Harold Jenkins, The Arden Shakespeare (London: Methuen, 1982), IV, v, 146-47: "And, like the kind life-rend'ring pelican,/Repast them with my blood."
7. Cf. Freeman, *English Emblem Books*, pp. 145-46.
8. The *Physiologus* was written between the 3rd and 4th century. Francis J. Carmody, ed., *Physiologus Latinus* (Paris: Librairie E. Droz, 1939). Translation into modern English: J. Curley, trans. & introd., *Physiologus* (Austin: Univ. of Texas Press, 1979), which includes a useful bibliography.

Ages".[9] The story of the pelican does not occur in the Old
English version of the *Physiologus*, which includes sketches of three
animals only, nor does it appear in the Middle English *Bestiary*, which
contains poems on thirteen animals.[10] The Latin *Physiologus* was the
most commonly known version in medieval Western Europe. This is the
story of the Pelican we find there, translated into English:

> David says in Psalm 101, "I am like the pelican in loneliness" [Ps. 102:7].
> Physiologus says of the pelican that it is an exceeding lover of its young. If the
> pelican brings forth young and the little ones grow, they take to striking their
> parents in the face. The parents, however, hitting back kill their young ones and
> then, moved by compassion, they weep over them for three days, lamenting over
> those whom they killed. On the third day, their mother strikes her side and spills
> her own blood over their dead bodies (that is, of the chicks) and the blood itself
> awakens them from death.
>   Thus did our Lord speaking through Isaiah say, "I have brought forth sons and
> have lifted them up, but they have scorned me" [Is. 1:2]. The Maker of every
> creature brought us forth and we struck him. How did we strike him? Because we
> served the creature rather than the creator [cf. Rom. 1:25]. The Lord ascended the
> height of the cross and the impious ones struck his side and opened it and blood
> and water came forth for eternal life [cf. John 19:34 and 6:55], blood because it is
> said, "Taking the chalice he gave thanks" [Matt. 26:27 and Lk. 22:17],
> and water because of the baptism of repentance [Mk. 1:4 and Lk. 3:3]. The Lord said,
> "They have forsaken me, the fountain of living water," and so on [Jer. 2:13].
> Physiologus, therefore, spoke well of the pelican.[11]

The final conclusion applies to the parent bird, but, as I intimated above,
Physiologus also introduces the idea of the ungrateful behaviour of the
"young ones." *Physiologus* is responsible for the specifically Christian
application of the legend.

The connection between *Physiologus,* Wither and *Lear* is clear. The text
of Isaiah 1:2 quoted in *Physiologus*—the Authorized Version reads: ". . . I
have nourished and brought up children, and they have rebelled against
me." — is an adequate paraphrase of Lear's words, although it does not
at all match the bitter vehemence and pithiness of Shakespeare's lines.
Wither's emblem, which is analogous to the text in *Lear,* reveals more
of its intended meaning than does the play which is its direct source.

Nor is our investigation completed once we have found that *Physiologus* rather than the Chronicle play is the true source of the pelican
image in *King Lear*. The point is that we are dealing with a cluster of

9. Curley, p. ix.
10. A.S. Cook, ed., *The Old English Elene, Phoenix and Physiologus* (New Haven:
Yale Univ. Press, 1919). Cf. also David M. Zesmer, *Guide to English Literature* (New
York: Barnes & Noble, 1961), p. 64 (Old E. Physiologus), pp. 179-80 (Mi. E. Bestiary);
P.A. Robin, *Animal Lore in English Literature* (London: John Murray, 1932); and
Beatrice White, "Medieval Animal Lore," *Anglia*, 72 (1954), 21-30.
11. Curley, pp. 9-10.

traditional meanings — Biblical and other — that have gone on developing. The metaphor Shakespeare uses has remained alive and in order to determine its meaning it is at least as relevant to find out what was "in the air" in the age of Shakespeare as to go a-source-hunting. For an author who may have known little Latin and less Greek, the climates of opinion current in his day may well have been more important determinants of his imagery than its ultimate source(s).[12]

Images still had a strongly traditional character and public function in the late Renaissance. The Bible and the classics were universally accepted sources of imagery and there was a continuous tradition lasting through the Middle Ages and the Renaissance, till well into the seventeenth century.[13] The pelican's self-sacrifice could be encountered in poems, plays and sermons. We would expect to find the image in emblems and paintings, in embroidery, carving and the stained glass windows of churches. 'Commonly felt cultural heritage' and 'shared cultural climate' are no meaningless phrases when used in connection with the art of the Renaissance.

12. Cf. Glanvill's statement in *The Vanity of Dogmatizing* (1661):

they that never peep'd beyond the common belief in which their easie under-standings were at first indoctrinated, are indubitably assur'd of the Truth, and comparative excellency of their receptions . . . the larger Souls, that have travail'd the divers *Climates* of *Opinions*, are more cautious in their *resolves*, and more sparing to determine (p. 227).

Qu. in Basil Willey, *Seventeenth Century Background* (London: Chatto & Windus, 1934), p. 193. This brief account of the pelican image serves a methodological purpose and is by no means intended to be historically complete. I chose to follow the Bible/ Physiologus/Wither trail but an equally interesting development of the image runs from Pliny's *Naturalis Historia* through Trevisa's translation of Bartholomaeus Anglicus' *De Proprietatibus Rerum* to translations/editions of both works in the English Renaissance. Pliny/Trevisa distinguish between the grateful and ungrateful behaviour of the pelican's brood and note a corresponding reaction from the mother bird. Pliny's 'Natural History' was translated into English by Philemon Holland (1601) and Trevisa's translation was re-edited as 'Batman vppon Bartholome' in 1582 (rpt. ed. Ann Arbor, 1933). The reference to the pelican can be found in the modern edition of Trevisa's work: M.C. Seymour, ed., *On the Properties of Things,* 2 vols. (Oxford: Oxford Univ. Press, 1975), I, 636-37. Cf. also H.S. Bennett, *Chaucer and the Fifteenth Century* (Oxford: Oxford Univ. Press, 1947), pp. 263-64.

13. Cf. C.S. Lewis, *The Discarded Image* (Cambridge: Cambridge Univ. Press, 1964); Jean Seznec, *The Survival of the Pagan Gods*, trans. B. Sessions (London, 1940; rpt. Princeton: Princeton Univ. Press, 1972); John R. Mulder, *The Temple of the Mind* (New York: Pegasus, 1969); Rosemond Tuve, *Allegorical Imagery* (Princeton: Princeton Univ. Press, 1966); Isabel Rivers, *Classical and Christian Ideas in English Renaissance Poetry* (London: George Allen & Unwin, 1979). These are some of the more stimulating books dealing with various aspects of the continuity of classical and medieval, pagan and Christian traditions into the Renaissance.

For a literary interpreter to ignore this public character of images is as dangerous as the other extreme, to believe that it is only the public aspect that determines meaning in a work of art. For the interpretation of the literature of Renaissance England an awareness of the medieval, Elizabethan and Jacobean world pictures is as indispensable for the modern reader as is his knowledge of and responsiveness to the ways in which the language works in specific instances. The tone, for example, of a poem like William Cartwright's "No Platonic Love,"[14] written in a dying tradition, can only be fully appreciated if one is familiar with the permeating influence of (neo-)Platonic philosophy on English love poetry from Chaucer onwards:

> Tell me no more of minds embracing minds,
>   And hearts exchanged for hearts;
> That spirits spirits meet, as winds do winds,
>   And mix their subtlest parts;
> That two unbodied essences may kiss,
> And then like angels, twist and feel one bliss.
>
> I was that silly thing that once was wrought
>   To practise this thin love;
> I climbed from sex to soul, from soul to thought;
>   But thinking there to move,
> Headlong I rolled from thought to soul, and then
> From soul I lighted at the sex again. (ll. 1-12)

Cartwright clearly appeals to his reader's knowledge of the philosophy he is parodying — and of the famous poem he is parodying as well, of course. If one does not know anything about that philosophy one is bound to miss the point; a modern reader, having grown up in what is so oddly called the permissive society, may well wonder what poor Mr. Cartwright is worried about. If, on the other hand, one does know something about the philosophy referred to the poem makes sense and one is able to grasp a large part of its tone and intended meaning. Of course, any moderately sensitive reader will recognize that the tone of "Tell me no more . . ." is one of protest, but the weariness of the statement gains in dramatic power when one realizes that the odds the poet is up against are the ideas expressed not only in Donne's poem "The Exstasie" but in centuries of Platonic love poetry. Similarly, the lightness of tone of "I was that silly thing . . ." is part of the parody in the narrow sense but it also stands in strong relief against the seriousness of a whole tradition. Knowledge of the place of Cartwright's poem in the tradition will enhance the relevance of one's interpretation.

14. *The Literature of Renaissance England*, eds. John Hollander & Frank Kermode, vol. II of *The Oxford Anthology of English Literature* (New York: Oxford Univ. Press, 1973), 610.

16

In some cases the awareness that there must be a shared intent between
reader and writer helps to corroborate what one had already concluded
on the basis of a purely semantic analysis.[15] In other instances it may be
helpful in preventing the reader from ascribing implications to words that
do not belong to their intended meaning.

2.2. Panofsky and the problem of meaning.

In the introductory chapter of *Studies in Iconology* (1939) Panofsky
illustrates the problem of the meaning of "meaning" with the everyday
example of a man lifting his hat to greet an acquaintance.[16] Panofsky
distinguishes three strata of meaning: a) the factual meaning which
enables one to identify what one sees on the basis of previous experience;
on this level of primary or natural meaning the hat is recognized as a hat
and not as something else; b) the level of secondary or conventional
meaning which includes images, stories and allegories. At this level the
raising of the hat is connected with medieval chivalry, when armed men
used to remove their helmets to show their peaceful intentions;[17] c) the
level of intrinsic, essential meaning. At this level the removal of the hat is

15. My use of the word "shared" approximates what E.D. Hirsch calls the "shared
type." The principle of sharing and sharability establishes a relation between author
and reader in the process of interpretation by demanding from the reader an
awareness of the generic aspects of a text:

> If verbal meaning is a willed type that can be conveyed through linguistic signs, it
> follows that the possibility of conveying the willed type depends on the interpreter's
> prior experience of the willed type. Otherwise, the interpreter could not generate
> implications; he would not know which implications belonged to the meaning and
> which did not. The willed type must be a shared type in order for communication
> to occur.

Validity in Interpretation (New Haven: Yale Univ. Press, 1967), p. 66.
16. Erwin Panofsky, *Studies in Iconology* (1939; rpt. New York: Harper & Row,
1972), pp. 3-31. The introductory chapter, "Iconography and Iconology: An Introduction to the Study of Renaissance Art" was reprinted in E. Panofsky, *Meaning in the
Visual Arts*, pp. 51-81. Critical appraisals of Panofsky's method have been written by
Bernard Teyssèdre, "Iconologie: "réflexion sur un concept d' Erwin Panofsky," *Revue
philosophiques de la France et de l'étranger,* 89 (1964), 321-40, and David Mannings,
"Panofsky and the Interpretation of Images," *BJA*, 13 (1973), 146-62. A useful survey of
the iconographical method is Jan Białostocki, "Iconography," in the *Dictionary of the
History of Ideas,* II (New York: Charles Scribner's Sons, 1973), 524-541, rpt. with the title
"Skizze einer Geschichte der beabsichtigten und der interpretierenden Ikonographie", in
Ikonographie und Ikonologie, ed. Ekkehard Kaemmerling (Köln: Dumont, 1979),
pp. 15-63.
17. See, for instance, the scene in *Sir Gawain and the Green Knight* in which the
forbidding appearance of the Green Knight is mitigated by his entering Arthur's court
without a helmet:

the expression of certain attitudes, habits and conventions constituting the social and cultural climate of a period. Panofsky concludes that it is particularly "in the search for *intrinsic meanings* or *content* that the various humanistic disciplines meet on a common plane instead of serving as hand-maidens to each other."[18]

Panofsky's scheme of levels of meaning is not only a theoretical proposition; it also provides a method of interpretation whereby the interpreter proceeds from one level to another. On the first level a purely textual approach is used in which he mainly applies his knowledge of semantics, of the relation between words and their referents. On the second level the approach becomes comparative; the interpreter applies his knowledge of the relation between aspects of different texts or pictures. Finally, on the third level, his insight into the relations between various expressions of the cultural climate of a period or of a nation or group of nations comes into operation. Applied to the passage in *Lear* that I discussed above, the method of interpretation outlined here would entail that the interpreter first establishes the relation between the words on the page and the world he knows. He knows that the pelican is a species of bird and he knows what daughters are. He also knows that the speaker is Lear and that "Those pelican daughters" refers to Regan and Goneril. On this level, too, his linguistic competence enables him to realize that "this flesh" is a metonymy for the King himself and to recognize the bitterness of the contrast between the intimacy and proximity suggested by "*this* flesh" and the estrangement and distance of "*Those* . . . daughters" (emphasis added).

Having established the natural meaning the interpreter proceeds to the level of the conventional meaning. At this level he demonstrates his awareness of the iconography of pelicans and of the mythological and Christian backgrounds of the particular configuration of details he finds in the *Lear* passage. The knowledge he applies at this level helps the interpreter to ascertain in how far Shakespeare's text resembles and differs from other texts. On the third level, finally, the interpreter realizes that

---

> It seemed that no man might
> His deadly dints withstand.
> Yet had he no helm, nor hauberk neither (ll. 201-03).

and:

> . . . I pass here in peace, and would part friends,
> For had I come to this court on combat bent,
> I have a hauberk at home, and a helm beside (ll. 266-68).

Trans. Marie Borroff (New York: W.W. Norton, 1967).
18. *Studies in Iconology*, p. 16; *Meaning in the Visual Arts*, p. 65.

18

the bitterness of Lear's attitude derives part of its significance from ideas about loyalty, kingship and political stability that were current in Shakespeare's time and which made the playwright express his ideas about filial ingratitude in this particular way.

To attempt analyses of this kind is a hazardous undertaking. Notwithstanding the fact that more or less objective standards such as the rules of *imitatio*, rhetorical principles, rules of genre and decorum help to distinguish relevant from irrelevant material, and thus reduce the likelihood of the interpreter going astray, it will always remain possible for him to attribute significances to a text that were never intended to form part of its meaning. As Mannings (1973) points out the three-part scheme proposed by Panofsky may leave a number of problems unsolved, especially the problem of the criteria on the basis of which the interpreter decides that a particular interpretation is correct, and the danger of mis- or over-interpretation.[19] For this risk there is no easy solution. As Gombrich (1972) formulates it: ". . . all iconological research depends on our prior conviction of what we may look for, in other words, on our feeling for what is or is not possible within a given period or milieu."[20]

Relevance would seem to be a key term here. Only a properly developed sense of relevance enables the interpreter to sift evidence that clarifies the poem's meaning from material that does not. The public aspect of meaning is the concern of the "informed reader" (Fish, 1972),[21] who is willing to trace the concepts and texts relevant for an adequate and valid interpretation of a particular text. In this sense interpretation becomes, in Gombrich's words: "reconstruction of a lost piece of evidence."[22] For the present study Panofsky's scheme of the levels of interpretation has proved a useful guide. It should be emphasized that the scheme is not adhered to in any rigid way, but occasional references in the chapters that follow will point at the relation between Panofsky's model and the analysis in progress.

2.3. Herbert's "The Sacrifice" and literary criticism.

Herbert called his poetry "private ejaculations." It is probably this description and the fact that his work appeared in print posthumously that led Vendler (1975) to introduce her book on the poet thus:

An expressive theory of poetry suits *The Temple* best: no matter how exquisitely

19. Mannings, pp. 146-47.
20. E.H. Gombrich, *Symbolic Images* (London: Phaidon, 1972), p. 5.
21. Stanley E. Fish, *Self-Consuming Artifacts* (Berkeley: Univ. of California Press, 1972), pp. 406-07.
22. *Symbolic Images*, p. 6.

written a poem by Herbert is in its final form, it seems usually to have begun in experience, and aims at recreating or recalling that experience. To approach such private poetry as an exercise in public communication with an audience is to misconstrue its emphasis. . . . My care in examining Herbert's art will, I hope, prevent my appearing to take poetry as the equivalent of life, but I do not think that there is significant help to be had in understanding Herbert by invoking theories of poetry that detach artefact, as a system of formal signs, from lived experience recreated in a mimetic form of speech.[23]

Vendler writes that Herbert's intention in writing poetry was to recreate or recall his experience in life "in a mimetic form of speech." One question that arises from her point of departure is whether the process of recreation does not *per se* turn private experience into an artefact with sharable, public qualities. The process of recreation *is* an exercise in public communication, because the poet can hardly avoid using publicly recognized and recognizable codes and signs.

Vendler's statement also raises questions of a literary-historical kind. Her ideas about the creative process seem too modern and are ill-suited to Herbert's poetics. As late as 1710 Pope could define "true wit" as: "...*Nature* to Advantage drest,/What oft was *Thought,* but ne'er so well *Exprest.*"[24] As my discussion of the pelican image in *King Lear* demonstrated, imagery in the Renaissance was still to a large extent a public matter because of its conventionality and, as the subsequent analyses will show, Herbert's images are no exceptions. In this connection Vendler's phrase "a mimetic form of speech" is misleading. One cannot introduce a term like "mimetic" and ignore the specific "period" significance of the word in an age when scores of treatises on poetry were available in which the Aristotelian notion of *mimesis* had a prominent place.

Moreover, if one considers the way in which Herbert presents his own poetry, it is obvious that the poet meant his work to be an exercise in public communication, although what he had to communicate was often derived from his private experience. What is "The Church-porch" addressed to if not to an audience; who else than the audience, faithful flock or reader, are exhorted to "avoid profaneness" and "to approach and taste/The Churches mysticall repast" in "Superliminare"?[25] Herbert was a priest. He wrote *in extenso* about the life and responsibilities of the priest in *A Priest to the Temple.*[26] *The Temple*, too, shows Herbert's awareness of his priestly office, both in its general framework and in many individual poems.

23. Helen Vendler, *The Poetry of George Herbert* (Cambridge, Mass.: Harvard Univ. Press, 1975), p. 5.
24. Alexander Pope, "An Essay on Criticism," ll. 297-98, in *The Poems*, ed. John Butt (London: Methuen, 1965), p. 153.
25. *Works*, p. 25.
26. *Works*, pp. 223-290.

In view of Vendler's "expressive theory" it is hardly surprising that she shows little appreciation for a poem like "The Sacrifice." It is, after all, one of Herbert's most manifestly public poems. "The Sacrifice" with its 63 stanzas of four lines each is the longest poem of *The Church*. Each stanza ends with the refrain: "Was ever grief like mine?" except for the last, which ends: "Never was grief like mine." The speaker is Christ complaining to His people from the Cross. Both the subject and the tone of the poem as a whole are firmly established in the very first stanza:

> *Oh all ye, who passe by*, whose eyes and minde
> To wordly things are sharp, but to me blinde;
> To me, who took eyes that I might you finde:
> Was ever grief like mine? (*Works*, p. 26)

The public nature of Christ's complaint is emphasized by the italicized quotation from Lamentations 1:12 with which the poem begins. Its form is conventional and is based on commonly known liturgical traditions.[27] The subject is one of the most crucial, public events in the history of Christianity. The poem is exceptional in the Herbert canon both by its length and by the fact that Christ is the speaker throughout.

This is what Vendler writes about "The Sacrifice":

> Though no one can deny the finished elegance of *The Sacrifice*, it is not, in spite of its subject, one of Herbert's immediately moving poems. Its rather frigid ingenuity and stylization is at odds with the literary tradition of verbal simplicity in poetic treatments of Christ's Passion. (p. 137)

As anyone who has read Rosemond Tuve's essay on "The Sacrifice" knows, the traditions drawn on in the poem are not restricted to the poetry Vendler alludes to. Consequently, one would wish for a more precise definition of what the poem is "at odds with." I believe Vendler deprecates "The Sacrifice" for the lack of qualities it was never meant to possess. Perhaps the poem is not "immediately moving." But is that a valid criterion to judge a poem by? Are poems that are "immediately moving" necessarily better than poems that are not? It may be that Vendler's conception of Herbert's best achievement makes her single out "The Sacrifice" in this way, but then it places the poem in a category it does not belong to. To emphasize, as Vendler does, that the type of public poetry exemplified by "The Sacrifice" belongs to an early mode of Herbert's from which he dissociated himself later on does not in itself warrant a qualitative distinction between one type and another.[28]

27. See R. Tuve's seminal essay "'The Sacrifice' and modern criticism" in her book *A Reading of George Herbert* (Chicago: Univ. of Chicago Press, 1952), pp. 19-99.
28. An argument against attaching too much weight to the time of composition of the poems is that Herbert clearly saw *The Temple* as an organic unity. In revising the collection he discarded certain poems, revised others and incorporated new ones.

It is a pity that Vendler did not devote more attention to "The Sacrifice" because the poem had been the subject of an instructive debate between William Empson and Rosemond Tuve, some decades before Vendler's book was published. Their exchange has a direct bearing on our discussion of the public aspect of poetry. When placed side by side with Vendler's comment on "The Sacrifice" Empson's (1947) seems to be about a different poem altogether:

> In "The Sacrifice," with a magnificence he never excelled, the various sets of conflicts in the Christian doctrine of the Sacrifice are stated with an assured and easy simplicity, a reliable and unassuming grandeur, extraordinary in any material, but unique as achieved by successive fireworks of contradiction, and a mind jumping like a flea.[29]

Empson's analysis was refuted by Tuve (1952), who successfully demonstrated that several of the, modern, ambiguities Empson read into "The Sacrifice" were unlikely to have been intended by the poet, because certain words and phrases had implications in Herbert's day that have been lost sight of since. Knowledge of the traditions and conventions the poem is based on enable the interpreter to decide on the relevance of specific readings. Tuve, who shares Empson's view of the poem's intrinsic quality, postpones textual criticism until she is sufficiently assured that she has established the generic quality of Herbert's text. Her interpretation is based on an attempt to reconstruct what must have gone into the poem by defining to what extent it is embedded in the shared religious and cultural climate of the time. Empson's response, for all its brilliance, makes one feel that it is Empson's rather than Herbert's mind that is jumping like a flea. Thus, the line:

> Man stole the fruit, but I must climbe the tree (l. 202)

makes him compare Christ not only to an apple-thief but to Prometheus, Jack and the Beanstalk, and an incestuous child into the bargain.

The debate between Empson and Tuve is too well-known to be discussed in all its detail here. But, since this appraisal of some critical attitudes is intended as a prelude to my own approach, a few more words on the essence of the controversy will not be out of place. The opposition between Empson and Tuve is not so straightforward as I have suggested. To define it in terms of a distinction between criticism and scholarship would be a simplification. Empson, too, repeatedly refers to sources of

---

Viewed in this light, a discussion about "early" and "later" modes becomes problematic. Cf. *Works*, pp. liii-lv and Amy M. Charles, "The Williams Manuscript and *The Temple*," *RenP* (1972), 59-77.

29. William Empson, *Seven Types of Ambiguity*, rev. ed. (New York: New Directions, 1947), p. 226.

Herbert's poem in order to substantiate his ideas about it. Both approaches are in a sense historical. The difference between the two becomes most clearly apparent in the way in which historical information is used and the purpose it is made to serve. The controversy is essentially about the proper aims and tools of literary interpretation.

Tuve's approach is founded on what one might call 'circumstantial reconstruction' of the intentions of the author, Empson's creates its own intentions. The discussion about "The Sacrifice" focuses on the 51st stanza:

> O all ye, who passe by, behold and see;
> Man stole the fruit, but I must climbe the tree;
> The tree of life to all, but onely me:
> Was ever grief like mine?

To Empson's analysis of this stanza Tuve reacted thus:

> . . . there is no such thing as 'the phrase in itself.' The locution marks a modern critical error, and philology should have taught us all to be wary of it. 'The son stealing from his father's orchard is a symbol of incest,' says Empson; 'Jesus seems a child in this metaphor.' But to whom? Perhaps it is the answer to this last question which every critic has a responsibility to make clear. (p. 30)

Tuve's interest is directed towards an interpretation that is controlled by the conventions of the cultural heritage which she considers the poem to be the product of. In the "Note for the third edition" of *Seven Types of Ambiguity* Empson concedes a few points to Tuve — without mentioning her name — , notably in the matter of the 'uniqueness' he had originally claimed for "The Sacrifice," but he maintains that: "An objector cannot really deny that Herbert's style is different from that of his medieval models." This is true, of course, but I do not regard the statement as a support for Empson's own analysis. Since he does not define how precisely Herbert should be read differently from medieval poetry, Tuve's criticism of Empson's method still holds true.

I have narrowed down the dispute between Tuve and Empson to a difference between *conformity* and *transformation*. It should be borne in mind, however, that even when Herbert transformed his sources, he did so as a poet writing religious verse in the seventeenth century. It is obviously true that Herbert is not a medieval poet. But he is not a twentieth century poet either, which is essentially what Empson tries to turn him into.

2.4. Conformity, transformation and applied scholarship.

A drawback or, more fairly, a possible weakness of Tuve's method is its tacit assumption that the whole scholarly apparatus that is brought to bear on the poetic text is actually geared to the intended meaning. The method, if used without Tuve's customary circumspection, may cause the search for meaning to deteriorate into indiscriminate source-hunting.[30] Another danger of a disproportionate emphasis on the efficacy of source material in determining meaning is that it will tend to highlight the extent to which a text conforms to other texts and thus obscure the way existing ideas and forms are transformed into the individual work of art.[31]

A poem like "The Sacrifice" has a predominantly public appeal. Tuve has shown that many of the phrases and images, and even the tone and irony of the poem are part of established religious and poetic habits and conventions. "The Sacrifice" thus demonstrates Herbert's versatility in using these traditions. The poet's subtle manipulation of the reader's expectations raised by the poem's public aspect constitutes its individual haecceity, which only reveals itself after the conventional, public side has been accounted for. In the final analysis we do not read Herbert because he resembles his medieval or other sources but because he transcends them.

What conclusions does this comparative analysis of critical procedures lead to? We have seen that the three critics we quoted for their appraisal of "The Sacrifice" represent three distinct approaches. Vendler requires the poem to be what it was never supposed to be, namely "immediately moving." Empson's approach, with all its originality, leans towards idiosyncrasy and Tuve's scholarly method, however useful as a means of transmitting information, has a tendency to crush the poem through sheer weight of annotation. Of course my critical notes are intended as comments on certain methods of interpretation rather than on the critics themselves from whose work the examples were taken. The analysis was meant to demarcate the boundaries of the scholarly and critical arena within which the following study is presented. This demarcation process has yielded a method and an aim. The aim is to establish the intended meaning of certain poems by George Herbert. My analyses of Herbert's poems will try to steer a careful middle course between conformity and transformation. The method could perhaps best be called that of *applied scholarship*. The object of the study cannot be attained without the proposed method. I suggest that applied scholarship can fill the gap between scholarship and criticism. It recognizes the necessity of postu-

30. Tuve's circumspection appears, for instance, from her "Note on the accessibility of materials used, to the sixteenth- and seventeenth-century reader," in which she takes great care to show that most of the texts she had mentioned previously were accessible to the readers of Herbert's poetry (*A Reading of George Herbert*, pp. 204-210).

31. Cf. Vendler: "I wish to show that Herbert also provides inventive transformations of the original *donnée* of a poem, whether it be a passage of Scripture, a liturgical prayer, a feast, a ritual, or a hymn" (*The Poetry of George Herbert*, p. 4).

lating an intention on the part of the author that must be reconstrued before any valid interpretation can be arrived at. An important step in the reconstruction of this intention, particularly when one is dealing with older texts, consists of the careful tracing and weighing of historical data that are no longer readily accessible to the modern reader because they have been lost or forgotten. But the results of the scholarly quest should always be compared with the individual characteristics of the particular text that is being analysed. That is where "applied" comes in. The best result that one can hope for in pursuing applied scholarship is that it will help to turn readers into informed readers and random guesses at meanings into guess-work that is at least as educated as possible.

Our **Pelican,** *by bleeding, thus,* **Fulfil'd** *the* **Law,** *and cured* **Vs.**

GREGE PROLEGE ETPRO

ILLVSTR. XX. *Book.*3

5

CHAPTER TWO

A STUDY OF HERBERT'S PATTERN POEMS

Part One: What Herbert Knew.

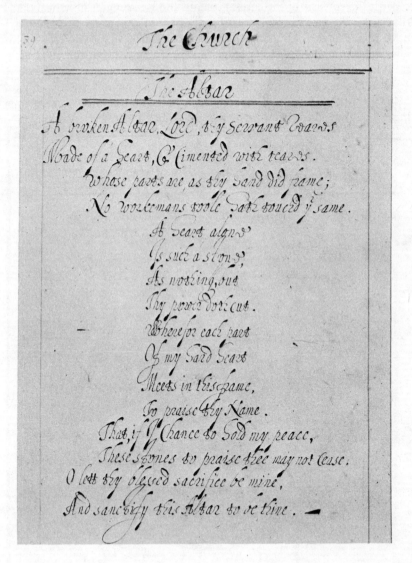

Easter wings.

Lord, who createdst man in wealth and store,
Though foolishly he lost the same,
Decaying more and more,
Till he became
Most poore:
With thee
O let me rise
As larks, harmoniously,
And sing this day thy victories:
Then shall the fall further the flight in mee.

7a

The Church

Easter wings

My tender age in sorrow did beginne:
And still with sicknesses & shame
Thou didst so punish sinne,
That I became
Most thinne.
With thee
Let mee Combine,
And feele this day thy victorie:
For if I imp my wing on thine,
Affliction shall advance the flight in mee.

7b

0. Introductory.

Although this chapter is mainly concerned with the context of Herbert's pattern poems, it is also intended to serve as framework for subsequent chapters. The concepts and conventions introduced here and applied primarily to the interpretation of the pattern poems are, *mutatis mutandis*, equally relevant for an understanding of the context of Herbert's other poetry. These concepts and conventions which relate to broad and general ideas help to an understanding at what Panofsky would call the third level of interpretation, that which is concerned with the intrinsic or essential meaning.[1]

The following pages address themselves to the problem as to why an altogether serious and devotedly religious poet like Herbert, who carefully selected the poems he thought worthy of inclusion in *The Temple* and who carefully arranged and revised these poems, why a poet like this should have decided to keep the pattern poems among what he apparently considered the best products of his poetic art. Was it just because, in Palmer's words, "embroidery pleased" and because "probably Herbert himself did on occasion enjoy a ruffled shirt"?[2] Or did the form appear less eccentric to Herbert and to his contemporaries than it does to us?

Gombrich raised a similar question relating to the popularity of emblems and, in the same breath, suggested a possible answer:

> The gravity with which the casuistry of the emblem and device was discussed by otherwise sane and intelligent people remains an inexplicable freak unless we understand that for them a truth condensed into a visual image was somehow nearer the realm of absolute truth than one explained in words.[3]

Gombrich's remark refers to the impact made by Neoplatonic philosophy on Renaissance thinking and Renaissance modes of expressing thoughts and ideas in emblems and devices. There can be no doubt that for Herbert the pattern poems, his other emblematic verse, his imagery of the senses and the concreteness of many of his other images were essential means to give poetic definition to the relationship between man the pilgrim and God, who is both cause and purpose of his pilgrimage. Plotinus, a chief exponent of early Neoplatonism, describes the perfection of Heaven thus:

1. See Chapter One, 2.2.
2. George Herbert Palmer, ed., *The English Works of George Herbert,* 3 vols., 3rd ed. (Boston: Houghton Mifflin, 1915), I, 147.
3. E.H. Gombrich, "Icones Symbolicae: The Visual Image in Neo-Platonic Thought," *JWCI,* 11 (1948), 163-188.

It must not be thought that in the Intelligible World the gods and the blessed see propositions; everything expressed there is a beautiful image.[4]

In "Prayer (I)" Herbert shows that prayer, the communication between man and God, can be concretely defined:

> Prayer the Churches banquet, Angels age,
> Gods breath in man returning to his birth,
> The soul in paraphrase, heart in pilgrimage,
> The Christian plummet sounding heav'n and earth;
> Engine against th' Almightie, sinners towre,
> Reversed thunder, Christ-side-piercing spear,
> The six-daies world transposing in an houre,
> A kinde of tune, which all things heare and fear;
> Softnesse, and peace, and joy, and love, and blisse,
> Exalted Manna, gladnesse of the best,
> Heaven in ordinarie, man well drest,
> The milkie way, the bird of Paradise,
> Church-bels beyond the starres heard, the souls bloud,
> The land of spices; something understood. (*Works*, p. 51)

Summers writes about this "sonnet without statement":

> The last three lines, with their 'definition' of that state of being which surpasses knowledge and logic, depend not only on the pattern of ideas and imagery of which they are a part, but also on the subtle changes of the rhythm and the dislocation of the language: the rhythmical daring of 'Church-bels beyond the starres heard' is matched by the phrase's startling ambiguity of reference. The peace of 'The land of spices; something understood' is both an abandonment of metaphor and its final crowning.[5]

The poem, we might say, exemplifies what Summers elsewhere describes as ". . . Herbert's religious and poetic concern with what we may call the hieroglyph."[6]

1. The hieroglyphic view of the universe.

The 'hieroglyphic image,' as Summers aptly called the type of metaphor most frequently used by Herbert, was to the poet a more effective instrument than the mere argumentation of logic or the persuasion of rhetoric. Herbert's concern to avoid ornate language and ambiguous metaphors on the one hand and his awareness of the limitations of an exclusively rational approach on the other find frequent expression in his poetry. The best known example of the former concern is "Jordan (II)":

---

4. Plotinus, *Ennead*, V, 8; qu. in Gombrich, *Symbolic Images*, p. 158.
5. Summers, pp. 182-83.
6. Summers, p. 123.

When first my lines of heav'nly joyes made mention,
Such was their lustre, they did so excell,
That I sought out quaint words, and trim invention;
My thoughts began to burnish, sprout, and swell,
Curling with metaphors a plain intention,
Decking the sense, as if it were to sell.

Thousands of notions in my brain did runne,
Off'ring their service, if I were not sped:
I often blotted what I had begunne;
This was not quick enough, and that was dead.
Nothing could seem too rich to clothe the sunne,
Much lesse those joyes which trample on his head.

As flames do work and winde, when they ascend,
So did I weave my self into the sense.
But while I bustled, I might heare a friend
Whisper, *How wide is all this long pretence!*
There is in love a sweetnesse readie penn'd:
Copie out onely that, and save expense. (*Works*, pp. 102-3)[7]

The poem nicely illustrates the problems Herbert must have encountered when he exchanged his office of Public Orator at Cambridge University for that of rector at Bemerton.

In "The Posie" the poet's wish for directness in his dealings with God is expressed in a clearly emblematic way:

Let wits contest
And with their words and posies windows fill:
Lesse then the least
Of all thy mercies, is my posie still.

This on my ring,
This by my picture, in my book I write:
Whether I sing,
Or say, or dictate, this is my delight.

7. Cf. "A True Hymne," (*Works*, p. 168):

. . . if th'heart be moved
Although the verse be somewhat scant,
    God doth supplie the want.
As when th'heart sayes (sighing to be approved)
O, could I love! and stops: God writeth, *Loved*. (ll. 16-20)

Herbert's metaphor of Divine Love writing in the human heart is the religious counterpart of the final line of Sidney's sonnet 1 in *Astrophel and Stella*: "'Foole,' said my Muse to me, 'looke in thy heart and write'" (*The Poems*, ed. William A. Ringler, Jr. (Oxford: Oxford Univ. Press, 1962), p. 165).

> Invention rest,
> Comparisons go play, wit use thy will:
> *Lesse then the least*
> *Of all Gods mercies*, is my posie still. (*Works*, pp. 182-3)

The posy here has a function similar to that of the motto of an emblem,
but in addition it is a *reductio ad essentiam* of the intense rhetorical
activity mentioned in the opening lines.

In "Jordan (II)" and "The Posie" Herbert shows that rhetoric is
inadequate to characterize the communion between man and God. In
other poems the poet points out that rational disputation is also
insufficient, or rather irrelevant in the light of true faith. Consider, for
instance "The Rose":

> Presse me not to take more pleasure
>   In this world of sugred lies,
> And to use a larger measure
>   Then my strict, yet welcome size.
>
> First, there is no pleasure here:
>   Colour'd griefs indeed there are,
> Blushing woes, that look as cleare
>   As if they could beautie spare.
>
> Or if such deceits there be,
>   Such delights I meant to say;
> There are no such things to me,
>   Who have pass'd my right away.
>
> But I will not much oppose
>   Unto what you now advise:
> Onely take this gentle rose,
>   And therein my answer lies.
>
> What is fairer then a rose?
>   What is sweeter? yet it purgeth.
> Purgings enmitie disclose,
>   Enmitie forbearance urgeth.
>
> If then all that worldlings prize
>   Be contracted to a rose;
> Sweetly there indeed it lies,
>   But it biteth in the close.
>
> So this flower doth judge and sentence
>   Worldly joyes to be a scourge:
> For they all produce repentance,
>   And repentance is a purge.

But I health, not physick choose:
 Onely though I you oppose,
Say that fairly I refuse,
 For my answer is a rose. (*Works*, pp. 177-8)

The intricate debate which the poem consists of is resolved in the quasi-simple statement of the final line. Through its concreteness and its brevity the image of the rose has a much more immediate appeal than the intellectual debate that precedes it; at the same time the image of the rose clinches the argument and contains the most essential statement of the poem. Notwithstanding its superficial simplicity this final statement has a profundity that goes far beyond the significance of the emblematic comparisons of the rest of the poem. Allen (1960) has shown that the simplicity of the poem is deceptive and that it is, on the contrary, highly complex.[8] The beauty of the metaphor of the rose resides in its inclusiveness: the rose is an emblem of the "deceits" of worldly pleasures and of the world's sweetness; it is, simultaneously, an emblem of penance (through its thorns that remind us of the Fall from Paradise where roses grew without thorns) and of heavenly love (the virgin Mary's flower is the rose without thorns; the Celestial Rose is Dante's ultimate goal in the *Divina Commedia*). The final line of the poem carries the full burden of all these implications. The solution is not, as Allen suggests, that there are two roses, the one pagan, the other Christian; there is just the one rose.[9] It is not the gentle, fair and sweet rose that leads to man's downfall but the "worldly joyes" he succumbs to. The rose is just a rose and it is incumbent upon man to learn from the contemplation of the flower's qualities.[10] The ramifications of this central symbol cannot be adequately described by discursive means — this is what the poem says and what the reader is supposed to think. The contraction of a whole argument into a single visual image thus functions as a means of concentrating ideas rather than of simplifying them.

 It would not be difficult to quote and discuss several other poems in

8. Don C. Allen, "George Herbert's 'The Rose,'" in *Image and Meaning: Metaphoric Traditions in Renaissance Poetry* (Baltimore: Johns Hopkins, 1960), pp. 67-79. Allen's essay brings together a number of classical and contemporary texts that exemplify the wide range of possible meanings of the rose metaphor. Notwithstanding Allen's erudition his essay does not invariably apply the scholarship to the text. There is no distinction between relevant and less relevant background material. I fail to see, for instance, that the rose of virginity (Allen, p. 76) has anything in common with Herbert's poem.

9. See Vendler (1975), p. 289 n. 13: "There is no evidence in the poem that the proffered and returned rose is anything but a natural rose, which by its innate qualities alone (of beauty and purgative effect) both displays and "sentences" wordly joys."

10. Cf. Herbert's poems "Vertue" and "Life" where the rose also fulfils the double task of "instruction and delight."

which Herbert stresses the limitations of rhetoric and reasoning for an adequate rendering of his religious themes. Such examples, however, would not bring us much further in our attempt to find out why Herbert used the pattern poem with its primarily visual appeal rather than other, primarily verbal, devices. The only explanation that does justice to both the pattern poems and the visual aspects of the other poems must be that for Herbert, too, "a truth condensed into a visual image was somehow nearer the realm of absolute truth than one explained in words."

Gombrich's "truth condensed into a visual image" is not very different from what the Renaissance understood by 'hieroglyph.' In the Preamble I have already indicated briefly that the interest of the Renaissance man of letters in the meaning of the Egyptian hieroglyphs went hand in hand with an increasing emphasis on the visual aspect of imagery. The word 'hieroglyph' had gradually acquired a wide range of meanings in the course of the sixteenth century. Giovanni Pierio Valeriano summed up its various aspects in his *Hieroglyphicorum Collectanea* (1556):

> Ad hieroglyphica accedunt emblemata, symbola, insignia, quae quamvis nomine differant; reipsa multis modis convenire videntur.[11]

The title of one of Francis Quarles' emblem books, *Hieroglyphikes of the Life of Man* (London, 1638), also shows that the words 'emblem' and 'hieroglyph' could be used almost interchangeably.[12]

Perhaps the best description of the significance attributed to the term 'hieroglyph(ic)' in the Renaissance was given by Henri Estienne in the introductory *Epistre* to his *L'Art de Faire les Devises* (quoted in the Preamble, n. 12). In England Bacon wrote the following about hieroglyphs as expressions of 'Parabolical wisedome':

> . . . ALLVSIVE, or PARABOLICALL, is a NARRATION applied onely to expresse some speciall purpose or conceit: Which later kind of Parabolical wisedome was much more in vse in the ancient times, as by the Fables of *Aesope*, and the briefe sentences of the seuen, and the *use* of *Hieroglyphikes* may appeare. And the cause was for that it was then of necessitie to expresse any point of reason which was more sharpe or subtile then the vulgar in that maner, because men in those times wanted both varietie of examples and subtiltie of conceit: And as *Hierogliphikes* were before Letters, so parables were before arguments: And neuerthelesse now and at all times they doe retaine much life and vigor, because reason cannot bee so sensible, nor examples so fit.[13]

11. "Hieroglyphics include emblems, symbols, insignia, which, although they differ in name, are seen to be similar in many ways." I consulted an edition of Pierio's work published in Köln in 1631; this qu. p. 7. See also Summers, p. 224 n. 2. Summers (mis-?)quotes from the Lyon edition of 1626.

12. Cf. also Wither (1635), p. A2: ". . . and in the Proprieties due to some other Hieroglyphicks; . . ."

13. Francis Bacon, *The Twoo Bookes of the Proficience and Advancement of Learning, Divine and Hvmane* (1605), in J.E. Spingarn, ed., *Critical Essays of the Seventeenth Century*, I. (Oxford: Oxford Univ. Press, 1908), 7.

The widespread interest in hieroglyphics was no doubt an important factor in Herbert's choice of images and helped to determine the emblematic quality of that imagery in particular. It is against this background that his use of the pattern poem must also be seen. In a chapter called "The Poem as Hieroglyph," Summers discusses a number of Herbert's poems which are either about a 'hieroglyph,' an emblematic object ("The Church-floore"), or use the hieroglyph as a central image ("The Bunch of Grapes") or, like "Church Monuments," "Deniall," "Aaron," and many others, are hieroglyphs themselves because "the form imaged the subject."[14] About the pattern poems Summers writes:

> In 'The Altar' and 'Easter-wings' Herbert extended the principle of the hieroglyph to a third level. If the natural or religious hieroglyph was valuable as content (used either as the object which the poem explained or as the image which crystallized the meaning of the poem), and if the poem could be constructed as a formal hieroglyph which mirrored the structural relationship between the natural hieroglyph, the poem, and the individual's life, it was but a further step to make the poem a visual hieroglyph, to create it in a shape which formed an immediately apparent image relevant both to content and structure.[15]

When the pattern poems are understood as expressions of Herbert's hieroglyphic disposition, they need no longer be seen as poems whose "eccentricity of form seems to have no inner justification" or as the epitomes of false wit.[16] They then seem to be characteristic examples of Herbert's method rather than exceptions. Summers' argument indicates that the difference between the pattern poems and many other poems in *The Church* is one of degree, not kind, and it proves that the use of the pattern poem meant something more important to Herbert than putting on "a ruffled shirt."

The emphatically concrete nature of his poetry can be adequately explained by referring to the hieroglyphic spirit in which he himself and many of his contemporaries wrote their poetry. It provides a philosophical background for Herbert's pattern poems. Within the broad framework of that background other phenomena can be mentioned that exemplify in a more specific way the general tendency towards visualisation.

In the context of a discussion of the pattern poems, two concepts will be introduced and briefly touched on in the remainder of this chapter: *utile dulce* and *opsis*. The former is a well-known Horatian adage and belongs to the equally well-known doctrine of *ut pictura poesis*. The latter is an aspect of rhetoric and stems from Aristotle. Neither has, as far as I

14. Summers, p. 135.
15. Summers, p. 140.
16. Palmer, I, 147; Addison, "False Wit," *The Spectator*, May 7, 1711.

am aware, been specifically related to Herbert's work or to his pattern poems.

2. *Ut pictura poesis* and *utile dulce*.

2.1. *Ut pictura poesis*.

The parallel between poetry and painting was a topic frequently discussed in Renaissance treatises on the visual arts and literature. It retained its appeal until well into the eighteenth century.[17] In Ripa's *Iconologia* (1603) the description of Painting ("Pittura") incorporates the basic ingredients of the *ut pictura poesis* doctrine as it was understood in the Renaissance:

> Donna, bella, . . . si cuopra la bocca, con una fascia ligata dietro à gli orecchi . . . & habbia scritto nella fronte, *imitatio*. . . . La bocca ricoperta, è inditio, che non è cosa che giovi quanto il silentio, & la solitudine; . . . essendo vero quel detto triviale, che la Poesia tace nella Pittura, & la Pittura nella Poesia ragiona . . .[18]

In later editions of the *Iconologia* the text was accompanied by a picture in which Painting was personified as a woman with a cloth bound over her mouth.[19] In the famous Hertel edition (Augsburg, 1758-60) the

17. A useful and succinct survey of *ut pictura poesis* is Rensselaer W. Lee, *Ut Pictura Poesis: the Humanistic Theory of Painting* (New York: Norton, 1967). Cf. also Irving Babbitt, *The New Laokoon* (Boston: Houghton Mifflin, 1910); Thomas Munro, *The Arts & Their Interrelations* (New York: Liberal Arts Press, 1949); Jean H. Hagstrum, *The Sister Arts: The Tradition of Literary Pictorialism and English Poetry from Dryden to Gray* (Chicago: Chicago Univ. Press, 1958): Mario Praz, *Mnemosyne: The Parallel between Literature and the Visual Arts* (Princeton: Princeton Univ. Press, 1970); René Wellek & Austin Warren, "Literature and the Other Arts," in *Theory of Literature,* 3rd ed. (Harmondsworth: Penguin, 1963), pp. 125-35; William K. Wimsatt Jr. & Cleanth Brooks, "Addison & Lessing: Poetry as Pictures," in *Literary Criticism: A Short History* (New York: Alfred A. Knopf, 1957), pp. 252-82; Cicely Davies, "Ut Pictura Poesis," *MLR,* 30 (1935), 159-69; Helmut A. Hatzfeld, "Literary Criticism through Art and Art Criticism through Literature," *JAAC,* 6 (1947), 1-21; G. Giovannini, "Method in the Study of Literature in its Relation to the Other Fine Arts," *JAAC,* 8 (1950), 185-95; John R. Spencer, "Ut rhetorica pictura," *JWCI,* 20 (1957), 26-44. See also Chapter One, 1, n. 19.

18. Cesare Ripa, *Iconologia* (Roma, 1603), pp. 404-5. Summary from Edward A. Maser, ed., *Baroque and Rococo Pictorial Imagery: The 1758-60 Hertel edition of Ripa's 'Iconologia'* (New York: Dover, 1971):

> The personification of Painting is a very beautiful woman . . . A cloth is bound over her mouth . . . a bit of rocaille bears the inscription "Imitatio" (Imitation). [Maser refers to the Hertel engraving] . . . The cloth bound over her mouth indicates that painting is a silent art, conveying its message by other means than words — it is mute poetry (p. 197).

19. In this way she appears in Baudouin's French version of 1644, holding a palette, brushes and a ribbon with the word *Imitatio* in her left hand and balancing a painting

details of the engraving of *Painting* coincide more or less with those of the
original edition but the close association of the sister arts is further
emphasized by the fact that the figure in the painting the allegorized
woman is leaning on is that of Poetry.[20]

The *Iconologia* points to the three *auctores intellectuales* of the *ut
pictura poesis*-doctrine: Aristotle, Simonides and Horace. The inscription
"Imitatio" refers, of course, to the *mimesis* of Aristotle's *Poetica*. The
cloth over the mouth of the woman who personifies Painting pictures the
adage, attributed by Plutarch to Simonides, that painting is mute poetry,
poetry a speaking picture.[21] The 'painting within the painting' in the
Hertel edition depicting Poetry illustrates the Horatian concept *ut pictura
poesis*.[22] The close relation between the two arts suggested by these three
authors caused them to be regarded as the 'sister arts.'

In treatises on art and on literature the *ut pictura poesis* doctrine was
reiterated time and again from the sixteenth century onwards until well
into the eighteenth, both on the continent and in England. I shall restrict
myself here to two typical examples from English treatises on the art of
writing poetry, Sir Philip Sidney's *Defence of Poetry* (1579-80) and Henry
Reynolds' *Mythomystes* (1632). Sidney's reference to the doctrine is part
of his definition of poetry. In accordance with Aristotle's ideas on the
subject Sidney writes that poetry surpasses philosophy and history in its
power to 'teach and delight' by means of memorable visual images:

---

on an easel with the other. A mask dangling from a chain on her breast emphasizes
that Imitation and Painting are inseparable (pp. 182-4).

20. The Hertel edition is of special interest in the history of Ripa's book: it consists
of engravings only and is therefore the exact opposite of Ripa's original edition of 1593
which did not contain any pictures. In a way this transformation illustrates the
parallellism of the two arts.

21. *De Gloria Atheniensium*, iii, 346f-347c.

22. Horace, *Ars Poetica*, 361-365:

> Ut pictura poesis: erit quae, si propius stes,
> te capiat magis, et quaedam, si longius abstes.
> haec amat obscurum, volet haec sub luce videri,
> iudicis argutum quae non formidat acumen;
> haec placuit semel, haec deciens repetita placebit.

Horace, *Satires, Epistles, Ars Poetica*, ed. H. Rushton Fairclough (London: Heinemann, 1970), p. 480.

> (A poem is like a painting: the closer you stand to this one the more it will impress you,
> whereas you have to stand a good distance from that one; this one demands a rather dark
> corner, but that one needs to be seen in full light, and will stand up to the keen-eyed
> scrutiny of the art-critic; this one only pleased you the first time you saw it, but that one
> will go on giving pleasure however often it is looked at. (T.S. Dorsch, trans., *Classical
> Literary Criticism* (Harmondsworth: Penguin, 1965), pp. 91-2)).

Poesy therefore is an art of imitation, for so Aristotle termeth it in the word μίμησις — that is to say, a representing, counterfeiting, or figuring forth — to speak metaphorically, a speaking picture — with this end, to teach and delight. . . . The philosopher, therefore, and the historian are they which would win the goal, the one by precept, the other by example. But both, not having both, do both halt. . . . Now doth the peerless poet perform both: for whatsoever the philosopher saith should be done, he giveth a perfect picture of it in someone by whom he presupposeth it was done, so as he coupleth the general notion with the particular example. A perfect picture I say, for he yieldeth to the powers of the mind an image of that whereof the philosopher bestoweth but a wordish description, which doth neither strike, pierce, nor possess the sight of the soul so much as that other doth. . . . the question is, whether the feigned image of poetry or the regular instruction of philosophy hath the more force in teaching: . . . For conclusion, I say the philosopher teacheth, but he teacheth obscurely, so as the learned only can understand him, that is to say, he teacheth them that are already taught; but the poet is the food for the tenderest stomachs, the poet is indeed the right popular philosopher, whereof Aesop's tales give good proof: whose pretty allegories, stealing under the formal tales of beasts, make many, more beastly than beasts, begin to hear the sound of virtue from these dumb speakers.[23]

Reynolds wrote his treatise, "wherein a short Survey is taken of the Nature and Value of True Poesy and Depth of the Ancients above our Moderne Poets," in 1632. He mentions *ut pictura poesis* in a prefatory letter, "To the Right hon[11] and my euer-honor'd Lord, Henry Lord Matrauers." Although the matter of the letter is trivial, it shows that the doctrine was still literally applied in Herbert's day:

My Lord,
    As I haue euer beene a louer (though ignorant one) of the Art of Painting, a frute of the Fancy that may be fitly called a silent Poësy, so of necessity must I loue her Sister the Art of Poësy, which is no other then a speaking Painting or Picture. And because I presume your LoP, fauoring and so well vnderstanding the one, cannot but vnderstand and like the other, I aduenture to present a slight drafte of her to your LoP, that, as you haue daily before your eyes one of the best suruayes of what is or can be in Picture, you may haue likewise limned, though in little, by a creature no lesse your owne then they are (how artfully I dare not auouch, but sure) a true picture of her Sister, Poësy: A Birth, my Lord, some moneths since conceiued, and euen as soone borne; and which, though now ope to other eyes, yet askes no other honour then your acceptance; to whome, in gratefull acknowledgment of your noble fauours, are (no lesse then this his slight issue is) for euer dedicated the best of the poore indeauors of the parent,

Your LoPs humble and most
affectionate seruant,
H.R.[24]

23. Sir Philip Sidney, "A Defence of Poetry" in *Miscellaneous Prose*, eds. K. Duncan-Jones & J. van Dorsten (Oxford: Oxford Univ. Press, 1973), pp. 79-80, p. 85, p. 87.
24. Henry Reynolds, *Mythomystes, wherein a short Svrvay is taken of the Natvre and Valve of Trve Poesy and Depth of the Ancients above ovr Moderne Poets* (1632) in Spingarn, *Critical Essays*, I, 141.

The doctrine of *ut pictura poesis* was not only formulated in treatises on poetry such as those by Sidney and Reynolds; it also found its way into literature itself. Thus it is dramatised in the well-known dialogue between painter and poet in Shakespeare's *Timon of Athens,* I, i:

> *Poet.* ... What have you there?
> *Pain.* A picture, sir. When comes your book forth?
> *Poet.* Upon the heels of my presentment, sir.
>   Let's see your piece.
> *Pain.*   'Tis a good piece.
> *Poet.* So 'tis; this comes off well and excellent.
> *Pain.* Indifferent.
> *Poet.*   Admirable. How this grace
>   Speaks his own standing! What a mental power
>   This eye shoots forth! How big imagination
>   Moves in this lip! To th' dumbness of the gesture
>   One might interpret.
> *Pain.* It is a pretty mocking of the life.
>   Here is a touch: is 't good?
> *Poet.*   I will say of it,
>   It tutors nature; artificial strife
>   Lives in these touches, livelier than life.
> ....
> *Pain.* 'Tis common.
>   A thousand moral paintings I can show
>   That shall demonstrate these quick blows of Fortune's
>   More pregnantly than words. ...[25]

This passage only makes sense if the reader is aware of concepts like *ut pictura poesis* and *imitatio* and the rhetorical principle of *inventio,* all of which would be common knowledge to the learned members of Shakespeare's audience. The painter's brevity and the poet's power of description illustrate Simonides' saying that painting is dumb poetry and poetry a speaking picture. When the painter introduces the subject of *imitatio* ("a pretty mocking of the life") the poet, in his rhetorical fervour, turns the dictum *artis natura magistra* into *naturae ars magistra.* In the dialogue from *Timon of Athens* Shakespeare dramatizes the relation between the sister arts, presenting it in the traditional form of a debate about the respective values of the two arts. As Anthony Blunt (1938-39) explains, the "audience of that time . . . would have seen in it an allusion to the "Paragone," or the quarrel and rivalry which had set the painter and poets of Italy against each other for two centuries. . .[26] This competitive element had its origin in discussions about the relative merits of the two

25. *Timon of Athens,* ed. H.J. Oliver (London: Methuen, 1959), pp. 5-6; p. 10, ll. 25-38; ll. 91-94.
26. Anthony Blunt, "An Echo of the 'Paragone' in Shakespeare," *JWI,* 2 (1938-39), 260-62.

senses associated with the arts of painting and poetry, the eye and the ear. Horace clearly expressed his preference in a passage from the *Ars Poetica* dealing with dramatic performance:

> However, the mind is less actively stimulated by what it takes in through the ear than by what is presented to it through the trustworthy agency of the eyes — something that the spectator can see for himself.[27]

In the Renaissance the *paragone* often led to outright family quarrels between the two arts.[28]

Ut pictura poesis provided the theoretical and aesthetic basis for a comparison between the aims and methods of the arts of literature and painting. Its influence went hand in hand with the growing popularity of emblem books and the revival of pattern poetry. On a more concrete level *ut pictura poesis* influenced the nature of the imagery used in both arts. As Tuve (1947) formulates it:

> When we recognize the demand for expressiveness that lay behind their demand for lifelikeness, and remember the parallel demand for significant abstractions portrayed through the vivid concretions in a poem, it does not seem to me that we can

27. *Ars Poetica*, 180-182, in *Classical Literary Criticism*, p. 85.
28. Jean Paul Richter, trans. and ed., *The Literary Works of Leonardo da Vinci*, 2 vols., 2nd ed. (London: Oxford Univ. Press, 1939), I, 49; cf. also *Trattato*, 22, 23 in Richter, I, 55-6. Leonardo's reasoning is basically Aristotelian. It is interesting to compare his Renaissance point of view on the matter with that of Shelley in the 19th century. This is Leonardo's view on the relative merits of the two arts (Trattato, 23):

> 'How Painting surpasses all works of men by the subtle speculations connected with it': The eye, which is the window of the soul, is the chief organ whereby the understanding can have the most complete and magnificent view of the infinite works of nature; and the ear comes second, which acquires dignity by hearing the things the eye has seen . . . And if you call painting dumb poetry, the painter may call poetry blind painting.

Shelley wrote:

> Poetry . . . expresses those arrangements of language, and especially metrical language, which are created by that imperial faculty, whose throne is curtained within the invisible nature of man. And this springs from the nature itself of language, which is a more direct representation of the actions and passions of our internal being, and is susceptible of more various and delicate combinations, than colour, form, or motion, and is more plastic and obedient to the control of that faculty of which it is the creation. For language is arbitrarily produced by the imagination, and has relation to thoughts alone; but all other materials, instruments, and conditions of art have relations among each other, which limit and interpose between conception and expression . . . (qu. in Richter, I, 49).

It would be difficult to find a more unequivocal instance of the radical difference between the Renaissance philosophy of art based on *imitatio* and the Romantic emphasis on the imagination, a faculty that is allowed to roam freely where once even Angels feared to tread. See also Irma Richter, introd. & trans., *Paragone: A Comparison of the Arts by Leonardo da Vinci* (London: Oxford Univ. Press, 1949).

think of *ut pictura poesis* as inducing either decorative or appliquéd images. *Ut pictura poesis* emphasizes the 'individual frame of reference' which characterizes both these arts, and it emphasized graphic liveliness in poetry when that was proper to the poet's ends.[29]

It is on this level that the visual shape of a poem like "The Altar" is in keeping with other images. In terms of Renaissance poetics there is no essential difference between the 'graphic liveliness' of the pattern poem in which the poet 'rears' an altar of words and that of an image such as "I made a posie, while the day ran by" ("Life", 1. 1; *Works,* p. 94).

2.2. *Utile dulce.*

Like *ut pictura poesis, utile dulce* as a phrase derives from Horace; both concepts are of course modifications of the Aristotelian theory of imitation.[30] Rensselaer W. Lee explained why the notion of 'instruction and delight' had such a great appeal for the Renaissance mind:

> Directly adapted from Horace who as a satirist had held up the mirror of his art to human foibles, and had a serious, if urbane and detached, concern for the improvement of human life, came the admonition that painting like poetry (Horace had been thinking of the effect of dramatic art on the audience) should instruct as well as delight. This half-moralistic definition of the purpose of art might not be consistent with the Aristotelian position that art as ideal imitation is founded on its own principles of structure and has no conscious didactic intent; but it was accepted axiomatically, if uncritically, by most Renaissance and Baroque critics both of poetry and painting, for the excellent reason that it provided an ethical sanction, fortunately in the words of an ancient critic, for those arts which, if the subject matter were profane, the Middle Ages had accepted only with the aid of allegorical or moral interpretation, and which the divine Plato had excoriated, in a way frequently embarrassing to the Renaissance, as feeding and watering the passions.[31]

Utile dulce provides the moral justification for the practice of both the art

29. *"Ut Pictura Poesis* and Functional Sensuous Imagery" in Rosemond Tuve, *Elizabethan and Metaphysical Imagery* (Chicago: Chicago Univ. Press, 1947), pp. 50-60; this qu. p. 60.
30. Horace, *Ars Poetica*, 333-34 and 343-44:

Aut prodesse volunt aut delectare poetae
aut simul et iucunda et idonea dicere vitae.
. . . .
omne tulit punctum qui miscuit utile dulci,
lectorem delectando pariterque monendo.

(Poets aim at giving either profit or delight, or at combining the giving of pleasure with some useful precepts for life ... The man who has managed to blend profit with delight wins everyone's approbation, for he gives his reader pleasure at the same time as he instructs him (*Classical Literary Criticism*, pp. 90-1)).

31. Rensselaer W. Lee, pp. 32-3.

of painting and that of poetry. In the passage from *Timons of Athens* quoted in the previous section Shakespeare remains fairly close to the Aristotelian notion of imitation. Sir Philip Sidney, on the other hand, explicitly combines the notion of the art of imitation with *ut pictura poesis* and *utile dulce*: "Poesy therefore is an art of imitation. . . a speaking picture — with this end, to teach and delight. . .".

It is hardly surprising that the maxim *utile dulce* with its moralistic-didactic intention had a strong appeal for Herbert, not only as emblematic poet, but also as poet/priest. Herbert makes use of the concept both in his prose and his poetry. Horace saw *utile dulce* primarily as a means for the dramatist to be persuasive and convincing in front of an audience and Herbert saw its function for the priest in a similar light:

> The Country Parson, as soon as he awakes on Sunday morning, presently falls to work, and seems to himselfe so as a Market-man is, when the Market day comes, or a shopkeeper, when customers use to come in.

In Herbert's opinion the parson as preacher should interweave the heavy stuff of his sermon with more lively material:

> Sometimes he tells them stories, and sayings of others, according as his text invites him; for them also men heed, and remember better then exhortations; which though earnest, yet often dy with the Sermon, especially with Countrey people; which are thick, and heavy, and hard to raise to a poynt of Zeal, and fervency, and need a mountaine of fire to kindle them; but stories and sayings they will well remember.

Even when the parson is enjoying the company of his neighbours of a Sunday evening:

> he takes occasion to discourse *of such things as are both profitable, and pleasant* . . .[32]

---

32. *A Priest to the Temple* in *Works*, p. 235, p. 233, p. 236. Cf. Chaucer's *Pardoner's Prologue* in *The Canterbury Tales*:

> Thanne telle I hem ensamples many oon
> Of olde stories longe tyme agoon.
> For lewed peple loven tales olde;
> Swiche thynges kan they wel reporte and holde. (ll. 435-38)

Geoffrey Chaucer, *The Works,* ed. F.N. Robinson, 2nd ed. (London: Oxford Univ. Press, 1957), p. 149. As Robinson's note to l. 435 of the quoted passage explains "ensamples" refers to 'exempla,' a term regularly applied to the illustrative anecdotes of preachers. On this tradition see "Fiction and Instruction in the Sermon "Exempla'" in G.R. Owst, *Literature and Pulpit in Medieval England*, 2nd ed. (Oxford: Blackwell, 1961), pp. 149-209. Owst reports that

> ... the Venerable Bede had told in his *Historia Anglorum* how a "very subtle and learned" bishop sent to convert the English had failed miserably in the task "with his subtlety in sermons"; but how a less literate successor with his anecdotes and *examples* "converted well nigh the whole of England" (p. 152).

Utile dulce is also presented by Herbert as a way in which the religious poet can persuade and convince his audience. The very first stanza of "The Church-porch" reads:

> Thou, whose sweet youth and early hopes inhance
> Thy rate and price, and mark thee for a treasure;
> Hearken unto a Verser, who may chance
> Ryme thee to good, and make a bait of pleasure.
>   A verse may finde him, who a sermon flies,
>   And turn delight into a sacrifice.

The concept befits the tone and content of "The Church-porch," which is an overtly didactic poem introducing the 'delight' of *The Church*.[33] In "Praise (III)" *utile dulce* is seen as a way of converting the hearts of sinners:

> Wherefore I sing. Yet since my heart,
>   Though press'd, runnes thin;
> O that I might some other hearts convert,
>   And so take up at use good store:
> That to thy chest there might be coming in
>   Both all my praise, and more![34]

As Owst points out in another part of his study, there is a long native tradition of realism in sermons:

> Writers of pulpit manuals and treatises, from the thirteenth century onwards, were accustomed to illustrate each separate "branch" of Vice or Virtue, treated in turn, with ... vivid little sketches of contemporary men and women and their ways (p. 87).

33. In the opening lines of "The Church-porch" Herbert indicates his moral and religious purpose on the one hand and the rhetoric mode by means of which he intends to achieve his ends on the other. The beginning of "The Church-porch" is written in words that underline the nature of the poetry that is to follow. The point is a generic one and we can best illustrate it by means of a comparison. Milton chose the epic as a vehicle for the 'grand design' of *Paradise Lost* and used the lofty style befitting that genre. Herbert used the lyric as the genre for the main body of his poetry and chose a simple, homely vocabulary to suit it. Both Herbert and Milton make their respective purposes and the literary genres they have adopted clear right from the start. The invocation of the "Heav'nly Muse" in the first lines of *Paradise Lost* 'places' the poem rhetorically and causes the reader to expect an epic on a grand scale to follow. The first lines of *The Temple* also determine the generic qualities of the poetry that is to follow. The phrase "Hearken unto a Verser" by itself precludes the possibility of an epic to follow; after such an opening line the reader expects rather the "private ejaculations" promised him by the author on the title-page and a style and vocabulary that is simple and homely. These expectations are diametrically opposed to those raised by Milton who invokes the aid of the Muse for his "adventrous Song, / That with no middle flight intends to soar / Above the *Aonian* Mount; while it persues / Things unattempted yet in Prose or Rime." (John Milton, *The Poetical Works*, ed. Helen Darbishire, I (Oxford: Oxford Univ. Press, 1952), 5-6).

34. *Works*, pp. 157-59, ll. 37-42.

Herbert's attitude is comparable to that of the emblem writers who used and transformed the emblem tradition — originally a humanistic venture with predominantly allegorical and mythological subject-matter — for didactic/religious purposes. Wither recommends his book of emblems to his readers in this way:

> For, when levitie, or a childish delight, in trifling Objects, hath allured them to looke on the Pictures; Curiositie may urge them to peepe further, that they may seeke out also their Meanings, in our annexed Illustrations.[35]

Wither's words are perfectly analogous with the first stanza of "The Church-porch."[36]

The first stanza of "The Church-porch" is in a sense the *scholium* to the typographical pattern of the pattern poems. Herbert used the pattern poem because its form would attract the reader's attention and lead him then from delight to instruction. *Utile dulce* is part of Herbert's poetic strategy of persuasion, a strategy that has a public function. It invites the reader to enter into the poet's concerns, to enter *The Church*.

As was pointed out before the battle between Poetry and Painting was waged on the battlefield of *imitatio* and under the banner of *ut pictura poesis.* The claim made by theorists of art that the eye reigned supreme over the other senses and its corollary that painting, because of its primary appeal to the eyes, was superior to poetry, influenced the formation of imagery in the sixteenth and seventeenth centuries. Tuve (1947) has also analysed the relation between *ut pictura poesis* as part of the theory of imitation and 'functional sensuous imagery.' Writing about certain highly detailed images in Spenser and Marlowe she comes to the conclusion that

> ... they please only by virtue of the habit (in both writer and reader) of seeing the

---

35. Wither, "To the Reader," in *A Collection of Emblemes* (1635), sig. A2. Cf. the mixture of *ut pictura poesis* and *utile dulce* in the following passage:

> If they [i.e. the engravings] were worthy of the Gravers and Printers cost, being only dumbe Figures, little usefull to any but to young Gravers or Painters; and as little delightfull, except, to Children, and Childish-gazers: they may now be much more worthy; seeing the life of Speach being added unto them, may make them Teachers, and Remembrancers of profitable things (sigs. A1[v] and A2).

As Praz indicates, *utile dulce* is part of the vocabulary of most emblematists: "Stichten met vermakelijkheid," to edify while amusing, (Jacob Cats; *Studies in Seventeenth-Century Imagery,* p. 169).

36. *Utile dulce* was also at the centre of the debate between the poet Francesco Petrarca and his brother, the Carthusian mon Gherardo. When the latter wrote to Francesco: "The sweetness of your poetry is inconsistent with the severity of my life," Francesco aptly answered: "Poetry is far from being opposed to theology; indeed one may say that theology actually is poetry — poetry concerning God."; qu. in Richter, ed., *The Literary Works of Leonardo da Vinci,* p. 19.

intelligible in the visible — a habit shared by most of the arts in an era like the Renaissance, and of which the extreme example is the emblem.[37]

Herbert's pattern poems are extreme examples of the poet's concern to express in visual terms his conception of the hieroglyphic nature of the universe. The time-hallowed concept of *imitatio* and the related notions of *ut pictura poesis* and *utile dulce* may have influenced the poet's decision to give these poems their distinctive shapes.

3. *Opsis.*

A specific aspect, the visual appeal of poetry as it appears on the page, has its place within the realm of rhetoric, too. In his book on Greek metaphor W. Bedell Stanford advanced the theory that the *technopaegnia,* the pattern poems of the Alexandrians in the *Greek Anthology,* depended for their visual effect on the element of ὄψις, *opsis.* The word occurs in Aristotle's *Rhetoric,* III, ii, 13, where Aristotle, quoting Licymnius, writes:

> The beauty of words is either in their sound or in their sense; ... The materials of metaphor must be beautiful to the ear, to the understanding, to the eye, or to some other physical sense.[38]

Stanford interprets *opsis* as "the direct visual effect of the shape of letters and words to the reader's eye" (p. 64) and he compares what he calls iconic or picture-writing with onomatopoeia, the former appealing to the visual sphere, the latter to sound:

> ... In fact onomatopoeic words are in the sphere of sound what iconic or picture writing is in the visual sphere, and both belong to the small class of linguistic symbols which *directly* represent their objects of reference to the senses with the minimum of mental mediation — rare survivals of the primeval stages of speech and writing. Without the use of picture-writing ... the only possible way of reproducing to the reader's *eye* what *murmur maris* does for the hearer's *ear* would be to print the word *green* in Marvell's
> 'Annihilating all that's made
> to a *green* thought in a *green* shade.'

37. *Elizabethan and Metaphysical Imagery*, p. 53. Art theorists were frequently involved in the emblematic movement. Thus Lodovico Dolce, one of the most influential theorists of art in the Italian Renaissance, wrote the explanatory stanzas to the three editions of *Imprese* of the painter Battista Pittoni (see Robert J. Clements, *Picta Poesis: Literary and Humanistic Theory in Renaissance Emblem Books*, Temi e testi, 6 (Roma: Ed. di Storia e letteratura, 1960), p. 26.

38. W. Bedell Stanford, *Greek Metaphor: Studies in Theory and Practice* (Oxford: Blackwell, 1936), p. 43. I owe the reference to Stanford to a suggestion made to me several years ago by Prof. Dr. J.J.A. Mooij. For the Greek text see, Aristotle, *The "Art" of Rhetoric,* The Loeb Classical Library, 193 (London: Heinemann, 1967), p. 358.

in green ink, or to use tricoloured inks in Shakespeare's 'making the *green* one *red*' (Macbeth, II, 2, 64) . . .[39]

In *Rage for Order* (1948) Austin Warren makes the same comparison between pattern poetry and onomatopoeia, although he does not refer to Aristotle's notion of *opsis* in that context:

> . . . "The Altar" and "Easter Wings" visualise the objects they signify. These innocent ingenuities have been duly chastised in Addison's essay on "False Wit" and elsewhere in neoclassical criticism. Relatively few in number, they proceed from a principle analogous to onomatopoeia and equally harmless in moderation: the expressive adjustment of structure, phonetic or typographical, to theme.[40]

In *Anatomy of Criticism* (1957) Northrop Frye uses the terms *opsis* and *melos* within the framework of a theoretical discussion about the distinction between the visual and the aural element in lyrical poetry:

> The two elements of subconscious association which form the basis for lyrical *melos* and *opsis* respectively have never been given names. We may call them, if the terms are thought dignified enough, babble and doodle. . . . The radical of *melos* is *charm*: the hypnotic incantation that, through its pulsing dance rhythm, appeals to involuntary physical response, and is hence not far from the sense of magic, or physically compelling power. . . . We have several times noticed the close relation between the visual and the conceptual in poetry, and the radical of *opsis* in the lyric is *riddle*, which is characteristically a fusion of sensation and reflection, the use of

---

39. Bedell Stanford, p. 42. An interesting parallel to what Stanford describes here can be found in musical notation. Einstein describes the 16th c. setting of Petrarch's sonnet against the papal court in Avignon, "Fiamma del ciel," in which occur these two lines:

> Per le camere tue fanciulle e vecchi
> Vanno trescando e Beel-ze-bub in mezzo.

("Through the rooms, you young women and old men / Go dancing the tresca and Beelzebub in your midst."). My dictionary tells me that one of the meanings of *trescare* is "avere un amorazzo" (to have an illicit love-affair), which seems quite relevant here (Zingarelli, *Vocabulario della lingua italiana,* 10th ed. (Bologna: Zanichelli, 1970). In the musical notation the second line consists solely of black notes. Einstein comments: "Zweifellos malt der Rhythmus den Tanz der alten Pfaffen mit den Huren; aber ohne Beelzebub wäre die Stelle schwerlich so "schwarz" ausgefallen" (Alfred Einstein, "Augenmusik im Madrigal," *Zeitschrift der Internationalen Musikgesellschaft,* 14 (1912-13), p. 18. Cf. Willi Apel, *The Notation of Polyphonic Music, 900-1600* (Cambr., Mass.: Harvard Univ. Press, 1953), pp. 403-4. Grout writes about French composers of the late 14th c.: "Their musical style is matched by the visual appearance of some pages in the manuscripts, with their fanciful decorations, intermingled red and black notes, ingenious complications of notation, and occasional caprices such as the writing of a love song in the shape of a heart . . . or a canon in the shape of a circle" (*A History of Western Music,* p. 135). Cf. Baude Cordier, "Belle bonne," Chapter One, 1, fig. 4.

40. Austin Warren, *Rage for Order: Essays in Criticism* (Chicago: Univ. of Chicago Press, 1948), p. 31.

an object of sense experience to stimulate a mental activity in connection with it.[41]

It is tempting to associate Frye's use of the word 'riddle' with the riddle-element in the *technopaegnia* of the *Greek Anthology*. But, although Frye does mention Herbert's pattern poems as extreme manifestations of *opsis*, the meaning he attaches to it is more comprehensive than the word 'riddle' suggests:

> In such emblems as Herbert's *The Altar* and *Easter Wings,* where the pictorial shape of the subject is suggested in the shape of the lines of the poem, we begin to approach the pictorial boundary of the lyric. The absorption of words by pictures, corresponding to the madrigal's absorption of words by music, is picture-writing, of the kind most familiar to us in comic strips, captioned cartoons, posters, and other emblematic forms. A further stage of absorption is represented by Hogarth's *Rake's Progress* and similar narrative sequences of pictures, in the scroll pictures of the Orient, or in the novels in woodcuts that occasionally appear. Pictorial arrangements of the visible basis of literature, which is alphabetical writing, have had a more fitful and sporadic existence, ranging from capitals in illuminated manuscripts to surrealist experiments in collage, and have not had much specifically literary importance. They would have had more, of course, if our writing had remained in the hieroglyphic stage, as in hieroglyphics writing and drawing are much the same art.[42]

Frye's analysis is exceptional in that it relates *opsis* with hieroglyphics, although he does not use "hieroglyphics" in the broad philosophical way that Summers did.

Frye mentions a number of possible ways in which what he calls the "absorption of words by pictures" can manifest itself. In recent years several anthologies have appeared in which the pattern poem occurs as one among many expressions of the visual element in language. *Letter and Image* by Massin, *The Word as Image* by Berjouhi Bowler and *Speaking Pictures* by Milton Klonsky are the most prominent of these collections.[43] The publication of anthologies of this particular kind is probably partly due to the influence of the concrete poetry movement in the fifties and sixties of our own century. Massin's book contains a great variety of illustrations that show the manifold expressive relations between the abstract sign and the pictured idea. The book teems with figured alphabets, initials from illuminated manuscripts, pattern poems, 'calligrammes,' reproductions of paintings in which collage techniques are used, modern advertisements and concrete poems. All the categories mentioned by Frye and more are represented. Bowler's book also contains many fine examples of the pictorial quality of language. He emphasizes the magnificent freedom and flowing quality of Arabic and

41. Northrop Frye, *Anatomy of Criticism* (Princeton: Princeton Univ. Press, 1957), p. 275, p. 278, p. 280.
42. Frye, pp. 274-75.
43. See Chapter One, 1, n. 1.

Chinese pictograms and describe their calligraphic technique which by virtue of the nature and shape of the letters of their alphabets lends itself to much more elaborate designs than its Western equivalents. Klonsky's edition, finally, takes the emblematic tradition for its starting-point. Klonsky assumes, erroneously, that the tradition of figured poetry originates in the Renaissance. His anthology does not contain material dating further back than the sixteenth century; there are no *technopaegnia* from the *Greek Anthology,* no *carmina figurata* by Hrabanus Maurus or Optatianus Porfirius, who kept the tradition of the patterned poem alive in the Middle Ages. The book does contain several emblems, not only from the sixteenth and seventeenth centuries but also by Bunyan in the eighteenth and Robert Louis Stevenson in the nineteenth. Klonsky includes English translations of the *Coup de Dés* by Mallarmé and some of Apollinaire's 'calligrammes.' Modern cartoons, poems illustrated by the poet, and some concrete poems conclude his rather chaotic collection.

The above described anthologies are interesting because they show how widespread and widely practised is the art of ideographic writing in which the written sign and that which is signified are expressed simultaneously on the page. Bowler and Klonsky see two main causes for the persistent urge to combine sign and signified, letter and image: the magical power that has always been attributed to patterned language and the mystical, Hermetic tradition. This explanation is in accordance with the hieroglyphic view of the universe that pervaded almost every aspect of Renaissance thinking and writing. It was expressed in emblems, devices and patterned language and was grounded on a firm belief in the mystical relation between the individual and the universe surrounding him. Bowler and Klonsky are far too one-sided, however, in their heavy emphasis on the occult aspect of this philosophy. They fail to pay sufficient attention to the public function of these visual elements. Court masques, pageants, tapestries, and the architecture of the Renaissance all illustrate that images also found an outlet in public display. In a different but comparable way the Roman-Catholic, and particularly the Jesuit, development of the emblem book had a clearly defined public function, because the Jesuits used the popular emblematic tradition for didactic purposes. Many of the images and symbols that were public property in the 16th and 17th centuries seem quite obscure to the modern mind. Hence epithets like 'mystical' or 'magical' should not be used without proper definition since they can easily be misunderstood.[44]

44. On the subject of patterned language and magic see also Alfons A. Barb, "St. Zacharias the prophet and martyr. A study in charms and incantations," *JWCI*, 11 (1948), 35-67. About the public nature of imagery see Chapter One, 2.3. and 2.4. *passim.*

The pattern poem is but one of the many possible relations between babble and doodle; as Frye indicates, the "absorption of words by pictures" could assume many forms. In 1930 Ludwig Volkmann, one of the pioneers of emblem studies, tried to capture all these manifestations in one diagram.[45] Since the diagram is not readily available, I reproduce it here:

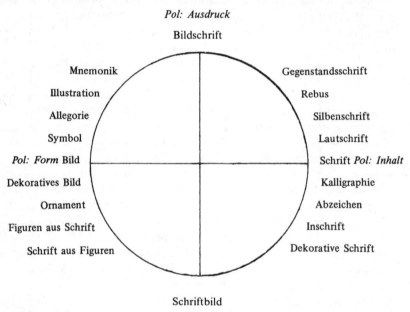

Volkmann calls pattern poems "Erzeugnisse ... ,worin aus Schrift oder Drucktypen durch bildmäszige Anordnung recht eigentliche "Schriftbilder" hergestellt wurden."[46] The diagram makes abundantly clear that pattern poetry did not and does not exist in isolation, either in theory or in practice.

Even if it could be demonstrated that Stanford's interpretation of Aristotle's word *opsis* is incorrect, the fact remains that visual aspects of the printed word have frequently and consciously been employed as integrated elements in works of literature. Therefore any theory of literature should at least pay some attention to the direct visual appeal of the graphic aspect of poetry. Wellek and Warren only touch upon the subject in their *Theory of Literature*. In a section dealing with the role of print in poetry they mention

45. Ludwig Volkmann, "Bild und Schrift," *Buch und Schrift*, 4 (1930), 9-18.
46. Volkmann, pp. 17-8.

the pattern poems of the *Greek Anthology*, Herbert's pattern poems, Sterne's blank and marbled pages, and the modern poetry of e.e. cummings, Apollinaire and Arno Holz. Wellek and Warren call these phenomena "rare extravaganzas," though they admit that the graphic aspect of the works concerned is an essential part of their total meaning.[47]

Frye assigns a more important place to the visual element in literature than Wellek and Warren do. In the introduction to the chapter I quoted from above, Frye defines his approach to the Aristotelian notions *opsis* and *melos*:

> Considered as a verbal structure, literature presents a *lexis* which combines two other elements: *melos*, an element analogous to or otherwise connected with music, and *opsis*, which has a similar connection with the plastic arts.[48]

The anthologies in which the manifestations of the visual element in literature are deliberately introduced do not discuss *opsis*. To say that *opsis* is a feature of written or printed language does not explain why in certain periods of literary history this element was more prominently and more frequently used than in others. For our purposes Bedell Stanford's interpretation of Aristotle's term is more relevant than Frye's theory, since we are not dealing with the timeless dimension of the concept so much as with the extent to which it can be considered part of the specific historical background of Herbert's pattern poems. One source that certainly forms part of that background, is Puttenham's treatise *The Arte of English Poesie* (1589).[49]

Puttenham's book is divided into three main sections: "The first of Poets and Poesie, the second of Proportion, the third of Ornament" (title page). The second of these sections, the book of "Proportion Poetical" begins thus:

> It is said by such as professe the Mathematicall sciences, that all things stand by proportion, and that without it nothing could stand to be good or beautiful (p. 64).

Puttenham distinguishes five elements that fall under the heading of proportion: "Staffe, Measure, Concord, Scituation and figure" (p. 65). These categories correspond more or less with the modern terms stanzaic form, number, rhyme, metrical and/or rhyme pattern, and typographical

47. Wellek & Warren, *Theory of Literature* (1963), pp. 142-44.
48. Frye, p. 244; J.J.A. Mooij devoted a chapter of his book *Tekst en Lezer* (Amsterdam: Polak & van Gennep, 1979), pp. 106-153, to the role of the written/printed word in poetry. It is a very useful survey of the literary theoretical approach to the matter. The chapter contains a wealth of references. Although Mooij does not use the terms *melos* and *opsis* explicitly, the body of his chapter concentrates on the tension between visual and aural aspects of poetry.
49. George Puttenham, *The Arte of English Poesie* (1589), eds. G.D. Willcock & A. Walker (Cambridge: Cambridge Univ. Press, 1936).

pattern (i.e. pattern poetry). It is this last type of proportion that concerns us here:

> Your last proportion is that of figure, so called for that it yelds an ocular representation, your meeters being by good symmetrie reduced into certaine Geometricall figures, whereby the maker is restrained to keepe him within his bounds, and sheweth not onely more art, but serueth also much better for briefenesse and subtiltie of deuice. And for the same respect are also fittest for the pretie amourets in Court to entertaine their servants and the time withall, their delicate wits requiring some commendable exercise to keepe them from idlenesse. I find not of this proportion vsed by any of the Greeke or Latine Poets, or in any vulgar writer, sauing of that one forme which they cal *Anacreons egge*. But being in Italie conuersant with a certaine gentleman, who had long trauailed the Orientall parts of the world, and seene the Courts of the great Princes of China and Tartarie. I being very inquisitiue to know of the subtillities of those countreyes, and especially in matter of learning and of their vulgar Poesie, he told me that they are in all their inuentions most wittie, and haue the vse of Poesie or riming, but do not delight so much as we do in long tedious descriptions, and therefore when they will vtter any pretie conceit, they reduce it into metricall feet, and put it in forme of a *Lozange* or square, or such other figure, and so engrauen in gold, siluer or iuorie, and sometimes with letters of ametist, rubie, emeralde or topas curiousely cemented and peeced together, they sende them in chaines, bracelets, collars and girdles to their mistresses to weare for a remembrance. Some fewe measures composed in this sort this gentleman gaue me, which I translated word for word and as neere as I could followed both the phrase and the figure, which is somewhat hard to performe, because of the restraint of the figure from which ye may not digresse. At the beginning they wil seeme nothing pleasant to an English eare, but time and vsage wil make them acceptable inough, as it doth in all other new guises, be it for wearing of apparell or otherwise (pp. 91-2).

This introduction of the subject is followed by illustrations of the various geometrical shapes and short essays on each of these shapes. Each geometrical shape is said to represent a particular moral virtue, natural inclination or element:

> The square is of all other accompted the figure of most solliditie and stedfastnesse, and for his owne stay and firmitie requireth none other base then himselfe, and therefore as the roundell or Spheare is appropriat to the heauens, the Spire to the element of the fire: the Triangle to the ayre, and the Lozange to the water: so is the square for his inconcussable steadinesse likened to the earth, which perchaunce might be the reason that the Prince of Philosophers in his first booke of the *Ethicks*, termeth a constant minded man, euen egal and direct on all sides, and not easily overthrowne by every litle aduersitie, *hominem quadratū*, a square man (p. 100).

In the next section of the same chapter Puttenham discusses "the deuice or embleme, and that other which the Greekes call Anagramma, and we the Posie transposed" (p. 102), in which he sums up the hieroglyphic bent that characterized the age he lived in:

> This may suffice for deuices, a terme which includes in his generality all those other, viz. liueries, cognizāces, emblemes, enseigns and impreses. For though the termes be diuers, the vse and intent is but one whether they rest in colour or figure

or both, or in word or in muet shew, and that is to insinuat some secret, wittie, morall and braue purpose presented to the beholder, either to recreate his eye, or please his phantasie, or examine his iudgement, or occupie his braine or to manage his will either by hope or by dread, euery of which respectes be of no litle moment to the interest and ornament of the ciuill life: and therefore giue them no litle commendation (pp. 107-8).

Puttenham inclines more towards *dulce* than towards *utile*. His views on the purpose of literature are closely related to his social views. Puttenham regards literature as part of the "ciuill life," a phrase that recurs time and again in his treatise and by which he means the courtier's life.[50] Puttenham's historical information about the origins of pattern poetry is quite amusing but largely wrong. Apparently he had no direct knowledge of the *Greek Anthology*. The egg-shaped poem from the *Anthology* was generally attributed to Simmias, not Anacreon, in Puttenham's day. The identity of the mysterious "gentleman, who had long trauailed the Orientall parts of the world" is unknown, but, although it is doubtful that the origin of the European pattern poem is to be found in the East, Puttenham may have seen Persian *ghazals* or Chinese calligraphy.[51]

Whatever the status of his scholarship, however, Puttenham is a useful source of information. His discussion of the proportion of figure shows that in the late sixteenth century *opsis* as manifested in pattern poetry was regarded as a rhetorical principle worthy of serious consideration. If we compare Puttenham's description of the use and aim of the device with Stanford's interpretation of Aristotle's term *opsis*, the resemblance is obvious.[52] Whereas we cannot be sure that Aristotle meant the word *opsis* to be understood as the direct visual effect of the words on the page, Puttenham's "ocular representation" was certainly meant to be understood in that way.

We can safely assume that Herbert knew the traditional Aristotelian division of poetry into six elements: *mythos*, *ethos*, *dianoia*, *melos*, *lexis*, and *opsis*. That he knew Puttenham's *Arte* is quite plausible. Puttenham's treatise shows that at the end of the sixteenth century *opsis* could be interpreted as referring to "ocular representation," i.e. a direct visual

50. The paragon of courtly virtue in the English Renaissance was Sir Philip Sidney, his model being the perfect courtier as described in Baldassar Castiglione's book *The Book of the Courtier* (1528), well-known in England through the English translation by Sir Thomas Hoby of 1561.

51. See Church, *The Pattern Poem*, pp. 1-8 and A.L. Korn, "Puttenham and the Oriental Pattern-Poem," for a survey of the Oriental line of development of the pattern poem. Cf. the ghazal reproduced in Chapter One, 1, fig. 1.

52. Although Puttenham does not refer at all frequently to his sources, classical or otherwise, he mentions Aristotle, "the Prince of Philosophers," in the quoted passage on the square (p. 100; see Willcock & Walker, p. lix, p. lxii).

effect of poetry rather than to the more indirect appeal to the imagination, the mind's eye, as most commentators of Aristotle's have interpreted the word.[53]

4. Conclusions.

In this chapter we have attempted to find an answer to the question as to why a serious poet like Herbert would use the form of the pattern poem. We have found that a number of concepts were current in Herbert's day that demonstrate that to Herbert and his reading public the pattern poem came more naturally than it did in later ages and that it could be used as a vehicle for deeply felt religious sentiments and convictions. The basic *rationale* of the visual element in Herbert's verse of which the pattern poems are but special instances, is the hieroglyphic view of the universe. Within the context of this special way of looking at reality the visual pattern of these poems reflects something of the order and beauty of God's universe as a whole. The moral and didactic corollary of the hieroglypic view is the notion of *utile dulce*. Several poems in *The Church* show Herbert's concern to 'instruct' and 'delight' in his dual function as priest and poet. Thus the direct visual appeal of the pattern poems can also be regarded as forming part of the persuasive strategy of the poet by means of which he prepares the ground for the serious and involved intention of his poems. The concept of *ut pictura poesis* postulates a comparison between the arts of poetry and painting. The concept did not only exert its influence on art and literature but it found expression in many ways and at many levels. Emblems and pattern poems are just two of the many manifestations of the doctrine.[54] *Opsis*, finally, provides a rhetorical justification for Herbert's use of the pattern poem. *Opsis* operates in the vivid, sensuous imagery of Herbert's poetry; the direct visual appeal of the pattern poem is an extreme instance of this concept. For a modern reader approaching the poetry with the aesthetic principles of Herbert's day rather than his own, the difference between a line like

> My answer is a rose.

and the possible representation of a rose in the typography on the page should be regarded as one of degree, not of kind.[55]

---

53. Bedell Stanford, p. 63.

54. Some emblem writers wrote pattern poems to accompany the pictures of their emblems. Thus Christopher Harvey's *Schola Cordis* (London, 1647) contains several pattern poems (see Chapter Three, n. 66).

55. See section 1 above. Cf. Palmer's remark: " ... Herbert has a final group of poems which have done much to alienate from him the sympathy of modern readers, though they commended him to his own generation." (I, 147).

CHAPTER THREE

A STUDY OF HERBERT'S PATTERN POEMS

Part Two: Analysis.

The   Altar.

A broken ALTAR, Lord, thy servant reares,
Made of a heart, and cemented with teares:
  Whose parts are as thy hand did frame;
 No workmans tool hath touch'd the same.
      A   HEART   alone
      Is   such   a   stone,
      As   nothing   but
      Thy pow'r doth cut.
      Wherefore each part
      Of   my   hard   heart
      Meets in this frame,
      To praise thy Name:
  That, if I chance to hold my peace,
 These stones to praise thee may not cease.
O let thy blessed SACRIFICE be mine,
And sanctifie this ALTAR to be thine.

Easter-wings.

Lord, who createdst man in wealth and store,
Though foolishly he lost the same,
Decaying more and more,
Till he became
Most poore:
With thee
O let me rise
As larks, harmoniously,
And sing this day thy victories:
Then shall the fall further the flight in me.

My tender age in sorrow did beginne :
And still with sicknesses and shame
Thou didst so punish sinne,
That I became
Most thinne.
With thee
Let me combine
And feel this day thy victorie:
For, if I imp my wing on thine,
Affliction shall advance the flight in me.

0. Introductory.

"The Altar" is the first poem of *The Church* and it is a pattern poem. This combination makes it doubly worthwhile to study the poem closely: such a study will, one hopes, both yield an interpretation of the poem itself and provide information about the poetry that is to follow. As Eliot (1962) observed "'The Temple' is ... a structure, and one which may have been worked over and elaborated, perhaps at intervals of time, before it reached its final form. We cannot judge Herbert, or savour fully his genius and his art, by any selection to be found in an anthology; we must study *The Temple* as a whole."[1] "The Altar" and "Easter-wings," the other poem to be discussed in this chapter, are pattern poems, but they are also part of the cycle of poems called *The Temple*.

The latter aspect received hardly any attention in the past. The typographical shape drew all the attention away from other aspects of the two poems. Until fairly recently they have been treated, more than any

1. T.S. Eliot, *George Herbert* (London: Longmans, Green & Co., 1962), p. 17.

other poem in *The Temple*, as if they were eccentric oddities, uncharacteristic of Herbert's poetic method. Hutchinson, the editor of the standard modern edition of Herbert's works, summed up the pattern poem's progress through the centuries:

> Conceits, which pleased in the seventeenth century, gave offence in the eighteenth, and elicited a half-hearted defence in the nineteenth century, are again seen to be no idle exercise of ingenuity but an effective way of expressing that blend of thought and passion which characterized such poetry.[2]

The phrase "blend of thought and passion" shows the extent to which Eliot's essay on the metaphysical poets of 1921 still influenced critical thinking in the forties, but the change in critical approach had, as far as Herbert's pattern poetry is concerned, already set in before that trend-setting essay was published.[3] In 1915 Palmer wrote in his edition of Herbert's work:

> ... Herbert has a final group of poems which have done much to alienate from him the sympathy of modern readers, though they commended him to his own generation. They are poems whose eccentricity of form seems to have no inner justification. Of course we know that every species of elaborate artificiality was then in fashion. Embroidery pleased. Probably Herbert himself did on occasion enjoy a ruffled shirt. I will not attempt fully to defend him. I merely say the number of such poems is small. I count but nine: *The Altar, An Anagram, Easter Wings, Heaven, Hope, Jesu, Love-Joy, Our Life is Hid, A Wreath*. And are these all artificial? I am willing to throw over *An Anagram, Heaven*, and *Jesu*, as badly marked with the time-spirit. But I maintain that the others are at worst pretty play, while often their strange forms are closely connected with their passionate matter .... Let any one study sympathetically *Hope, Paradise, A Wreath, Easter Wings, Love-Joy*, and he will discover how exquisite poetry can be when most remote from present habits of thought.[4]

Hutchinson and Palmer reacted against the condescending, derogatory manner in which critics had dismissed pattern poetry as Procrustean efforts or the by-products of 'false wit.'[5] The negative attitude towards the pattern poem persisted, however. Bennett wrote as condescendingly about pattern poetry in 1966 as Dryden, Pope, Addison and Hobbes had done in the 18th century:

> Poets of more complex mood cannot deal so simply with the problem of relating sound to sense, their pattern cannot be predetermined with the same completeness. But what Herbert had to say was usually simple ... It is a naïve device but adequate to the simple mood in which it was conceived.[6]

2. *Works*, p. xlix.
3. T.S. Eliot, "The Metaphysical Poets," (1921), in *Selected Essays*, 3rd ed. (London: Faber and Faber, 1951), pp. 281-291.
4. Palmer, I, 147.
5. See *Works*, pp. xxxix-1 for an account of the way in which the tides of taste affected the appreciation of Herbert's poetry.
6. Joan Bennett, *Five Metaphysical Poets*, 3rd ed. (Cambridge: Cambridge Univ. Press, 1963), p. 62.

Fortunately, other critics have dealt more seriously with Herbert's pattern poems. In the course of the past fifteen years a number of scholarly and critical articles and parts of books have been devoted to various aspects of these poems.[7] In virtually all these studies both Herbert's debt to the *Greek Anthology* and the popularity of the form in the age he lived in are mentioned. In none of them, however, has the exact relation between Herbert's pattern poems and either his classical examples or contemporary parallels been worked out. Only Rickey (1966) made an attempt to point out parallels between Herbert's "The Altar" and its immediate predecessors.[8] Moreover, although many commentators have remarked on the structural unity of *The Temple* and on the prominent position in it of "The Altar," the relation between "The Altar" and "Easter-wings" within that structure has elicited relatively little comment.[9] This is all the more surprising because they are the only immediately recognizable pattern poems in *The Church*.

Finally, the emblematic aspect of the pattern poems has not been studied sufficiently either. Colie (1973) points out Herbert's debt to the

---

7. The most important articles and parts of books devoted to the pattern poems are,
a) on "The Altar":
Tuve, *A Reading of George Herbert*, p. 152; Summers, *George Herbert: His Religion and Art*, pp. 140-143; Mary Ellen Rickey, *Utmost Art* (Lexington: Univ. of Kentucky Press, 1966), pp. 9-16; Coburn Freer, *Music for a King* (Baltimore: Johns Hopkins Univ. Press, 1972), pp. 119-121; Fish, *Self-Consuming Artifacts*, pp. 207-215; Vendler, *The Poetry of George Herbert*, pp. 61-63; Thomas B. Stroup, "'A Reasonable, Holy, and Living Sacrifice': Herbert's 'The Altar',", in *Essays in Literature*, 2 (Western Illinois Univ., 1975), pp. 149-63; Barbara K. Lewalski, "Typology and Poetry: A Consideration of Herbert, Vaughan and Marvell," in Earl Miner, ed., *Illustrious Evidence: Approaches to English Literature of the Early Seventeenth Century* (Berkeley: Univ. of California Press, 1975), pp. 45-7.
b) on "Easter-wings":
W.C.B., "George Herbert's 'Easter Wings,'" *N&Q*, 8th Ser., 7 (26 Jan., 1895), 66; T.O. Beachcroft, "Nicholas Ferrar and George Herbert," *The Criterion*, 12 (1933), 40; E. de Selincourt, "George Herbert," *The Hibbert Journal*, 39 (1940-41), 389-397; Tuve, p. 157; Summers, pp. 140-43; Boultenhouse, "Poems in the Shapes of Things"; Walker, "The Architectonics of George Herbert's *The Temple*"; Robert Hastings, "Easter Wings as a Model of Herbert's Method," *Thoth*, 4 (1963), 15-23; Bennett, pp. 62-3; C.C. Brown & W.P. Ingoldsby, "George Herbert's 'Easter-Wings,'" *HLQ*, 35 (1971-72), 131-142; P. Chossonery, "Les 'Poèmes figurés' de George Herbert et ses prétendues fantaisies poétiques," *EA*, 26 (1973), 1-11.
General:
Higgins, *George Herbert's Pattern Poems*; Rosemary Freeman, "George Herbert," in *English Emblem Books*, pp. 153-168.
8. Rickey, pp. 9-14.
9. Eliot, *George Herbert*, p. 17; Walker, pp. 289-306; Amy M. Charles, "The Williams Manuscript and *The Temple*,"; Louis L. Martz, *The Poetry of Meditation*, rev. ed. (New Haven: Yale Univ. Press, 1962), pp. 288-320; Barbara K. Lewalski, "Typology and Poetry," in Earl Miner, ed., *Illustrious Evidence*, pp. 45-7. See n. 25.

Schola Cordis emblem tradition but does not mention "The Altar" within that context.[10] Freeman (1948), Tuve (1952) and Summers (1954) discuss the relation between the emblematic method and the pattern poems in general terms but they do not compare them with specific emblems. Hastings, whose article on "Easter-wings" (1963) purports to demonstrate the emblematic vein in Herbert, concludes that "while making relatively sparse use of specific emblems or allusions to emblems of this kind, *Easter Wings* is full of the allusive suggestion characteristic of that method of viewing reality."[11] Had Hastings actually consulted the emblem books available to Herbert his conclusion would no doubt have been quite different.

The structural relation between Herbert's pattern poems and *The Church*, the emblematic aspect of the pattern poems and their connection with classical and contemporary sources will constitute the bulk of this chapter.

1. Herbert's pattern poems in *The Church*.

1.1. Introductory.

"The Altar" and "Easter-wings" should be analysed both as individual poems and as poems belonging to a cycle. The individual characteristics of the two poems will be analysed in later sections of this chapter. This first part will be devoted to determining the place of "The Altar" and "Easter-wings" within the structure of *The Temple* as a whole.

The architectonic aspect of *The Church* is part of its significance. This aspect has been studied for *The Temple* as a whole by Walker (1962).[12] Walker argues that the tri-partite division of *The Temple* into "The Church-porch," *The Church* and "The Church Militant" reflects the analogous divisions of the Hebraic temple of Solomon into porch, holy place and holy of holies. Walker's argument was partly refuted by Rickey who has pointed out that only two of Herbert's divisions are spatial; the association of "The Church Militant" with the holy of holies would seem to be far-fetched and indefensible.[13]

Summers sees *The Temple* metaphorically, as a record of the living temple of the Holy Spirit in the human heart.[14] The unity of the work, according to Summers, is derived from the exploration in the poetry of

---

10. Rosalie L. Colie, *The Resources of Kind* (Berkeley: Univ. of California Press, 1973), pp. 48-67.
11. Hastings, p. 19.
12. Walker, pp. 289-306.
13. Rickey, p. 4.
14. Summers, pp. 85-87.

the relationship between the Christian, God and the Church mystical, the body of Christ. Praz (1964) sees the unity of *The Temple* in its emblematic aspect. According to him "George Herbert's *Temple* is a conspicuous case of a mute emblem book (i.e. wanting only the plates)."[15] Eliot, too, sees *The Temple* as a structural unity that no anthology can do full justice to: "we must study *The Temple* as a whole."[16]

Whatever their critical or scholarly approach, all commentators seem to agree that *The Temple* shows remarkable coherence and that it is intended to be read as a whole. Within the structural unity of the work as a whole it is possible to discern several groups of poems that belong together in one way or another. Several poems, for instance, have titles denoting parts of the church, others relate to church-festivals or the liturgy of the church.[17] There are also series of poems that, through their order and succession, point to stages in the pilgrimage of life. Thus, the final set of poems of *The Church*: "Death," "Dooms-day," "Judgement," "Heaven," "Love (III)" forms a chronological chain which starts with death and ends with a poem celebrating the arrival of the soul at Heaven's Inn.

That "The Altar" occupies a conspicuous position within the structure of *The Church* is not a very original observation. Virtually every commentator who mentions the poem at all has remarked that its initial position in *The Church,* in combination with the fact that it is a pattern poem, is a noteworthy phenomenon. Within the spatial framework of *The Church* "The Altar" follows naturally after "The Church-porch" and "Superliminare." The titles of all three poems refer to *physical* aspects of a church. The typographical shape of "The Altar" emphasizes this aspect. The effect of all this is that the reader is given the idea that he

---

15. Mario Praz, *Studies in Seventeenth-Century Imagery*, p. 226.

16. Eliot, *George Herbert*, p. 17.

17. Herbert always eludes the commentator who wishes to label or categorize his poetry in a rigid way. One cannot say that *The Church* is a series of poems 'about' parts of a church. Even in the case of the poems with titles referring to parts of the church-building those titles are invariably used in more ways than one. The subtlety of Herbert's method contrasts with the crudeness of his imitator Christopher Harvey. Harvey's volume of verse, *The Synagogue, or, The Shadow of the Temple* (1640) was written "in imitation of Mr George Herbert" and frequently accompanied Herbert's poetry. It contains an exhaustive and exhaustingly tedious catalogue of poems about parts of the church, such as subterliminare, churchyard, church-stile, church-gate, church-walls, church-porch, the font, the reading-pew. I consulted two editions of Harvey's poems: Pickering's edition of Herbert's poetry which still incorporated Harvey's book, *The Temple: Sacred Poems and Private Ejaculations*, ed. William Pickering, 2nd ed. (London, 1838), pp. 273-354, and *The Complete Poems of Christopher Harvey M.A.*, ed. Alexander B. Grosart (London, 1874).

is actually approaching and entering a church in which the first 'object' he is confronted with is the altar.[18]

With respect to content "The Altar" follows naturally after the moralizing poems "The Church-porch" and "Superliminare." Herbert writes this poem of praise in the double function of artist and priest; in one sense "The Altar" is the artistic product which Herbert presents to God in order that "These stones to praise thee may not cease," but in another sense Herbert as priest, God's "servant," humbly asks Him to sanctify the altar on which he commemorates the Sacrifice at Holy Communion. Summers argues that "... it is well to remember that the word 'altar' was not applied to the Communion Table in the Book of Common Prayer, and that the canons of Herbert's time directed that the Table should be made of wood rather than stone ... ".[19] Neither of these arguments, however, disproves that part of the significance of "The Altar" lies in its sacramental function. Even though in the Book of Common Prayer the word 'altar' is not used for the Communion Table, it is a common enough notion in the liturgical vocabulary of the Eucharist.

Herbert not only presents himself as a man, but also as the Lord's servant, who functions as intermediary between God and man. It is in this function as priest that the poet addresses his audience in "The Church-porch" and "Superliminare"; it is in this function, too, that he asks for the altar to be sanctified through the mediation of Christ's Sacrifice. Lancelot Andrewes, whose influence on Herbert was extensive, wrote:

> The Holy Eucharist ... is fitly called an *Altar*; which again is as fitly called a *Table*, the Eucharist being considered as a *Sacrament*, which is nothing else but a distribution and an application of the Sacrifice to the several receivers.[20]

"The Altar" stands between "Superliminare" and "The Sacrifice." "Superliminare" prepares "the churches mysticall repast," "The Sacri-

18. The fact that the shape of "The Altar" resembles that of a pagan, classical altar rather than the Christian communion table does not essentially affect the argument that the title and shape of the poem are related to a material object; see Summers, pp. 140-42.

19. Summers, p. 141.

20. C.A. Patrides, ed., *The English Poems of George Herbert* (London: Dent, 1974), p. 47n. Herbert first met Andrewes in London when Andrewes was still dean of Westminster Abbey. Herbert went to Westminster School and remained a close friend of Andrewes until the latter's death in 1626. A letter that Herbert wrote from Cambridge to Andrewes, then Bishop of Winchester, is printed in *Works*, "Epistolae," XVII, pp. 471-73. On the relation between Herbert and Andrewes see a.o. *Works*, p. xxiv and Amy M. Charles, *A Life of George Herbert* (Ithaca: Cornell Univ. Press, 1977), p. 49, pp. 51-53 and *passim*. Cf. also Douglas Bush, *English Literature in the Earlier Seventeenth Century: 1600-1660*, 2nd ed. (Oxford: Oxford Univ. Press, 1962), p. 316.

fice" dramatizes Christ's suffering on the Cross. Surely the altar and the Sacrifice celebrated on it make more sense if viewed as expressions of the Anglican priest's duties towards God and man. To see the altar only as a place for the poet to lay down his divine poetry, as some critics have done, is to misjudge Herbert's method and intention.[21]

I agree with Summers that the "shape of Herbert's poem was intended to hieroglyph the relevance of the old altar to the new Christian altar within the heart"; the typological function of the typographical form of the poem is that of creating a balance between the two Covenants.[22] Herbert's altar is not a pagan altar, it is the Mosaic altar of Exodus 20:25:

> And if thou wilt make me an altar of stone, thou shalt not build it of hewn stone: for if thou lift up thy tool upon it, thou hast polluted it.

It has to bear both the heart of man broken by God and Christ's Sacrifice

---

21. Although the comparison may, at first sight, seem far-fetched the most apposite parallel of this sacramental function of "The Altar" in English literature is the opening passage of James Joyce's *Ulysses*:

> Stately, plump Buck Mulligan came from the stairhead, bearing a bowl of lather on which a mirror and a razor lay crossed. A yellow dressing-gown, ungirdled, was sustained gently behind him by the mild morning air. He held the bowl aloft and intoned:
> - *Introibo ad altare Dei.*
> Halted, he peered down the dark winding stairs and called up coarsely:
> - Come up, Kinch. Come up, you fearful jesuit. (London: Bodley Head, 1960), p. 1.

The Latin text quoted by Mulligan is from Psalm 43 (42):4 and belongs to the Preparation in the liturgy of the Roman Catholic Church, which is a prayer said just before the *Introit*, when the priest approaches the altar. If, as Levin writes, "The problem of *Ulysses* is the age-old attempt to put Christian precept into practice," the altar 'approached' by the mock-priest Mulligan is as much a metaphor for Joyce's creation as is the altar on which Herbert lays his priestly and creative burden (Harry Levin, ed., *The Essential James Joyce* (Harmondsworth: Penguin, 1963), p. 13). The occasion of these words is Mulligan's morning shave, but on a metaphoric level the shaving utensils suggest, beside the obvious religious connotation of their lying 'crossed,' a cleansing process similar to the 'sprinkling' in Herbert's "Superliminare," the poem linking "The Church-porch" with *The Church* and immediately preceding "The Altar":

> Thou, whom the former precepts have
> Sprinkled and taught, how to behave
> Thy self in church; approach, and taste
> The churches mysticall repast.

Herbert, the poet and priest, who has first taught the precepts of "The Church-porch" now asks the congregation of readers to follow him into the church and approach the altar of praise and sacrifice.

22. Summers, p. 142. The relation between *altar* and *heart* will be discussed in subsequent sections of this chapter.

brought about by man. This paradox gives additional significance to the pattern. The distribution of the Eucharist is the outward sign of the resolution of the paradox:

> We do not presume to come to this thy Table, O merciful Lord, trusting in our own righteousness, but in thy manifold and great mercies. We are not worthy so much as to gather up the crumbs under thy Table. But thou art the same Lord, whose property is always to have mercy: Grant us therefore, gracious Lord, so to eat the flesh of thy dear Son Jesus Christ, and to drink his blood, that our sinful bodies may be made clean by his body, and our souls washed through his most precious blood, and that we may evermore dwell in him, and he in us.[23]

This prayer from the Anglican service is said by the priest just before the prayer of consecration. The last sentence has some relevance to the final lines of "The Altar." These lines should not, I think, be read as an appeal from the poet to God to sanctify his verse — he had already asked for that in "The Dedication" — but rather as a prayer from the priest asking God to make him worthy of his sacramental function. The "mysticall repast" promised in "Superliminare" is approached in liturgical terms in "The Altar."

This interpretation does not imply that the altar in "The Altar" refers to the Communion Table directly. The altar is a metaphor for the Eucharist as it is in the passage by Lancelot Andrewes quoted above. This reading also adds to the structural unity of *The Church*. The Eucharist is celebrated both in its first poem "The Altar" and in its last "Love (III)," where the 'repast' is offered, appropriately, by Christ Himself as host in Heaven.

"The Altar" is a poem the religious significance of which is revealed step by step. The shape of the poem is reminiscent of pagan altars, the unhewn stones it is made of bring Exodus to mind, and the Sacrifice mentioned in the last line is the typological fulfilment of the Old Law in the Covenant of grace of the New Testament.[24] Whereas in "The Altar"

---

23. All quotations of the Book of Common Prayer are taken from the 1604 edition, unless specified otherwise. See William Keeling, *Liturgiae Britannicae* (London: Pickering, 1842).

24. My reading is diametrically opposed to Rickey's. Rickey writes:

> It is a mistake, I feel, to regard these two poems ["The Altar" and "The Sacrifice"] as the counterparts of the church altar and the sacrament of Holy Communion. For Herbert, the Eucharist never suggested a reenactment of the Passion. Following the mode of his fellow churchmen, he regularly characterized this sacrament as the one affording spiritual nourishment for the Christian, providing the most immediate possible communication between him and Christ. For him it memorialized the Passion, but did not recreate it (Rickey, pp. 15-16).

I prefer the comment of Patrides, who writes:

the correlation between Sacrifice, Communion, and the two Covenants is only hinted at, they are connected quite explicitly in "The Bunch of Grapes":

> Blessed be God, who prosper'd *Noahs* vine,
> And made it bring forth grapes good store.
> But much more him I must adore,
> Who of the Laws sowre juice sweet wine did make,
> Ev'n God himself being pressed for my sake. (ll. 22-26; *Works*, p. 128)

I suggested above that in "The Altar" Herbert not only presents himself as Everyman and poet but also as an ordained priest. In *A Priest to the Temple* Herbert expressed his views on "The Countrey Parson his Character, and Rule of Holy Life" (*Works*, p. 223). In the first chapter, "Of a Pastor," the main duty and dignity of a priest is set forth:

> ... And therefore St. *Paul* in the beginning of his Epistles, professeth this: and in the first to the *Colossians* plainly avoucheth, that he *fils up that which is behinde of the afflictions of Christ in his flesh, for his Bodie's sake, which is the Church.* Wherein is contained the complete definition of a Minister. Out of this Chartre of the Priesthood may be plainly gathered both the Dignity thereof, and the Duty: The Dignity, in that a Priest may do that which Christ did, and by his auctority, and as his Viceregent. The Duty, in that a Priest is to do that which Christ did, and after his manner, both for Doctrine and Life. (*Works*, p. 225)

Within 'The Church' proper, moreover, the first poem is 'The Altar,' promptly and significantly followed by the sixty-three stanzas of 'The Sacrifice' ... whose liturgical rhythms re-enact *and* commemorate the original historical event, even as they suggest the ideal response demanded of man (Patrides, p. 18).

Herbert's poetry exemplifies the *Imitatio Christi* and the metaphors of the Eucharist he uses are no exception. Thus in "Divinitie":

> But he doth bid us take his bloud for wine.
> Bid what he please; yet I am sure,
> To take and taste what he doth there designe,
> Is all that saves, and not obscure (ll. 21-24; *Works*, p. 135).

In "The Agonie":

> Who knows not Love, let him assay
> And taste that juice, which on the crosse a pike
> Did set again abroach; then let him say
> If ever he did taste the like.
> Love is that liquour sweet and most divine,
> Which my God feels as bloud; but I, as wine (ll. 13-18; *Works*, p. 37).

"Love unknown," one of Herbert's most overtly emblematic poems, is about man's heart, his tears, Christ's blood and Passion, and the Eucharist. The eucharistic metaphors in these examples are highly dramatic. Their quality and effect is determined to a large extent by the suggestion that man's experience in life should run parallel with that of Christ on earth.

In chapter XXII, "The Parson in Sacraments," Herbert writes:

> The Countrey Parson being to administer the Sacraments, is at a stand with himself, how or what behaviour to assume for so holy things. Especially at Communion times he is in a great confusion, as being not only to receive God, but to break, and administer him. Neither finds he any issue in this, but to throw himself down at the throne of grace, saying, Lord, thou knowest what thou didst, when thou appointedst it to be done thus; therefore doe thou fulfill what thou didst appoint; for thou art not only the feast, but the way to it. (*Works*, pp. 257-8)

The humble attitude of the priest as a sinner among sinners is also apparent in "The Authour's Prayer before Sermon":

> ... Especially, blesse this portion here assembled together, with thy unworthy Servant speaking unto them: Lord Jesu! teach thou me, that I may teach them: Sanctifie, and inable all my powers, that in their full strength they may deliver thy message reverently, readily, faithfully, & fruitfully. (*Works*, p. 289)

In the spatial structure of *The Church* "The Altar" is a truly transitional poem and should be analysed accordingly. On the one hand it follows naturally after the moralizing poems "The Church-porch" and "Superliminare," because Herbert writes it in the double function of poet *and* priest while on the other hand it prepares naturally for the highly personal lyrics of affliction and faith which constitute the core of *The Church*. These afflictions are always subordinated to the example of Christ's Passion and Sacrifice, which is mentioned in "The Altar" and is the main subject of "The Sacrifice," the poem following it.

1.2. The cycle of Holy Week in *The Church*.

The subtlety with which Herbert prepares for transitions in tone, subject-matter and point of view manifests itself in the way in which the first poems of *The Church* are arranged. Herbert's two pattern poems mark off a group of poems that are related in theme, expression and time.[25]

The first poems of *The Church*, from "The Altar" to "Easter-wings," are all centred around Christ's Passion and are all related to Holy Week. These poems in a sense describe the progress from the dramatic and painful impact of Calvary to the joyful release of the Resurrection.

25. The idea that the poems at the beginning of *The Church* form a sequence is not original. Fredson Bowers sees a sequence in the poems from "The Altar" up to "Jordan (I)." Some of the verbal echoes I refer to are also mentioned by Bowers. My analysis differs from his in two respects: I argue for a sequence with the pattern poems at its beginning and end and I have used the order of the (early) MS. from Dr. Williams' Library (*W*) to support my argument. See Fredson Bowers, "Herbert's Sequential Imagery: 'The Temper,'" *MP*, 59 (1962), 202-13; also Charles, pp. 59-77. Martz has the first section of *The Temple* end after the two poems on Baptism (Martz, p. 295). Summers (p. 143) and Lewalski (p. 47) share my idea that the pattern poems begin and end a unified group of poems.

Between "The Altar" and "Easter-wings" we find a number of poems that lead from sacrifice to resurrection. These poems vary widely in tone, syllabic structure and point of view, but are linked together by the sequence of events they commemorate and the verbal echoes which act as stepping-stones from one poem to the next. The sequential character of this series of poems is particularly clear in the Williams manuscript (*W*), an early version of *The Temple* with corrections in the poet's hand. The pairing of poems with the same title and the placing of related poems on facing or succeeding pages is a pronounced feature of *W*.[26] Some of the verbal echoes linking one poem to the next in *W* are preserved in the manuscript of Herbert's poems in the Bodleian library (*B*) and in the first edition of 1633. The final lines of "The Altar" contain the word "Sacrifice" which is also the title of the poem following it. The final line of "The Sacrifice" contains the word "grief" that reappears in the first line of the next poem, "The Thanksgiving." "The Thanksgiving" enumerates the various ways in which the poet tries to imitate God's life on earth in commemoration of the suffering of His Son, the "King of grief." The final lines of the poem:

> Then for thy passion — I will do for that —
> Alas, my God, I know not what. (ll. 49-50; *Works*, p. 36)

lead directly to the beginning of "The Reprisall":

> I have consider'd it, and finde
> There is no dealing with thy mighty passion: (ll. 1-2; *Works*, p. 36)

The more rigid patterning of the cycle of poems on Holy Week in the early manuscript as compared to *B* and 1633 is also demonstrated by the position of "The Sinner." In the later arrangement "The Sinner" comes between "The Agonie," a poem not found in *W*, and "Good Friday"; in *W* it is preceded by "Good Friday" and followed by the three "Easter" poems. Just like "The Altar" and "The Sacrifice," "Good Friday" and "The Sinner" are linked by a word in the final line of the former poem being repeated in the title of the latter. In *W* the final stanza of "Good Friday" reads:

> Or rather lett
> My several sinnes their sorrows gett.
> That as each beast his cure doth know
> Each sinne may so.[27]

"The Sinner" is in the first place intended as a review of the past life of

---

26. Hutchinson provides a list that allows one to compare the number of poems and the order in which they appeared in *W* on the one hand and *B* and 1633 on the other (*Works*, pp. liv-lv). Charles also gives a comparative list (pp. 60-64).
27. Jones MS. B 62, sig. 25ᵛ.

the poet. But if one considers its position in *W* it can also be interpreted as a comment on the poetry itself:

> Lord, how I am all ague, when I seek
> What I have treasur'd in my memorie!

The pain of the poet/'sinner' increases when he ponders the implications of what he has written so far, "treasur'd" in his "memorie"; it increases because he realizes the extent of his unworthiness to receive the grace he is praying for. This feeling of unworthiness has been enhanced by the poignancy of the events described in the poems between "The Altar" and "The Sinner":

> Since, if my soul make even with the week,
> Each seventh note by right is due to thee. (ll. 3-4)

"The Sinner" is the seventh poem after "The Altar." It may well be that this fact brings to mind the prayer for sanctification in that poem.[28] Consequently the poet writes in the opening lines of the second quatrain:

> I finde there quarries of pil'd vanities,
> But shreds of holinesse, that dare not venture
> To shew their face, since crosse to thy decrees: (ll. 5-7)

The "broken Altar" of the heart, untouched by any "workman's tool" is contrasted with the quarry from which the useless stones of vanity are extracted and piled up in the memory of sinning man. "The Sinner" ends:

> Yet Lord restore thine image, heare my call:
> And though my hard heart scarce to thee can grone,
> Remember that thou once didst write in stone. (ll. 12-14)

The end of the poem, we notice, returns to the themes and phraseology of "The Altar." The phrase "hard heart" is repeated in the final couplet of "The Sinner" and the poem ends with the image of the stony heart, although in this case the Biblical reference is not to the altar of stone of Exodus, 20:25, but to Exodus 31:18:

> And he gave unto Moses, when he had made an end of communing with him upon mount Sinai, two tables of testimony, tables of stone, written with the finger of God.

and to the counterpart of that text in the New Testament:

---

28. Herbert frequently demonstrates his predilection for numerology: "Sunday" consists of *seven*-line stanzas (*Works*, pp. 75-77); "Trinitie Sunday" of *three* stanzas of *three* lines each (*Works*, p. 68). In the final, *third* stanza of this last poem each line contains an enumeration of *three* nouns or verbs:

> Enrich my heart, mouth, hands in me,
> With faith, with hope, with charitie;
> That I may runne, rise, rest with thee.

... written not with ink, but with the Spirit of the living God; not in tables of stone, but in fleshy tables of the heart. (2 Corinthians, 3:3)

By returning to the themes and wording of "The Altar," "The Sinner" concludes the set of poems dealing with the Passion and leads up to the set of three Easter poems that follow in *W*. The common denominator of those three poems and "The Sinner" is the notion of *heart*. Whereas "The Sinner" is still concerned with the hardness of the heart, "Easter (I)" begins on a new tone entirely, that of the *sursum corda*:

> Rise heart; thy Lord is risen. Sing his praise
>   Without delayes,
> Who takes thee by the hand, that thou likewise
>   With him mayst rise: (ll. 1-4; *Works*, p. 41)[29]

"Easter (I)" is the first poem in *The Church* in which the 'hard heart' is replaced by a zealous heart; the relation between man and God changes accordingly. The distance between sinner and God diminishes within this new relationship because of the direct contact between the human soul and Christ.

In "Easter-wings," finally, harmony is achieved or rather prayed for; both the resurrection of Christ and the harmonious music produced by the concord between Christ and man are caught in the beautiful image of the larks, whose music is ever melodious and harmonious and whose movement is continuously upwards. The 'victory' of "Easter-wings" has replaced or rather borne out the 'sacrifice' of "The Altar."

If, as I have suggested, the pattern poems are considered to be in conjunction with one another, namely as boundary-marks of the most crucial events in Christianity — the Passion and the Resurrection — the poems and their typographical patterns make much more sense. The structural coherence of this first section of *The Church*, once it has been recognized, at least partly accounts for Herbert's use of the pattern poems and fully accounts for the place allotted them within the total structure of *The Temple*. The revisions Herbert made in his manuscript — he added "The Agonie" and "Sepulchre," drastically changed "Easter (II)" and re-ordered the poems — do not affect the essence of the argument. Charles (1972) writes about Herbert's revisions: "The order of *W* is obviously simpler and more literal than that of its successor, less imaginative and less subtle in its more direct approach, its linkings and

---

29. Another interesting aspect of the beginning of "Easter (I)" is the connection between "hand" and "heart." Although the poem is connected with the preceding one by the motif of the heart, it prepares for poems like "Life" in which the proximity of "hand" and "heart" is likewise emphasized:

My hand was next to them, and then my heart: (l. 7; *Works*, p. 94)

pairings of poems, ..." and Martz (1962) qualifies the changes from *W* to
B and 1633 in terms of Herbert's "changing his style from the 'winding' of
wit to a witty simplicity."[30] Even though the 'chaining' of the poems by
means of verbal echoes is less conspicuous in *B* and 1633 than it is in *W*
the later order still makes the relative position of "The Altar" and
"Easter-wings" significant and the pattern poems invariably retain their
function of demarcating the two most important events in Christian
religion. It is useful to point out Herbert's method as manifested in the
Williams manuscript, because it shows the author's intentions at that
stage of composition when the skeleton of the ultimate product was
clearly visible but the verse had not yet found its finished form.

2. Herbert's pattern poems and their ancestry.

2.1. Classical examples and Christian emulation.

Herbert knew the pattern poems in the *Greek Anthology*. There is both
circumstantial and textual evidence that supports this assertion. The
collection of poetry known as the *Greek Anthology* was printed numerous
times in the Renaissance in various editions, since it was virtually the only
Greek poetry available at the time.[31] Besides complete editions of the
Anthology, separate editions appeared of parts of it. The handful of
pattern poems in the *Greek Anthology* were the frequent subject of these
separate volumes and several humanist scholars produced impressive
tomes full of learning about them.[32] Herbert may well have come across
one or more of these editions in the course of his studies at Cambridge.

Herbert did not have to depend on continental sources only for his
knowledge of the poems from the *Greek Anthology*. Among the English
humanists Thomas More had produced popular translations and Richard
Willis had rewritten the pattern poems, adding efforts of his own in which

30. Charles, p. 65; Martz, p. 321.
31. For the various editions and the printing history of the *Greek Anthology* see
Church, "The Pattern Poem," pp. 16-21. Also James Hutton, *The Greek Anthology in
Italy* (Ithaca: Cornell Univ. Press, 1935).
32. Church mentions Crispin and Scaliger as editors of the pattern poems; I myself
have consulted 16th and 17th century editions by Stephanus and Licetus respectively.
Henricus Stephanus belongs to the famous and influential printers' family of the
Estiennes and edited *Theocriti Aliorumque Poetarum Idyllia ... Simmiae Rhodii Ovum,
Alae, Securis, Fistula, Dosiadis Ara* (n.p., 1579). Fortunius Licetus wrote separate volumes on each of the Greek pattern poems: *Ad Epei Securim* (1637), *Ad Syringam* (1655),
etc. I shall quote one title fully to show how seriously and scholarly the editor approached
his subject: Fortunii Liceti/Genuensis/In Archigymnasio Patavino/Medici Theorici
Primarij ex L. Com./. *Ad Syringam,/A Theocrito Syracusio compactam & inflatam,/
Encyclopaedia:/In qua Theocritus, celebrans laudes & munera Poetices, vetustiones/
historias conplures, & Poetarum figmenta, & Philosophicas/contemplationes abditiones
attingit, quae latius explicantur./... /Utini, ... MDCLV.

he adapted the pagan examples to make them suit a Christian purpose.[33] In addition to the fact that the pattern poems had circulated widely before Herbert wrote his contributions to the genre, there are verbal and thematic correspondences between the classical examples and Herbert's poems that substantiate the claim that he was familiar with the classical source.

2.1.1. "The Altar" and the Greek Anthology.

There are two altar poems in the *Greek Anthology*, one by Dosiados (*c.* 150 B.C.) and another by Besantinus or Vestinus, a high-priest of Alexandria, who lived in the reign of Hadrian (117-138) (figs. 8,9).[34] The shape of Herbert's poem is different from that of the two Greek examples. The most notable difference is the absence of the top 'slab' of the altar in Herbert's poem. There is no relation in content between Dosiados' altar and Herbert's, apart from the fact that in both poems the construction of the altar is mentioned. The poem by Dosiados is a puzzle poem in which the names of various mythological gods and heroes are given in a coded form.[35] Vestinus' altar poem resembles that of his predecessor to a certain extent. It, too, is a puzzle poem in which the reader's knowledge of mythology is put to the test. This resemblance is

---

33. About Thomas More's translations of the Greek epigrams into Latin, which he wrote in gentle competition with Lily (*c.* 1508), see R.W. Chambers, *Thomas More* (1935; rpt. Harmondsworth: Penguin, 1963), p. 83; H.A. Mason, *Humanism and Poetry in the Early Tudor Period* (London: Routledge & Kegan Paul, 1959), p. 39; also E.E. Reynolds, *The Life and Death of St. Thomas More* (London: Burns & Oates, 1968), p. 132. About Richard Willis and his adaptations of the Greek pattern poems see section 2.2.1.1. *post*. Also Church, pp. 37-54 and Rickey, pp. 10-12.

34. Church, pp. 14-15.

35. The following translation is by J.M. Edmonds:

I am the work of the husband [Jason] of a mannish-mantled quean [Medea], of a twice-young mortal, not Empusa's [Thetis] cinder-bedded scion [Achilles], who was the killing of a Teucrian neatherd [Paris] and of the childing of a bitch [Hector, son of Hecuba], but the leman of a golden woman [Jason, who built this altar to Chrysè (=Golden)]; and he made me when the husband-boiler [Medea] smote down the brazen-leggèd breeze [Talos the brazen man] wrought of the twice-wed mother-hurtled virgin-born [Hephaestus]; and when the slaughterman [Philoctetes] of Theocritus [Paris] and burner of the three-nighted [Heracles] gazed upon this wrought piece [the Altar], a full dolorous shriek he shright, for a belly-creeping shedder of age [serpent] did him despite with enshafted venom [poison=arrow]; but when he was alack-adaying in the wave-ywashen [isle of Lemnos], Pan's mother's [Penelopè] thievish twy-lived bedfellow [Odysseus] came with the scion of a cannibal [Diomed], and carried him into the thrice-sacked [by Heracles, the Amazons, the Greeks] daughter of Teucer [land of Troy] for the sake of Ilus-shivering arrow-heads [the arrows of Heracles brought by Philoctetes caused (Troy's fall and) the destruction of the tomb (and corpse) of Ilus]. J.M. Edmonds, trans., *The Greek Bucolic Poets*, p. 507.

ΒΗΣΤΙΝΟΥ[1]

ΒΩΜΟΣ

Ο λὸς οὔ με λιβρὸς ἱρῶν
Λ ιβάδεσσιν οἷα κάλχης[2]
Υ ποφοινίσσι τέγγει,
Μ αὖλες δ' ὕπερθε πέτρη Ναξίη[3] θοούμεναι
Π αμάτων φείδοντο Πανός, οὐ στροβίλῳ[4] λιγυΐ
Ι ξὸς εὐώδης μελαίνει τρεχνέων με Νυσίων·
Ε γὰρ βωμὸν ὄρη με μήτε γλούρου[5]
Π λάθεν[5], 'Αλύβης παγέντα[6] βώλοις,
Ο ὐδ' ὃν Κυνθογενὴς ἔτευξε φύτλη
Λ αβόντε μηκάδων κέρα,
Ο ισσαίσιν ἀμφὶ δειράσιν
Ι σσαι νέμονται Κυνθίαις,
Σ ύρρος πος πελοιτό μοι·
Ε ἰνάς μ', ἔτευξε γηγενής,
Τ άων ἀείζρον τέχνην
Ε νευσε πάλμυς ἀφθίτων·
Σ ὺ δ', ὦ πιὼν κρηπῖθεν ἣν
Ι κόλαψε Γοργόνος,
Θ οίης τ' ἐπισπεύδοις τ', ἐμοὶ
μητιπάδαον πολὺ λαροτέρην
Υ πουδὴν ἄδην ἰθὶ θαρσέων
Ε ἰς ἐμήν· τεύξειν καθαρμοῖ θᾶβρον ῥά δράμῃ ἐγὼ
Α μφὶ Νέας Θρηϊκίαης ὃν σχεδόθεν Μυρίνης
Σ οί, Τριπάτωρ, πορφύρεον φὼρ ἀνέθηκε κροιό.

10

20

6

ΔΩΣΙΑΔΑ ΔΩΡΙΕΩΣ

ΒΩΜΟΣ

Εἱμάρσενός με στήτας
πόσις, μέροψ δίσαβος,
τεῦξ', οὐ σποδεύνας ἶνις 'Εμπούσας μόρος
Τεύκροιο βούτα καὶ κυνὸς τεκνώματος,
Χρυσᾶς δ'[1] ὔτας, ἅμος ἑψιάδρα
τὸν γυιόχαλκον οὖρον ἔρρωσεν,
ὃν ἀπάτωρ δίσευνος
μόγησε ματρόριπτος·
ἐμὸν δὲ τεῦγμ' ἀθρήσας
Θεοκρίτοιο κτάντας
τρεσσπέρτεροιο καύστας
θώυξεν αἶν' ἰύξας[2]
χάλεψε γάρ νιν ἰῷ
σύργαστρος ἐκδυθήρας[3]
τὸν δ' αἰλινεῦντ'[4] ἐν ἀμφικλύστῳ φὼρ
Πανός τε ματρὸς εὐνέτας φὼρ
ἤρ' ἀρδίων ἐς Τεύκρίδ' ἄγαγον τρίπορθον

8

not really remarkable, since Vestinus explicitly refers to the other poem in the comparison at the end of his poem.

There is a number of verbal correspondences between Herbert's altar and that of Vestinus, as the following translation makes clear:

> The murky flux of sacrifice bedews me not with ruddy trickles like the flux of a purple-fish, the whittles whetted upon Naxian stone spare over my head the possessions of Pan, and the fragrant ooze of Nysian boughs blackens me not with his twirling reek; for in me behold an altar knit neither of bricks aureate nor of nuggets Alybaean, nor yet that altar which the generation of two that was born upon Cynthus did build with the horns of such as bleat and browse over the smooth Cynthian ridges, be not that made my equal in the weighing, for I was builded with aid of certain offspring of Heaven by the Nine that were born of Earth, and the liege-lord of the deathless decreed their work should be eterne. And now, good drinker of the spring that was strucken of the scion of the Gorgon, I pray that thou mayst do sacrifice upon me and pour plentiful libation of far goodlier gust than the daughters of Hymettus; up and come boldly unto this wrought piece, for 'tis pure from venom-venting prodigies such as were hid in that other, which the thief who stole a purple ram set up unto the daughter of three sires in Thracian Neae over against Myrinè.[36]

Vestinus' altar is pagan, Herbert's is Christian: Vestinus' altar is hallowed by Zeus, Herbert's by God; like Herbert's Vestinus' poem is a poem of praise. Both altars are 'eternalized' by the divine workmanship that wrought them. Neither altar is made by human hands and in both poems this aspect is presented in the form of a negation: "... in me behold an altar knit neither of brick aureate nor ..." and: "A broken ALTAR, Lord, thy servant reares, / Made of a heart ... / No workmans tool hath touch'd the same." Vestinus' altar is not made of 'bricks aureate,' Herbert's altar is made of the stones of the heart. In both poems the word sacrifice occurs and in both cases the sacrifice offered on the altar is one of praise rather than of blood. In both poems, finally, the *purity* of the altar is emphasized: "... come boldly unto this wrought piece, for 'tis pure ..." and "... sanctifie this ALTAR to be thine."

Notwithstanding obvious and profound differences in tone and purpose between the two poems, these superficial resemblances seem worth pointing out. They show, I think, how profane subject-matter could be incorporated into a sacred context. This kind of application occurred in many religious poems of the early 17th century. Herbert even uses some of the metaphors of his classical example: only an altar made of a supernatural material is sacred and pure enough to carry the sacrifice of praise. By thus emulating the pagan examples Herbert emphasizes the superiority of the Christian faith over Greek pantheism.[37]

---

36. *The Greek Bucolic Poets*, p. 511.
37. The type of Christian emulation exemplified in Herbert's pattern poems was a

2.1.2. "The Altar" and Publius Optatianus Porfirius.

Vestinus, who was patronized by Hadrian, wrote his pattern poems c. 100 A.D.. Publius Optatianus Porfirius lived two centuries after Vestinus and in his case, too, an Emperor acted as patron. Constantine the Great was apparently quite fond of the poet since he called him "frater carissime."[38]

Porfirius wrote a great number of pattern poems, most of them *carmina quadrata*. These are poems that contain as many lines as each line contains letters. Within the resulting quadrangles acrostics, pictures or designs could be incorporated that were set off from the rest of the text by either capitalizing the letters which together form the figure, or by using different colours of ink. But besides these *carmina*, the writing of which remained a popular pastime of poets throughout the Middle Ages, Porfirius also wrote pattern poems in concrete shapes and among these we find an altar poem. The poem is clearly written in imitation of the Greek *technopaegnia*, as the pattern poems from the *Greek Anthology* are commonly called (fig. 10).

The verbal echoes of the altar poem by Porfirius ring even stronger in Herbert's "The Altar" than those of Vestinus' poem. This is its translation:

> You see how I stand, an altar consecrated to the Pythian god, polished by the craft of the musical art of the poet, so fair am I, bringing most sacred offerings, meet for Phoebus and fitted for these temples in which the choruses of poets make their acceptable gifts, adorned with so many woven flowers of the muse, of such kind as must be placed in the Heliconian groves of song. No workman polished me with sharp tool; I was not hewed out of the white rock of the mountain of Luna, nor from the shining peak of Paros. It was not because I was cut or forced with the hard chisel that I am straitly confined and hold back my edges as they attempt to grow and then, in the succeeding portion, let them spread more broadly. Cautiously I force each edge to be drawn in, line by line, by tiny steps, in lines turning in, thus following on, regulated everywhere by the measure, so that my margin, within the limit which rules it, is that of a square. Then again, continuing on to the bottom, my line, spreading more broadly, is artfully stretched according to the plan. I am made by the metre of ten feet. Provided that the number of feet is never changed, and the learned measure obeys its rules, the lines of such poems increase and decrease. Phoebus, may the supplicant who offers these pictures, made of metre, take his place joyfully in your temples and your sacred choruses.[39]

common phenomenon. See J.D.P. Warners, "Translatio-Imitatio-Aemulatio," *De Nieuwe Taalgids,* 49 (1956), 289-295 and 50 (1957), 82-88, 193-201. Also E. de Jongh, "The Spur of Wit: Rembrandt's Response to an Italian Challenge," *Delta,* 12, no. 2 (Summer, 1969), 49-67. Cf. Dryden: "Emulation is the spur of wit" ("An Essay of Dramatic Poesy," in W.P. Ker, ed., *Essays of John Dryden,* 2 vols. (New York: Russell & Russell, 1961), I, 37.

38. Church, p. 22.

39. Glanville Downey, trans. in Boultenhouse, "Poems in the Shapes of Things," p. 72.

II.—ΠΤΕΡΥΓΕΣ

Λεῦσσέ με τὸν Γᾶς τε βαθυστέρνου ἄνακτ' 'Ακμονίδαν τ' ἄλλυδις ἑδράσαντα
μηδὲ τρέσῃς, εἰ τόσος ὢν δάσκια βέβριθα λάχνᾳ γένεια.
τᾶμος ἐγὼ γὰρ γενόμαν, ἁνίκ' ἔκραιν' 'Ανάγκα
πάντα δ' ἕκας εἶχε φράδεσσι λυγροῖς [1]
ἑρπετά, πάνθ' ὅσ' εἶρπε [2]
δι' αἴθρας

Χάους τε·
οὔτι γε Κύπριδος παῖς
ὠκυπέτας   'Αρέϊος [3]   καλεῦμαι·
10 οὔτε γὰρ ἔκρανα βίᾳ, πραϋνόῳ [4] δὲ πειθοῖ,
εἰκέ τέ μοι γαῖα θαλάσσας τε μυχοὶ χάλκεος οὐρανός τε·
τῶν δ' ἐγὼ ἐκνοσφισάμαν ὠγύγιον σκᾶπτρον, ἔκρινον [5] δὲ θεοῖς θέμιστας.

11

XXVI.

```
        5        10       15       20       25       30       35
 5  VIDES·VT·ARA·STEM·DICAT·A·PYTHIIO
    FABRE·POLITA·VATIS·ARTEM·VSICA
SIC·PVLCHRA·SACRISSIM†A·GENS·PHOEBO·DECENS
IIS·APTA·TEMPLIS·QVI·8·LITANT·VATVM·CHORI
 5  TOT·COM·TA·SERT·I·SET·CAMENAE·FLORIBVS
    HELICONI·IS·LOCANDA·LVCIS·CARMINVM
    NON·CAVTED·VRA·ME·POLIVIT·ARTIFEX
    EXCIS·A·NON·S·VM·RV·PE·MONTIS·ALBIDI
    LVNA·ENITEN·TENE·C·PARI·DEVERTICE
10  NON·CAES·A·DVRON·EC·COACTA·SPICVLO
    ARTA·REP·RIMOS·EMINENTES·ANGVLOS
    ET·MOX·SECVNDOS·PROPAGARE·LATIVS
    EOS·QVE·CAVTES·INGVLOS·8·BDVCERE
    GRAD·V·MINVTO·PERRECVRVAS·LINEAS
15  NORMATA·V·BIQVE·SIC·DEINDE·REGVLA
    V·TORA·QVADRAE·SIT·RIGENTE·LIMITE
    VEL·INDE·A·DIMV·M·FVS·A·RV·RS·VM·LINEA
    TENDA·T·V·BAR·TE·LATIOR·PER·ORDINEM
    MEMETRA·PANG·VNT·DE·CAMENARVM·MODIS
20  MVTATON·VM·QVA·MN·V·MERO·D·VM·TA·XA·T·PEDVM
    QVAE·DOCTA·SERVAT·DVM·PRAECEPTIS·REGVLA
    ELEMENTA·CRESCVNT·ET·DECRESCVNT·CARMINVM
    IIAS·PHOEBE·BES·VPPLEX·DAN·S·METRORVM·IMAGINES
    TEMPLIS·CHORIS·QVE·LAETVS·INTERSIT·SACRIS
```

10

The phrase: "No workman polished me with sharp tool" ("non caute dura me polivit artifex") is repeated almost literally in Herbert's "No workmans tool hath touched the same." Porfirius' "Ara" celebrates the art of writing in beautiful patterns; Herbert's "The Altar" celebrates God's power to "work" in the poet's heart, turning it into an altar of praise. It is, I would say, a sign of Herbert's greatness that while emulating the pagan poem he not only adapts it to his Christian purposes but also manages to preserve some of the idioms of his classical examples, turning them into images with surprisingly fresh meanings. Whereas Porfirius' phrase "No workman ... tool" only explains that a pattern poem is written and not chiselled, the (almost) identical phrase in Herbert's poem functions on several levels at once. One level is that of its classical predecessor. Herbert, too, draws attention to the fact that this altar consists of words and that words are not the same as bricks or stones. In this sense he presents himself as poet.[40] But taken within its Christian context the phrase clearly refers to Exodus 20:25:

> And if thou wilt make me an altar of stone, thou shalt not build it of hewn stone: for if thou lift up thy tool upon it, thou hast polluted it.[41]

And, finally, if the phrase is read within the metaphoric development of the poem, it is proleptic and points forward to the equation with the heart in the next line: only God Himself is able to hew the 'hard heart' and Herbert, a mere mortal, cannot presume to be such a workman.

2.1.3. "Easter-wings" and the wing poem by Simmias of Rhodes.

Simmias of Rhodes, who lived c. 300 B.C., was closely connected with

40. Summers, p. 142: "In an important sense this, the first poem within 'The Church,' ... *is* the altar upon which the following poems (Herbert's 'sacrifice of praise') are offered, and it is an explanation of the reason for their composition."
41. Summers, p. 142: "There is hardly a phrase in 'The Altar' which does not derive from a specific biblical passage." Cf. Henry Ainsworth, *Annotations upon the Pentateuch* (Amsterdam, 1617-21). Ainsworth comments on the meaning of 'hewn stone': "of such the altar might not be built, but of whole stones, over which no man had lift up any yron; as Iesus did on mount Ebal" (*Annotations upon ... Exodus* (1617), sig. P4). In an annotation on Deuteronomy 27:6: "Thou shalt build the altar of the Lord thy God of whole stones: and thou shalt offer burnt offerings thereon unto the Lord thy God" Ainsworth explains that the "burnt offerings" serve "to obteyn of God by Christ, forgivenesse of sinnes; and sanctification of life" (*Annotations upon ... Deuteronomie* (1619), sig. Aa3ᵛ. Elsewhere the burnt offering presented to the Lord is explained thus:

> ... The signification was of Christ, that through the eternal spirit offered himself, unto God, *Hebr.* 9.14. & 10 8.10 and of Christians, that *present their bodies a living sacrifice, holy, acceptable unto God,* which is their *reasonable service, Rom.* 12.1.
> (*Annotations upon ... Leviticus* (1618), sig. A3)

Alexandria, as were the other writers of pattern poetry in the *Greek
Anthology*.[42] He is the reputed author of three pattern poems, called after
their shapes "The Axe," "The Wings" and "The Egg." We are here
concerned with "The Wings" (fig. 11):

> Behold the ruler of the deep-bosomed Earth, the turner upside-down of the Son of
> Acmon [i.e. Heaven], and have no fear that so little a person should have so
> plentiful a crop of beard to his chin. For I was born when Necessity bare rule, and
> all creatures, moved they in Air or in Chaos, were kept through her dismal
> government far apart. Swift-flying son of Cypris and war-lord Ares — I am not
> that at all; for by no force came I into rule, but by gentle-willed persuasion, and yet
> all alike, Earth, deep Sea, and brazen Heaven, bowed to my behest, and I took to
> myself their olden sceptre and made me a judge among Gods.[43]

Simmias' "Wings" is a much more sophisticated poem than the other
classical pattern poems we have analysed. For one thing it is more
successful in combining shape and sense. This appears most clearly in the
middle of the poem:

> δἰ αἴθρας
> χάους τε· (ll. 6-7)

The shortest lines of the poem describe the cheerless conditions of
existence into which the god of love was born. Chaos is the element from
which the eldest of the gods — that is why he is said to be bearded — was
created.[44]

The quintessence of the argument of Simmias' poem is found in the

42. Church, pp. 9-15.
43. J.M. Edmonds, trans., *The Greek Bucolic Poets*, p. 493. Edmonds explains:
"The poem seems to have been inscribed on the wings of a statue — perhaps a votive
statue — representing Love as a bearded child. ... The poem ... differs from the *Axe* in
making no reference, except by its shape, to the *wings* of Love" (p. 491).
44. The genealogy of the God of Love is well attested by the classical authors, e.g.
Plato:

> 'That the god should be one of the most ancient of all beings is a title to honour,' he said,
> 'and as evidence of this I can point to the fact that Love has no parents, and that parents
> are never ascribed to him by any writer either of prose or verse. Hesiod tells us that
> Chaos first came into existence,

>> but next
> Broad-breasted Earth, on whose foundation firm
> Creation stands, and Love.

> Acusilaus agrees with Hesiod in saying that after Chaos these two, Earth and Love,
> came into being. And Parmenides in speaking of creation says

>> First among all the gods she invented Love.

> So you see that there is widespread agreement about the extreme antiquity of Love.

(*The Symposium*, trans. W. Hamilton (Harmondsworth: Penguin, 1951), p. 42).

central, 'thinnest' lines. This is also the case in "Easter-wings." At the centre of its two stanzas we find two lines of two syllables each: "Most poore: / With thee" and "Most thinne. / With thee" respectively. The brevity of "Most poore" and "Most thinne" reflects the dejection of the poet at that point. The physical and mental constraint expressed in these lines is juxtaposed to the hope for relief that is implied in the "With thee" of the line that follows. Herbert uses the narrowing of the lines to achieve a double effect: it expresses most effectively what happens in the poem (typographically) and what happens to the poet (metaphorically).

The effective use of the shortness of the central lines is not the only justification for comparing Simmias and Herbert. In both wing-shaped poems the development of the argument follows the gradual shortening and lengthening of the lines. "Wings" begins boastfully and confidently: "Behold the ruler of the deep-bosomed Earth, the turner upside-down of [Heaven]" and continues by describing the miserable plight of creatures who had to live in a state of chaos, at which point the 'thinnest' part of the poem has been reached. After that chaos is said to have been overcome by love, and all the elements "bowed to my behest." The final line, through its length, emphasizes the power of love: "and I took to myself their olden sceptre and made me a judge among Gods." A similar effective way of using the "diminuendo and crescendo" of the stanza pattern is found in "Easter-wings."[45] The first stanza moves from the grand gesture of its opening: "Lord, who createdst man in wealth and store" to the desolation of "Most poore," at which point the help of Christ is invoked: "With thee," which leads to renewed courage and confidence in the final line of the stanza:

> Then shall the fall further the flight in me.

The first half of the first stanza describes the poverty of mankind in general contrasted with the 'wealth and store' man originally possessed. The second half applies the general situation to the destiny of the individual, culminating in the subtle statement of the final line. W had "my fall" instead of "the fall." The change from 'my' to 'the' enforces the generalizing effect of the line. Man's fall from Paradise can be overcome in Christ. Herbert's allusion to the paradox of the 'felix culpa,' the fortunate fall, is partly expressed in the typographical shape of the poem.

Whereas the first stanza of "Easter-wings" treats of the situation of mankind in general, the second stanza describes the condition of the individual man already burdened with sin from the moment of birth: "My tender age in sorrow did beginne." Now it is not the loss of 'wealth and store' that results in destitution ('most poore') but a continuing

45. Bennett, p. 63.

process of emaciation that leads from 'sorrow' to being "Most thinne."
Here not 'the fall' but 'affliction' is the focus of the poet's attention. By
using the strength of Christ's wing ("if I imp my wing on thine") all will
be well in the end ("Affliction shall advance the flight in me").

In Simmias' poem the god of love describes the world at the time of his
birth: "For I was born when Necessity bare rule"; in "Easter-wings" the
poet describes the world as he experienced it in his early youth: "My
tender age in sorrow did beginne." Herbert's line may be regarded as a
free rendering of Simmias', since both 'sorrow' and 'necessity' are
possible translations of the Greek word ἀνάγκη. The striking verbal
correspondence between the two poems should not make us disregard the
important differences between them, however. The most significant
difference lies in the points of view of the two poems; in Simmias' poem
the pagan god of love is the speaker, whereas in "Easter-wings" the
Christian god of love is addressed by the human soul.

2.1.4. Conclusions.

Do these comparisons help us in our interpretation of Herbert's pattern
poems? I believe they do. We have found that Herbert's pattern poems
not only derived their shape but also part of their idiom and imagery
from their classical predecessors. "The Altar" has several elements in
common with the altar-poems by Vestinus and Porfirius, notably the
emphasis on the relation between workmanship and the non-human
origin of the altar. "Easter-wings" shares, among other aspects, the
intricate relation between shape and sense with Simmias' "Wings."

Most of Herbert's contemporary readers would have known the
classical models of Herbert's pattern poems.[46] They would have realized
that Herbert was using them to set off the infinite superiority of Divine
Love against the pagan gods speaking or invoked in the classical pattern
poems. It is characteristic of Herbert's method that his pattern poems are
prayers directed towards God or Divine Love, i.e. Christ. The classical
pattern poems are self-centred; they are soliloquies of the altar or of the
bearded god of love, who do not doubt their own powers. Herbert's
pattern poems are dynamic interactions between the poet/priest and his
God; their classical counterparts are static monologues. Because Herbert
adheres to the shape and idiom of the classical examples, the superiority
of the Christian faith as a source for poetry stands out even more
strikingly than it would otherwise have done. Christian emulation must
have been at least part of Herbert's intention in writing pattern poems

---

46. See Kenneth Charlton, *Education in Renaissance England* (London: Routledge,
1965) and Mulder, *The Temple of the Mind*.

that go back directly to the examples in the *Greek Anthology* and would be recognized in that context by the poet's reading public.

2.2. Herbert's pattern poems and contemporary examples.

2.2.1. "The Altar."

The relation between "The Altar" and analogous pattern poems of the English Renaissance has received more critical attention than the analogy with the classical examples; I shall therefore discuss this relation only briefly and try as much as possible to avoid repetition, unless the reference to findings by others can serve to corroborate my own argument.[47]

2.2.1.1. Richard Willis.

The poems from the *Greek Anthology* were available to English poets and scholars in various editions. Continental editions by Scaliger, Crispin and Estienne — of the famous French printers' family — went through several printings and found their way to England as well. Thomas More made a popularized English version of parts of the *Anthology*. Richard Willis, one of the first English writers to imitate the Greek patterns, explicitly mentions Scaliger and Crispin in his *scholia* on the pattern poems.[48] Richard Willis, a member of the Society of Jesus and a learned scholar, taught Greek at Trier in 1569 and held the chair of rhetoric at Perugia. His *Disputatio de Re Poetica* (1573) was the first formal defence of poetry in the English Renaissance. It was published in one volume together with *Poematum Liber*, which contains the eight pattern poems.[49] Willis' altar imitates the shape of the altar by Dosiados, but the text is his (see fig. 12). The poem is an autobiography of the Pilgrim in Progress. The only thing apart from its shape that Willis' poem has in common with the classical example, is the fact that it is written in the first person singular. The only relation between Willis' altar and Herbert's is the fact that both are adaptations of a pagan convention to Christian purposes. It is not unlikely, however, that Herbert saw Willis' pattern poems in his

47. Rickey quotes and discusses altar poems that appeared before Herbert; she also mentions the wing-shaped poem by Richard Willis. Rickey suggests that "probably because the difficulties inherent in devising this pattern were greater than the rigors involved in composing altar verses, few English poets tried to imitate them" (p. 27).

48. Church, "The Pattern Poem" (1944), p. 40; also "The First English Pattern Poems" (1946).

49. The full title of Willis' book is: *Poematum liber ad Gulielmum Bar. Burghleium auratum nobilis ordinis equita sereniss. reg. consiliarum ac summum Angliae quaestorum* (London, 1573). Cf. Church, "The Pattern Poem," p. 38. See also A.D.S. Fowler, trans. & ed., *De Re Poetica* (Oxford: Blackwell, 1958).

INSCRIPTIO.

To England's, Scotland's, France & Ireland's KING:
Great Emperour of EVROPES greatest Iles:
Monarch of Hearts, and Artes, and every thing
Beneath BOOTES, maaie thousande myles.
Vpon whose Head Honour and Fortune smiles:
About whose browes clusters of Crowns do spring
VVhose Faith, Him Cham-
pion of the FAITH enstiles:
VVhose VViledome's Fame,
O're all the World doth ring:

MNEMOSYNE
&

Her faire Daughters bring
The DAPHNEAN Crowne,
To Crowne Him (Laureat)
VVhole and sole Soueraigne
Of the THESPIAN Spring,
Prince of PARNASSVS, and Pierian State:
And with their Crown, their kingdoms Arms they yeild:
Thrice Three Pennes Sun-like in a Cinthian field.
Sign'd by THEM-SELVES, and their High Treaforer
BARTAS, the great: In-grofs'd by SYLVESTER.

13

R. WILLEII
ARA
Christianæ religioni.
Θεοκαυσικῶς

Sancto rnatus infans
Baptismatis lauacro,
Deinde CONfirmatus in vera
Fide sacrata Præsulis manu,
Et lectus in sortem Dei puer:
AETATE vernali procellosa
Nostri per vndas Ponti,
Finesque Brabantinos,
RHENI per oras late,
Celsas & inter Alpes,
Taururumque Apenninique
Iuga p Hetruscas vrbes
Fassus polo TONantis
Sacru ac tremendu nicem.

Adultus inter GALLICAnas
Neces professus CHRISTIanum,
Viv CHRISTIANA Religione
Rtuam scelestus? Derelinquam
Senex?mori ab nncme ante malim.

LONDINI, CIƆ.IƆLXXIII.

12

Cambridge period. Willis was not only a very learned man, but also an avid collector of academic titles. By 1578 he had acquired M.A.'s in the Universities of Mainz, Perugia, Oxford and Cambridge. At Cambridge Willis enjoyed a considerable reputation which lasted into the seventeenth century. Of the eighteen extant copies of the *Poematum Liber* at least eight are in Cambridge libraries or were owned by Cambridge men.[50]

2.2.1.2. Sylvester.

The next altars to be written were the twelve (!) altar-shaped poems by Sylvester that serve as introduction to his translation of Guillaume Du Bartas' *Devine Weekes and Workes*.[51] They are altars of praise, the first dedicated to Mnemosyne, mother of the Muses, the second to a 'new Muse' born from the ashes of the Phoenix, followed by nine altars each dedicated to one of the Muses (see fig. 13). All of them are written in praise of King James I. The altars owe their shape more to the printer's effort than to that of the poet. They are linked together because the final line of each altar is repeated as the first line of the next. Although the altars themselves bear no direct resemblance to Herbert's altar, Sylvester is interesting because besides the altar poems he has another introductory poem, which may well have been the source of "Superliminare," the poem that precedes "The Altar" in *The Temple*. Sylvester's poem is printed on opposite pages and divided into two parts, entitled *Indignis* and *Optimis* respectively. The two poems are printed under two Roman arches (see fig. 14). The part on the left is directed to the 'unworthy,' who are warned to keep away from Du Bartas' work. All the lines except the last begin with the forbidding word: 'Hence':

> Hence profane Handes, factors for Hearts profane:
> Hence hissing *Atheists*, Hellish Misse-Creants:
> Hence Buzard Kites, daz'led with Beauties glance
> Hence itching Eares, with Toyes and Tales vp-taen:
> ....
> Hence Al vn holy, frō the WORLDs BIRTH-Feast
> VRANIA's Grace brookes no vn-worthy Guest. (ll. 1-4; ll. 13-14)

The sonnet under the arch on the right invites the deserving readers to partake of what is offered. Most lines begin with "Welcome":

50. See Fowler, p. 20. Like Herbert, Willis used the shaped poem to emulate his pagan example: "He wished to take over classical forms and purify them" (Fowler, p. 14). Willis himself writes: "Cupio enim et vehementer cupio libidinosa poemata vel omnino exulare, vel, Christianis moribus, caste ac pie in adolescētulorū oculis versari" (Scholia, 17).
51. Joshua Sylvester, trans., *Bartas: His Devine Weekes and Works* (1605; facs. rpt. Delmar, N.Y.: Scholars' Facsimiles & Reprints, 1965).

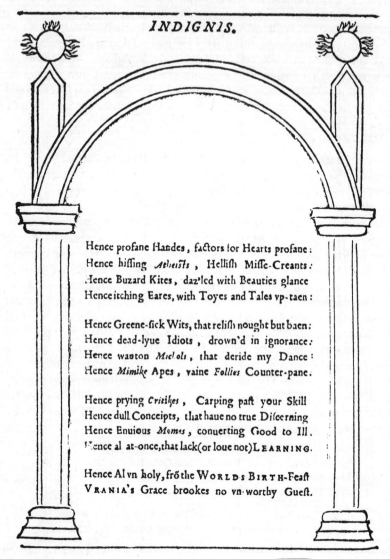

INDIGNIS.

Hence profane Handes, factors for Hearts profane:
Hence hissing *Atheists*, Hellish Misse-Creants:
Hence Buzard Kites, daz'led with Beauties glance
Hence itching Eares, with Toyes and Tales vp-taen:

Hence Greene-sick Wits, that relish nought but baen:
Hence dead-lyue Idiots, drown'd in ignorance:
Hence wanton *Mielols*, that deride my Dance:
Hence *Mimike* Apes, vaine *Follies* Counter-pane.

Hence prying *Critikes*, Carping past your Skill
Hence dull Conceipts, that haue no true Discerning
Hence Enuious *Momus*, conuerting Good to Ill.
Hence al at-once, that lack(or loue not)LEARNING.

Hence Al vn holy, frō the WORLDS BIRTH-Feast
VRANIA's Grace brookes no vn-worthy Guest.

14a

Welcome pure Hands whose Hearts are fixt aboue:
Welcome deere Soules that of Art's choise are charie:
Welcom chast Matrones whom true zeale doth moue:
Welcome good Wits that grace-full Mirth can varie:
....
Sit-downe (I pray) and taste of euerie Dish:
If Ought mis-like You, better Cooke I wish. (ll. 5-8; ll. 13-14)

Rickey quotes the first sonnet and explains that Sylvester makes use of

OPTIMIS.

But(my best Guest)welcome great King of FAIRIE:
Welcom faire QVEEN (his vertue's vertuous Loue);
Welcom right ÆGLETS of the ROYAL Eyrie:
Welcome found Eares that facred Tunes approue:

Welcome pure Hands whofe Hearts are fixt aboue:
Welcome deere Soules that of Art's choife are charie:
Welcom chaft Matrones whom true zeale doth moue:
Welcome good Wits that grace-full Mirth can varie:

Welcome milde Cenfors that meane flips can couer:
Welcome quicke Spirits that found the depth of Art:
Welcom MECÆNAS, & each LEARNING-louer:
Welcome All good: Welcome with all my Heart:

Sit--downe (I pray) and tafte of euerie Difh:
If Ought mif--like You , better Cooke I wifh·

14b

the *procul este profani* motif that was part of Roman rituals and was also used by Herbert in "Superliminare."[52] I do not think that the parallel between Herbert's poem and Sylvester stops there. The extent of the analogy can best be illustrated by quoting "Superliminare":

52. Rickey, p. 9.

Thou, whom the former precepts have
Sprinkled and taught, how to behave
Thy self in church; approach, and taste
The churches mysticall repast.

Avoid, Profaneness; come not here:
Nothing but holy, pure, and cleare,
Or that which groneth to be so,
May at his perill further go. (*Works*, p. 25)

In *W* the two stanzas were written on opposite pages so that the contrast between them stood out even more clearly. There is none of Sylvester's flippancy in Herbert's poem nor is the contrast between the two stanzas as clear-cut as it is between Sylvester's two sonnets. There are also clear resemblances between Sylvester and Herbert, however. Besides the *procul este profani* motif their poems share the emphasis on the virtues of holiness, purity and zeal that oppose the profaneness of the impure Christian. Both poets, finally, point out the Eucharistic quality of their 'offering':

Sit-downe (I pray) and taste of euerie Dish:

and:

... approach, and taste
The churches mysticall repast.[53]

In view of these similarities it is not at all unlikely that Herbert derived some basic ideas for "Superliminare" and the idea of beginning "The Church" with "Superliminare" and "The Altar" from Sylvester's way of introducing his translation of Du Bartas.

2.2.1.3. Francis Davison.

There is one more altar that deserves separate treatment because it may have influenced Herbert. It is an anonymous poem in *A Poetical Rhapsody*, a very popular anthology in Herbert's day, first published in 1602 and edited by Francis Davison. As Rickey points out, the altar from that anthology, although it is not religious, shows more verbal correspondences with Herbert's altar than any other English example:

An Altare and Sacrifice to Disdaine, for freeing him from Love.

My Muse by thee restor'd to life,
To thee Disdaine, this Altar reares,
Whereon she offers causlesse strife,
Self-spending sighs, and bootlesse teares.
Long sutes in vaine,

53. Cf. "Love (III)": "You must sit down, sayes Love, and taste my meat" (*Works*. p. 189.

83

Hate for good will:
Still dying paine,
Yet living still,
Selfe-loving pride,
Lookes coyly strange,
Will Reasons guide,
Desire of change.
And last of all,
Blinde Fancies fire;
False Beauties thrall
That bindes desire.
All these I offer to disdaine
By whome I life from fancie free.
With vow, that if I love againe,
My life the sacrifice shall bee.

Vicimus & domitum pedibus calcamus
amorem.   Anomos.[54]

Although no one could maintain that the altar by 'Anomos' is Herbert's main source, certain of its phrases do also occur in "The Altar." The 'rearing' of the altar, the 'teares' and 'sacrifice' are mentioned in both poems. If Herbert had 'Anomos'' altar in mind when he wrote "The Altar" he has not only transformed profane themes into sacred ones but also shown himself capable of infusing new significance into rather unpromising material.

2.2.1.4. Other altars.

Other altar-shaped poems are of relatively little importance since they do not throw new light on Herbert's use of the old form. William Browne of Tavistock wrote an altar-shaped poem in *The Shepherd's Pipe* (1614). In the poem he laments the loss of a friend. Two more altar-poems occur in a miscellany called *Witt's Recreations* (1641). The first altar from *Witt's Recreations* is dedicated to Cupid, the second is an epitaph for Andrew Turncoat.[55]

The final poem of Robert Herrick's collection of poetry, *Hesperides*, is called "The pillar of Fame." Since it is altar-shaped and slightly more relevant than the poems just mentioned, I shall quote it in full:

Fames pillar here, at last, we set,
Out-during *Marble, Brasse,* or *Jet,*
Charm'd and enchanted so,

---

54. Sig. I.3ᵛ, qu. in Church, p. 308. See Rickey, p. 13, p. 15.
55. Church had not seen the editions of 1645, 1650 and 1653; in the edition of 1654 the altar was present; Church, pp. 134-35.

```
        As to withstand the blow
        Of      overthrow:
        Nor shall the seas,
        Or    OUTRAGES
        Of storms orebear
        What we up-rear,
        Tho Kingdoms fal,
    This   pillar   never   shall
    Decline  or   waste   at   all;
    But stand for ever by his owne
    Firme and well fixt foundation.⁵⁶
```

Herrick makes a contrast between the pillar made of words and those made of "Marble, Brasse or Jet." We have seen that this concern with the poetic material from which the pattern poem is constructed is characteristic not only of Herbert's "The Altar" but of the classical examples as well.

The next poet to be mentioned in passing is Edward Benlowes (1605?-76), whose poetic versatility was ridiculed by Samuel Butler:

> There is not Feat of Activity, nor Gambol of Wit, that ever was performed by Man, from him that vaults on *Pegasus*, to him that tumbles through the Hoop of an Anagram, but *Benlows* has got the mastery in it.⁵⁷

Benlowes' chief work, "Theophila, or Loves Sacrifice" (1652) contains an altar-shaped poem, entitled "The Consecration," followed by a Latin translation of the same poem, also altar-shaped. The poem is a "Loves Offering" (l. 8) to Christ and is written in praise of Christ's love for mankind.

Finally, there is Samuel Speed. As Church (1944) remarks, "Samuel Speed's only distinction is his servile imitation of Herbert's verse." Vendler (1975) came to a similar conclusion in her comparison between Speed's and Herbert's altars.⁵⁸ In order to bring out the contrast between original and imitation, between real poet and hack poet, I shall end this short survey of the use of the altar-shaped pattern poem in England by quoting Speed's poem:

```
    A broken altar, Lord, to thee I raise,
    Made of a heart, to celebrate thy praise
    Thou that the onely Workman art,
    That canst cement a broken heart.
        For   such   is   mine
        O   make   it   thine:
        Take   out   the   Sin
```

---

56. Robert Herrick, *The Poetical Works*, ed. L.C. Martin (Oxford: Oxford Univ. Press, 1956), p. 335.
57. Qu. in Church, p. 181.
58. Church, p. 198; Vendler, pp. 109-10.

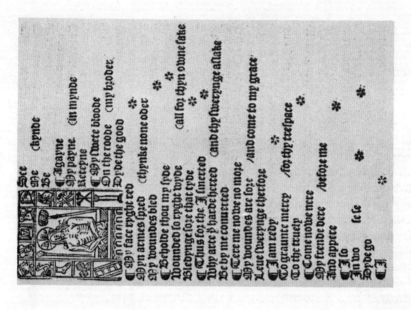

16

Summa colentes iuga Parnaſsia Nymphæ teneræ, Caſtalides puellæ,
Si latices haurio ſuaues, Helicon vertice quos ab alto
Murmure agit dulcisono, ſi colui ſacratam
Aoniam paruulus, & repoſta
Munera ſi quid a me
valebunt,

Hyblæam
Candidula tyaram
Ferte manu, lilia ferte pulchra,
Neapoleonem decorate, O, violis roſiſqué
Neapoleonem Peruſinæ decus vrbis, cui nomen auo
Par celebris fama dedit, perpeti agendum ſtudio cum pietate nomen.

15

```
Thats    hid    therein
Though   it  be  Stone
Make    it   to   groan,
That    so   the   same
      May praise thy Name.
   Melt it, O Lord, I thee desire,
   With flames from thy Coelestial fire;
   That it may ever speak thy Praise alone,
   Since thou hast changed into Flesh a Stone.⁵⁹
```

2.2.2. "Easter-wings."

Two wing-shaped poems written in England before Herbert made use of the form deserve mention; the one by Willis in *Poematum liber* invoking the Muses, the other the first known English pattern poem, by Stephen Hawes (see figs. 15 and 16).[60] Willis' wings need not engage our attention long; like his altar-shaped poem they are clearly written in imitation of the patterns in the *Greek Anthology* and do not add to our understanding of Herbert's "Easter-wings." Stephen Hawes' poem is more interesting and, since it has never been properly analysed or compared with Herbert's poem, I shall discuss it here.

2.2.2.1. Stephen Hawes.

Hawes' pattern poem is part of *The Convercyon of Swerers* (1509). From the picture it is not easy to discern that the poem is a pattern poem. The woodcut in the left-hand corner at the top has 'pushed' the poem aside, but it is a pattern poem of the traditional type in which the number of syllables determines the pattern. In this case the poem increases from monosyllabic lines to lines of six syllables and decreases again to monosyllables at the end. For the pattern to come out clearly the poem should have been printed thus:

```
See
Me                          (kynde
Be
Agayne
My payne                    (in mynde
Reteyne
My swete bloode
On the roode                (my broder
Dyde the good
My face ryght red
```

---

59. From *Prison Pietie*, p. 72; qu. in Church, p. 404.
60. On Willis' "Alae" see Church, p. 50; the wing-shaped poem by Stephen Hawes was discussed by Church in "The First English Pattern Poems."

```
Myn armes spred                        (thynke none oder
My woundes bled
Beholde thou my syde
Wounded so ryght wyde            (all for thyn owne sake
Bledynge sore that tyde
Thus for the I smerted
Why arte thou harde herted      (and thy swerynge aslake
Be by me conuerted
Tere me nowe no more
My woundes are sore              / and come to my grace
Leue swerynge therfore
I am redy
To graunte mercy                 / for thy trespace
To the truely
Come nowe nere
My frende dere                    / before me
And appere
I so
In wo                                          se se
Dyde go
I
Crye                                          (the
Hy
```

The poem represents a pair of wings. The left wing is composed of rhyming triplets. The first triplet consists of monosyllables, the next of disyllabic lines, the next of trisyllabic lines and so on to the middle triplet in which the lines have six syllables; after that the lines are gradually reduced again to the monosyllables of the final triplet. The right wing follows the same pattern, except that it has only one line for every three lines of the left wing. The lines of the right wing are organized in rhyming couplets. The first line of the right wing should be read after the first triplet of the left wing; the second line after the second triplet and so on. If one follows the sense rather than the visual pattern of the poem its rhyme scheme is aaabcccbdddefffe, etc.

Although the idiom and rhythm of the poem are traditional, even dull, the relation between pattern and poem is remarkably effective. In the first half of the poem Christ complains about the neglect by His people of the Passion. In this respect it is comparable to the tone and wording of Herbert's "The Sacrifice." The exact middle of the poem is a question: "Why arte thou harde herted." The second half of the poem is about grace and mercy. It begins with the gently spoken advice to leave off swearing. The final line of the poem forms the verbal link between the poem and the typographical pattern. Christ invites mankind to hurry ("Hy the") and join Him in Heaven. He addresses humanity from on high, i.e. after the Resurrection and the Ascension; the wings are the instruments to bring about the desired reunion between man and Christ. In some editions the woodcut supports this interpretation because it shows Christ enthroned in Heaven, speaking to mankind after the Ascension.[61]

Both Herbert's "Easter-wings" and Hawes' poem are religious pattern poems. "Easter-wings" is concerned with the hope of the resurrection in Christ and its point of view is that of the human being who desires to 'imp' his wing on the wing of Christ. In Hawes' poem the point of view is that of Christ enthroned in Heaven who is desirous to have mankind partake of the heavenly glory. In both poems the wings are the symbolic expression of the unification of man and Christ through the Resurrection. In "Easter-wings" the desired reunion is expressed in the poem by "With thee" and the image "imp my wing on thine"; in Hawes' poem by Christ's exhortation to man — "My frende dere" — to "Come now nere." It should be observed that the wing-shape of Hawes is composed differently from that of Herbert; in Hawes the wing-shape is vertical while the lines are horizontal; in Herbert's poem the visual pattern only appears if the lines are placed vertically, as they were in the first edition of 1633. This difference has obvious consequences for the relation between pattern and content of the respective poems.

2.2.2.2. Christopher Harvey and Patrick Carey.

After Herbert's work was published posthumously in 1633, many other wing-shaped poems appeared,[62] but two are particularly interesting in connection with Herbert's poem: a wing-poem by Christopher Harvey, Herbert's imitator, and another by Patrick Carey, a poet writing around the middle of the century.[63] Both are religious poems and show what Herbert's contemporaries or near-contemporaries did with wing-patterned poems on themes similar to that of "Easter-wings."

Christopher Harvey's doubtful claim to distinction is mainly based on the fact that he is an imitator of Herbert's. Harvey (1597-1663) jumped on the band-wagon when Herbert's work proved to be a success. From the sixth edition of 1640 onward many editions of Herbert's *The Temple*

61. This is the case, for instance, in the edition used by Church (Huntington Library, Hn 61308; *c.* 1530). The two earlier editions have the same woodcut of Christ surrounded by the instruments of his Passion; the edition of *c.* 1510 is also in the Huntington (Hn 61309), the earliest edition — the one I have consulted — is in the British Library (C.25.k.7) and dates from 1509. The latter edition was also used for the modern edition of *The Convercyon of Swerers* by the E.E.T.S.: Stephen Hawes, *The Minor Poems*, eds. Florence W. Gluck & Alice B. Morgan, E.E.T.S., 271 (London: Oxford Univ. Press, 1974), bibl. notes, pp. xvii, xviii; pp. 76-77 and pl. 12. The 1510 edition of the pattern poem is reprinted in Stephen Hawes, *The Works*, introd. Frank J. Spang (Delmar, N.Y.: Scholars' Facsimiles and Reprints, 1975), sig. A.iii^v.
62. E.g. by Robert Baron and William Bosworth; see Church, "The Pattern Poem," p. 363, p. 382.
63. I owe my knowledge about Carey to Church, "The Pattern Poem," pp. 176-78.

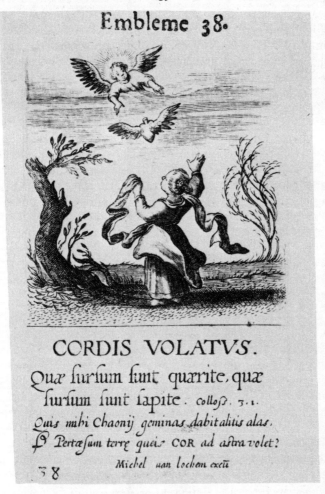

Embleme 38.

CORDIS VOLATVS.

Quæ surfum sunt quærite, quæ
surfum sunt sapite. *colloss. 3.1.*
Quis mihi Chaonij geminas dabit alitis alas.
S Pertæsum terræ quæs COR ad astra volet?

Michel uan lochom excū

38

17

were bound together with Harvey's *The Synagogue*, first published
without the author's name.[64] As late as 1835 Pickering's edition of
Herbert still included *The Synagogue*. Harvey also wrote a book of
emblems, called *Schola Cordis or The Heart of it Selfe, gone away from
God; brought back againe to him; instructed by him* (London, 1647),
written in imitation of the *Schola Cordis* by Benedictus van Haeften
(Antwerp, 1629).[65] Although Harvey copied the plates of van Haeften the

64. See n. 17.
65. The copy of the *Schola Cordis* I consulted in the Bodleian Library had the name
of Quarles written on the title-page in a contemporary (?) hand; nowadays Harvey is
generally recognized as the author of both the emblem book and *The Synagogue*. Cf.

text is his, and here, too, Herbert's influence is clearly felt. Several emblem-texts in Harvey's collection are pattern poems.[66] One of these is wing-shaped and clearly imitates "Easter-wings." It is called "Cordis Volatvs," "The Flying of the Heart" (see fig. 17):

> This way, though pleasant, yet me thinks is long:
> Step after step, makes little haste,
> And I am not so strong
> As still to last
> Among
> So great
> So many lets:
> Swelter'd and swill'd in sweat,
> My toyling soul both fumes and frets,
> As though she were inclin'd to a retreat.
>
> Corruption clogs my feet like filthy clay,
> And I am ready still to slip:
> Which makes me often stay,
> When I should trip
> Away.
> My fears
> And faults, are such,
> As challenge all my tears
> So justly, that it were not much,
> If I in weeping should spend all my years.
>
> This makes me weary of the world below,
> And greedy of a place above,
> On which I may bestow,
> My choicest love,
> And so
> Obtain
> That favour, which
> Excells all wordly gain,
> And maketh the possessour rich,
> In happiness of a transcendent strain.
>
> What? must I still be rooted here below,
> And riveted unto the ground,
> Wherein mine haste to grow

Pickering, ed., *The Temple*, (1838), "Advertisement to the Synagogue," sigs. T2 and T2ṽ; Freeman, p. 135.

66. Harvey frequently combined emblem and pattern poem. In Grosart's edition the dedicatory prose passage with which the book begins consists of two heart-shaped paragraphs; no. 23, "The Levelling of the Heart" is in the shape of an hour-glass (pp. 169-71); no. 24, "The Renewing of the Heart" is lozenge-shaped (pp. 171-76); no. 37, "The Ladder of the Heart" is shaped like a pyramid (pp. 205-7), and no. 38, "The Flying of the Heart" is composed of wing-shaped stanzas (pp. 207-10).

91

Will be though sound,
But slow?
I know
The Sun exhales
Gross vapours from below,
Which, scorning as it were the Vales,
On mountain-topping clouds themselves bestow.

But my fault-frozen heart is slow to move,
Makes poor proceedings at the best,
As though it did not love,
Nor long for rest
Above.
Mine eyes
Can upward look,
As though they did despise
All things on earth, and could not brook
Their presence: but mine heart is slow to rise.

Oh that it were once winged like the Dove,
That in a moment mounts on high,
Then should it soon remove,
Where it may lye
In love.
And loe,
This one desire
Me thinks hath imp'd it so,
That it already flies like fire,
And ev'n my verses into wings do grow.[67]

The poem is wordy and the pattern only supports the general theme of the poem. There is in Harvey's poem no correlation between the length of the lines and what is said in them. On the other hand several details help us understand Herbert's poem better, because Harvey states explicitly what Herbert only hints at. The second stanza is about the effects of sin. It describes in a diluted, lachrymose way what Herbert states so succinctly and dramatically in his second stanza:

My tender age in sorrow did beginne:
And still with sicknesses and shame
Thou didst so punish sinne,

67. Harvey, pp. 150-53; Grosart's ed., pp. 207-10. Harvey's emblem is preceded by the motto: "Who are these that fly as a Cloud, and as the Doves to their Windows?", a quotation of Isaiah 60:8, and an epigram:

Oh that mine heart had wings like to a Dove,
That I might quickly hasten hence, and move
With speedy flight tow'rds the celestial sphears,
As weary of this world, its faults, and fears!

> That I became
> Most thinne. (ll. 11-15)

The resemblance between Harvey's poem and Herbert's appears most clearly in the final stanza. Harvey uses the word 'imp' and he expresses the desire of the human heart to rise upward by referring to the wings which the poem consists of. In Harvey's poem the process of 'imping' takes place within the human heart and is a metaphor of the desire to rise, whereas in Herbert's poem the poet imps his wing on Christ. The dramatic interaction between Christ and the human soul in "Easter-wings" is totally absent from Harvey's poem. The final line of Harvey's emblem establishes beyond doubt how the typographical pattern should be understood, but its tone is flippant compared with the seriousness of the rest of the poem. "And e'en my verses into wings do grow" seems a petty reward for the zealous soul. The anti-climactic ending of Harvey's poem contrasts with the powerful paradox that ends Herbert's poem:

> Affliction shall advance the flight in me.

The beginning of the final stanza of Harvey's poem refers to the Bible text that is the source of Harvey's wing-image, Psalm 55:6:

> Oh that I had wings like a dove! for then would I fly away, and be at rest.

The same lines from Psalm 55:6 form the motto of the pattern poem by Patrick Carey, a poet whom Sir Walter Scott described as "a gentleman, a loyalist during the civil war, a lawyer, and a rigid high-churchman, if not a Roman Catholic."[68]

Although the imagery of Carey's poem is different from that in Herbert's, the two poems share the idea that human affliction and disappointment in worldly affairs can be overcome if man is reunited with Christ. In Carey's poem the reunion is expressed in the Biblical metaphor of the dove's wings. In "Easter-wings" the wings are mentioned too, but the reference to the dove is absent. In view of the obvious parallels between Herbert's poem and the pattern poems by Harvey and Carey it is not unlikely that the text of Psalm 55 is implied in the image of the wings in "Easter-wings" as well. In the section on the emblematic aspect of "Easter-wings" we shall have occasion to return to Herbert's use of this image.

2.2.3. Conclusions.

More pattern poems were written in England after Herbert had used the

---

68. Church, "The Pattern Poem," p. 176; Patrick Carey, *Trivial Poems and Triolets*, ed. Sir Walter Scott (1820), p. iii.

form than before. The success of a great poet must have stimulated several minor poets to imitation though none of them was able to emulate him. Herbert's debt to his classical precursors is easier to demonstrate than is a direct connection between Herbert's patterns and those of English poets before him. Some pattern poems written after the poet's death have proved to be more illuminating for certain aspects of "The Altar" and "Easter-wings" than the poems of his immediate predecessors.

A few conclusions can be drawn from the preceding account. As far as typography is concerned it is interesting to observe that "The Altar" lacks the top slab characteristic of the Greek examples, a feature it shares with several contemporary altar-shaped poems. One reason for this absence might be that the top slab would have been too suggestive of the sacrifice of blood celebrated on pagan altars to suit the taste of Anglican England.

The wing-shaped poem appeared in various forms in the course of the English Renaissance. Herbert's use of it is traditional; it imitates the typography of Simmias' "Wings" in that the pattern only comes out when the lines are printed vertically as they should be in Herbert's case. Hawes and Carey used different arrangements of lines to achieve the same visual effect of the wings on the page.

As far as content is concerned, Sylvester and 'Anomos' may have been in Herbert's mind when he set out to write *The Church*. Sylvester's introductory poems to his translation of Du Bartas may well have inspired both the tone of "Superliminare" and the architectonic structure of the beginning of *The Church*. The anonymous altar in Davison's anthology may have suggested some of the phrases in "The Altar." It is uncertain whether Herbert had read Hawes; in any case a comparison between their two wing-shaped poems is interesting because the themes are similar. Although Hawes was not a great poet he clearly attempted to use the pattern poem as effectively as possible, which cannot be said for any other poets writing wing-shaped poems in England except Herbert. Harvey's wing-shaped poem is interesting, finally, because it is a conscious imitation of "Easter-wings" and indirectly refers us to some of the possible sources for Herbert's poem.

Herbert used classical shapes for Christian purposes. No one in the field of pattern poetry has done this as successfully as he did. The juxtaposition of Herbert's poems with similar efforts by his contemporaries supports this conclusion. The use of profane elements for sacred purposes was not Herbert's invention, of course. A similar development had taken place in a phenomenon that, more extensively and successfully than the pattern poem, swept through Europe as comic books do today: I refer to the emblem book.

3. Herbert's pattern poems and the emblem tradition.

3.1. Definitions.

The transformation of the classical, mythological themes of the pattern poems in the *Greek Anthology* into religious, Christian ones was parallelled by a corresponding change in emblem books. The development of the pattern poem and the development of the emblem in the 16th and 17th centuries are closely related. One reason for their popularity was the enormous interest in the Egyptian hieroglyphs.[69]

Another reason for discussing pattern poetry and emblem writing together is the fact that both traditions are related to the *Greek Anthology*. Pattern poetry is rooted in the *technopaegnia* of the *Anthology,* one of the sources of emblems is the Greek epigram.[70]

Freeman has given a succinct and adequate definition of the emblem:

> Each emblem was made up of a symbolical picture, a brief motto or *sententia*, and an explanatory poem. The purpose of the motto was to complete and interpret the picture, while the picture gave meaning to the motto: neither could stand without the other. The purpose of the poem, the third essential feature, was to explain the whole and to point the moral. The three parts were called by the emblem writers and their critics the 'picture,' the 'word,' and the 'explanation' or 'mind' of the emblem, respectively ... There was never any necessary essential likeness between the picture and its meaning ... The details ... never illuminate the image: they merely extend it.[71]

Second-rate poets such as Whitney, Wither, Quarles, and Harvey clearly found the writing of emblems so inspiring that they devoted whole volumes to them. But they appealed to major poets as well: Donne, Herbert, Crashaw, and Vaughan made extensive use of emblems and the emblematic method, although to them the emblem was a means to an end rather than an end in itself. These poets, Eleanor James (1942) writes,

> applied in their imagery lessons drawn from the visual, almost tactual vividness of the emblem plate, the economy, point and pith of the emblem verse, and the high degree of memorability which could be obtained by an image, simple and sharp in outline, but highly figurative in meaning.[72]

69. As Quarles wrote: "And, indeed, what are the Heaven, the Earth, nay every Creature, but Hieroglyphics and Emblems of His Glory?" *Emblemes* (1635), sig. A3. See also Chapter One, 1 and Chapter Two, 1.

70. James Hutton demonstrated that Alciati's *Emblematum Liber* (1531) draws on the Planudean version of the *Greek Anthology* for a large number of its emblems; over fifty out of the 212 emblems go back directly to the *Anthology* (James Hutton, *The Greek Anthology in Italy*, p. 204).

71. Rosemary Freeman, "George Herbert and the Emblem Books," *RES*, 17 (1941), 150-165. This qu. p. 151, p. 154.

72. Eleanor James, "The Emblem as an Image-pattern in some metaphysical poets," Diss. Univ. of Wisconsin 1942, p. 2.

Dr. Johnson disparagingly defined metaphysical wit as "heterogeneous ideas ... yoked by violence together."[73] The metaphysical conceit, once thought to be so uniquely characteristic of the poetry of the time, owes a good deal of its expressiveness and compactness to the emblem.[74] Moreover, the metaphysical poet could depend on his reading-public's familiarity with emblem books.[75] It was a characteristic requirement of emblematic practice that an emblem should not be immediately comprehensible. Paolo Giovio writes: "The device should not be so obscure as to require the Sibyl to interpret it, nor yet so obvious that any literal-minded person can understand it."[76] Devices, impresas, emblems, hieroglyphs are all visual expressions of the same desire to mystify and yet explain, to be concise and yet complex, to show and yet to veil.

3.2. Sacred and profane.

In the early decades of the seventeenth century an important change took place in the development of the emblem book. Mainly due to the exertions of the Jesuits the emblem books developed into devoutly Christian collections. The Cupids of earlier profane emblems changed into the Amor Divinus and Anima of the religious emblem book. Whereas the earlier Cupids were fluttering around naked in the emblem plates, Divine Cupid and the Human Soul were decently clad and properly haloed. The religious emblem proved an ideal playground for the didactically inclined Jesuits. The fashion for religious emblem books spread so quickly that within a few years' time Vaenius published two emblem books, one on profane, the other on sacred love.[77]

3.2.1. Amor and Anima.

There are two types of devotional emblem books that are particularly relevant for the study of Herbert's verse: the Amor/Anima emblem book and the Schola Cordis emblem book. In the first of these Divine Cupid (i.e. Christ) is depicted as a little boy who teaches Anima, the human soul, depicted as a young girl, the way to salvation. Each emblem shows a different aspect of religious life and devotion: Christ shoots arrows at a

---

73. Samuel Johnson, *Lives of the Poets* in *Selected Poetry and Prose*, ed. Frank Brady and W.K. Wimsatt (Berkeley: Univ. of California Press, 1977), p. 348.

74. "... emblems serve as a median stage between old and worn poetic metaphor and the peculiarly vivid and graphic seventeenth century poetic conceit" (James, p. 33).

75. Clements notes that by 1616 700 different editions of emblem books had appeared (*Picta Poesis*, p. 220).

76. Qu. in Clements, p. 194.

77. Otho Vaenius, *Amorum Emblemata* (Antwerp, 1608) and *Amoris Divini Emblemata* (Antwerp, 1615).

broken heart; He shows the way to Heaven; He shows Anima the way out of a labyrinth by means of a rope let down from Heaven, etc. The two most influential emblem books in this tradition are *Pia Desideria* by the Jesuit Hermannus Hugo (Antwerp, 1624) and *Typus Mundi*, compiled by the College of Rhetoric of the Society of Jesus at Antwerp and published in 1627. Hugo's book especially went through numerous editions and was frequently imitated. These two popular works inspired the Englishman Francis Quarles to write his famous *Emblemes* (London, 1635), one of the few emblem books that are also widely known outside the little circle of specialists. The illustrations of Quarles' emblem book are derived both from the *Pia Desideria* and the *Typus Mundi*.[78]

3.2.2. Schola Cordis.

The school-of-the-heart type is another kind of devotional emblem book that became popular in the seventeenth century. Here the human heart is the focus of attention; it is made to undergo tortures, is swept, purified, refined, pressed, etc. All these penitential activities are intended to make the heart fit for grace. Although the motif was already used by Georgette de Montenay in *Emblemes, ou Devises Chrestiennes* (Lyon, 1571) and several other emblem writers, the best known collection of emblems devoted exclusively to the teaching of the heart was Benedictus van Haeften's *Schola Cordis* (Antwerp, 1629). Van Haeften's book was imitated in English by Christopher Harvey (1647). Another English emblem book that belongs to this tradition is Henry Hawkins, *The Devout Hart* (Rouen, 1634). Frequently a mixture of elements from the Amor/Anima and the Schola Cordis traditions is found in one and the same emblem book. This is the case, for instance, in Hugo's *Pia Desideria*, where Amor Divinus shoots an arrow at a broken heart while Anima watches. Quarles copied this emblem. Several other examples that show a mixture of the two devotional emblem traditions can be found in John Hall, *Emblems with Elegant Figures. Sparkles of Divine Love* (London, 1648), which is also inspired by the continental tradition.[79]

3.3. Herbert and the emblematic method.

When dealing with English emblem books one should realize that they appeared relatively late and that most of them were copies, imitations or

78. Quarles' engravers, W. Marshall and W. Simpson, used the illustrations of Boetius à Bolswert, the illustrator of *Pia Desideria*, for three of the five parts of *Emblemes*. See Freeman, pp. 117-18.
79. For further information about the *schola cordis* tradition and the relation between continental and English emblem books see the bibliographies in Praz and Freeman; also Praz, chapter III and Freeman, pp. 134-39.

adaptations of continental originals. In view of this I have felt free to quote more or less indiscriminately from emblem books by Alciati, Whitney and Hugo, which appeared before Herbert wrote *The Temple* and from Wither, Quarles, Harvey and Hall, whose emblem books were published after Herbert's death but were based on material that had appeared in continental emblem books well before.[80] In many instances it seems more sensible to refer to and quote from English parallels rather than their continental sources as the former can be expected to illustrate better how these sources, mostly Roman Catholic, were transformed by English poets to suit Anglo-Catholic or Anglican taste and needs. What English poets wrote may often inform us better about Herbert's intentions in his own verse than earlier, non-English sources could. An exception should be made for Hugo's emblem book which I am convinced Herbert knew and which I shall refer to directly and regularly.

In a passage from *Studies in Seventeenth-Century Imagery* that we quoted before Praz calls Herbert's *Temple* "a mute emblem-book." Freeman argues that no other poet in the English language made such an extensive use of emblematic conceits as Herbert did. She describes how the art of emblem writing, which itself had hardly yielded any great poetry, could affect the imagery of a great poet:

> ... Herbert's work as a whole constitutes the transformation of the methods of the emblematists into a form for poetry ... characterized by a simplicity of image, an extreme unobtrusiveness, and a concentration of meaning in which the complexity becomes only gradually apparent.[81]

But Freeman also writes:

> Apart from one noteworthy exception, however, Herbert cannot be said to have confined himself in any poem to the material of the emblematists. Memories of Amor and Anima are perhaps behind the *Dialogue* and the better known 'Love bade me welcome but my soul drew back ...' ... In all these, however, the influence of the emblems is reflected in only a general way. The sole exception is *Love unknown*.[82]

Praz oversimplifies matters when he says that Herbert's *The Temple* is really an emblem book without plates; Freeman explains quite convincingly how emblems were transformed into poetic images in Herbert's work. However, she does not allow for evidence that Herbert occasionally used actual emblems from specific emblem books for certain images in

---

80. There are two reasons that justify the reference to emblem books published after Herbert's death. The first is given in the text: most English emblem books derive their substance from earlier, continental sources; the second is that, even when an English emblem book could not have been a *source* for Herbert's poetry, it may be very useful as an *analogue* (cf. Chapter One, 2).

81. Freeman, "George Herbert and the Emblem Books," p. 157.

82. Freeman, *English Emblem Books*, p. 164.

his work. Two scholarly critics who realized and, to a certain extent, have
demonstrated that comparisons between those images and the emblems
might well help us to understand the poetry better are James (1942) and
Colie (1973).[83] In the following sections we shall pay attention to both
specific and general resemblances between Herbert's pattern poems,
certain images in those poems, and the emblematic mode. By way of
introduction I shall analyse a passage from a "normal" Herbert poem in
which his particular method of transforming emblem into metaphor is
clearly evident.

3.3.1. "Love unknowne," "The Temper (I)" and the Schola Cordis
tradition.

In *The Resources of Kind* (1973) Colie writes this about *The Temple*:

> I want to suggest that there is a major emblematic sub-theme in Herbert's Temple
> as a whole; that the collection is, among other things, a "school of the heart" much
> like the continental devotional emblem books.[84]

Colie supports her thesis by mentioning several poems in which emblematic imagery of the heart plays an important part but, oddly enough,
without referring to "The Altar."

The most orthodox and elaborate example of an emblematic heart-
poem in Herbert's work is "Love unknowne" (*Works*, pp. 129-131). Colie
compares its imagery of the heart that has to undergo various tortures
with *Emblemata Sacra* (Frankfurt, 1624), a continental emblem book by
Daniel Cramer, in which we also see "the heart detached, to suffer
severely and alone" (Colie, p. 57). The heart at work or "worked upon"
occurs in a good many other poems by Herbert, though rarely as
elaborately as in "Love unknowne":

> It is instructive to enumerate the various heart-images in Herbert's book: the heart
> has a mouth, "runs mutt'ring up and downe" ("A True Hymne"); it is busy and
> enquiring ("The Discharge"); it can spin; it is pressed and runs thin ("Praise III");
> it is wrung out; it has hands ("The Collar"), knees ("The Deniall"), and feet ("A
> True Hymne"), like that odd picture in Haeftanus' *Schola Cordis*, where the heart
> reflected in a mirror sprouts two little hands and two little feet; it has eyes ("The
> Discharge," "Ephes. 4.30," "The Dawning"). It can sleep and rise, with and
> without the wings it often asks for. This heart is hard, sometimes softened,
> sometimes hardened by a hammer; it is cut by cords as in the *Schola Cordis*; its

83. Eleanor James suggests that Herbert owes several of his images to Hugo's *Pia
Desideria*; she mentions the labyrinth in "The Pearl" (Hugo, Book II, pl. II), the image of
the potter in "The Priesthood" (Hugo, Book I, pl. V), the image of
sighs and groans in combination with that of arrows in "Longing" (Hugo,
frontispiece) and several other parallels (James, pp. 271-75). For Rosalie Colie see the
next footnote and section 3.3.1. of the text.
84. Colie, p. 53, p. 57; the quotation is part of a chapter about Herbert entitled
"*Small Forms*: Multo in Parvo" (pp. 32-75).

thoughts are as a case of knives wounding it, but it is relieved when "suppling grace" drops from above.

In several poems, the heart asks to be written on, or carved on as stone, most notably in the poem called "IESU"; the heart is "shrivel'd," but recovers greenness, as in the picture from Johann Mannich's book in which the heart sprouts grain afresh. God's "strong hand" (as in "Prayer (II)") works in some of Herbert's poems as it does characteristically in the emblems, where a mighty hand emerges from a cloud to do one or another remarkable thing — unlock the heart, as in "Church lock and key," or plumb heaven and earth or the human heart ... (Colie, p. 57, p. 62)

Colie's account demonstrates that Herbert's debt to the emblematic method was extensive and the illustrations from emblem books she includes show the affinity of Herbert's imagery with the Schola Cordis tradition.

There is also biographical evidence to show that Herbert was aware of the Schola Cordis type of emblem book and liked its method. In the life of his brother Nicholas, Herbert's closest friend, John Ferrar describes how the ladies of Little Gidding used to make Concordances:

One of these Books was sent to Mr Herbert, wch he sayd, he prized most highly, as a rich jewel worthy to be worne in ye heart of all Xtians, & in his letter to them expresses himself thus, y^t he most humbly blessed God, y^t he had lived now to see womens scizzers brought to so rare an use as to serve at Gods altar, & incouraged them to proceed in ye like works as y^r most happy employment of theyr times & to keep y^r Book allwayes wthout Book in their hearts, as well as they had it in their heads, memories, & tongues dayly. (*Works*, p. 577)

As Freeman (1948) explains, these concordances consisted of "the Book of Revelation, illustrated with a number of engravings of the type of the school of the heart, which Nicholas Ferrar had probably collected among the books and engravings which we know he brought back from his travels abroad" (p. 166).

About "Love unknowne" Freeman writes that it "is the only poem which versifies the material of that particular group of emblem books so consistently and obviously. It is the *Schola Cordis* in little" (pp. 166-7). A little further on she indicates in a more general way what to her is the relation between Herbert and the emblematic method:

These connections with specific emblem books are only occasional and while they do establish incontrovertibly Herbert's closeness to the form, scattered parallels are never a very fruitful method of comment. And the emblem mode had for Herbert a wider application in that in all the poems ideas are constantly formulated through images, each of which is brief and completed, yet fully investigated (p. 167).

Although Colie seems to do exactly what Freeman warns against, she too, is aware that the mere summing-up of specific parallels will not quite do:

... I think that both this immediacy and this incalculability derive from the psychological appeal of the emblem to its reader, inducing a set for solving problems. The kind of implied meaning noted in Marvell's tortoise-imagery in *Upon Appleton House,* where many things are drawn into a single hieroglyph, we may find paralleled in Herbert's very different equivalencies for the heart he educates in his book. The true temple of God is not a temple, but the human heart — for all its architectural poems, Herbert's book *The Temple* is written out of and for that metaphor: it is a school for the heart, teaching it to become a temple fit for God's dwelling (pp. 62, 67).

There is more to the influence of the emblematic method on the formation and scope of imagery in literature than the mere tracing of images to specific emblems. It is difficult, anyhow, to prove conclusively that an image in a poem derives from a specific emblem. More often than not both image and emblem spring from the hieroglyphic mode of thinking that pervaded the culture. A recognition of that hieroglyphic turn of mind is more essential for the understanding of Renaissance literature and art than the chase after parallels.

On the other hand I think that Freeman is too dismissive about the specific one to one relationship between images in Herbert's poems and emblems in emblem books, mainly because she does not distinguish between source and parallel or analogy. The connections between Herbert and emblem books are not occasional, but extensive and regular, as Colie has shown and as I shall illustrate further in the course of this study. The provision of examples illustrating this connection is not an aim in itself, but may help determine the 'landscape' of Herbert's mind that made him prefer a certain type of imagery, the type that is "brief and completed, yet fully investigated" (Freeman, p. 167).

It is beyond doubt that *The Temple* has affinities with the *Schola Cordis* emblem books. Nonetheless it is an exaggeration to call *The Temple* "a mute emblem book." The difference becomes clear as soon as one compares the method of the *Schola Cordis* with that of *The Temple.* Take, for instance, the following lines from "The Temper (I)" (*Works,* p. 55):

> Yet take thy way; for sure thy way is best:
> Stretch or contract me, thy poore debter:
> This is but tuning of my breast, ,
> To make the musick better. (ll. 21-24)

Several layers of imagery serve to illustrate Herbert's point in these four lines: the sinner will undergo the agony of penance with more acquiescence if he realizes that this is just a preparation for eternal peace and joy in the future. The imagery employed by Herbert derives from the Scriptures: "As for God, his way is perfect;" (2 Sam. 22:31; Ps. 18:30) which he paraphrases in the line:

> Yet take thy way; for sure thy way is best:

But the imagery also refers to the mythological story of Procrustes, the giant who punished the travellers whom he set upon by either stretching their limbs if they were too short or chopping them off if they were too long. This torture took place on a bed that served as a yardstick for the ideal size Procrustes wished the poor prisoner to conform to. This myth underlies l. 22 of "The Temper (I)":

> Stretch or contract me, thy poore debter:

Simultaneously the verbs that evoke the myth — "stretch or contract" — prepare for the musical image in the line following, because stretching and contracting also refer to the tuning of string instruments. Nor is that all, because 'contract' is also connected with the word 'debter' (he contracts debts). Together the two verbs are an image-pattern in themselves and express the fealty of man to God. The emblem of the tuning of the heart is implicit in l. 23:

> This is but tuning of my breast,
> To make the musick better.

Harmony can be achieved only after man has become attuned to God. The cluster of images briefly examined here serves to show once again that myth is used by Herbert as the handmaiden of Christianity. The Procrustean torture is transformed into, 'embedded in,' a penitential preparation for heavenly harmony.

The treatment of the image of the tuning of the heart in emblem books does not allow for complexities of this nature. This can be demonstrated by comparing Herbert's use of the image with that of Hawkins, who used it for one of the emblems in *The Devout Hart* (see fig. 18). The emblem in question is entitled "Iesus the Sonne of David, playes on the harp in the hart, while the Angels sing," and the picture shows Christ playing the harp in the human heart.[85] The picture of each emblem in Hawkins' book

---

85. pp. 185-198. Hawkins' emblem book belongs to one of the three sub-types of emblem books in the School of the Heart tradition. In Harvey's emblem book the heart undergoes various tortures; in this type the heart is a metaphor for the several stages and states of man in his pilgrimage of life. Divine Love functions as the teacher and guide of the human soul. Hawkins' book belongs to the other type in which the heart is not so much "worked upon" as "operated in." In this type the heart is shown as a place (*locus*) in which Christ performs various allegorical actions: he sweeps with a broom, he knocks at the door, he crowns, etc. Herbert's image of the "tuning of my breast" in "The Temper (I)" belongs to the latter type. On the place of Hawkins' emblem book within the meditative tradition see Freeman, pp. 173-198. Cf. Chapter Five, 3.2.2. As Colie points out Cramer's *Emblemata Sacra* (1624) represents a third sub-type: "... the heart so treated is made to seem utterly separate from the speaker, its ostensible possessor, who watches the strange signs as in a trance or dream" (p. 57). Herbert's "Love unknown" belongs to this category.

Pulsa chordas, sonet chelys,　Dulce melos intonabunt
Dum nos recreas de cœlis　Nuum nobis excitabunt
IESV cordis gaudium:　Angeli tripudium.

18

is followed by a "Hymne." The final lines of the Hymne to this particular emblem read:

> ... *Euermore*
> *IESV be al in al, my part,*
>   *My God, musitian to my hart,*
> *And harmony, which solace brings,*
>   *Ah touch my hart, & tune it's strings.*

Hawkins' interest is primarily didactic and devotional, not literary; a poem alone is not enough for him: the hymn of each emblem is followed by lengthy prose passages the first of which is invariably called "The Incentive." In the 'Incentive' to the emblem under discussion those metaphors of the hymn that might be open to ambiguous readings are explained unequivocally:

1. If IESVS touch alone and mooue affects, which are the strings of our hart, good God! how sweet, how diuine a musike he makes therein. But if self-loue once play the Harper, and medle with the quil, and touch the springs but neuer so litle, ah me! it is a hellish horrour, and no musike.
2. When IESVS with a soft modulation steals into my hart there is streight such a sweetnes in the marrow and bowels, as al things satisfy and please alike; life, death, prosperity, aduersity: You would verily say my miseries were charmed by IESUS and his Angels.

3. Touch but the harp, litle *Dauid*, giue it a lick with the quil, twang that only, I say, twang the domestical harp but neuer so lightly, whereon thy Gransier *Dauid* playd so long a goe, and it is enough. It was it dispersed the horrid clouds of sadnes and melancholy, & draue away the wicked Genius. O God, when I heare this *Dauid* both father and sonne of the Royal Psalmist, playing on his harp, how my hart iumps the while, yea how ready it is to leap out of it-self.

After the reader's attention has thus been properly focused, he is ready for the "Preamble" to the "Meditation":

The heauenly *Dauid* in the midst of the Hale of the hart, with nimble fingers, tickles the harp, to the musical numbers. Come hither Angels, then come you deare soules to IESVS, come you al: Cleare vp your voyces, and tune them to the pulse, and harmony of this harp. This sound, beleeue me, wil banish Sathan, and throughly purge away melancholy, that grateful seat of the wicked Genius.

But why the harp (most sweet IESUS) rather then another? Yet should I thinke thou takest it not by chaunce: vnles perhaps it be that the forme and sound of this Instrument. Ah! thou wouldst present that figure which in mount Caluary thou actedst so long a goe; playing the Chorus of that sad Tragedy, in the publike Theater of Heauen & earth, in view of al? Ah, now I remember how thine armes and feet were then stretched forth on the tentours, as in the harp the strings are wont. How stiff were then the nerues and sinewes of the whole body: But here loue playes the harper, and yealds so forth a sound most like the harp, reaching farr and wide, as farre I say, as the highest, midle, & nether orb extend heauen, earth, & hel
. . .
Therefore, o my hart, listen I pray, and when thou hearest the voice of thy God, anon being struck as it were and smil, giue a sound with al, and attemper and ply thy voyce to his, make his wil and mine to iump and sympathize together: take heed thou yealdst not a rustike musike; and a harsh vngrateful tone; sing to the numbers right, and dance with al whether aduersity maane thee, or prosperity play with thee. But especially lend thine empty eares to the most sweet ditty of the diuine Harper: who sweetly allures thee a farre of, and neerer hand puls thee with the sound of his harp.

Hawkins is your proper, tidy emblem writer; the configuration of details in the picture tallies completely with the imagery of the verse and the explanation of the prose following it. Every detail in the picture is given ample consideration in the verse and prose, but all the images and metaphors employed there never go beyond the details of the picture. Hawkins' method is one of equation, whereas Herbert's metaphors invite exploration. There is in Hawkins' emblem nothing of Herbert's complexity, a complexity arising mainly from a dense verbal structure and a mixture of metaphoric ingredients that causes the passage to be open to the different approaches I have traced above.

Hawkins' method, and that of the emblem writer in general, is unilateral; Herbert's method, and that of any great poet, is multilateral. Notwithstanding this basic difference in quality, a study of Hawkins' emblem may add to our understanding of the passage from "The Temper (I)." Hawkins writes: "Ah, now I remember how thine armes and feet were then stretched forth on the tentours, as in the harp the strings are wont." This sentence makes us aware of a further dimension of the analogical image in Herbert's poem:

> Stretch or contract me, thy poore debter:

If one interprets the line as a gloss on the Passion, an interpretation suggested by Hawkins' emblem text, the stretching and contracting of the poet's heart explains the poet's debt to Christ, Who paid for the sins of mankind by His crucifixion. Herbert's suffering is an *imitatio Christi*; the stretching and contracting of his heart's strings will bring him into harmony with the example of Christ's suffering.

Another element shared by emblem and poem is that the heart is willing to undergo the penance imposed on it. The hymn reads:

> . . . *Euermore*
> *IESU be al in al, my part,*
>   *My God, musitian to my hart,*
> *And harmony, which solace brings,*
>   *Ah touch my hart, & tune it's strings.*

Herbert's stanza:

> Yet take thy way; for sure thy way is best:
>   Stretch or contract me, thy poore debter:
> This is but tuning of my breast,
>   To make the musick better.

When considered in isolation this stanza from Herbert's "The Temper (I)" clearly belongs to that part of the Schola Cordis tradition in which the heart is the focus of penitential activity. If one analyses it, however, within the context of the poem it belongs to, the submission of the heart that is expressed in the stanza is seen to be infinitely more dramatic and complex than the passivity of the heart in the emblematic counterpart:

> How should I praise thee, Lord! how should my rymes
>   Gladly engrave thy love in steel,
> If what my soul doth feel sometimes,
>   My soul might ever feel!
>
> Although there were some fourtie heav'ns, or more,
>   Sometimes I peere above them all;
> Sometimes I hardly reach a score,
>   Sometimes to hell I fall.
>
> O rack me not to such a vast extent;
>   Those distances belong to thee:
> The world's too little for thy tent,
>   A grave too big for me.

Wilt thou meet arms with man, that thou dost stretch
    A crumme of dust from heav'n to hell?
Will great God measure with a wretch?
    Shall he thy stature spell?

O let me, when thy roof my soul hath hid,
    O let me roost and nestle there:
Then of a sinner thou art rid,
    And I of hope and fear.

Yet take thy way; for sure thy way is best:
    Stretch or contract me, thy poore debter:
This is but tuning of my breast,
    To make the musick better.

Whether I flie with angels, fall with dust,
    Thy hands made both, and I am there:
Thy power and love, my love and trust
    Make one place ev'ry where.

The penultimate stanza of the poem presents a solution to the problems posed in the stanzas 2 and 3. There the weakness of man's faith is presented in cosmic terms: man either overreaches himself or falls short of his aim. This unfortunate contrast in man's behaviour is set off against God's omnipotence:

    O rack me not to such a vast extent;
      Those distances belong to thee:

The Procrustean images in the poem are introduced by the word 'rack.' In the following stanza the string of images is continued:

    Wilt thou meet arms with man, that thou dost stretch
      A crumme of dust from heav'n .to hell?
    Will great God measure with a wretch?
      Shall. he thy stature spell?

Both the questions posed here and the double paradox in the lines preceding them:

    The world's too little for thy tent,
      A grave too big for me.

are resolved in the harmony achieved in the final stanzas. In the process the focus of attention has moved from the territory of the macrocosm to the microcosm of the human heart. These intricate adjustments of tone, subject-matter and metaphor go far beyond the range of the emblem proper. On the other hand, the emblematic aspect of the poem adds an element of clarity and terseness to a complex and gradually developing argument.

  This analysis of "The Temper (I)" is intended as a paradigm for many other poems in which the emblematic strain is particularly strong. "The Altar" and "Easter-wings" are no exceptions to the rule. They are only exceptional in Herbert's work because their typographical pattern seems to provide the 'picture' found 'wanting' in his other emblematic poems. A closer analysis of both the typographical patterns and what underlies them will show, however, that even these two seemingly extreme examples of Herbert's adherence to the emblematic method bear only a superficial likeness to their emblematic counterparts.

3.4. "The Altar" and the Schola Cordis tradition.

The shape of Herbert's altar recalls the classical altars from the *Greek Anthology*; in Herbert's poem, however, the altar is a metaphor of the broken heart which is offered to God as a sacrifice of praise. Emblem literature provides several examples in which a classically shaped altar served religious purposes. Thus Henkel/Schöne mention an emblem by Juandes Boria, *Empresas Morales* (Prague, 1581), bearing the motto: *Non sine igne*, in which "ein Altar / und Feuer zum Opffer angezündet / gesehen wird / weil nach der Meynung der Alten / kein Opffer ohne Feur / Gott gefallen mag / welches auch die Beyschrifft / Nicht ohne Feuer / andeutet..."[86] In the more widely known and influential emblem book by Gabriel Rollenhagen, *Nucleus Emblematum* (Arnhem, 1611) we find a similar emblem with the motto, *Sacrificivm Deo Cor Contribvlativm*, showing a flaming heart on an altar.[87]

This last emblem is also found in Wither, *A Collection of Emblemes* (1635). Wither used the plates of Rollenhagen's emblem book, which he considered so excellent that he did not mind waiting for several years until he could procure them from Holland.[88] The verses accompanying the plates are Wither's. To Rollenhagen's motto he added a heading of his own that is a free rendering of the former:

> *The* Sacrifice, *God loveth best,*
> *Are* Broken-hearts, *for* Sin, *opprest.*

---

86. Arthur Henkel & Albrecht Schöne, *Emblemata; Handbuch zur Sinnbildkunst des XVI. und XVII. Jahrhunderts* (Stuttgart: Metzlersche Verlagsbuchhandlung, 1967), p. 132: Juande S. Boria, *Empresas Morales* (Prague, 1581), [84, no. 83].

87. Henkel/Schöne, p. 1029: Gabriel Rollenhagen, *Nucleus Emblematum* (Arnhem, 1611), nr. 65, *Reue*.

88. See Chapter One, 1, text and n. 13. Wither himself wrote about the engravings by "Crispinus Passaeus":

> *These* Emblems, *graven in Copper by* Crispinus Passaeus ... *came to my hands, almost twentie yeares past. The* Verses *were so meane, that, they were afterward cut off from the* Plates; ... *the* Copper Prints *(which are now gotten) could not be procured out of* Holland, *upon any reasonable Conditions.* ("To the Reader," sig. A 1ᵛ)

Embleme 19.

20

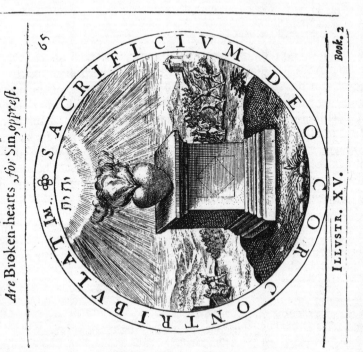

The Sacrifice, God loveth best,
Are Broken-hearts, for Sin, oppreſt.

65

SACRIFICIVM DEO COR CONTRIBVLATVM.

ILLVSTR. XV.

Book. 2

19

(see fig. 19). A similar combination of altar, heart and sacrifice can be found in Harvey's *School of the Heart,* Emblem 19 (see fig. 20). Its motto resembles Wither's: *The Sacrifices of God are a broken heart.* I quote three of its nine stanzas:

6.

But is this all? Must there not be
Peace-offerings, and sacrifices of
Thanksgiving tendered unto thee?
Yes, Lord, I know I should but mock, and scoffe
Thy sacrifice for sinne, should I
My sacrifice of praise deny.

8.

My self then I must sacrifice:
And so I will, mine heart, the onely thing
Thou dost above all other prize
As thine owne part, the best I have to bring.
An humble heart's a sacrifice,
Which I know thou wilt not despise.

9.

Lord, be my altar, sanctifie
Mine heart thy sacrifice, and let thy Spirit
Kindle thy fire of love, that I,
Burning with zeale to magnifie thy merit,
May both consume my sinnes, and raise
Eternall trophies to thy praise.[89]

Wither's and Harvey's mottoes might also have served for Herbert's poem "The Altar," although there the altar and the broken heart are telescoped into the single image of the broken altar made of the heart. The emblems by Rollenhagen/Wither and Harvey provide the circumstantial corroboration for the most probable interpretation of the word 'Sacrifice' in Herbert's poem. The 'broken heart,' oppressed by sin but full of religious zeal is man's ultimate offering on the altar which forms the link between man's sacrifice and the Sacrifice of Christ. The idea of the sacrifice of the broken heart that we find in the emblems and in Herbert's poem has a common source in Psalm 51:17:

> The sacrifices of God are a broken spirit: a broken and a contrite heart, O God, thou wilt not despise.

This verse is one of the sentences read at the beginning of Morning Prayer in the liturgy of the Church of England.[90]

89. Harvey, *Schola Cordis*, pp. 76-79.
90. The whole of Psalm 51 is relevant. Its subject is the cleansing process that we also find in Herbert's poem "Superliminare"; the Psalm mentions the "bones which

In one respect, however, Herbert's poem differs from both source and emblems; in his poem the heart is not placed on the altar, but it is the stuff the altar is made of. Part of the complexity and the difficulty of interpretation arises from the fact that the altar is actually constructed from a stony heart and thus does not seem to accord with the feeling of contrition that underlies the other texts. Herbert's heart is 'broken,' it has been cut by God's power (l. 8) but the emotions involved do not indicate contrition, but rather the poet's acceptance of the place assigned to man by God. Herbert needs the metaphor of the stony heart for two poetic reasons. For the logic of the first comparison of the poem to hold, the heart has to be made of stone: the altar is made of a heart, the heart is made of stone, the tears provide cement — hence the altar is made of stones and cement.

Besides the role assigned to the stony heart within the image cluster of "workmanship" it also plays an important part in the metaphor of praise the poem works towards:

> ... if I chance to hold my peace,
> These stones to praise thee may not cease. (ll. 13-4)

Francis Quarles, like Harvey an author of emblem books as well as pattern poems, wrote an elegiac poem in which the obdurate heart has a function similar to that in "The Altar":

> Hard stones,
> If hearts should not,
> Would cleave and split with grones
> Ere so much worth should lie forgot:
> At such a losse, should stones forbeare to breake
> Their flinty Silence; stones, the very stones would speake.
>
> (st. 11)

> Stone hearts
> Let me bespeake
> You all to play your parts:
> If you be too too hard to breake,
> Too stout for drops to pierce, yet come;
> You'l serve for stuffe, to build their honourable Tombe.[91]
>
> (st. 15)

These two stanzas from Quarles' poem form a parallel to ll. 9-14 of "The Altar." In both poems the heart of stone is used for building purposes

---

thou hast broken" (51:8) and it relates the cleansing process to the missionary function of the priest (51:13, 14, 15), both of which are also constituent elements of "The Altar."

91. Francis Quarles, *The Complete Works in Prose and Verse*, ed. Alexander B. Grosart, 3 vols. (Edinburgh: Edinburgh Univ. Press, 1880), III, 39-40.

and "the very stones would speake" is echoed in Herbert's line, "These stones to praise thee may not cease." Both phrases refer to Luke 19:40: "if these should hold their peace, the stones would immediately cry out." Herbert's masterly control over his source-material appears clearly when one compares his image of the 'speaking stones' with that in Quarles' poem. In Quarles the quotation from Luke is almost literal; the relation of the stones to the heart is that of a simple comparison: stones have certain qualities in common with stubborn hearts. The comparison leads to the hyperbole in the final line of his stanza: if the deceased beloved should ever be neglected by hard-hearted posterity stones will prove to be even more communicative than stony hearts. In Herbert's metaphor the transference between the stone and the heart is much more complete than in Quarles'. The comparison does not end in a hyperbole but the conclusion follows logically from the preceding argument: if the stony 'parts' of the heart (which is the altar and thus the poem) can do no better than form the 'frame' of the altar, they contribute at least to the construction of an altar of praise that will continue to celebrate its Creator long after the fallible poet has died. Thus the metaphor of the speaking stones is completely integrated within the argument of the poem as a whole. While Quarles has merely quoted from, Herbert has transformed the source-text.

The image of the broken heart, well-worn in secular love poetry, is put to characteristically good use in Herbert's religious love poetry. In the emblems we have considered, the desire to be united with God was epressed visually by flames rising from the heart placed on the altar as a sacrifice. "Non sine igne" was Boria's motto. The element of fire, another stock image borrowed from the treasure-box of Petrarchan love conceits, was invariably added by poets imitating or commenting on Herbert's poem "The Altar." Consider for instance, Crashaw's poem: "*On Mr. G. Herberts booke intituled the Temple of Sacred Poems, sent to a Gentlewoman*":

> Know you faire, on what you looke;
> Divinest love lyes in this booke:
> Expecting fire from your eyes,
> To kindle this his sacrifice.
> When your hands unty these strings,
> Thinke you have an Angell by th' wings.
> One that gladly will bee nigh,
> To wait upon each morning sigh.
> To flutter in the balmy aire,
> Of your well perfumed prayer.
> These white plumes of his heele lend you,
> Which every day to heaven will send you:
> To take acquaintance of the spheare,
> And all the smooth faced kindred there.

And though *Herberts* name doe owe
These devotions, fairest; know
That while I lay them on the shrine
Of your white hand, they are mine.[92]

Crashaw's tribute is a rather drastic example of the application of a profane idiom to a religious theme. One wonders whether Herbert himself would have appreciated Crashaw's 'well-perfumèd praiers' and 'smooth-fac'd kindred.' It is remarkable that Crashaw repeats or paraphrases words and phrases from the pattern poems in particular ("sacrifice," "wings," These ... plumes of his heele lend you"). The image of the "fire from your eyes," which combines the zeal of the Christian soul towards God and the fervour of a mistress in love exemplifies the obvious ease with which Crashaw could move from one poetic category to another without being aware of crossing border-lines.

The following passage, by a minor poet, is less ambivalent of tone and borrows from "The Altar" more directly:

In vain such praises I should strive to write,
Or for thy Temple's steps measures indite,
Till from the Blest Dove's wing a pen I steal,
Or a live coal from thine own altar feel;
Till I perceive, in fine, the sacred fire
Thy heart and mine with equal vein inspire.

(translation by Rev. Richard Wilton of a commemorative Latin poem by Dean Duport)[93]

Apart from the poem's obvious debt to "The Altar" it is noteworthy how much more clearly emblematic Duport's idiom is than Herbert's. The lines from Duport's poem could have served as *explicatio* to either Boria's emblem or Rollenhagen's.

"The Altar" differs from these emblematic examples in two respects. If we compare poem and emblems we see that, whereas the emblems show a heart placed *on* an altar, Herbert merged the two into one image and introduced a broken altar made of a heart. This was done by the poet for a particular reason to achieve a particular effect as I indicated previously. The point will perhaps become even clearer when we compare the

---

92. From "Steps to the Temple," in Richard Crashaw, *The Poems*, ed. L.C. Martin, 2nd ed. (Oxford: Oxford Univ. Press, 1957), pp. 130-1. Crashaw's poem is also quoted in Walton's *Lives*: Izaak Walton, *The Lives of John Donne, Sir Henry Wotton, Richard Hooker, George Herbert and Robert Sanderson* (London: Oxford Univ. Press, 1927), pp. 337-38.

93. From *Musae Subsecivae seu Poetica Stromata* (Cantabrigiensi, 1676), pp. 357-58; qu. in Alexander B. Grosart, ed., *The Complete Works in Verse and Prose of George Herbert*, 3 vols. (London, 1874), II, cix.

imagery of "The Altar" with that of one of Herbert's Latin epigrams, bearing the Greek title: "Λογικὴ Θυσία":

> Ararúmque Hominúmque ortum si mente pererres,
> Cespes vivus, Homo; mortuus, Ara fuit:
> Quae diuisa nocent, Christi per foedus, in vnum
> Conueniunt; & Homo viua fit Ara Dei.

(translation: "Reasonable Sacrifice":

> If one considers the rise of men and altars,
> Earth breathed upon was man, dead earth
> An altar. Those, which separated
> From one another make for harm, through Christ's compacts
> Were put together: so man becomes
> The living altar of God.)[94]

The reasonable sacrifice is the sacrifice described in Romans 12:1: "... present your bodies a living sacrifice, holy, acceptable unto God, which is your reasonable service." If we read the sacrifice of the heart in "The Altar" with the above poem and the underlying text from Romans in mind, all the pieces of the puzzle fall into place. The sacrifice of the heart which is an altar, is to be regarded as a part of a larger framework in which the human body is seen as a temple: "What? know ye not that your body is the temple of the Holy Ghost which is in you, which ye have of God, and ye are not your own?" (1 Corinthians, 6:19; similarly 1 Cor., 3:16). In terms of Herbert's work as a whole we might even describe these relations in the form of an equation: "The Altar" is to *The Temple* what the heart is to the body. At this stage of 'the heart's progress,' right at the beginning of "The Church" it is fitting that Herbert commemorates the stuff the altar is made of and its sacrificial and sacramental functions. The fact that in Herbert's poem the altar actually *is* a heart turns it into a corollary of the scriptures rather than an appendage to a familiar emblem.

A similar reason may underlie the second point of difference between "The Altar" and its emblematic counterparts: the absence of the element of fire in Herbert's poem. A comparison with another poem by Herbert will make this difference clear. In the second of the sonnets entitled "Love" Herbert writes:

> Immortall Heat, O let thy greater flame
> Attract the lesser to it: let those fires,
> Which shall consume the world, first make it tame;
> And kindle in our hearts such true desires,
> As may consume our lusts, and make thee way.

94. From "Lucus," 29 in M. McCloskey and P.R. Murphy, eds. & trans., *The Latin Poetry of George Herbert* (Athens, Ohio: Ohio Univ. Press, 1965), pp. 106-7.

Then shall our hearts pant thee; then shall our brain
All her invention on thine Altar lay,
And there in hymnes send back thy fire again:
("Love (II)," ll. 1-8; *Works*, p. 54)

"Love (II)" is about religious zeal. "The Altar," introducing the cycle of poems commemorating Holy Week is about the sacrifice of the human heart, that is, the altar in God's temple, the body of man. The sacrifice is penitential and is made *in imitatione Christi*. The metaphor of the heart enflamed with religious zeal does not figure in *The Temple* before "Love (II)." It does not once occur in the set of poems that begins with the pattern poem "The Altar" and ends with the other pattern poem "Easter-wings."[95]

3.5. "Easter-wings" and the Amor/Anima tradition.

3.5.1. Introductory.

That the word 'fire' is absent from "The Altar" is perhaps contrary to what one would expect but its absence from "Easter-wings" is even more surprising. The former poem emphasizes both by its metaphors and by its typography the 'stony,' i.e. sinful aspect of the heart. "Easter-wings," on the other hand, is about man's wish to be released from the earthly bonds of sin. This desire for release was commonly expressed by the emblem of the flaming heart. Whereas "The Altar" is a corollary of Christ's Sacrifice, "Easter-wings" is a corollary of the Resurrection.

Like "The Altar" "Easter-wings" is a poem that would immediately remind a contemporary reader of emblematic counterparts. The comparison of "The Altar" with analogical emblems showed a certain kinship of the poem with the school-of-the-heart tradition, while "Easter-wings" has affinity with the Amor/Anima emblem books. In "Easter-wings" the soul wishes to be reunited with Christ in Heaven. The first stanza elaborates on the concept of *felix culpa* (the Fortunate Fall) and its effects on the general condition of mankind. The second stanza describes the consequences of this condition for the personal situation of the poet and his relation with Christ. The theme of the Christian, whether he be priest or layman, engaged in a personal search for a harmonious relationship with his God, is characteristic of the whole cycle of Herbert's

---

95. Even within the context of the altar of sacrifice the element of fire is something to be expected. The sacrifices on the altar "of whole stones" consisted of "burnt offerings" (Deut. 27:6). As Ainsworth (1618/19) explains the burnt offerings are intended "to obteyn of God by Christ, forgivenesse of sinnes; and sanctification of life" and they signify the "living sacrifice" of the Christian's body that is described in Rom. 12:1. See n. 41 *ante* for fuller reference.

Zelus in Deum.

To my Father, Mr. Henry Peacham, of Leverton in
Holland, in the Countie of Linc:

poems. In this respect his intentions and the Amor/Anima emblems overlap.

There are, I think, at least three popular emblems or emblem-types within the Amor/Anima tradition that show affinities with the imagery of Herbert's pattern poem. The first two are related to "Easter-wings" in theme as well as metaphor. Herbert's choice of metaphors is partly derived from or at least analogous to the emblems concerned. Whether the third emblem exerted any direct influence on "Easter-wings" is more doubtful. The relation is general and thematic rather than specific and textual. The reasons for discussing it will be given later on.

3.5.2. Zelus in deum.

Religious zeal is the motivating force of the soul in "Easter-wings." In his *Iconologia* Ripa had dictated the proper attributes of the personification of religious zeal (see fig. 21) and his recipe was faithfully followed by later emblem writers.[96] In England Peacham imitated Ripa's picture and added verses of his own (see fig. 22). The picture shows *Zeal* as a winged woman. The eyes cast upwards indicate her desire to rise towards Heaven. The wings attached to her back attest to her velocity. One hand is stretched out as if to ward off the evils of the world, the other is pressed to her bosom to show that the source of her devotional zeal is to be found there, in the "Breast enflam'd" (l. 1):

> ... the soule, by Sinne pursu'de and chas'd,
> Thee, thee, (oh Lord) desires, who dost surmount
> All treasures, pleasures, which we here possesse,
> The summe and substance, of our happines. (ll. 9-12)[97]

Both Peacham and Herbert set off the "heartes desire" (l. 1) against the limitations of man's earthly existence. In Peacham this is done by negating, "loathing what the world doth most admire" (l. 3), but in Herbert the contrast is brought out in the poet's own experience, most clearly and dramatically expressed in the paradox of the final line of the poem: "Affliction shall advance the flight in me."

3.5.3. Paupertas.

The contrast between reality and desire, between a sinful state and a state of grace, between earth and Heaven are the subject of a very popular emblem, which usually bears the motto "Paupertatem summis ingeniis obesse, ne provehantur" ("Poverty mars the full development of the

96. Ripa, (1603), pp. 101-103.
97. Henry Peacham, *Minerva Britanna* (London, 1612; facs. rpt. Menston: Scolar Press, 1966), p. 170.

Paupertatem summis ingenijs
obesse, ne prouehantur.

Dextra tenet lapidem: manus altera suftinet alas.
Vt me pluma leuat: sic graue mergit onus.
Ingenio poteram superas volitare per arces,
Me nisi paupertas inuida deprimeret.

23

117

My Wit got Wings; and, high had flowne;,
But, Povertie did keepe mee downe.

PAVPERTATE PREMOR, SVBLEVOR INGENIO.

Book. 3

ILLVSTR. XLII.

25

24

greatest talents").[98] In Alciati's *Emblematum Liber* (1531) the emblem occurs in the section about Fortuna (see fig. 23).[99] The picture shows a man with a large stone attached to his right hand, dragging him down while his left hand is winged and stretched out towards Heaven where God the Father can be seen reaching out towards him with a gesture of blessing. The accompanying text complains that poverty prevents great talents from coming to full bloom. It is in fact an exhortation to patrons of the arts to be more liberal in their financial support of the artist. In Alciati and later imitators the text should be taken literally rather than metaphorically. 'Poverty' is used to describe a physical rather than a mental state, although the two are obviously related.[100] Whitney, in *A Choice of Emblemes* (1586), follows the original rather closely; the picture is virtually identical with Alciati's (see fig. 24). The poem still refers to the profane theme of poverty:

> One hande with winges, woulde flie unto the starres,
> And raise mee vp to winne immortall fame:
> But my desire, necessitie still barres,
> And in the duste doth burie vp my name:
> That hande woulde flie, th'other still is bounde,
> With heauie stone, which houldes it to the ground.

> My wishe, and will, are still to mounte alofte.
> My wante, and woe, denie me my desire:
> I shewe theire state, whose witte, and learninge, ofte
> Excell, and woulde to highe estate aspire:
> But pouertie, with heauie clogge of care,
> Still pulles them downe, when they ascending are. (p. 152)

When we look at the analogous emblem in Wither's *A Collection of Emblemes* (1635), we notice that most of the details of the picture still match those of Alciati's and Whitney's emblems (see fig. 25). The first part of the text reiterates the traditional ideas:

> You little thinke, what plague it is to bee,
> In plight like *him*, whom pictur'd here you see.

98. See Praz, pp. 35-58. Prof. E. de Jongh kindly referred me to an article by Hana Sefertová, "Paupertate premor, sublevor ingenio," which summarizes the history of this particular emblem, *Umění*, 25 (1977), 224-241.

99. This picture from the Lyon edition of 1551 in Henry Green, ed., *Andreae Alciati Emblematum Flumen abundans, or, Alciat's Emblems in their Full Stream*, facs. ed. (Manchester, 1871), p. 132. Alciati derived the idea for this emblem from the *Hypnerotomachia* by Francesco Colonna published by Altus in 1499, fol. h.vii, in which a woman is shown holding a turtle in one hand and having wings attached to the other. The dichotomy between velocity and sluggishness expressed by the picture is defined in this motto: "Velocitatem sedendo, tardidatem tempera surgendo." The picture is reproduced in Praz, p. 36.

100. See Clements, pp. 25-26, p. 164, p. 169.

His *winged-Arme*, and his *up-lifted-eyes*,
Declare, that hee hath *Wit*, and *Will*, to rise:
The *Stone*, which clogs his other *hand*, may show
That, *Povertie* and *Fortune*, keepe him low: (ll. 1-6)

The end of the poem introduces a moral note that was absent in Alciati and Whitney:

... But, God be prais'd.
The *Clog* which kept me downe, from being rais'd,
Was chain'd so fast, that (if such *Dreames* I had)
My *thoughts*, and *longings*, are not now so mad.
For, plaine I see, that, had my *Fortunes* brought
Such *Wealth*, at first, as my small *Wit* hath sought;
I might my selfe, and others, have undone,
Instead of *Courses*, which I thought to runne.
I finde my *Povertie*, for mee was fit;
Yea and a *Blessing*, greater than my *Wit*:
  And, whether, now, I *rich* or *poore* become,
  Tis nor much *pleasing*, nor much *troublesome*. (ll. 19-30)

Poverty is here regarded as a means of preventing harm, as a blessing rather than a punishment. A moral emphasis had already been added to the *Paupertas* emblem in Ripa. *Povertà* is depicted as a woman with the usual attributes of wings and stone (see fig. 26). The text explains that the wings indicate the desire of those who are talented but poor to overcome all difficulties and attain virtue.[101] This positive attitude is also expressed in the circular motto around the picture: "Pavpertate premor subleuor ingenio" (I am weighed down by poverty but I find relief in my talents).

Wither's emblem points a moral but it cannot be called specifically religious. Long before Wither wrote his emblems, however, the *Paupertas* emblem had become part of the Amor/Anima tradition.[102] It occurs, for instance, in Hugo's *Pia Desideria*, the most popular of the Amor/Anima emblem books (see fig. 27). We see Anima trying to soar upwards to Heaven where Christ is waiting for her with open arms. The large weight attached to her left foot is the globe. In the background a little boy shows how the bird he is training tries in vain to escape from the stick it is attached to by a leash. In the process of transformation from profane to sacred the emblem has undergone some significant changes. The wings are now attached to Anima's back instead of her wrist and the weight has been transferred from her hand to her left foot. The weight is no longer a

101. *Iconologia*, pp. 409-10. "L'ali, nella mano sinistra, significano il desiderio d'alcuni poueri ingegnosi, i quali aspirano alle difficultà della virtù, ma oppressi dalle proprie necessità ...".
102. See Chew, *The Pilgrimage of Life*, p. 177; Freeman, *English Emblem Books*, p. 119; Praz, p. 146.

27

26

simple stone but it represents the earth. Finally the motto has changed from profane to Biblical: "Coarctor è duobus, desiderium habens dissolui, & esse cum CHRISTO" (Philip. 1:23).

The same motto introduces the parallel emblem in Quarles' *Emblemes* (1635): "*I am in a streight betweene two, having a desire to be dissolv'd, and to be with Christ.*" The following stanzas provide a useful background for Herbert's "Easter-wings":

5

Ev'n like the Hawlk, (whose keepers wary hands
  Have made a prisner to her wethring stock)
Forgetting quite the pow'r of her fast bands,
  Makes a rank Bate from her forsaken Block,
    But her too faithfull Leash doth soone restraine
    Her broken flight, attempted oft in vaine,
It gives her loynes a twitch, and tugs her back againe.

6

So, when my soule directs her better eye
  To heav'ns bright Pallace (where my treasure lies)
I spread my willing wings, but cannot flie,
  Earth hales me downe, I cannot, cannot rise;
    When I but strive to mount the least degree,
    Earth gives a jerk, and foiles me on my knee;
Lord, how my soule is rackt, betwixt the world and Thee.

7

Great God, I spread my feeble wings, in vaine;
  In vaine I offer my extended hands;
I cannot mount till thou unlink my chain;
  I cannot come till thou release my Bands:
    Which if thou please to break, and then supply
    My wings with spirit, th' Eagle shall not flie
A pitch that's half so faire, nor half so swift as I.[103]

Although the picture of Quarles' emblem still recalls the *Paupertas* emblem the text is completely different. Poverty is no longer a condition that thwarts the free exercise of talent but a condition that facilitates the passage to Heaven. We are dealing here not with physical but with spiritual needs and consequently the function of the poverty described in Quarles' religious emblem is different from that in Alciati's profane original.

Quarles' text concentrates on the contrast between the soul's desire and its impediment, the body. The wings of the soul are feeble and the poet prays for them to be strengthened by God's "spirit." Both the conflict between flight and imprisonment and the weakness of the wings of the

103. Francis Quarles, *Emblemes* (London, 1635), Book V, Emblem IX, pp. 276-79. Cf. Daniel, "Ode XVII," stanza 2 (qu. in section 3.5.4. of this chapter).

soul are essential elements of "Easter-wings" too.[104] In one respect
Herbert follows the earlier *Paupertas* emblem. He uses the word "poore"
in the middle of the first stanza. Viewed within its context Herbert's "Till
he became / Most poore," for all its briefness and simplicity, carries
much more metaphorical power and meaning than did the word 'poverty'
in Alciati and Whitney. Herbert's use of the idea of poverty is based on
the loss of Paradise, man's squandering of the riches which God had
originally provided him with.

3.5.3.1. 'Oh that I had wings like a dove.'

We have seen how the *Paupertas*-emblem which originally had a worldly
meaning and a limited scope was combined by later emblem writers with
the text from Philippians to form emblems of a much wider, religious and
metaphorical significance and application. Within the Amor/Anima
tradition the *Paupertas* emblem was also frequently combined with a text
from the Psalms: "Oh that I had wings like a dove! for then would I fly
away, and be at rest" (Psalm 55:6). It readily found its way into both
emblems and pattern poems. We have already mentioned the pattern
poem for which Carey, its author, used the quotation as a motto (see
section 2.2.2.2. of this chapter).

Hugo, too, used Psalm 55:6 as the motto for one of his emblems (see
fig. 28). In this emblem Anima is depicted with wings attached to her
arms; she tries to fly upwards to join Christ who has already taken wing
and points the way to the source of the sunbeams that shine down on
Him. A dove is perched on a rock to the left of Anima flapping its wings
as if it wishes to teach Anima the art of flying.

Harvey, Herbert's imitator, used the text in "The Flying of the Heart,"
which is an emblem and a pattern poem at once (qu. in section 2.2.2.2. of
this chapter). The poem imitates "Easter-wings," but unlike Herbert's
poem it conflates the *Paupertas* motif with the emblem of the winged dove.
The first five stanzas of Harvey's poem all emphasize the barriers of
worldly corruption: "Corruption clogs my feet like filthy clay" (l. 11);
"What? must I still be rooted here below" (l. 31); "... mine heart is slow
to rise" (l. 50). The final stanza offers the resolution to the problems
presented earlier. Religious zeal replaces lack of faith and Harvey uses the
image of the winged dove to express this resolution.

Whereas the connection of "Easter-wings" with the *Paupertas* emblems is clearly traceable, its relation with the wings of the dove is less

---

104. Similarly in "Miserie": "... Now he is/ A lump of flesh, without a foot or wing
/ To raise him to a glimpse of blisse" (ll. 73-75; *Works*, p. 102); also "Mans medley,"
particularly ll. 12-14: "With th'one hand touching heav'n, with th'other earth. / In
soul he mounts and flies, / In flesh he dies." (*Works*, p. 131).

28

straightforward. Tuve (1952) suggests that there might well be a connection between the wings in "Easter-wings" and Herbert's function as a
priest. In the *Glossa ordinaria* the silver wings of the dove (Psalm 68) are
said to represent the preachers who "carry aloft the glory of the Church."
Tuve adds that St. Augustine in his comment on this Psalm wrote that
"the Church is borne up, as on wings, by the preaching of the faithful..."
(p. 157). In "Praise (I)" Herbert seems to refer to this idea:

> I go to Church; help me to wings, and I
> > Will thither flie. (*Works*, p. 61)[105]

In other poems the dove is mentioned occasionally in connection with the
idea of the zealous soul. Not surprisingly, it occurs in "Whitsunday":

> Listen sweet Dove unto my song,
> And spread thy golden wings in me;
> Hatching my tender heart so long,
> Till it get wing, and flie away with thee. (ll. 1-4; *Works*, p. 59)

and in "The Invitation":

---

105. Cf. Duport's poem, the translation of which was quoted from in section 3.4.
of this chapter.

> Come ye hither All, whose love
> Is your dove,
> And exalts you to the skie: (ll. 25-7; *Works,* p. 180)[106]

Although in "Easter-wings" the only bird mentioned explicitly is not the dove but the lark, I think that both birds 'lent their plumes' to the poem. It is not exceptional to find the dove and the lark referred to together. Quarles' version of Hugo's "Dove" emblem has the same picture and the same motto as its model. The poem describes the Dove and the Lark as emblems of religious fervour:

1

...

> O that I had the pineons of a Dove
> That I might quit my Bands, and sore above,
> And powre my just Complaints before the great JEHOVA!

2

...

> How happy is the Lark, that ev'ry howre,
> Leaves earth, and then for joy, mounts up and sings!
> Had my dull soule but wings as well as they,
> How I would spring from earth, and clip away,
> As wise *Astraea* did, and scorne this ball of Clay![107]

3.5.3.2. 'Oh let me rise / As larks, harmoniously.'

The image of the larks in "Easter-wings" can be understood in various ways. The most literal interpretation is based on the Latin name of the bird, *alauda.* The Middle English *Pilgrimage of the Soul* explains:

> This be called larkes, which þat in Latyn han the name of praysyng and of

---

106. Cf. Stengel's *Ova Paschalia,* a curious emblem book in which each emblem is placed within the oval shape of an egg. Emblem XII shows the Dove of the Holy Spirit hovering above an egg placed on an altar. An angel to the left of the altar and the Virgin Mary to the right complete this extraordinary Annunciation scene (Georg Stengel, *Ova Paschalia* (Ingolstadium, 1678), p. 64).

107. *Emblemes* (1635), Book V, Emblem XIII, pp. 292-95. Quarles added a comment by St. Augustine on Psalm 38 to this emblem:

> What wings should I desire but the two precepts of love, on which the Law and the Prophets depend! O if I could obtaine these wings, I could flye from thy face to thy face, from the face of thy Justice to the face of thy Mercy: Let us find those wings by love which we have lost by lust.

The emblem concludes with an "Epigram":

> Tell me, my wishing soul, didst ever trie
> How fast the wings of Red-crost Faith can flie?
> Why beg'st thou then the pineons of a Dove?
> Faiths wings are swifter, but the swiftest, Love.

worshepyng, and be called 'alaude' ... and purely thei prayse God with hire mery song.[108]

Another attractive interpretation is that of the lark as a symbol of the humility of priesthood, a meaning attached to it because it flies high and sings only on its flight toward Heaven.[109] Such an interpretation concurs with the possible interpretation of the wings as the preachers of the Church which we mentioned above. The fact that Herbert uses the plural 'larks' may also support this reading. Such an interpretation fits in with Herbert's concern to express himself in his poetry both as a believer and as a priest. In *Piers Plowman* the lark is described as a type of humility and poverty as opposed to the peacock that represents pride and wealth:

> The larke þat is a lasse fowel is moore louelich of ledene,
> And wel awey of wynge swifter þan þe Pecock,
> And of flessh by fele fold fatter and swetter;
> To lowe libbynge men þe larke is resembled.
> [Swiche tales telleþ Aristotle þe grete clerk];
> Thus he likneþ in his logik þe leeste fowel oute.[110]

Whether or not Herbert presents himself as priest in "Easter-wings" may be difficult to establish beyond doubt; but that he is concerned about his role and attitude as an individual Christian who has to find a way to accommodate the hopeful message of Easter to the knowledge of his own sinful state, is certain. The image of the larks has a clearly defined function in this dilemma. The larks are mentioned after the 'thinnest' part of the first stanza. Man has forfeited his fortune and has fallen from bliss. The image of the larks reflects the hope of a resurrection in Christ. The lenghthening of the lines coincides with the flight of the larks, which has the effect of a release from bondage. Herbert emphasizes two characteristics of the lark: *rising* and *singing*. Rising with Christ produces harmony; the harmony produces circumstances that are conducive to song. In "Sion" Herbert uses the image of the lark with similar connotations:

> But grones are quick, and full of wings,
> And all their motions upward be;

108. *Pilgrimage of the Soul* (c. 1450); qu. in *MED*, pp. 668-69.
109. Ferguson, *Signs & Symbols*, p. 21.
110. George Kane & Talbot Donaldson, eds., *Piers Plowman: The B Version* (London: Univ. of London, The Athlone Press, 1975), p. 481, ll. 264-69. The passage from Langland is discussed in Francis Klingender, *Animals in art and thought* (London: Routledge & Kegan Paul, 1971), p. 371. Klingender also informs us that at the death of St. Francis "a flock of larks, his favourite birds, kept vigil and at the moment of his death 'made a wheel like a circle around the roof, and sweetly singing, seemed likewise to praise the Lord,'" (p. 444; the quotation within the quotation is from the *Mirror of Perfection*, Temple Classics, trans. Robert Steele (London, 1903), ch. CXIII). St. Francis, we should recall, is the paragon of poverty and humility.

> And ever as they mount, like larks they sing;
> The note is sad, yet musick for a King. (ll. 21-4; *Works*, p. 107)

In this passage the double function of the lark so briefly intimated in "Easter-wings" is expounded in greater detail.

The comparison between the soul and the lark gains in significance because of the implied contrast between the fetters of sin and the freedom of flight, or, in religious terms, between lack of faith and religious zeal. Herbert could have found inspiration for this contrast in the *Paupertas* emblem and its various offshoots. Even the specific combination of *Paupertas* and the lark is represented in emblem literature. In "Invocation," the introductory emblem to Quarles' collection, the picture shows a lark flying towards Heaven. The text uses the same configuration of visual images that Herbert employed much more tersely in "Easter-wings":

> Rowze thee, my soul; and drein thee from the dregs
> Of vulgar thoughts: Skrue up the heightned pegs
> Of thy sublime Theorboe foure notes higher,
> And higher yet; that so, the shrill-mouth'd Quire
> Of swift-wing'd Seraphims may come and joyn,
> And make thy consort more than halfe divine.
> Invoke no Muse; Let heav'n be thy *Apollo*;
> And let his sacred influences hallow
> Thy high-bred strains; Let his full beams inspire
> Thy ravish'd brains with more heroick fire:
> Snatch thee a Quill from the spread Eagle's wing,
> And, like the morning Lark, mount up and sing:
> Cast off these dangling plummets, that so clog
> Thy lab'ring heart, which gropes in this dark fog
> Of dungeon-earth; Let flesh and bloud forbear
> To stop thy flight, till this base world appear
> A thin blew Lanskip ... (ll. 1-17)[111]

Quarles' emblem combines a number of emblematic images that are frequently found separately: the soul or the heart used as a musical instrument, the consort of the heart, the heart clogged by 'dangling plummets,' the soul trapped in the prison ('dungeon') of the body, the flight of the soul — all these images occur in the Schola Cordis and Amor/Anima emblem books. One image in Quarles' poem deserves special attention because it is related to a phrase in "Easter-wings" that has not been given its due yet, namely, "Snatch thee a Quill from the spread Eagle's wing."

---

111. Quarles, *Emblemes*, ed. Grosart, I, 46.

3.5.3.3. 'imp my wing on thine.'

> For, if I imp my wing on thine,
> Affliction shall advance the flight in me.

The image of the 'imping' of the wing is a regularly recurring feature in *Paupertas* emblems. We have already come across the image in Harvey's wing-shaped poem and in Quarles' "Invocation." The verb 'to imp' derives from falconry and means "to engraft feathers in the wing of a bird so as to make good losses or deficiencies, and thus restore or improve the powers of flight; hence, allusively, with reference to 'taking higher flights,' enlarging one's powers, and the like" (*OED*, s.v. *imp*, 4). The background of these lines of Herbert's poem is partly Platonic, partly Scriptural.[112] The Platonic reference is to the myth of the winged soul in the *Phaedrus* and the Biblical analogy is the text from Malachi 4:2:

> But unto you that fear my name shall the Sun of righteousness arise with healing in his wings; and ye shall go forth, and grow up as calves of the stall.

Isaiah 40:31 carries the same message:

> But they that wait upon the Lord shall renew their strength; they shall mount up with wings as eagles;

The line "Snatch thee a Quill from the spread Eagle's wing" from Quarles' poem should be interpreted against the background of these passages.[113] Occasionally poets quote the Bible even more literally. This is how Harvey quotes the image from Malachi in one of his *Schola Cordis* emblems:

> I must confess,
> And I can do no less,
> Thou art the Sun of righteousness:
> There's healing in thy wings; thy light is life;
> My darkness death. To end all strife,
> Be thou mine husband, let me be thy wife;
> So light and life divine
> Will all be thine.[114]

Although commentators have pointed out the affinity between Herbert's phrase: "if I imp my wing on thine," and the texts from Malachi and Isaiah, the exact nature of the affinity has not been established. Nor has the fact that the wings in Isaiah are those of an eagle been related to

112. See Brown and Ingoldsby, (1971-72), pp. 131-142.
113. Cf. "These white plumes of his heele lend you" from Crashaw's poem "On Mr. G. Herberts booke intituled the Temple ..." (see section 3.4. of this chapter). The eagle's wings also occur, although within a different context, in Drayton's "Heroic Epistle," V, l. 78: "Their Buzzard-wings, imp'd with our Eagles Plumes" (qu. in *OED*, s.v. "imp").
114. "Ode XXV," stanza 6, in Harvey, *Complete Poems*, ed. Grosart, p. 80.

the wing-images in "Easter-wings." In the related texts we have studied
so far, for example "The Invocation" by Quarles, the lark and the eagle
are sometimes mentioned together. The passages from Malachi and from
Isaiah are both implicitly present in Quarles' *Paupertas* emblem, the final
three stanzas of which were quoted in section 3.5.3. of this chapter. In the
final stanza of that poem the poet asks Christ to add strength to (i.e. to
'imp') the wings of his soul so that it will be able to fly even better than
the eagle. In contrast with the eagle as an emblem of liberty Quarles
introduced in the fifth and sixth stanzas the image of the hawk as an
emblem of the imprisonment of the soul:

> Ev'n like the Hawlk, (whose keepers wary hands
>   Have made a prisner to her wethring stock)
> Forgetting quite the pow'r of her fast bands,
>   Makes a rank Bate from her forsaken Block,
>   But her too faithfull Leash doth soone restraine
>   Her broken flight, attempted oft in vaine,
> It gives her loynes a twitch, and tugs her back againe.
>
> So, when my soule directs her better eye
>   To heav'ns bright Pallace (where my treasure lies)
> I spread my willing wings, but cannot flie,
>   Earth hales me downe, I cannot, cannot rise;
>   When I but strive to mount the least degree,
>   Earth gives a jerk, and foiles me on my knee;
> Lord, how my soule is rackt, betwixt the world and Thee.

Quarles' method is as always that of the true emblem writer — his
imagery is based on equations and similarities: "E'en as... So ... ". The
second of the stanzas quoted above explains faithfully, point by point the
spiritual significance of every detail of the picture described in the first.
Herbert uses the emblematic details but transforms them into new images
with a significance all their own. This essential difference in the formation
of images can be nicely illustrated by comparing Quarles' two stanzas
with "Easter-wings" or with the following passage from Herbert's poem
"Home":

> Oh loose this frame, this knot of man untie!
>   That my free soul may use her wing,
> Which now is pinion'd with mortalitie,
>   As an intangled, hamper'd thing. (ll. 61-4; *Works*, p. 109)

Here, too, bird-images are used. They remind us of the Amor/Anima
emblems. "Pinion'd with mortalitie" is the crucial phrase in these lines.
"Pinion'd," the exact opposite of "imped," means: "a) of a bird: Having
the wings maimed or confined. b) Having the arms bound so as not to be
moved; shackled." (*OED*, *s.v.* 'Pinioned').

Herbert's use of the word recalls the emblem but does not repeat it. He uses the emblematic image to add visual clarity to his ideas. But his choice of the word 'pinion'd' is not solely determined by the picture of an emblem. It is in the first place part of the metaphoric structure of the stanza as a whole. Because of its double meaning it forms the link between two clusters of images in the stanza: those connected with the winged soul on the one hand ("loose," "*untie*," "free soul," "wing"), and those that have to do with the mortal body on the other ("frame," "knot," "un*tie*," "mortalitie," "intangled," "hamper'd"). The effect of the lines is further enhanced by the words "knot" and "intangled" which suggest a string that wants an expert hand to unravel it. The use of the word "thing" rather than 'bird' or 'hawk' adds to the pathos of the soul's situation. By being 'pinion'd' the winged soul is reduced to a 'thing,' and this has a powerfully dramatic effect.[115]

A similar argument to that presented above could be advanced to explain why Herbert does not mention any particular bird's name in the second stanza of "Easter-wings." In the Amor/Anima emblems that form the background of "Easter-wings" the hawk, as we saw, is used to express the captive state of the soul. But what is the significance of the eagle as emblem of the 'free soul'? The answer to this question will take us to the Platonic element in "Easter-wings" and to the last of the three emblems that are relevant to a proper understanding of Herbert's imagery in the poem. We have discussed the *Zelus in deum* and the *Paupertas* emblems. The third will take us back to Greek mythology.

3.5.4. Ganymede and the eagle; Platonism.

The story of Ganymede and the eagle is one of the many examples of a mythological story that was used for sacred purposes in the art and literature of the Renaissance. The emblems in which the story is used may explain why the eagle frequently occurs in poems that treat of religious zeal.

The subject of one of the emblems in Wither's collection is the story of Ganymede, the beautiful youth who was ravished by Zeus in the guise of an eagle (see fig. 29). The motto of the emblem is:

> *Take wing, my* Soule, *and mount up higher*;
> *For*, Earth, *fulfills not my* Desire.

The picture shows Ganymede, face uplifted, riding an eagle which is carrying him straight to Heaven. The text leaves nothing to the imagination of the reader:

---

115. Cf. Wordsworth, "A Slumber did my Spirit Seal": "She seemed a thing that could not feel / The touch of earthly years," where the word "thing" has a similar effect.

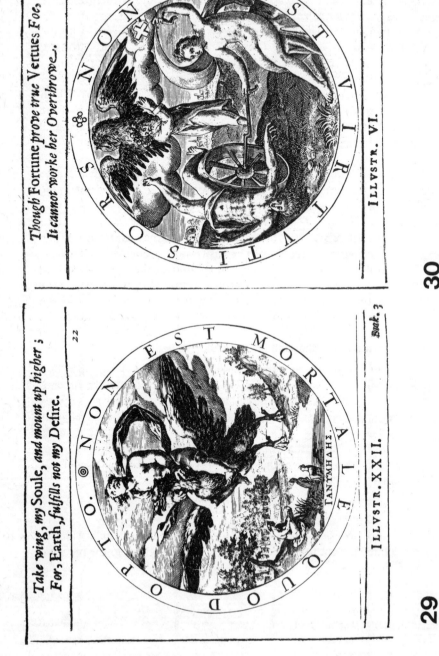

Though Fortune prove true Vertues Foe,
It cannot worke her Overthrowe.

6

NON OBEST VIRTVTI SORS

Book. 1.

ILLVSTR. VI.

30

Take wing, my Soule, and mount up higher;
For, Earth, fulfills not my Defire.

22

NON EST MORTALE QUOD OPTO

ΓΑΝΥΜΗΔΗΣ

Book. 3

ILLVSTR. XXII.

29

When *Ganymed*, himselfe was purifying,
Great *Iupiter,* his naked beauty spying,
Sent forth his *Aegle* (from below to take him)
A blest Inhabitant, in Heav'n to make him:
And, there (as Poets feigned) he doth still,
To *Iove*, and other *God-heads*, Nectar fill.
   Though this be but a *Fable*, of their feigning,
The *Morall* is a *Reall truth*, pertayning
To ev'ry one (which harbours a desire
Above the Starry *Circles*, to aspire.)
By *Ganymed*, the *Soule* is understood,
That's washed in the *Purifying flood*
Of sacred *Baptisme* (which doth make her seeme
Both pure and beautifull, in *God's* esteeme.)
The *Aegle*, meanes that Heav'nly *Contemplation*,
Which, after Washings of *Regeneration*,
Lifts up the *Minde*, from things that earthly bee,
To view those *Objects*, which *Faith's* Eyes doe see.
The *Nectar*, which is filled out, and given
To all the blest *Inhabitants of Heaven*,
Are those *Delights*, which (*Christ* hath sayd) they have,
When some *Repentant soule* beginnes to leave
Her foulnesse; by renewing of her *birth*,
And, slighting all the *Pleasures* of the Earth.
   I aske not, *Lord*, those Blessings to receive,
Which any Man hath pow'r to take, or give;
Nor, what this World affords; for, I contemne
Her Favours; and have seen the best of them:
   Nay, *Heav'n* it selfe, will unsufficient bee,
   Vnlesse, *Thou*, also, give *Thy selfe,* to mee.[116]

The poem's division into three parts indicates the structure of the argument. Wither first retells the mythological story, then provides the moral and philosophical interpretation and ends up by applying the message to the situation of an individual Christian.

In another of Wither's emblems the same motif is used with a slightly different context. The motto is:

> *Though* Fortune *prove true* Vertues *Foe*,
> *It cannot worke her Overthrowe.*

The picture shows Fortune, her gown blown by the wind, turning her wheel on which a poor suffering mortal is 'pinion'd' (see fig. 30). The turning of the wheel causes the ups and downs of his life. In the middle of the scene an old man is carried aloft by an eagle who clutches him by the venerable, grizzled head. The text explains that for a man to depend on Fortune's wheel is a hazardous experience, whereas on the other hand:

---

116. Wither, p. 156.

... he that's *Vertuous,* whether high or low
His *Fortune* seemes (or whether foule or faire
His *Path* he findes) or whether friend, or foe,
The *World* doth prove; regards it not a haire.
His *Losse* is *Gaine*; his *Poverty* is *Wealth*;
....
Above all Earthly powres his *Vertue* reares him;
And, up with *Eglets* wings, to Heav'n it beares him.[117]

The paradox in this poem is reminiscent of "Easter-wings" in which 'poverty' and 'loss' are used likewise as stepping-stones to future bliss: "Affliction shall advance the flight in me."

Ganymede, who is already to be found in Alciati's emblem book, stands for the pure "unsullied soul finding its joy in God."[118] The ideas behind Wither's Ganymede emblem as well as its phrasing are Platonic. The connection between the elevation of the soul and the growing of wings has its source in Plato's *Phaedrus*:

> The wing is the corporeal element which is most akin to the divine, and which by nature tends to soar aloft and carry that which gravitates downwards into the upper region, which is the habitation of the gods. The divine is beauty, wisdom, goodness, and the like; and by these the wing of the soul is nourished, and grows apace; but when fed upon evil and foulness and the opposite of good, wastes and falls away.[119]

These Platonic ideas were readily assimilated into English poetry of the sixteenth and seventeenth centuries and combined with the images of the eagle and the falcon. Thus both elements are found in Spenser's "An Hymne of Heavenly Beavtie":

> Beginning then below, with th'easie vew
> Of this base world, subiect to fleshly eye,
> From thence to mount aloft by order dew,
> To contemplation of th'immortall sky,
> Of the soare faulcon so I learne to fly,
> That flags awhile her fluttering wings beneath,
> Till she her selfe for stronger flight can breath. (ll. 22-8)

and:

> Thence gathering plumes of perfect speculation,
> To impe the wings of thy high flying mynd,

117. Wither, p. 6. Rickey suggests that the wings in Herbert's poem celebrating Christ's victory over death and corruption are reminiscent of the classical personifications of victory, Nike and her counterpart Victoria, both of whom were traditionally represented as winged (Rickey, p. 28).
118. Jean Seznec, *The Survival of the Pagan Gods*, p. 101; also p. 103.
119. Plato, *The Works,* ed. I. Edman, trans. B. Jowett (New York: Random House, 1956), p. 287. In Alciati (1531) the emblem of Ganymede occurs with the motto "In Deo Laetandvm" (Henry Green, ed., *Andreae Alciati, Emblematum Fontes Quatuor,* facs. ed. (Manchester: Brothers, 1870), sig. B6).

133

Mount vp aloft through heauenly contemplation,
From this darke world, whose damps the soule do blynd,
And like the natiue brood of Eagles kynd,
On that bright Sunne of glorie fixe thine eyes,
Clear'd from grosse mists of fraile infirmities. (ll. 134-40)[120]

The Platonic ascent towards the contemplation of eternal Beauty is expressed in terms of the flight of the falcon and the even higher flight of the eagle, the only bird that can look at the sun without being blinded. This supposed ability often turned the eagle into a symbol of Christ himself.[121]

The imagery of Spenser's "Hymne" not only reappears in emblems such as the *Paupertas* emblem by Quarles discussed above, but it also finds its way into the meditative, Platonic poetry of Marvell:

Here at the Fountains sliding foot,
Or at some Fruit-trees mossy root,
Casting the Bodies Vest aside,
My Soul into the boughs does glide:
There like a Bird it sits, and sings,
Then whets, and combs its silver Wings;
And, till prepar'd for longer flight,
Waves in its Plumes the various Light. ("The Garden", ll. 48-55)[122]

The soul's preparation for 'longer flight' may be expressed in various ways. Sometimes, as in Spenser's "Hymne," it is part of a purely Platonic ascent. Sometimes the Platonic element is embedded in other forms, such as the time-hallowed tradition of the garden-poem. The Platonic element can also merge with Biblical references. This is the case in "Easter-wings," but also in the highly emblematic poem by George Daniel, "Ode XVII":

When I my Clod
Would kicke, oh God,
How am I fettered;
At either heele,
Methinks I feele
A plummet, heavier far then Lead;
Or like the Falcon knit
Unto the Perch, I flitt,
And make a bayte;
I pick my Jesses; and assay

120. Edmund Spenser, *Minor Poems*, ed. E. de Sélincourt (Oxford: Oxford Univ. Press, 1910), p. 464, p. 468. On the Neoplatonic context of these passages see Richard Cody, *The Landscape of the Mind* (Oxford: Oxford Univ. Press, 1969), pp. 156-57.
121. Ferguson, p. 17.
122. Andrew Marvell, *The Poems and Letters*, ed. H.M. Margoliouth (Oxford: Oxford Univ. Press, 1971), p. 52.

For Libertie, in everie way;
But cannot hitt.
I toyle and flutter; faine would break the grate,
Where I am mewed, of Clay.
. . . .
Poore helples Man
What number can
Expresse thy weaknesse? Had
All Quills bene bent,
To this intent,
How were it more then yet a Shade?
There is a Dismall Screene
Of Earth and Sin betweene
Us and the bright
Objects we would discerne.
How farre are wee to learne
The yet unknowne
Beauties of Truth? and onlie hope a Light
For which our Bowells yerne.
Leave me awhile
Officious Quill;
For I have a great Thought
Unformed yet;
Nor can I fitt
It to the better Formes I ought
Let me awhile retire,
Till warmed with Sacred Fire,
My Active nerves
Secure a stronger flight,
To gather (from that Light)
Which I admire)
Some ray; . . .[123]

Daniel's poem is one more proof of the many ways in which different concepts, emblems, traditions could be combined for an equally varied number of poetic purposes. The poem, by its imagery of fetters and falconry, reminds us of several *Paupertas* emblems we have discussed. The Platonic element appears in the images of the 'Shade' and the flight towards the sun, but the latter image could just as well derive from the text in Malachi.

The wings of religious zeal also occur in the poetry of Herbert's great contemporary, Donne. In the following passage from "To Mr. Tilman after he had taken orders" the Platonic concept has become part of a self-contained argument:

123. George Daniel, *The Poems*, ed. Alexander B. Grosart (1878), II, 44; qu. in Church, pp. 349-50.

> ... as we paint Angels with wings, because
> They beare Gods message, and proclaime his lawes,
> Since thou must doe the like, and so must move,
> Art thou new feather'd with coelestiall love? (ll. 19-22)[124]

The wings of the newly ordained clergyman have been imped with religious zeal. The meaning of "new feathered" is not 'explained' in the way of the *zelus in deum* type of emblem nor is the Bible quoted overtly as in Harvey's emblem, or a direct reference made to Plato's myth as in Spenser's "Hymne." Nevertheless these stories and allegories were all part of the intellectual awareness of both Donne and his audience and they would be felt to constitute part of the background of the imagery employed in the poem. But, although the significance of the phrase "new feathered" is partly determined by this background. Donne has also made it part of the rhetorical structure of the poem. By embedding the image in a chain of reasoning: "as ... because ... Since ... so ..." Donne has decreased its referential aspect and has integrated it into the argument of the poem. The reader's attention will be caught by the logic of the argument rather than the genesis of the imagery and the stories and allegories it is associated with.

In another poem by Donne the distance between the image and the stories and allegories underlying it is even greater. I shall quote it in full because it deals with problems and conflicting urges similar to those in "Easter-wings":

> Thou hast made me, And shall thy worke decay?
> Repaire me now, for now mine end doth haste,
> I runne to death, and death meets me as fast,
> And all my pleasures are like yesterday,
> I dare not move my dimme eyes any way,
> Despaire behind, and death before doth cast
> Such terrour, and my feebled flesh doth waste
> By sinne in it, which it t'wards hell doth weigh;
> Onely thou art above, and when towards thee
> By thy leave I can looke, I rise againe;
> But our old subtle foe so tempteth me,
> That not one houre I can my selfe sustaine;
> Thy Grace may wing me to prevent his art,
> And thou like Adamant draw mine iron heart.[125]

Here the verb 'to wing' has become almost synonymous with more neutral words such as 'teach' or 'lift up.' The connection of the image with its conventional background is weakened even more because it is followed immediately by a new comparison, ("like Adamant"), with

124. John Donne, *The Divine Poems*, ed. Helen Gardner, 2nd ed. (Oxford: Oxford Univ. Press, 1978), p. 32.
125. Donne, "Divine Meditations" 1, *The Divine Poems*, p. 12.

associations all its own. Nevertheless the meaning of the word 'wing' is still determined largely by the traditions that we have discussed.

In Herbert's poetry, too, the image of the wings is used in the various ways described above. A direct reference to the Platonic myth is found in "Death":

> We lookt on this side of thee, shooting short;
>   Where we did finde
>   The shells of fledge souls left behinde,
> Dry dust, which sheds no tears, but may...
>
> ... Therefore we can go die as sleep, and trust
>   Half that we have
>   Unto an honest faithfull grave;
> Making our pillows either down, or dust. (ll. 9-12; ll. 21-4; *Works*, p. 186)

Herbert uses the traditional Platonic image ("fledge souls") and the stock comparison ("we can go die as sleep") to prepare for that marvellous clinching image at the end of the poem:

> Making our pillows either down, or dust.

The word "down" is most effectively placed here. Its proximity to "grave" and "dust" makes the reader doubt for a moment whether he is to take it as an adverb (which it is not) or as a noun (which it is).[126]

In some poems the Platonic concept of the winged soul is applied by Herbert in a decidedly emblematic way, as in the passage from "Home" quoted above in section 3.5.3.3. and in "Miserie":

> But sinne hath fool'd him. Now he is
> A lump of flesh, without a foot or wing
> To raise him to a glimpse of blisse: (ll. 73-5; *Works*, p. 102)

In other poems the wings of the Dove are mentioned and, although these images are based on the Scriptures, their presentation is usually emblematic. This may be illustrated by another passage from "Miserie": "... thy love / ... doth cover / Their follies with the wing of thy milde Dove," (ll. 26-28), and the first stanza of "Whitsunday":

> Listen sweet Dove unto my song,
> And spread thy golden wings in me;
> Hatching my tender heart so long,
> Till it get wing, and flie away with thee. (*Works*, p. 59)[127]

3.5.5. "Easter-wings" — In conclusion.

The image of the wings in "Easter-wings" is complex, as the variety of

---

126. Cf. "The Church-porch," ll. 83-84: "God gave thy soul brave wings; put not those feathers / Into a bed, to sleep out all ill weathers."

127. Cf. Stengel, p. 64 (see n. 106 *ante* and section 3.5.3.1. of this chapter).

analogies discussed in the previous sub-sections indicates. After considering the range of possible analogies we are now better equipped to interpret it. In the first place we should avoid talking about the image of the wings as if there were only one such image in the poem. Actually there are three wing-images in "Easter-wings," each with its own specific background. The first image is the typography of the poem. There is an obvious analogy here with the classical pattern poem by Simmias of Rhodes. Considered against this background the poem is an example of Christian emulation showing the superiority of sacred over profane themes, of the Resurrection of the Christian God of Love over the birth of pagan Eros. The second wing-image is implicit in the comparison of the lark in the first stanza of the poem. The reader will associate the shape of the poem with the image of the rising and singing of the lark, which in its turn refers to the Easter event celebrated in the poem. This image is supported by emblems in the Amor/Anima tradition. The stanza is about the virtue of humility and the lark is its symbol. The word "poore" epitomizes the attitude of humility that pervades the first stanza; it recalls the first beatitude of the Sermon on the Mount: "Blessed are the poor in spirit: for theirs is the kingdom of heaven" (Matthew, 5:3). *Humilitas* is the concomitant virtue of this beatitude.[128] Poverty has become a *condition* for fulfilment rather than an obstacle to it. Herbert attaches the same value to poverty in "Easter-wings" as do the Christian versions of the *Paupertas* emblem. This interpretation turns the stanza into a tightly organized structure leading from Fall to Resurrection and from the Old Law to its fulfilment in the New Dispensation of which the Sermon of the Mount is the epitome.

In the second stanza a quite different wing-image is used. Whereas in the first a bird is mentioned but not its wing, in the second stanza a wing is mentioned but not the bird. This has led commentators to believe that the wings of stanza two belong to the bird of stanza one. But I am convinced that they do not. As I have tried to indicate, the second stanza is founded on a Biblical context and on stories and emblems that are different from those of the first. The word 'imp' stems from the world of falconry. In some of the *Paupertas* emblems we have discussed the falcon or hawk is depicted, attached to its keeper by a leash, or is described in the text as a prisoner. Thus, to be a hawk or falcon will not suffice to reach Heaven. The soul's wings must be 'imped' with feathers from a stronger bird if it is to achieve its goal. The only bird that can serve this high purpose is the eagle, a symbol both of Christ and of the Resurrection. As Ganymede was carried aloft by the eagle, so Herbert wishes

---

128. See Tuve, "Allegory of Vices and Virtues," in *Allegorical Imagery*, pp. 57-143 and Appendix.

likewise to imp the wings of his soul on those of Christ. "With thee / Let me combine," he writes, using the word 'combine' in its Latin sense of 'joining two by two.' This is, essentially, what "Easter-wings" is about: one should join forces with Christ, imp one's wings on those of Christ in order to reach salvation. The first stanza of the poem indicates the proper attitude of the human soul towards the Resurrection; the second stanza provides the impetus and the means enabling man to fully share that event.

4. Conclusions.

This study of Herbert's two pattern poems has yielded some interesting results. The remarkable absence of the mention of fire in two poems in which religious zeal plays such an important role, the total absence of any reference to zealous fire in the entire section of *The Church* that is bounded by the two pattern poems, and the analogy with the *Paupertas* emblems all serve to emphasize Herbert's main concern in the section: it is to establish man's position in relation to his God. This position has been made precarious by the Fall; yet the Fall is fortunate (*felix culpa*), because of Christ's Passion and the resulting hope of redemption. Penitence and prayer serve as the human answer to the sacrifice of the Saviour. Considering that in a sense *The Church* describes a pilgrim's progress, it is appropriate that the metaphor of fire is reserved for a somewhat later stage of that pilgrimage. The whole cycle from "The Altar" to "Easter-wings" is concerned with Holy Week. The zeal for God is described by Herbert in metaphors expressive of man's desire to do penitence in imitation of Christ: "O let thy blessed SACRIFICE be mine," he writes in "The Altar." "But how then shall I imitate thee, and / Copie thy fair, though bloudie hand?" is his question in "The Thanksgiving." "Yet by confession will I come / Into thy conquest: though I can do nought / Against thee, in thee I will overcome / The man, who once against thee fought" is his assertion in "The Reprisall." And finally in "Easter-wings": "if I imp my wing on thine, / Affliction shall advance the flight in me."

Another result is that we have been able to establish how and to what extent Herbert made use of the concepts, texts and pictures that were part of his cultural heritage. As we have seen, the classics, literary and rhetorical tradition, emblems, the Scriptures, Platonism, and the liturgy of the Church, are all behind these two poems in one way or another. It is a sign of Herbert's power and control as a poet that he managed to transcend and transform his sources. "Easter-wings" in particular exhibits this poetic mastery. The wing-images in the poem belong together; they form a harmonious chain, but the 'worlds' they represent or refer to are diverse and clearly defined. Although the image-cluster in "Easter-wings" is truly complex and sophistiated, the typography and the smooth surface of the poem have for a long time deceived critics into thinking that the poem was a simple and naive contraption.

The imagery of "The Altar" and "Easter-wings" has affinities with emblem literature. Herbert is clearly indebted to the Schola Cordis and the Amor/Anima traditions. James (1942) describes Herbert's way of using emblems thus:

> ... in images drawn from the poetry of George Herbert ... one can trace figures which began as vivid metaphors, which were given graphic representation in religious emblems, to reappear as arresting poetic conceits. For the writer of religious emblems, no source was more fecund than the Bible with its highly metaphorical expression .... Thus can be seen the completed circuit; from poetic metaphor, to graphic representation in the emblem, and then back into the body of poetry in a kind of metaphor which in its concreteness of detail, its completeness of realization for all its compression and economy of words, shows the trace of the emblem method.[129]

The comparative analysis in this chapter has attempted to show how the transformation from emblem to metaphor actually works in the case of Herbert's pattern poems.

129. James, p. 36, p. 38.

CHAPTER FOUR

A STUDY OF "THE PILGRIMAGE"

The Pilgrimage.

I travell'd on, seeing the hill, where lay
          My expectation.
A long it was and weary way.
The gloomy cave of Desperation
I left on th' one, and on the other side
          The rock of Pride.

And so I came to Fancies medow strow'd
          With many a flower:
Fain would I here have made abode,
But I was quicken'd by my houre.
So to Cares cops I came, and there got through
          With much ado.

That led me to the wilde of Passion, which
          Some call the wold;
A wasted place, but sometimes rich.
Here I was robb'd of all my gold,
Save one good Angell, which a friend had ti'd
          Close to my side.

At length I got unto the gladsome hill,
          Where lay my hope,
Where lay my heart; and climbing still,
When I had gain'd the brow and top,
A lake of brackish waters on the ground
          Was all I found.

With that abash'd and struck with many a sting
          Of swarming fears,
I fell, and cry'd, Alas my King!
Can both the way and end be tears?
Yet taking heart I rose, and then perceiv'd
          I was deceiv'd:

My hill was further: so I flung away,
          Yet heard a crie,
Just as I went, *None goes that way*
And lives: If that be all, said I,
After so foul a journey death is fair,
          And but a chair.

0. Introductory.

Herbert's pattern poems occupy a special place in the poet's work, written as they are in a genre the poet made no further use of. Yet they are representative of the main themes in the early part of *The Church*. Like the pattern poems, "The Pilgrimage," too, is exceptional in one way and representative in another; generically exceptional and thematically representative.

As its title indicates, the poem is about the pilgrimage of life. It is, in fact, a Pilgrim's Progress in miniature. The first half of the poem describes a journey through an allegorical landscape the most prominent landmark of which is a hill. The soul-errant passes some of the pitfalls and by-paths common to all allegorical pilgrimages and reaches his goal, only to discover that the hill he has climbed is not the one he had expected; his hill "was further." Although he is warned by a mysterious voice that the journey awaiting him is even more perilous than the one just undergone he goes forward confidently, considering his future hardships "fair" compared to the "foul"-ness of the past journey. Thus the theme of "The Pilgrimage" reflects the main concern of the central section of *The Church*: the trials and errors of the itinerant Christian. The corollary of the poem, in terms of its theme, is "Love (III)," the final poem of *The Church*, in which the arrival of the human soul at Heaven's door is described.[1]

The poem is exceptional in the Herbert canon for the literary mode it uses. As several critics have pointed out, allegory is one of Herbert's favourite literary techniques. But the explicitness with which the obstacles along the pilgrim's road are named, or rather labelled, is peculiar to "The Pilgrimage."[2] Because of this labelling the poem makes a simple and straightforward impression which may account for the fact that "The Pilgrimage" has not received the scholarly and critical attention it deserves. In this chapter I hope to show that the poem both merits and requires as close an analysis as some of the better known Herbert poems.

1. Charles A. Pennel and William P. Williams argue that "the progress of the pilgrim soul, under the care of Christ's Church, is the *leit-motif* of the central portion of *The Temple*." They call "The Pilgrimage" "a useful trope for illuminating *The Church*. "The Unity of *The Temple*," *Xavier University Studies*, 5(1966), 37-45; qu. in John R. Roberts, *George Herbert: An Annotated Bibliography of Modern Criticism, 1905-1974* (Columbia: Univ. of Missouri Press, 1978), p. 182.
2. See Saad El-Gabalawy, "The Pilgrimage: George Herbert's Favourite Allegorical Technique," *College Language Association Bulletin*, 13 (1970), 408-19; also Robert L. Montgomery, Jr., "The Province of Allegory in George Herbert's Verse," *Texas Studies in Literature and Language*, 1 (1960), 457-72.

142

1. "The Pilgrimage" and criticism.

Literary critics have not always recognized Herbert's poetic genius in "The Pilgrimage." Most commentators only mention the poem in passing or select one aspect for discussion. Two elements in particular have been singled out for critical attention: the tone of the poem and the contents of the third stanza.

1.1. Tone.

In 1930 Empson writes about the tone of "The Pilgrimage":

> The most striking thing about the verse is its tone, prosaic, arid, without momentum, whose contrast with the feeling and experience conveyed gives a prophetic importance to this flat writing; there is the same even-voiced understatement in the language of the Gospels.[3]

Some twenty years later Margaret Bottrall writes:

> Even when we might legitimately expect description, we do not get it. The first verse of *The Pilgrimage,* for instance, could scarcely be starker ... If we imagine for a moment what Spenser would have made of this material, it seems scarcely just to describe Herbert as a visual poet.[4]

Both Bottrall and Empson refer to the starkness of the poem that results from its dryness of tone. Their conclusions are different in that Bottrall's assessment of the first stanza is based on expectations derived from the reading of Spenser, whereas Empson approaches the tone of the poem on the basis of what he assumes to be Herbert's intentions; the word "understatement" points to this. The contrast between Herbert and Spenser remarked upon by Bottrall is more interesting than appears from her own words. It may well have been part of Herbert's poetic strategy to evoke the kind of response shown by Bottrall. In the following section I shall explore this possibility.

Other critics, too, have commented on the flatness of the poem's tone. According to Summers (1954) it is caused partly by what he calls the "weariness of the introductory past imperfect" and Vendler (1975) connects it with the way Herbert presents his allegory:

> The initial gestures toward description in Herbert ... are fatigued; the phases of the journey are labeled before we even have a chance to experience them ... Herbert cannot wait to gloss his allegory, which he does more baldly and retrospectively here than anywhere else in *The Temple.* We can hardly imagine an allegory more perfunctory.[5]

Vendler is the only one of these critics who does not merely describe the

---

3. Empson, *Seven Types of Ambiguity*, p. 129.
4. Margaret Bottrall, *George Herbert* (London: John Murray, 1954), p. 112.
5. Summers, *George Herbert: His Religion and Art*, p. 173; Vendler, *The Poetry of George Herbert*, p. 95.

tone of the poem but also attempts an explanation. She finds it in the contrast between the general and the personal, between the allegorical journey of the first half of the poem and the personal experience of the second. To this extent I fully agree with Vendler. I do not agree, however, with her description of the theme of the poem which is, in her words, ". . . the foul journey, whose insight is the despairing one that both the way and end are tears" (p. 97). I believe Vendler misinterprets the poem. My reasons will be given in section 2, which concentrates on the "gladsome hill."

1.2. The "wilde of Passion."

It is not unlikely that Empson's remarks about the tone of the poem have influenced later comments on it. Similarly, most critics feel obliged, apparently, to discuss what to Empson constitutes the most interesting and "exceedingly beautiful" passage of the poem: the third stanza and, more specifically, the phrase "wilde of Passion." Empson's discussion of the ambiguity of the word "Passion" has triggered off a number of reactions. Summers (1954), Martz (1954), Rickey (1966) and Freer (1972) all examine Herbert's punning in greater or lesser detail. An even more obvious pun in the passage concerned is that of the "good Angell" which "a friend had ti'd / Close to my side." Grosart already in 1874 pointed out that the word "Angell" could refer both to a gold coin current in Herbert's day and to the pilgrim's guardian angel.[6] In section 6.3.3. of this chapter we shall discuss the implications of Grosart's gloss for the reading of the rest of the poem. Hutchinson saw a pun on "would" in the phrase "the wilde of Passion, which / Some call the wold."[7] That this pun was intentional is made more likely by the fact that the Bodleian manuscript reads "would" instead of the word "wold" of the *editio princeps*.[8] Empson, like Hutchinson, sees a pun on "willed/would." I am not altogether clear about the meaning of the line that would then result.[9]

Empson's most intriguing suggestion about the third stanza is that about the implications of the word "Passion." He suggests that the poetical meaning of the word includes meanings such as "lack of patience, the loves of the flesh, and the ambitions at Court which he had abandoned; nor is it easy to map out its underground connections, by opposites, with the *Passion* of the Christ."[10] This interpretation has been

6. George Herbert, *The Complete Works*, I, 132.
7. *Works*, p. 527n.
8. *W* does not include "The Pilgrimage."
9. My feelings of doubt are apparently shared by Summers who finds some of Empson's readings "improbable if the stanza is read within its context" (pp. 173-4). Summers probably refers to this particular instance.
10. Empson, pp. 129-30.

accepted by most later critics. Yet I wonder if the ambiguities Empson ascribed to the word really fit the context. I think it unlikely that the word "Passion" would have been intended by Herbert to convey simultaneously both the ideas of the sinful passions of this world and Christ's suffering and crucifixion. If we interpret the word in the former sense it is clearly part of the allegorical landscape described in the first two stanzas. The "good Angell" is in that case the only helper in a world beset with the dangers and pitfalls of sinful temptations.[11] In this interpretation "sometimes rich" refers to the former, innocent state of Paradise which man has lost by his own doing.[12] If, however, we read "Passion" as referring to the suffering of Christ it points forward to the redemption that awaits the pilgrim after death, on the second hill.

Empson suggests that the word "Passion" carries both meanings. Outside the poem the word may be ambiguous in the sense he describes, but within the poem it does not work in that way. For one thing, this reading would affect the allegorical unity of the first part of the poem, for another it would confuse the dramatic development that is, as I hope to demonstrate, the poem's strength. Finally, an interpretation such as Empson's would mean the violent yoking together of heterogeneous ideas that for a religious poet like Herbert would belong to mutually exclusive categories. Unless one believes that any complication adds to a poem's "richness," Empson's claim that "Passion" is ambiguous in the way he indicates is incompatible with the poet's intentions as realized in "The Pilgrimage."

If there is ambiguity at all in the word "Passion," a suggestion made by Martz seems more plausible than Empson's. Whereas in Empson's reading the worldly and religious connotations of the word are conjoined, Martz sees an ambiguity within a more strictly religious framework:

> The "Passion" of Herbert's poem refers to "the passions" in this sense: that is, to "the sufferings of this present time" (Romans 8:18); with simultaneous reference to the sufferings of Christ and to the similar "crosses" which the Christian must bear in the imitation of Christ.[13]

In other words, "the wilde of Passion" refers to the tribulations the human pilgrim meets with in the course of his earthly existence, tribulations that derive their significance and relevance from the example of Christ's suffering.

Martz's interpretation is more persuasive than Empson's and it would

---

11. All editions from 1656 onwards have the emendation "world" for the earlier "wold."
12. *OED*, *s.v.* Somtimes † 2 = Sometime = at a certain time in the past; once; formerly.
13. Martz, *The Poetry of Meditation*, p. 305.

be difficult to disprove it. Personally, I tend to read the phrase and the passage it forms part of in the worldly sense only. I think that the stanza should be allowed to take its place in the allegorical framework that determines the structure of the poem. "Passion" is a logical fifth in the series "Desperation," "Pride," "Fancy," and "Care." The passion that the pilgrim has to overcome is of the kind described by St. Gregorius in his *Moralia*:

> The valour of a just man is to conquer the flesh, to contradict his owne will, to quench the delights of this present life, to indure and love the miseries of this world for the reward of a better, to contemne the flatteries of prosperity, and inwardly to overcome the feares of adversity.[14]

There is also a syntactic similarity between "the wilde of Passion" and the other allegorical landmarks of the first two stanzas: each of these is connected with the worldly sin to which it belongs by an 'of' construction: "cave of Desperation," "rock of Pride," etc. On the basis of these parallel constructions it would seem to fit in with the rest of the series.

The evidence of the concordance, though not conclusive by itself, also points to an interpretation along the lines I suggest. In addition to its occurrence in "The Pilgrimage" the word "Passion(s)" is used fourteen times in Herbert's writings. Of these fourteen occurrences five refer to the Passion in the sense of the suffering of Christ, the other nine clearly refer to the sinful passions of this world. In none of these instances is there an ambiguity of the kind indicated by Empson.[15]

The 'willed/would' pun some critics see in "wilde/wold" does not in my opinion fit the context either. It seems more likely that "wold," apart from its literal meaning of 'elevated tract of open country,' suggests "world." The passage contrasts the pre- and post-lapsarian states. The

---

14. Book 8; quoted in Francis Quarles, *Emblemes* (1635), p. 107, appended to Book 2, emblem XI, an emblem bearing the text from Matthew 7:14 for a motto: "Narrow is the way that leadeth unto life, and few there be that find it." The circumstance that the robbery takes place in the "wilde of Passion" does not contradict a worldly interpretation nor does the "good Angell" who, like Good Deeds in *Everyman*, remains with the pilgrim even when the latter has been robbed of all his worldly possessions.

15. See Mario A. di Cesare & Rigo Mignani, *A Concordance to the Complete Writings of George Herbert* (Ithaca: Cornell Univ. Press, 1977). Of the nine instances in which Herbert uses "passion" in the worldly sense five have the plural "passions." In all five instances in which the word is used in the religious sense a possessive pronoun is attached to it: three times "thy" and twice "his." In only one instance, not included in our analysis because it only occurs in *W*, the definite article is used in the title "The Passion" (i.e. the Crucifixion), introducing the poem that bears the title "Redemption" in *B* and 1633. It must be said, in fairness, that other arguments may tip the scale for Martz's interpretation: a) the fact that "Passion," unlike the previous obstacles, is allotted a whole stanza, b) the tears of stanza 4, and c) the ultimate fulfilment.

world that used to be a well-ordered and "rich" Paradise has turned into a wild place, laid waste by man's sins.

Most later critics, in the footsteps of Empson, have emphasized the importance of the third stanza within the total structure of the poem. This critical bias has led to the neglect of a number of other aspects of the poem's structure and imagery. These aspects and the interpretative problems raised by them will be dealt with in the main body of this chapter.

2. The gladsome hill.

As I suggested above, the structure of the poem is based on the allegorical pilgrimage that is its subject. The stages of the journey are demarcated by fundamental changes in tone and vocabulary. The landmarks that bring about these changes are the two hills mentioned, one of which is climbed, the other descried in the distance. The concept of the two hills will be studied in the next section. For the moment we shall concern ourselves with the basic division of the poem into two parts.

As we have seen, the way Herbert describes the allegorical landscape in the first two and a half stanzas has caused critics to call the tone of the poem "dry," arid," and "without momentum." The poem begins:

> I travell'd on, seeing the hill, where lay
> My expectation.
> A long it was and weary way.

Part of the length and the weariness of the journey lies in the past, which we as readers know nothing about. We meet the pilgrim when he is half-way through his journey; his emotional state fluctuates between exhaustion because of the hardships he has already encountered and eager expectation because he is now within sight of the hill that he sees as his destination. The way the poem begins, *in medias res,* is characteristic of epic rather than lyric poetry.[16] As I shall demonstrate there is reason to assume that Herbert is parodying the genre of the allegorical epic.

The second and third lines of the poem also seem to suggest that an elaborate allegorical description is to be expected. The enjambment increases the intensity of "My expectation" and the halting rhythm of the third line, caused by the change of the regular word order, adds to the suspense. Had the line read "It was a long and weary way" the statement would have been flat and without interest. After such an opening the

16. Cf. *The Faerie Queene*: "A gentle Knight was pricking on the plaine." Also T.S. Eliot's "The Journey of the Magi": "A cold coming we had of it, / Just the worst time of the year / For a journey, and such a long journey:". Like Herbert, Eliot uses inversion to enhance the feeling of expectancy on the part of the reader.

readers of Herbert's day might well expect a narrative on a grand scale. The description that follows would, however, hardly satisfy the well-trained allegorical mind of a seventeenth-century reader. The snares and pitfalls that the pilgrim encounters and overcomes in the course of his journey are enumerated rather than described. In two and a half stanzas we speed past the Scylla and Charybdis of Despair and Pride, Fancy's meadow, the copse of Care and the wild/wold of Passion. The respective allegorical landscapes appropriate to each of these worldly dangers are merely mentioned; there is hardly a description in these lines that would enable us to visualize the pilgrim's progress.

The only element that receives any emphasis at all is the actual progress. All the verbs in the passage under discussion express or imply some kind of activity or movement: "left," "came," "quicken'd," "got through," "led to." It is as if Herbert is hurrying the reader through the well-worn steps that form an inevitable part of any allegorical pilgrimage in order to get him as quickly as possible to the main end of this particular pilgrimage: the discovery that the hill which all along the pilgrim had seen as his goal, is just another stage of the pilgrimage, and that his ultimate destination lies on a yet further hill, located beyond death.

The lack of descriptive detail in the first part of the poem made Bottrall compare Herbert with Spenser and characterize Herbert as a non-visual poet. The comparison with Spenser is interesting but the conclusion that Herbert is not a visual poet is in my opinion unwarranted. For a just appreciation of the flatness of tone caused by the absence of striking images and lack of variation in the initial description the reader should first determine the proper place and function of the tone in the poem as a whole. In all probability Herbert deliberately avoided the abundance of a Spenserian fairyland, while at the same time including some of the features characteristic of the allegorical epic. These assumptions about Herbert's intentions are supported by the sudden change of tone and direction that occurs half-way through the poem which marks a change in the poet's attitude towards the scene described. From a mechanical catalogue of allegorical commonplaces the poem develops into a highly personal and involved statement. In the process the allegorical detail of the two hills turns into a complex metaphor.

This transition from general to personal is prepared for in the second half of the third stanza and takes place in the fourth. The change might even be said to hinge on one word right at the beginning of the fourth stanza, which sums up perfectly the allegorical expectation built up in the earlier stanzas and leads directly to the pilgrim's discovery of his having been deceived. The word is "gladsome."

The Spenserian word "gladsome" is unique in Herbert's poetry.[17] Although none of the critics of Herbert has to my knowledge singled out the word for comment, it seems to me a crucial word and, incidentally, quite an ambiguous one. The poet uses the word "gladsome," I would suggest, to underline the fact that the traditionally allegorical part of the poem, describing "the way" of the traveller, has ended. The remainder of the poem is concerned with "the end" of the allegorical journey and concentrates on the personal experience of the pilgrim.

The word "gladsome" was rarely used in the poetry of Herbert's day and it must therefore have been chosen deliberately.[18] The poets roughly contemporary with Herbert — Donne, Marvell and Herrick — do not use the word at all. Milton uses it twice, both times in versions of Psalms.[19] Among earlier poets the word was perhaps a little more common: Wyatt used it four times, Sidney once. Shakespeare, however, did not use it at all. The only poet who used "gladsome" with some frequency was Spenser, in whose work it occurs twelve times. Seven of these twelve occurrences are to be found in *The Faerie Queene*. On the basis of this evidence, however meagre, I risk the conclusion that Herbert's selection of the word "gladsome" in this explicitly allegorical poem was made in deliberate imitation of Spenser.

The word "gladsome" as Herbert uses it clearly indicates what attitude the reader should adopt towards the first half of the poem. The use of a word that has already acquired slightly archaic overtones has the effect of increasing the distance between the reader and the subject. Herbert seems to suggest that the allegorical view will not suffice for a presentation of true eternal life, which is the ultimate goal of the "soul in pilgrimage." The 'gladsome hill' is the end of the earthly part of the pilgrimage; this is as far as allegory can 'accompany' the soul; beyond death there is no room for allegory and only God's grace can bring about the ultimate fulfilment. This interpretation would explain the lack-lustre quality of the metaphors in the first stanzas: Herbert intended to present them thus, as dull emblems, because they are not at the centre of his real interest. Whereas in other instances he was capable of bringing emblematic material to life with unequalled vividness, here he purposely uses it in the most arid way possible to bring out all the more strikingly the contrast with the

17. In *W* the word occurs once more, in "The Sacrifice," l. 199: "The gladsome burden of a mortall saint."
18. For the concordances on which these conclusions are based see the Bibliographical Index, under *Concordances*; the *OED* quotes the line from "The Pilgrimage" *s.v.* Gladsome, 2b. "Of looks and feelings: Expressive of, or characterized by, gladness." Only one example anterior to Herbert is listed, from Douglas' translation of the Aeneid.
19. Psalm 84, l. 26 and Psalm 136, l. 1.

dramatic and triumphant final part of the poem.

One other poet should be mentioned in this context. Vaughan used the word "gladsome" four times in his poetry. Like Milton, he used it twice in versions of Psalms. Vaughan deserves to be singled out for two reasons. In the first place his debt to Herbert is extensive and well-known; any local resemblance between Vaughan and Herbert therefore deserves special attention.[20] In the second place Vaughan is the only poet besides Herbert who uses "gladsome" as an adjunct to "hill." He does so in his version of Psalm 121:

> Up to those bright, and gladsome hils
> Whence flowes my weal, and mirth,
> I look, and sigh for him, who fils
> (Unseen,) both heaven, and earth.
>
> He is alone my help, and hope,
> That I shall not be moved,
> His watchful Eye is ever ope,
> And guardeth his beloved;[21]

Vaughan's rendering of the Psalm is as it were a footnote to "The Pilgrimage," pointing the way to one of its (possible) sources. Even though the Authorized Version does not have the word "gladsome" it may well have served as the model for the metaphor of the hills in Herbert's poem:

> I will lift up mine eyes unto the hills, from whence cometh my help.
> My help cometh from the Lord, which made heaven and earth.

Vaughan's version is interesting because the relative neutrality of the original has been made more dramatic and turned into an incitement to the speaker to allegorical action.[22]

"The Pilgrimage" resembles Psalm 121 and Vaughan's version of it in relating the hope of the Christian pilgrim to the metaphor of hills. On the

---

20. Hutchinson writes that there is "no example in English literature of one poet adopting another poet's words so extensively" (*Works*, p. xlii).

21. *The Works of Henry Vaughan*, ed. L.C. Martin (Oxford: Oxford Univ. Press, 1957), pp. 458-9.

22. It is noteworthy that all the 16th century examples (*i.e.* Wyatt 4 times, Spenser 12 times) but one (Sidney) are used in profane contexts whereas all the 17th century examples (i.e. Herbert once, Vaughan 4 times, Milton twice) are used in religious contexts. Bearing in mind that the word occurs with relatively negligible frequency which makes any statistical conclusion tentative at best, one could conclude that the word "gladsome" received a Biblical aura in the 17th century which it did not have in the 16th. The King James Version not only inspired a profusion of Psalm versions but also the development of a new vocabulary for religious poetry. The word "gladsome" found its (modest) place there. Four of the seven occurrences of the word in 17th century literature are in Psalm versions.

other hand the word "gladsome" as used by Herbert recalls the idiom of traditional allegory. Herbert was a learned poet and wrote for an erudite audience; his poetry works by implication rather than reference. It would therefore be difficult to call Psalm 121 the one and only source for the metaphor of the hills in "The Pilgrimage," although it is part of the background of the poem. It would be less difficult but still problematical to call *The Faerie Queene* the source text for the word "gladsome" in the poem. Notwithstanding these uncertainties the conclusion seems warranted that an informed reader in Herbert's day would respond to the subtle way the poet manipulates the allegorical mode here, assuming that the word had already become archaic at the time. This supposition gains strength from the fact that after Herbert it was used almost exclusively in versions of the Psalms. "Gladsome" is the word that triggers off this response. It is the key to the genre the poem starts out from.

3. The concept of the two hills.

3.1. Introductory.

In the previous section we compared "The Pilgrimage" with Psalm 121 and Vaughan's version of it. I have not as yet pointed out that there is one difference that is at least as significant as the resemblances. Whereas the Authorized Version and Vaughan have "hills" and "gladsome hils" respectively, Herbert not only uses the singular, "gladsome hill," but also makes a clear distinction between that hill and another hill in his poem. When the pilgrim has left the initial obstacles of his journey behind, he arrives, full of eager expectation, at the hill he had already seen from far off:

> At length I got unto the gladsome hill,
> > Where lay my hope,
> Where lay my heart; · · ·

The only thing he finds on top of the hill after his arduous ascent is "A lake of brackish waters on the ground."[23] The disappointment causes a temporary dampening of his spirits:

> I fell, and cry'd, Alas my King!
> Can both the way and end be tears?
> Yet taking heart I rose, and then perceiv'd
> > I was deceiv'd:

> My hill was further · · ·

23. See Francis Quarles, *Emblemes* (1635), Book 2, Emblem XI:

> The true-bred Spark, to hoise his name
> Upon the waxen wings of Fame,
> Will fight undaunted in a Flood
> That's rais'd with brackish drops, and blood: (p. 106)

The space between the stanzas emphasizes the distance between the pilgrim's present situation and his newly discovered goal. He is the victim of an optical illusion; in retrospect the first confident lines of the poem suddenly acquire an ironic overtone:

> I travell'd on, *seeing* the hill, where lay ...
>   (emphasis added)

Human sight is a limited faculty; it is significant that the verb 'to see' in l. 1, with its possibility of delusion, has been replaced by the less ambiguous verb 'to perceive' in l. 29. The pilgrim can only perceive the true state of affairs when he has 'taken heart' again. Only then does he realize that the right hill lies beyond, and the ominous voice that says:

> ... *None goes that way*
> *And lives ...*

becomes a spur rather than an obstacle to the itinerant, faithful soul:

> ... If that be all, said I,
> After so foul a journey death is fair,
>   And but a chair.

In the final part of the poem hope and faith, the abstract conditions for reaching heaven's gate, are characteristically transformed into personal experience.

"The Pilgrimage" is generally interesting for its judicious mixture of allegorical and personal elements. The favourable outcome of the pilgrimage depends largely on the pilgrim's perception of his true goal, which is contrasted with the limited vision afforded by his mortal eyes so that, to quote T.S. Eliot, himself an admirer of Herbert's verse, "the purpose is beyond the end you figured / And is altered in fulfilment."[24] The 'objective correlative' of the pilgrim's growth towards a true insight into his situation is the metaphor of the two hills.

3.2. Problems, questions, and an answer.

Critics have commented on the function of the two hills in "The Pilgrimage," although this aspect of the poem has not received the attention it deserves. My paraphrastic account of the poem has shown that the metaphor of the two hills determines the allegorical structure, the dramatic progression and the *dénouement* of the poem. The poem moves from the described journey and ascent of the first hill towards the prescribed journey and ascent of the second.

Of the major critics of Herbert's work only Summers and Martz discuss the phenomenon of the two hills.[25] Others either repeat the ideas

---

24. T.S. Eliot, "Little Gidding," I, ll. 35-6.
25. Summers, pp. 174-75; Martz, p. 306.

152

expressed by Summers or Martz, or ignore the matter entirely. We shall first juxtapose the glosses of Summers and Martz on the hills. This is Summers' account:

> We have not been led directly from the vales of Sin to the Heavenly City on the Hill. The hill which the pilgrim had thought would provide his goal has furnished only tears; the first hill was not off the path, but his true hill was 'further,' and it could only be reached by death ... the first hill clearly represents within the poem that state of grace or service which the Christian may falsely hope can assure him of continuous beatitude on this earth. The pilgrim has not reached the end of his journey at the end of the poem, for no man can describe the end except by means of a dream; but in his willingness to lose his life, we are assured that he will find it.

Martz writes:

> The advancement continues ... It is a Calvary: where else could this *via dolorosa* end but in a pool of tears? Yet the speaker misunderstands the meaning of this hill, and he cries out, stung with fears as with vicious insects arising from a stagnant pool ... It is so, yet something more lies beyond: the speaker has, we might say, mistaken Calvary for Mount Zion: and yet for all this, he has gone by the right road ...

Before commenting on these two critical views I wish to add one more opinion on the poem which, though it does not deal explicitly with the concept of the hills, provides a convenient starting-point for my own investigation. In her study of Herbert's poetry Vendler writes about "The Pilgrimage":

> "Is this the promised end?" we ask when we find first the brackish waters, next the inaccessible "further" hill, and finally the taunt of death. This is a grisly set of "dissolves," made more so by the perspective thus cast on the whole preceding "plot." This sequence of experiences has been, says Herbert, "so foul a journey." Such revulsion at the total Christian pilgrimage is, so far as I know unheard-of outside this poem. The true wayfaring Christian may have his trials and his sloughs of despond, but it is unthinkable that Piers Plowman or Christian should fling out in anger, "After so foul a journey, death is fair." ... the journey is simply foul, in itself and in its result. It neither strengthens resolve, braces the soul, cleanses the heart, nor has any other moral effect ... Whether the two perspectives — "the Christian pilgrimage" and "this foul journey" — can be reconciled, I am not sure ... In this poem, Herbert re-examines the *Imitatio Christi:* the crucifixion is less painful finally, says Herbert, than the *via dolorosa.*[26]

These three opinions raise a number of questions. On the basis of the quoted passages it is not at all easy to determine the exact function of the first hill ascended by the pilgrim. The second hill does not present any problem: it may be regarded as Mount Zion on the top of which the Heavenly Jerusalem is situated. The interpretations of the first hill vary considerably. There is an appreciable difference between Martz who interprets it as "a Calvary" and Summers who calls it the hill of "grace or

26. Vendler, p. 94, p. 98.

service." Vendler's interpretation complicates matters even more; she seems to place the crucifixion somewhere beyond the first hill. One reason for these contradictory views may be the fact that the hills, unlike the other landmarks in the first half of the poem, are not provided with allegorical tags.

Another interpretative problem that needs sorting out is that of the exact quality of the journey towards the first hill. Summers and Martz see a clear-cut caesura in the pilgrimage of the Christian soul as it is presented in the poem, whereas to Vendler the ascent of the first hill represents "the total Christian pilgrimage." Consequently, Summers and Martz foresee the possibility of a favourable outcome of the pilgrimage once the top of the second hill has been gained, but Vendler can only see gloom in the poem, both in "the journey . . . itself and in its result."

One issue can be cleared up here and now. When Vendler says that the journey "neither strengthens resolve, braces the soul, cleanses the heart, nor has any other moral effect" the poem itself would seem to contradict her view. After the despondent outcry of the pilgrim:

> . . . Alas my King!
> Can both the way and end be tears?

the poem continues:

> Yet taking heart I rose, and then perceiv'd
> I was deceiv'd:

The pilgrim has almost fallen into the snares of Despair, but he pulls himself together just in time, "taking heart." The idiomatic phrase "taking heart" has the effect of vivid immediacy characteristic of emblematic verse. This effect has been carefully prepared by the poet as is witnessed by the earlier reference to the heart: ". . . the gladsome hill . . . where lay my heart." When the two phrases in which the heart is mentioned are considered separately they are simply two dead metaphors; together they become emblems from a *Schola Cordis*, in which the heart is actually placed on top of the hill and picked up by the pilgrim who discovers it through his fall. Only the pilgrim's act of will and his faith enable him to rise and behold the "further hill" that opens the way of grace to him. "For a just man falleth seven times, and riseth up again: but the wicked shall fall into mischief" (Proverbs, 24:16). The text would have been an appropriate gloss to this part of the poem. Quarles used it as a motto for one of his emblems, a passage from which is particularly relevant:

> . . . the Righteous man falls oft,
>   Yet falls but soft:
> There may be dirt to mire him; but no stones,
>   To crush his bones:
> What, if he staggers? Nay, put case he be
>   Foyl'd on his knee;

That very knee will bend to heav'n, and woo
   For mercy too.
The true-bred Gamester ups a fresh; and then,
   Falls to't agen;
Whereas the leaden-hearted Coward lies,
And yeelds his conquer'd life; or cravend, dies.[27]

Both the falling and the rising are part of the experience of a just man in search of his heavenly destination. This idea is illustrated in an emblem from Georgette de Montenay's *Emblemes, ou Devises Chrestiennes* (Lyon, 1571), p. 94, that bears the motto "Facile Difficile" (see fig. 31).

3.3. Hills and tradition.

   Herbert's use of hills in an allegorical context was not without precedent nor was he the last to use them thus. It is almost a commonplace to say that the pilgrimage of life often involves climbing; mountains have always been reserved for spiritually elevated matters. In Greek mythology Mount Helicon, Parnassus, and Olympus fulfilled important sacred and inspirational functions. In the Old Testament Moses had to climb Mount Sinai in order to receive the Ten Commandments; the life and Passion of Christ are inextricably interwoven with the Mount of Olives and Calvary; finally the Hereafter, the New Jerusalem, is situated on Mount Zion, the typological counterpart of Mount Sinai.

   The most famous and elaborate allegorical account of a mountain is Dante's ascent of Mount Purgatory in the *Divina Commedia*. Petrarch made a quite different, but equally influential contribution to the theme of mountains in literature. In a famous letter to Dionigi da Borgo San Sepolcro, Professor of Theology in Paris, written in 1336, he describes

---

27. *Emblemes* (1635), Book 2, Emblem XIV, pp. 116-119. Quarles added to his emblem a passage from a sermon by St. Ambrose: "Peter stood more firmly after he had lamented his fall, than before he fell: Insomuch that he found more grace than he lost grace." Cf. also Herbert's "The Church-porch," ll. 331-342:

Pitch thy behaviour low, thy projects high;
So shalt thou humble and magnanimous be:
Sink not in spirit: who aimeth at the sky,
Shoots higher much then he that means a tree.
   A grain of glorie mixt with humblenesse
   Cures both a fever and lethargicknesse.

Let thy minde still be bent, still plotting where,
And when, and how the businesse may be done.
Slacknesse breeds worms; but the sure traveller,
Though he alight sometimes, still goeth on.
   Active and stirring spirits live alone,
   Write on the others, Here lies such a one.

155

31

how he and his brother climbed Mont Ventoux in Southern France.
Because of its unusual vividness of description and its many naturalistic
details, the letter was regarded for a long time as one of the first realistic
accounts of a difficult journey; now it is recognized as yet another
spiritual pilgrimage.[28] That Petrarch intended his letter to be read
metaphorically rather than literally is indicated most clearly by the many
references to the Scriptures and the Church Fathers — in particular St.
Augustine's *Confessiones* — , and by the meditative attitude of the author
towards his subject. The following passage illustrates these ideas:

> ... Would that I might achieve with my mind the journey for which I am longing
> day and night as I achieved with the feet of my body my journey today after
> overcoming all obstacles. And I wonder whether it ought not to be much easier to
> accomplish what can be done by means of the agile and immortal mind without

28. Petrarch's letter is translated and introduced by Hans Nachod in Ernst Cassirer
et al., eds., *The Renaissance Philosophy of Man* (Chicago: Univ. of Chicago Press,
1948), pp. 36-46. See also Marjorie Hope Nicolson, *Mountain Gloom and Mountain
Glory* (Ithaca: Cornell Univ. Press, 1959), pp. 49-50. Although Hope Nicolson's book
has a different purpose from mine, I owe several quotations in this section to her.

any local motion "in the twinkling of the trembling eye" than what is to be performed in the succession of time by the service of the frail body that is doomed to die and under the heavy load of the limbs.

There is a summit, higher than all the others ... On its top is a small level stretch. There at last we rested from our fatigue. ... Then another thought took possession of my mind, leading it from the contemplation of space to that of time. ... The time will perhaps come when I can review all this in the order in which it happened, using as a prologue that passage of your favourite Augustine: "Let me remember my past mean acts and the carnal corruption of my soul, not that I love them, but that I may love Thee, my God."[29]

The occurrence of mountains in religious allegory is a persistent tradition. Bunyan's *Pilgrim's Progress* was written more than 300 years after Dante's *Divine Comedy*, but the mountains in Bunyan's work still fulfill the same allegorical function. Any reader will remember Hill Difficulty and the Delectable Mountains where Christian ascends Hill Clear and, through a "perspective glass," gets a blurred view of the Celestial City that is situated on "a mighty hill." The hills in Herbert's poem belong to an allegorical tradition that was persistently and consistently alive from the Middle Ages up to the end of the seventeenth century. It would therefore be quite correct to compare the ascent of Herbert's pilgrim to Dante's ascent of Mount Purgatory, the insight he gains on top of the hill to that of Petrarch on top of Mont Ventoux, and to name the two hills of "The Pilgrimage" Hill Difficulty and Mount Zion respectively, as in Bunyan's allegory.

These comparisons could even be extended to the level of verbal correspondences. Thus the wording of Christian's song at the outset of his ascent of Hill Difficulty resembles Herbert's poem closely:

Christian now went to the spring and drank thereof to refresh himself, and then began to go up the Hill, saying,

> *This Hill, though high, I covet to ascend,*
> *The difficulty will not me offend,*
> *For I perceive the way to life lies here;*
> *Come, pluck up, heart; let's neither faint nor fear:*
> *Better, though difficult, the right way to go,*
> *Than wrong, though easy, where the end is woe.*[30]

Throughout the first half of "The Pilgrimage," too, the difficulty of the journey is emphasized. On his arrival at the top of the first hill the pilgrim faints, "struck with many a sting / Of swarming fears," but, "taking heart," he rises and discovers, "perceives" his mistake.

But, although these comparisons show that Herbert's poem is firmly rooted in an allegorical tradition, they do not sufficiently explain the

29. *The Renaissance Philosophy of Man*, pp. 40-42.
30. John Bunyan, *The Pilgrim's Progress* (Harmondsworth: Penguin, 1965), p. 74.

specific metaphoric structure of "The Pilgrimage." The dramatic tension between the high-strung expectations of the pilgrim, the difficulty of his ascent and his disappointment and temporary despondency after he has gained the top in particular are not found in the examples mentioned. Nor can the subsequent, sudden change of attitude from despair to renewed faith be explained by reference to these parallels only. Finally, the dichotomy caused by the specific number of *two* hills is characteristic of Herbert's poem but not of other texts. We will have to cast our nets wider.

3.4. Hills and mountains as metaphors.

Hills and mountains readily combined with other motifs and they were used within the general framework of the pilgrimage of life to express various ideas. In Renaissance literature we find two basic contexts in which hills occur. In the one they are regarded as positive, in the other as negative elements. In the positive case their elevation above the common earthly level is emphasized; the summits of hills and mountains are closer to Heaven than anything else on earth. Moreover, the religious writer found a wealth of support in the Scriptures for regarding hills and mountains with respect and awe. Both Dante's Mount Purgatory and Petrarch's Mont Ventoux exemplify this attitude. Vaughan's version of Psalm 121, which we quoted from earlier, is a good example of the use of the hill as an emblem of man's hope of Heaven.

On the other hand hills and mountains, because of their height, were frequently associated with pride, whereas the valleys represented humility. The basic text for this idea is Isaiah 40:4: "Every valley shall be exalted, and every mountain and hill shall be made low: and the crooked shall be made straight, and the rough places plain."[31] In many instances, however, the positive and the negative views are blended together. The metaphor of the hills, moreover, readily absorbed or combined with

31. St. Augustine expounded the idea thus:

Hills and mountains are elevations of the earth; but valleys are depressions of the earth. Do not despise the depressions, for from them springs flow.... The heavens are indeed the higher bodies of the world.... But it is not written that God is near to tall men, or to those who dwell on the mountains, but it is written, 'The Lord is nigh unto them that are of a broken heart,' which refers to humility. (qu. in Hope Nicolson, pp. 47-8)

This attitude towards mountains also found its way into emblem literature. Henry Peacham has an emblem on the subject in *Minerva Britanna* (1612) with the motto *Humilibus dat gratiam* (He gives grace to the humble). The picture shows two mountains whose barrenness contrasts with the flowers of the fertile valley (Peacham, p. 55).

concepts like Kingship, Fortune, Truth, or Virtue.[32]

When mountains or hills are mentioned within an allegorical context as in Dante, Petrarch, Herbert, or Bunyan, they are mostly used to mark a stage of the total pilgrimage of life. The basic Bible-text for all Christian pilgrimages is Hebrews 11:13-16:

> 13 These all died in faith, not having received the promises, but having seen them afar off, and were persuaded of them, and embraced them, and confessed that they were strangers and pilgrims on the earth.
> 14 For they that say such things declare plainly that they seek a country.
> 15 And truly, if they had been mindful of that country from whence they came out, they might have had opportunity to have returned.
> 16 But now they desire a better country, that is, an heavenly: wherefore God is not ashamed to be called their God: for he hath prepared for them a city.

This passage contains the essential ingredients of the pilgrimage of life; both the incentive for and the goal of the journey are described in allegorical terms. The desire of the true Christian to be reunited with God in Heaven is expressed in the spatial metaphor of a pilgrim's journey from one country to another, and from his earthly abode to the Heavenly City.

A little further, in Hebrews 12:22, the city of God is said to be located on top of a mountain:

---

32. Mountains and kingship combine, for instance, in Drayton's *Poly-Olbion* (1612-13):

> ... This stoutlie I maintaine
> 'Gainst Forrests, Valleys, Fields, Groves, Rivers, Pasture, Plaine...
>   The Mountaine is the King....
> For Mountaines be like Men of brave heroique mind,
> With eyes erect to heaven, of whence themselves they find...

(qu. in Hope Nicolson, p. 54). In *King Lear*, II, iv, ll. 71-74, hills are associated with kingship and Fortune:

> Let go thy hold when a great wheel runs down a hill, lest it break thy neck with following; but the great one that goes upward, let him draw thee after.

Here the Fool gives a mock-warning to Kent not to let his loyalty to the King ruin him.

In *Emblemata Politica* by Jacobus â Bruck (Köln, 1618) we find an emblem bearing the motto "Integritate" (emblem 18, p. 69). The picture shows three hills; on top of the hill in the middle are a sceptre and a crown; on the hills to the left and right are two mirrors, each reflecting the sceptre and the crown. In the background, to the right, a lofty building is shown in front of which we see a king and his train. Further back there is a hilly landscape with an amphitheatre. The text of the emblem explains that a king, being elevated above the common level, is visible to both God and his (the king's) subjects. Consequently, he should take care to lead an unsullied life, devoted to furthering the cause of justice, because "Integritas, vitae, & recti mens Conscia; coelo/Pondus habet, terris praemia certa capit" (Integrity and a mind intent on leading a just life carry weight in heaven and earn an assured reward on earth). The

But ye are come unto mount Sion, and unto the city of the living God, the heavenly Jerusalem, and to an innumerable company of angels.[33]

These texts inspired Vaughan's poem "The Pilgrimage" which has Hebrews 11:13 for a motto. The poem ends thus:

> O feed me then! and since I may
> Have yet more days, more nights to Count,
> So strengthen me, Lord, all the way,
> That I may travel to thy Mount.[34]

Clearly the general background of Vaughan's poem is the same as that of Herbert's. For a more specific analysis of the function of the hills in Herbert's poem it is useful to realize that hills and mountains could be and were used in the various ways briefly indicated in the preceding paragraphs.

When we approach these variations in a more systematic way several things come to the fore. Basically three aspects of hills/mountains return

---

two mirrors stand for the reflection of the sovereign's deeds in heaven and on earth, respectively; the hills emphasize the precarious nature of a high, public office.
   In other instances the hill is associated with Truth as in Donne's "Satyre III":

> ... On a huge hill,
> Cragged, and steep, Truth stands, and hee that will
> Reach her, about must, and about must goe;
> And what th'hills suddennes resists, winne so;
> Yet strive so, that before age, deaths twilight,
> Thy Soule rest, for none can worke in that night. (ll. 79-84)

John Donne, *The Satires, Epigrams and Verse Letters*, ed. W. Milgate (Oxford: Oxford Univ. Press, 1967), p. 13. The hill of Truth is also mentioned in the Bible, in Zech. 8:3, where Jerusalem is called "a city of Truth" located on top of "the holy mountain." Milton combines the metaphor of the hill of Truth with the theme of the choice of the Two Paths:

> Lady that in the prime of earliest youth,
> Wisely hast shun'd the broad way and the green,
> And with those few art eminently seen,
> That labour up the Hill of heav'nly Truth ...

Sonnets, IX, ll. 1-4 in Milton, *The Poetical Works,* II, 150. It is clear that the meaning of mountain/hills in Renaissance literature varied depending on the context and intention of the text in which they occurred. This idea is confirmed by contemporary encyclopaedias; for instance in Picinellus' *Mundus Symbolicus* (Köln, 1681).

Mons ... est symbolum Sapientiae, Meriti, ... Vitae Contemplativae, Spei in Deo ponendae, Humilitatis, quae est mensura meritorum, ... Peccatoris foelicis, Paupertatis securae, ... Auxilii divini.

(facs. rpt. in Henkel/Schöne, p. 2164 *s.v. Mons*).
33. See also Psalm 48:1-2.
34. *The Works of Henry Vaughan*, pp. 464-65.

time and again: height, ascent and perspective. Mountains can only be climbed with a certain amount of effort, they obscure the sight of what is beyond them until the ascent is achieved. After that they allow a panoramic view of the world. Applied to the pilgrimage of life each of these basic aspects may have either a positive or a negative moral effect on the pilgrim depending on their allegorical significance and the virtue or vice that is at stake. Thus, if the aspect of height is emphasized the moral effect may be positive if the allegorical significance is that mountains are nearer to Heaven than anything else on earth. In that case the concomitant virtue is religious aspiration or Zeal. On the other hand the effect may be negative if the allegory emphasizes that mountains are higher than their surroundings thus indicating that the Deadly sin of Pride prevails. For clarity's sake and by way of transition to the following section it will be convenient to arrange the possible variants in a diagram:[35]

natural level	function	moral effect	allegorical significance	Virtue/Vice
Mountains are elevations of the earth	height	positive	nearest to Heaven	Zeal
Mountains are elevations of the earth	height	negative	higher than surroundings	Pride
Mountains can only be climbed with effort	ascent	positive	challenge	Perseverance
Mountains can only be climbed with effort	ascent	negative	in the way of fulfilment	Sloth
Mountains allow panoramic view	perspective	positive	insight into spiritual destiny	Hope
Mountains prevent panoramic view	perspective	negative	'psycho-optic' illusion	Despair

3.5. Hills and mountains in Herbert's work.

It would not be an arduous task to find examples of allegorical texts illustrating each of the categories in the diagram; some were mentioned in the previous section. But how does all this fit in with "The Pilgrimage"?

From the start of the poem the hill is introduced as the goal of the allegorical journey and the difficulty of the journey is emphasized. The effort involved in climbing the first hill is described in the fourth stanza:

35. The table is not intended to be exhaustive. I have limited it to those metaphoric uses of mountains/hills that occur regularly in allegories of the pilgrimage of life. Other notions, such as that of the mountain disturbing the perfectly circular symmetry of the world, are left out of consideration (see Hope Nicolson, pp. 34 ff.).

> *At length* I got unto the gladsome hill,
>   Where lay may hope,
>   Where lay my heart; and *climbing still,*
>   When I had *gain'd* the brow and top ...
>   (emphasis added)

The poetic economy of this passage is remarkable. Both the height and the difficulty of the ascent are emphasized. The height is indicated in the first place by the word "still" but also, more indirectly, by the rhetorical repetition of "Where lay my ..." It is as if the poet wishes to make us feel that he is coming step by step closer to his goal.[36] The difficulty of the ascent is reflected in "At length," "gain'd," and perhaps in the tautology of "brow and top." Moreover, when he has reached the top, the pilgrim becomes aware that he has been deluded by the false perspective of the hill and is also made to realize that only by overcoming the difficulties of the ascent can he get a proper view of what lies beyond it.

In the effect of the journey on the pilgrim both the negative and the positive aspects of the hill metaphor are reflected. The pilgrim's attitude changes from despair to hope, from lack of faith to renewed faith; the lesson he learns by climbing the hill and overcoming his disappointment is a penitential one. The road up the hill is the way of virtue, although the pilgrim is threatened by the deadly sin of despair which almost causes him to give up.

We find, then, that the poem touches on most of the categories in the diagram presented above — proof once again of Herbert's remarkable power of poetic concentration. The economy of the rhetorical means used by the poet tends to make one neglect a complexity that is indicated rather than elaborated upon. For each of these categories Herbert could rely on firmly established traditions. Before indicating some of the possible sources and analogues to specific passages of "The Pilgrimage" I shall pay some attention to Herbert's use of the image of the hill in the rest of his work.

The word "hill(s)" occurs eight times in Herbert's poetry. The first thing that strikes us is that three instances out of these eight are to be found in "The Pilgrimage." In three of the other five instances the moral effect of the image is negative: in "The Church-porch" the climbing of a hill is regarded as a futile effort (l. 111); in "The British Church" the hill is the dwelling-place of Roman Catholicism (l. 13). Its pomp and

36. Cf. Donne, "Satyre III": "... hee that will/ Reach her, about must, and about must goe." Also Quarles, *Emblemes* (1635), Book 4, Emblem II, Epig. 2:

> Pilgrim trudge on: What makes thy soule complaine,
> Crownes thy complaint. The way to rest is paine:
> The road to Resolution lies by doubt:
> The next way Home's the farthest way about.

vainglory are contrasted with the valley of Calvinism. Herbert, as a staunch Anglican, can approve of neither. In "Sinnes Round" "the Sicilian Hill" (l. 8) is compared to the "inflamed thoughts" of the poet. In one instance Herbert praises the qualities of both hill and valley, namely in "Providence," where he attributes wealth and abundance to hills and valleys alike (l. 95), a dispensation which he regards as a sign of the Providence of God in His creation.

The final example is rather more relevant to our understanding of the significance of the hills in "The Pilgrimage." It occurs in the fourth stanza of "The Size":

> Great joyes are all at once;
> But little do reserve themselves for more:
> Those have their hopes; these what they have renounce,
>   And live on score:
> Those are at home; these journey still,
> And meet the rest on Sions hill.

Here Herbert states as philosophy what he formulates as allegorical and personal experience in "The Pilgrimage." In both poems renunciation and effort are presented as positive values. A temporary postponement of fulfilment makes the ultimate reunion "on Sions hill" all the more desirable.[37] The realization of this Christian tenet no doubt strengthens the pilgrim's courageous resolve to resume his journey.

4. The ascent.

> At length I got unto the gladsome hill,
>   Where lay my hope,
> Where lay my heart; and climbing still,
> When I had gain'd the brow and top,
> A lake of brackish waters on the ground
>   Was all I found.

The ascent of the "gladsome hill" is by no means easy and in retrospect the speaker is quite justified in calling the journey "foul." It is one of the characteristics of the allegorical journey that the going is rough. The top of Virtue's hill is almost by definition only reached through hardship. "The Pilgrimage" is about the ascent of the one hill and the preparation for the ascent of Mount Zion. What is intriguing about the third and fourth stanzas is not so much the difficulty of the ascent *per se* or the disappointment experienced by the pilgrim after he has "gain'd the brow and top," nor even his subsequent fall and outcry, but the motivating force behind the renewed courage that makes him rise again. The

---

37. "The Size" actually provides some of the positive evidence that Vendler could not find in "The Pilgrimage" when she wrote that "the journey is simply foul, in itself and in its result" (see section 3.2. of this chapter).

incitement does *not* come from his perceiving the further hill — the order
of events precludes this possibility: "... I rose, and *then* perceiv'd / I was
deceiv'd" (emphasis added). If there is a causal connection here, it is the
rising that leads to perception and not the other way round.

So far we have analysed this line from the angle of the Theological
Virtue of Faith opposing Despair, the Deadly Sin. I now propose
approaching the ascent and what it leads up to in terms of other
conventions.

4.1. *Quieta sedes.*

The idea of a certain relief awaiting the pilgrim who has chosen the
arduous path of virtue is very old and occurs in some of the oldest
versions of the Choice of the Two Paths. Panofsky (1930) points to
Hesiod's description:

> ... der Pfad zur "Tugend" aber ist lang, steil und anfänglich schmal, aber wenn
> man zur Höhe gelangt ist, erscheint er hinterher leicht trotz seiner Schwere.[38]

The *bivium* tradition is frequently associated with a mountain landscape.[39] There is no choice between two paths in "The Pilgrimage,"
however. The distinction between the two hills in the poem cannot be
explained in terms of a division between Pleasure and Virtue or between
Death and Eternal Life, the Christian corollary of the pagan myth. The
road taken by the pilgrim is the right one from the start. There are, to be
sure, two hills in the poem and the contrast between them is clearly
emphasized, but the contrast lies in the attitude of the pilgrim towards his
experience rather than in the moral quality inherent in the hills themselves. The climbing of Hill Difficulty is a penitential journey and an
indispensable prelude to the ascent of Mount Zion.

Notwithstanding these differences the ascent described in "The Pilgrimage" has much in common with that of Virtue's hill. Panofsky
quotes the *Satires* of Persius in which the path of virtue is described thus:

---

38. Erwin Panofsky, *Hercules am Scheidewege* (Leipzig, 1930), p. 46. Panofsky here
refers to Hesiod, *Opera et Dies*, 287 ff. See also Chew, *The Pilgrimage of Life*, pp. 17-
81; Hope Nicolson, *Mountain Gloom and Mountain Glory*, pp. 50-1.

39. See, for instance, Barclay's *The Ship of Fools* (1509), which has a woodcut
showing Pleasure and Virtue ("Voluptuosyte" and "vertue") on top of their respective
hills (Alexander Barclay, trans., *The Ship of Fools, by Sebastian Brant* (1509), ed. T.H.
Jamieson, 2 vols. (Edinburgh, 1874; rpt New York: AMS Press, 1966), II, 286).
Barclay's rendering of Brant's *Narrenschiff* is a very free one, adapted to the tastes and
circumstances of early 16th c. England. It was "translated out of Laten, French, and
Doche ..." Barclay's purpose being "to redres the errours and vyces of this oure
royalme of England" (Jamieson, I, xviii). The woodcuts are derived from the Basle
edition in Latin of 1497, supervised by Brant himself. There is a modern translation of
Brant's work by Edwin H. Zeydel, *The Ship of Fools* (New York: Dover, 1962).

Et altera est dextra, in qua virtutis opera celebrantur, *arduum* ac difficilem *limitem pandens*. Quem qui evaderint, quieta sede excipiuntur.[40]

The *quieta sedes* motif is repeated in many later pilgrimages. In Dante's *Purgatory*, for instance, Virgil, Dante's faithful companion, compares the heavy strain of the ascent that lies behind them and the repose now awaiting Dante:

> ... Il temporal fuoco e l'eterno
> Veduto hai, figlio, e sei venuto in parte
> Dov' io per me più oltre non discerno.
>
> Tratto t' ho qui con ingegno e con arte;
> Lo tuo piacere omai prendi per duce:
> Fuor sei dell' erte vie, fuor sei dell' arte.
>
> ... Seder ti puoi e puoi andar tra elli.

(Canto XXVII, ll. 127-132; ll. 137-38)[41]

Spenser has *Contemplation*, "that godly aged Sire," show Redcrosse the uphill road to the heavenly Jerusalem:

> Then come thou man of earth, and see the way,
> That neuer yet was seene of Faeries sonne,
> That neuer leads the traueiler astray,
> But after labours long, and sad delay,
> Brings them to ioyous rest and endlesse blis.

(*The Faerie Queene*, I, x, 52).

A century after Spenser Bunyan uses the *quieta sedes* motif in *The Pilgrim's Progress*. In Part Two Christiana advises Mr. Ready-to-halt to

---

40. "And the other is the one on the right on which the works of virtue are celebrated, leading to an arduous and difficult path. Those who climb it awaits an easy resting-place/chair." The Latin text is taken from Panofsky (1930), pp. 65-6. Richard Lattimore quotes a Latin epitaph also using the word "chair" in connection with the pilgrimage of life: "Multis annis navigando et peregrinando hanc sede peti" ("Themes in Greek and Latin Epitaphs," in *Illinois Studies in Language and Literature*, 28 (Urbana, 1942), 167).

41.   ... "The temporal fire and the eterne
        Thou hast beheld, my son, and reached a place
        Where, of myself, no further I discern.

        I've brought thee here by wit and by address;
        Make pleasure now thy guide — thou art well sped
        Forth of the steep, forth of the narrow ways ....

        ... thou may'st prospect
        At large, or sit at ease to view all this ...."

Dorothy L. Sayers, trans., *The Comedy of Dante Alighieri the Florentine*, II (Harmonsworth: Penguin, 1955), 284-85.

complete his journey: "So she said to him, 'Thy travel hither has been with difficulty, but that will make thy rest the sweeter'."[42]

4.2. Post amara dulcia.

One way of expressing relief after hardships in the pilgrimage of life is by means of the idea of the *quieta sedes*. This idea is possibly what Herbert had in mind when he used the word "chair" at the end of "The Pilgrimage," although this word suggests other ideas besides, as will be explained in section 7.

Another, related way of expressing relief after the hardships of the journey is in the emblematic image *post amara dulcia,* which may partly explain the pilgrim's exclamation: "After so foul a journey, death is fair." *Post amara dulcia* frequently occurs in the same context as the *quieta sedes* motif. This is the case, for instance, in the same part of *The Pilgrim's Progress* quoted from before, in Bunyan's description of the Land óf Beulah and the River of Death:

> In this land they heard nothing, saw nothing, felt nothing, smelt nothing, tasted nothing that was offensive to their stomach or mind; only when they tasted of the water of the River over which they were to go, they thought that tasted a little bitterish to the palate, but it proved sweeter when 'twas down.[43]

Here the image is used, quite literally, to describe the taste of the water of the river. It occurs frequently, too, with a slightly different emphasis, in emblems.

"Post amara dulcia" is the motto of an emblem in Whitney (see fig. 32) and a similar emblem occurs in Wither, bearing the motto, "*Hee that enjoyes* a patient Minde, / *Can* Pleasures *in* Afflictions *finde*." (see fig. 33)[44] In continental emblem books analogous emblems had appeared. In Georgette de Montenay's *Emblemes, ou Devises Chrestiennes* (1571) an emblem occurs with the motto "ex malo bonum" (see fig. 34).[45] The engravings of all three emblems show a human being picking thorny or prickly flowers (roses in Montenay and Whitney, thistles in Wither). The emblems differ from one another with regard to the function of the flowers, as is expressed in the accompanying verses. Whereas the thorns in Montenay's emblem represent human sin ("oeuures meschantes") and the rose God's grace that will overcome and heal all sin, the English counterparts of the emblem use the image of the flower and the thorns to express penitence and patience: the person picking the flower will at first

42. *The Pilgrim's Progress*, II, p. 366.
43. *ibid.*, p. 364.
44. Whitney, p. 165; Wither, p. 232.
45. Georgette de Montenay, *Emblemes, ou Devises Chrestiennes* (Lyon, 1571), p. 66.

GAVDET PATIENTIA DVRIS.

Hee that enioyes a patient Minde,
Can Pleasures in Afflictions finde.

74

Book. 4.

ILLVSTR. XXIV.

33

32

34

feel the pricks caused by the thorns but this will be only a temporary infliction because, once the flower is picked, "it makes him straight amendes / It is so freshe, and pleasant to the smell, / Thoughe he was prick'd, he thinkes he ventur'd well" (Whitney).

Montenay advises the reader to bear his pains patiently, because "Dieu fait tout bien: que nul n'en doute plus." Whitney's message is directed at the action of man rather than the glory of God:

> None merites sweete, who tasted not the sower,
> Who feares to climbe, deserues no fruicte, nor flower.
> ... For after paine, comes pleasure, and delighte.
> ... So after paines, our pleasures make vs glad,
> But without sower, the sweete is hardlie had.

Although neither the picture nor the context calls for it, Whitney uses the verb "to climbe" as a metaphor of the penitential journey, which demonstrates the extent to which the word had become accepted as the means *par excellence* to express human effort in the context of the pilgrimage of life.

Wither's picture resembles Whitney's. In both pictures the man picking the flower is depicted in the middle of his pilgrimage, in the act of walking. Moreover, the index-finger of the left hand is extended and points both upward and forward to underline the idea that the pilgrim does not heed his present afflictions but bears his future glory in mind.[46] Both Whitney's and Wither's emblems emphasize the penitential implications of the picture: perseverance will lead to ultimate bliss. In this respect the emblems resemble the theme of "The Pilgrimage."

When we take a closer look at the text of Wither's emblem we find that the resemblance between it and Herbert's poem is not restricted to the general theme:

> So, Men, assured that *Afflictions* paine
> Comes not for vengeance to them, nor in vaine;
> But, to prepare, and fit them for the place,
> To which, they willingly direct their pace;
> In Troubles, are so farre from being sad,
> That, of their *Suffring*, they are truely glad.
> What ever others thinke, I thus beleeve;
> And, therefore, *joy*, when they suppose I *grieve*. (ll. 23-30)

In this passage Wither explains why the pilgrim willingly submits to "Troubles" and "Suffring." In Herbert's poem the act of faith expressed by "Yet taking heart I rose" and ". . . so I flung away" is presented rather than explained. Herbert leaves it to the reader to determine what it is that makes the pilgrim summon all his courage and get up again. In the poem itself all the attention is focused on the progress of the pilgrimage and the experience of the pilgrim, in other words on allegorical action rather than reflection. Nevertheless, there can be no doubt that the pilgrim is prompted to action by religious zeal. The hardships and pain suffered in the initial stage of his pilgrimage are penitential, as the picking of the thorny flowers in the *post amara dulcia* emblems is penitential; and the rising of the pilgrim is an expression of religious expectation comparable to the upward pointing finger in the emblems.

There are other more literal resemblances between Wither's text and Herbert's poem. In ll. 25-27 Herbert writes:

> With that abash'd and struck with many a sting
> Of swarming fears,
> I fell, and cry'd, Alas my King!

Wither, more explicit and less ambiguous than Herbert, writes:

---

46. In a way these emblems recall the *zelus in deum* or *coarctor in duobus* emblems discussed in a previous chapter. In both types there is a contrast between a downward and an upward movement expressed in physical terms. Herbert's "fall" may hint at the *zelus in deum* motif, which may be supported by means of a comparison with Dante's *Purgatory*, XII, ll. 95-6: "O human race, born to take flight and soar, / Why fall ye, for one breath of wind, to earth?"

> I, oft have sayd (and, have as oft, beene thought
> To speake a *Paradox*, that savours nought
> Of likely truth) that, some *Afflictions* bring
> A *Honey-bag*, which cureth ev'ry Sting
> (That wounds the *Flesh*) by giving to the *Mind*,
> A pleasing taste of *Sweetnesses* refin'd.
> Nor can it other be, except in those,
> Whose Better part, quite stupifyed growes,
> By being Cauterized in the Fires
> Of childish *Feares*, or temporall *Desires*.
> For, as the *Valiant* (when the *Coward* swounds)
> With gladnesse lets the *Surgion* search his *Wounds*;
> And, though they smart, yet cheerefully indures
> The Plaisters, and, the Probe, in hope of Cures...

What does "Sting" refer to in Wither's emblem? If one bases one's interpretation on the picture the most likely possibility would be the effect of the thorny flowers. If, on the other hand, the interpretation is based on the text of the emblem, words like "Honey-bag" and "Sweetnesses" suggest bees as the cause of the stings. It is even more difficult to determine the cause of the stings in Herbert's poem than it is in the emblem. Although the context seems to indicate that they are inflicted by insects ("swarming") it is not impossible that there is an echo here of the thorny flowers of the *post amara dulcia* emblems whose stings represent the penitential aspect of the pilgrimage. Such an ambiguity would also enhance the significance of "I fell." It would then not only describe the act of this particular pilgrim but be representative of the Fall, which, according to an early legend related by St. Ambrose, caused roses to bear thorns as a reminder of man's sins and his fall from grace.[47]

It should be pointed out that the resemblances and analogues described here only partially serve to clarify Herbert's poem. He does not of course mention thorny flowers or bees and the notion of *post amara dulcia* does not occur explicitly in the poem. As we said before, the reader's attention is focused entirely on the experience of an individual pilgrim in a particular situation. Nevertheless the fact that almost every word in the lines under consideration is rooted in tradition is proof of Herbert's remarkable powers of transformation.

5. The false and the true perspective.

"The Pilgrimage" contains two perspectives, one false, the other true. The false perspective is brought about by the first hill, which the pilgrim

---

47. St. Ambrose is also associated with bees; he is frequently depicted carrying a beehive as a sign of his eloquence. See James Hall, *Dictionary of Subjects and Symbols in Art*, rev. ed. (New York: Harper & Row, 1979), and Ferguson, *op. cit.* in relevant lemmata.

takes to be the only one. It is a natural enough phenomenon: standing at the bottom of a hill or mountain, one can never be sure that there is not a higher mountain behind it. The only way to find out is by climbing it. Long before Herbert wrote "The Pilgrimage" the visual aspect of hills and/or mountain ranges had been used as a metaphor in the pilgrimage of life. As far as I know, the meaning of this metaphor in Herbert's poem has not been studied before.

5.1. Visual deception.

In early versions of the myth of the Choice of the Two Paths the deceptive nature of mountain ranges is emphasized. In these versions by the old Greek rhetoricians the visual aspect of the hills of Voluptas and of Virtus as Hercules, the protagonist of the myth, sees them is described. In Panofsky's words:

> Er sieht zwei Hügel, die — aus einem gemeinsamen Massiv sich erhebend, *so daß sie von ferne trüglicherweise als Einheit erscheinen* — zu ungleicher Höhe emporragen (emphasis added).[48]

The deceptive unity of the two hills is easier to describe in words than to delineate in a picture; in most pictures that illustrate the *bivium* tradition the two hills are seen to rise from a common foundation but the reader/spectator has an unobstructed view of both hill-tops. The illustrations invariably show a *frontal* view of the two hills, whereas the description of the Greek rhetoricians and the words of Herbert's poem call for a *side*-view. I suppose that these distinctions between pictures and words reflect an essential difference between the two sister arts, one depending for its effect mainly on simultaneity and immediacy, the other on succession and duration.

In the development of the *bivium* tradition the pictures usually emphasize the element of choice.[49] In verbal descriptions, on the other hand, the psychological difficulty of the choice may be indicated by an author's accenting the proximity or even the apparent unity of the two hills. Occasionally artists have complicated the fairly straightforward situation of the Choice, particularly in the Christian version of the broad and narrow ways in the pilgrimage of life. Thus, an engraving by Hieronimus Wierex from a design by H.V. Bael (*c.* 1600) shows the Two Paths diverging at the bottom of Calvary, at the top of which the crucified Christ is seen. A little further back a row of skeletons is dancing a macabre Dance of Death. As usual the Broad Way leads to the yawning

---

48. Panofsky (1930), p. 48.
49. This is the case, for instance, in the woodcut in Barclay's *The Ship of Fools* described before (see n. 39) or in the elaborate frontispiece of Wither's emblem book showing the Broad and Narrow Ways of Matt. 7:13.

mouth of Hell and the Narrow Way to the gates of Heaven. But beyond the gate of Hell there is yet another way that leads towards the Celestial City. This 'emergency route' leads across a range of hills and the pilgrim who has chosen to follow it has to pass the huts of Humility and Repentance before he can reach Heaven.[50]

The engraving by Wierex illustrates what Petrarch had written some two and a half centuries earlier in the letter about his ascent of Mont Ventoux quoted from before (see section 3.3.):

> What you have so often experienced today while climbing this mountain happens to you, you must know, and to many others who are making their way toward the blessed life. This is not easily understood by us men, because the motions of the body lie open, while those of the mind are invisible and hidden. The life we call blessed is located on a high peak. 'A narrow way,' they say, leads up to it. Many hilltops intervene, and we must proceed 'from virtue to virtue' with exalted steps. On the highest summit is set the end of all, the goal toward which our pilgrimage is directed .... you must either ascend to the summit of the blessed life under the heavy burden of hard striving, ill deferred, or lie prostrate in your slothfulness in the valleys of your sins. ... How often, do you think, did I turn back and look up to the summit of the mountain today while I was walking down? It seemed to me hardly higher than a cubit compared to the height of human contemplation, were the latter not plunged into the filth of earthly sordidness. This too occurred to me at every step: "If you do not regret undergoing so much sweat and hard labor to lift the body a bit nearer to heaven, ought any cross or jail or torture to frighten the mind that is trying to come nearer to God and set its feet upon the swollen summit of insolence and upon the fate of mortal men?" ... How intensely ought we to exert our strength to get under foot not a higher spot of earth but the passions which are puffed up by earthly instincts.[51]

In this passage the deceptive aspect of the mountain range has become a metaphor of a mental process. The allegorical phrase "Many hilltops intervene" mirrors the "motions ... of the mind" which are "invisible and hidden." Here there is no choice between good and evil but rather a progression from one level of existence to a higher, "hidden" one. The hills of virtue are presented as stepping-stones for the soul on its way towards its goal.

50. Chew, fig. 132. Chew's gloss on the picture is to be found on p. 178 of *The Pilgrimage of Life*.

51. *The Renaissance Philosophy of Man*, pp. 39-40; pp. 45-6. The metaphor "from virtue to virtue" is familiar to ecclesiastical writers; see Anselm of Canterbury, *Letters*, i, 43 in Migne, *Patrologia Latina*, CLVIII, 1113, who uses the metaphor as a friendly wish in salutations. See *The Renaissance Philosophy of Man*, p. 40. Martz writes about St. Bernard's *The Twelve Degrees of Humility and Pride*:

> In the terms of St. Bernard, self-scrutiny forms the first degree of Truth, because it leads away from curiosity and moves toward humility: "the characteristic virtue of those *who are disposed in their hearts to ascend by steps* from virtue to virtue, until they reach the summit of humility; where, standing on Sion as on a watch-tower, they may survey the truth" (*The Poetry of Meditation*, p. 118).

Petrarch's letter is full of references to St. Augustine and to his *Confessions* in particular. The following quotation from the *Confessions* is especially relevant here:

> A body inclines by its own weight towards the place that is fitting for it. Weight does not always tend towards the lowest place, but the one which suits it best, for though a stone falls, flame rises. . . . When things are displaced, they are always on the move until they come to rest where they are meant to be. In my case, love is the weight by which I act. To whatever place I go, I am drawn to it by love. By your Gift, the Holy Ghost, we are set aflame and borne aloft, and the fire within us carries us upward. *Our hearts are set on an upward journey*, (Ps. 83:6 (84:5)) as we sing the *song of ascents* (Ps. 119:33 (120:34)). It is your fire, your good fire, that sets us aflame and carries us upward. For our journey leads us upward to the peace of the heavenly Jerusalem . . . [52]

The passage, although not directly related to the idea of perspective, is relevant because of the distinction made in it between the movement of different bodies. The heart, being "displaced" on earth, is zealous to climb upward accompanied by the "song of ascents." Displacement is followed by ascent as the wrong perspective in "The Pilgrimage" is corrected by perception.

Even though in these examples visual deception plays a less conspicuous role than it does in "The Pilgrimage" the conditions of the pilgrimage are very much the same. If we are looking for examples in which perspective is used as it is in "The Pilgrimage" we must expect for reasons already indicated to find literary rather than pictorial parallels. Let us consider two texts that are in most respects quite different from Herbert's poem but share with it the element of perspective. The following passage by William Drummond describes the dilemma that Herbert's pilgrim found himself in:

> Ah! as a Pilgrime who the *Alpes* doth passe,
> Or *Atlas* Temples crown'd with winters glasse,
> The ayrie *Caucasus*, the *Apennine*,
> *Pyrenès* cliftes where Sunne doth neuer shine,
> When hee some heapes of Hilles hath ouer-went,
> Beginnes to thinke on rest, his Iourney spent,
> Till mounting some tall Mountaine hee doe finde,
> More hights before him than hee left behinde . . . [53]

It has been argued that one of the most famous passages from Pope's "Essay on Criticism" (1711) was modelled on Drummond's example:

52. St. Augustine, *Confessions*, trans. R.S. Pine-Coffin (Harmondsworth: Penguin, 1961), XIII, 9, p. 317.
53. "An Hymne of the Fairest Faire," ll. 149-156, in William Drummond, *The Poetical Works*, ed. L.E. Kastner, 2 vols. (Manchester, 1913; rpt. New York: Haskell, 1968), II, 41-2.

A *little Learning* is a dang'rous Thing;
Drink deep, or taste not the Pierian Spring:
There *shallow Draughts* intoxicate the Brain,
And drinking *largely* sobers us again.
Fir'd at first Sight with what the *Muse* imparts,
In *fearless Youth* we tempt the Heights of Arts,
While from the bounded *Level* of our Mind,
Short Views we take, nor see the *Lengths behind*,
But *more advanc'd*, behold with strange Surprize
New, distant Scenes of *endless* Science rise!
So pleas'd at first, the towring *Alps* we try,
Mount o'er the Vales, and seem to tread the Sky;
Th'Eternal Snows appear already past,
And the first *Clouds* and *Mountains* seem the last:
But *those attain'd*, we tremble to survey
The growing Labours of the lengthen'd Way,
Th' *increasing* Prospect *tires* our wandring Eyes,
Hills peep o'er Hills, and *Alps* on *Alps* arise![54]

Whereas in Drummond's poem the image of 'mountains behind mountains' is used to express the inability of the speaker to raise himself to "the vnbounded Circüits of thy [i.e. God's] praise" (l. 158), Pope applies it to the dangers of imperfect learning. Although the significance of the image in these texts is different from that in "The Pilgrimage" its *function* is similar in all three cases. Pope's words: "... from the bounded *Level* of our Mind, / *Short views* we take, nor see the *Lengths behind*" are in a way the most concise and pointed corollary of the situation in Herbert's poem.

5.2. Two hills.

What the quotations from Drummond and Pope have in common with Herbert's poem is the idea that the false perspective offered by a mountain range has the double effect of tempering man's ambitions and at the same time urging him on. But Drummond and Pope write about "heights" and "hills" in general terms, whereas Herbert is quite specific: his pilgrim has climbed one hill and realizes that he will have to ascend another — the final one. The idea will now be explored that the background to the number of two hills is religious and Scriptural.

54. "An Essay on Criticism," ll. 215-232, in Alexander Pope, *The Poems*, p. 151. The introduction of Pope here is not only justifiable because of the comparison with Drummond. Pope frequently used the emblems and iconography of an earlier age for his own purposes; cf. e.g. *The Dunciad*, Book IV: "When Reason doubtful, like the Samian letter, / Points him two ways, the narrower is the better" (ll. 151-52). The "Samian letter" is the letter Y, the *Litera Pythagorae* — Pythagoras was a native of Samos — , an emblem of the Choice of the Two Paths. Pope skilfully parodies the *bivium* tradition here.

35

The first example we shall consider is an emblem from a German emblem book, *Emblematum Ethico-Politicorum* ... by Jacob Bornitius (1664). The motto of the emblem is *Patria non nobis heîc est; quaerenda supernè / Hanc pete, sustuleris si grave Carnis onus,* paraphrased in German: "So dein Wandell im Himmel ist / Des Fleisches bürd leg ab zurüst." (see fig. 35)[55] The picture shows a pilgrim attempting to climb a ladder leading into the clouds from the top of a hill which he has ascended along a winding path. In the foreground we see another pilgrim, a staff in his hand, his hat on the ground and resting his burden on a low wall, while he overlooks the hilly landscape in front of him.

The motto of the emblem refers to Hebrews 11:13-16, quoted in section 3.4. Hebrews 11 is about faith and describes the tribulations which in the course of history the faithful in Christ have had to pass through without any certainty that they would be rewarded in the hereafter.

Faith is the common denominator of the emblem by Bornitius and Herbert's "The Pilgrimage." But the reason for their being compared here is the fact that they also have the aspect of the two hills in common.

55. Jacob Bornitius, *Emblematum Ethico-Politicorum sylloge prior (-posterior)* (Heidelberg, 1664), no. 6, sig. B2.

The source-texts for this aspect are also to be found in the Bible. One of them occurs in the next chapter of Hebrews where Mount Sinai is compared and contrasted with Mount Zion:

> For ye are not come unto the mount that might be touched, and that burned with fire, nor unto blackness, and darkness, and tempest,
> And the sound of a trumpet, and the voice of words; which voice they that heard intreated that the words should not be spoken to them any more.
> (For they could not endure that which was commanded, And if so much as a beast touch the mountain, it shall be stoned, or thrust through with a dart:
> And so terrible was the sight, that Moses said, I exceedingly fear and quake:)
> But ye are come unto mount Sion, and unto the city of the living God, the heavenly Jerusalem, and to an innumerable company of angels. (Hebrews, 12:18-22)[56]

In this passage Mount Sinai is presented as the epitome of the Law of the Old Testament whereas Mount Zion represents the Dispensation of Grace.[57] The terror instilled into man by "the mount that might be touched" is set off against the consolation of Mount Zion. The anagogical significance of the metaphor of the two hills is expounded in Galatians 4:22-26:

> For it is written, that Abraham had two sons, the one by a bondmaid, the other by a freewoman.
> But he who was of the bondwoman was born after the flesh; but he of the freewoman was by promise.

---

56. Cf. Gerhard Kittel, *Theologisches Wörterbuch zum Neuen Testament*, ed. Gerhard Friedrich, vol. 7 (Stuttgart: W. Kohlhammer Verlag, 1964), p. 285:

> ... Hagar = Sinai = jetziges Jerusalem. Diese Glieder sind dadurch zusammengehalten und zueinander in Beziehung gesetzt, daß von ihnen allen gemeinsam das Sklavesein ausgesagt wird. Der Bund vom Sinai übermittelt somit ein knechtendes Gesetz, das im oberen Jerusalem, in dem die Kinder der Freien leben und in dem die Freiheit waltet, nicht mehr gilt (Gal. 4:26-31). Damit ist der Bruch mit der jüdischen Überlieferung vollzogen und das Gesetz vom Sinai abgetan; denn Christus ist des Gesetzes Ende (Rom. 10:4).

In a note to this passage the special relation between Sinai and Zion for the Christian faith is explained:

> Die jüd Apokalyptik kennt den Gedanken einer Verbindung Sinai-Zion. Während aber in der Apokalyptik mit dieser Verbindung die Heiligkeit des Gottesberges ausgedrückt wird, ist für Paulus der Sinai nicht Stätte der Offenbarung Gottes, sondern die Gleichung Sinai = jetziges Jerusalem zeigt, daß das Gesetz knechtet.

57. Cf. Exodus, 19:12, 13:

> And thou shalt set bounds unto the people round about, saying, Take heed to yourselves, that ye go not up into the mount, or touch the border of it: whosoever toucheth the mount shall be surely put to death:
> There shall not an hand touch it, but he shall surely be stoned, or shot through; whether it be beast or man, it shall not live ...

> Which things are an allegory: for these are the two covenants; the one from the mount Sinai, which gendereth to bondage, which is Agar.
> For this Agar is mount Sinai in Arabia, and answereth to Jerusalem which now is, and is in bondage with her children.
> But Jerusalem which is above is free, which is the mother of us all.[58]

The chapters from Hebrews referred to above are about faith, "the substance of things hoped for, the evidence of things not seen" (Hebrews 11:1). The verses that lead up to the passage from Hebrews 12 just quoted explain that faith and patience are indispensable virtues for the pilgrim in his struggle with present tribulations:

> Now no chastening for the present seemeth to be joyous, but grievous: nevertheless afterward it yieldeth the peaceable fruit of righteousness unto them which are exercised thereby.
> Wherefore lift up the hands which hang down, and the feeble knees;
> And make straight paths for your feet, lest that which is lame be turned out of the way; but let it rather be healed. (Hebrews, 12:11-13)

These verses indicate how the idea of a pilgrimage through life in which the pilgrim encounters two mountains may be related to the apostolic teaching of the epistle to the Hebrews. The two mountains, Sinai and Zion, bear a typological relation to each other representing the covenant of Law and the covenant of Grace, respectively. The religious virtue involved is that of faith and the allegorical function of the two mountains in the pilgrimage is to make the pilgrim reach a state of true penitence on mount Sinai which will make him look forward to the ultimate fulfilment on top of mount Zion.

Spenser uses the typological relation between these two mountains in *The Faerie Queene*, I, x. In this canto the Redcross Knight is brought to the house of Holinesse, where "he is taught repentance, and / the way to heauenly blesse." He meets Dame Cœlia and her three daughters Fidelia, Speranza and Charissa, who represent the three Theological Virtues. Having endured the penitential trials in the house of Holinesse he recovers from his sins by "wise Patience, / and trew *Repentance*"; subsequently he is accompanied by Mercy, "an auncient matrone" and climbs the hill of Contemplation:

> That hill they scale with all their powre and might,
> That his frayle thighes nigh wearie and fordonne
> Gan faile, but by her helpe the top at last he wonne. (stanza 47)

58. Cf. Kittel, VII, 337:

Der Hebräerbrief stellt die διαθήκη vom Sinai der neuen, im Opfertode Jesu aufgerichteten διαθήκη gegenüber ... Der Weg des Gottesvolkes kommt von diesem Jerusalem her und führt dem himmlischen Ziel entgegen, das wiederum keinen anderen Namen trägt als Jerusalem.

After he has been introduced to Contemplation, "an aged holy man," the
latter leads the knight to a mountain:

> That done, he leads him to the highest Mount;
> Such one, as that same mighty man of God,
> That bloud-red billowes like a walled front
> On either side disparted with his rod,
> Till that his army dry-foot through them yod,
> Dwelt fortie dayes upon; where writ in stone
> With bloudy letters by the hand of God,
> The bitter doome of death and balefull mone
> He did receiue, whiles flashing fire about him shone.
>
> Or like that sacred hill, whose head full hie,
> Adornd with fruitfull Oliues all arownd,
> Is, as it were for endlesse memory
> Of that deare Lord, who oft thereon was fownd,
> For euer with a flowring girlond crownd:
> Or like that pleasant Mount, that is for ay
> Through famous Poets verse each where renownd,
> On which the thrise three learned Ladies play
> Their heauenly notes, and make full many a louely lay.
>
> From thence, far off he vnto him did shew
> A litle path, that was both steepe and long,
> Which to a goodly Citie led his vew;
> Whose wals and towres were builded high and strong
> Of perle and precious stone, that earthly tong
> Cannot describe, nor wit of man can tell;
> Too high a ditty for my simple song;
> The Citie of the great king hight it well,
> Wherein eternall peace and happinesse doth dwell.
>
> As he thereon stood gazing, he might see
> The blessed Angels to and fro descend
> From highest heauen, in gladsome companee,
> And with great ioy into that Citie wend,
> As commonly as friend does with his frend. (stanzas 53-56)[59]

There are three rather than two hills involved in this scene, viz. the hill of
Contemplation, the starting-point of this part of Redcross's journey; the
second, which is compared to Mount Sinai, the Mount of Olives and
Mount Parnassus, and finally the third on which the heavenly City is
situated, Mount Zion. Even though the number of hills is different in
Herbert's "The Pilgrimage," a comparison between Spenser and Herbert
is justified and relevant here. The first hill in "The Pilgrimage" shares its
most important characteristics with the first two hills in the passage from
The Faerie Queene. Like the hill of Contemplation its ascent is difficult

---

59. Spenser, *The Faerie Queene*, I, 135-36.

and serves a penitential purpose. But Herbert's first hill also affords the view that is only allowed to Spenser's knight after his second ascent. The two distinct experiences of the knight are telescoped into the single experience of the pilgrim. The consequence of this is that the ascent in Herbert's poem has the additional effect on the pilgrim of providing him with immediate and full insight into his own situation. The reader's attention is focused fully on the dramatic experience of the pilgrim and the mental process involved.

The absence of allegorical labels in the second half of Herbert's poem is one of the aspects that have the effect of 'internalizing' the events described. I have already commented on the striking difference between the first and the second half of the poem in this respect (see section 2 of this chapter). The comparison between Spenser and Herbert bears out this interpretation. Whereas Spenser offers a variety of possible comparisons which define the nature of the hills, Herbert does not do so at all. His hills remain hills and it is only because of the mysterious voice that the reader is reminded of the allegorical setting of the journey. In Herbert's poetry all the attention is directed to the pilgrim rather than to the pilgrimage. This conclusion is based partly on other aspects of the poem not yet discussed.

5.3. *"None goes that way/And lives."*

In most descriptions of ascents leading to a vision of Mount Zion or a promised land the pilgrim is aided by a guide or a guardian angel. Dante has his Virgil and Beatrice, Redcross has Mercy and Contemplation, Christian has Faithful and the shepherds. In "The Pilgrimage," too, the guardian angel is present but 'de-personified' as it were; he is referred to obliquely in "one good Angell," a gold coin with the device of St. Michael on it. The pun has been recognized before but its function in the total effect of the poem has not. This last point will be taken up in section 6.3.3. Here it will suffice to emphasize that the effect of the de-personification is to make the phrase "one good Angell" refer to stories and allegories outside the poem without disturbing its inner, psychological coherence.

Herbert's method and intention can also be seen at work in what one might call the 'displacement' of particular words and phrases. Compare, for instance, the use of the word "gladsome" in stanza 56 of the passage from *The Faerie Queene* discussed in the previous section with the occurrence of the same word in stanza 4 of "The Pilgrimage." In Spenser the word is used where it 'should' be; it is a fitting epithet for the company of angels that have their abode on Mount Zion. The word is unambiguous and straightforward. In "The Pilgrimage," on the other hand, there is a dramatic irony involved that is totally absent in Spenser.

The adjective "gladsome" is attributed by the pilgrim to the hill which he expects to be Mount Zion, or at least like Mount Zion, but which turns out to be something entirely different. The irony arises from the 'displacement' of "gladsome" from its appropriate position as an epithet of the second hill, to a qualification of the hill that does not prove "gladsome" at all.

Another instance of 'displacement' occurs in the final stanza when the pilgrim has overcome his temporary feeling of despondency and "flung away" towards the second hill. At that juncture a mysterious voice addresses him: "*None goes that way / And lives ...*"; the pilgrim, unabashed, takes this ominous pronouncement as a stimulus rather than a prohibition and pursues his way eagerly.

There are two comments to be made about the words of 'the voice.' In the first place we are not told who cries out to warn the pilgrim. This anonymity forms part of Herbert's poetic strategy. It is yet another element that helps to focus all the attention of the reader on the effect the cry has on the pilgrim. This is not to say that we should not at least attempt to identify the speaker, just as we tried to establish the names of the hills the pilgrim encounters in the course of his pilgrimage. By making the attempt one avoids a vagueness of interpretation that Herbert did not intend. After all, he could only afford to leave out the allegorical labels within a cultural milieu that was familiar with the allegorical method and the allegorical tools. Omission can only function as part of poetic strategy if the reader is aware of *what* has been left out or, to phrase it differently, what the poet could have put in but chose not to.

If we apply this argument to the cry in the final stanza of our poem, the fact that the speaker remains anonymous does not mean that the statement is made by an unidentifiable agent. It is incumbent on the modern reader to find out who is speaking in order to establish as precisely as possible what the poet's intentions must have been. Moreover, I submit that a determination of the specific meaning of this line will enable us to read the final lines of the poem more correctly, since there is a direct causal relation between those final lines and the warning statement that precedes them.

Apart from the anonymity of the cry, what strikes us in its wording is the resemblance between the commanding "None goes that way / And lives" and two texts from the Pentateuch. The first is Exodus 33:20, where God warns Moses: "... there shall no man see me, and live." The second is Deuteronomy 34:4 where God tells Moses just before his death that he will not be permitted to accompany his people into Canaan: "... I have caused thee to see it with thine eyes, but thou shalt not go over thither."[60]

60. In both instances Moses is on a mountain top. In Exodus on Mt. Sinai, in Deuteronomy on Mt. Nebo.

180

In a way the phrase in Herbert's poem is a conflation of the two Bible texts. It combines the generality and syntax of the first with the idea of pilgrimage of the second. The main difference is that, unlike the two analogical texts, Herbert does not use a verb expressing sense perception. Perhaps a verb of this kind would have been somewhat confusing at this stage of the poem's development; we argued earlier that there is a delicate balance between the phrases: "I travell'd on, *seeing* the hill ..." and "I rose, and then *perceiv'd* / I was deceiv'd" (emphasis added), where the spiritual progress of the pilgrim is reflected in the change from "see" to "perceive." The introduction of the verb "to see" into the final stanza would have obscured this aspect, whereas the verb "go" is perfectly in accordance with the physical progress of the pilgrim from hill to hill.

The juxtaposition of the Bible texts and the lines under discussion here not only suggests that the speaker is God but, more important, it helps us to establish a connection between the metaphor of the two hills and the tone of the final lines of the poem. The forbidding statement "None goes that way / And lives" belongs to the Old Testament, to the covenant of the Law. The reaction of the pilgrim, causally linked with God's words by the colon in l. 35, is not one of "desperate bravado."[61] It is a reaction of relief, coming as it does after that part of the poem in which the pilgrim has seen that his hill lay further and has continued on his pilgrimage with renewed courage.

The final four lines of the poem repeat, in different metaphors, the essential dichotomy of the poem. The second hill offers consolation and new hope for the pilgrim at a moment when he has almost succumbed to despair after the disappointment of his first ascent. In other words, it is the covenant of Grace that provides this consolation. The contrast between the two covenants is repeated in the final lines. First, the voice of God speaks as it had spoken to Moses on top of Mount Sinai which, as we saw previously, is the typological predecessor of Mount Zion. The pilgrim, who has come to recognize both the difference and the connection between those two hills, no longer doubts the glory awaiting him and he now takes death in his stride. The voice would have acted as a deterrent had the pilgrim not been aware of the redeeming quality of the New Dispensation. In order that God's words may function as an ultimate test of the extent of the pilgrim's faith Herbert 'displaced' them and put them at the end of the poem.[62]

61. Vendler, p. 97.
62. On the relation between 'the voice' and St. Michael see section 6.3.3. of this chapter.

6. "After so foul a journey death is fair."

6.1. Introductory.

One element that strikes the reader, or struck this reader at least, is the alliterating opposition "foul"/"fair" in l. 35 of the poem. The phrase has a proverbial air about it and reminds one, for instance, of the familiar "Fair is foul, and foul is fair" (*Macbeth*, I, i, 11). In the note to this line in the Arden edition Kenneth Muir refers to the proverbial nature of the phrase as it occurs in *Macbeth*.[63]

Herbert was an expert on proverbs and used or adapted them throughout his work. He was almost certainly connected with the compilation of *Outlandish Proverbs* (1640), one of the main collections of proverbs in the 17th century.[64] In *Outlandish Proverbs* the opposition fair (fine)/foul occurs several times:

> 119. To a fair day open the window, but make you ready as to a foule.
> 243. Fine dressing is a foule house swept before the doores.
> 829. No prison is faire, nor love foule.

In the poetry it occurs, besides the line in "The Pilgrimage," once more:

> Not a fair look, but thou dost call it foul.[65]

In most of these examples the opposition between "fair" and "foul" indicates what L.C. Knights, referring to the line in *Macbeth* quoted above, called a "reversal of values";[66] it can also indicate, I would add, a contrast between appearance and reality. This proverbial meaning applies very well to the phrase "After so foul a journey death is fair" in "The Pilgrimage." It would then mean something like: "The foulness of the journey behind me only serves to add a positive element to the death that awaits me," implying that, had the journey *not* been such a difficult one, death would have been more frightening and less attractive. The attitude of the pilgrim towards death is thus modified and newly defined by the penitential aspect of the journey. The journey is only "foul" if considered in isolation and, conversely, the value of the journey is modified by its outcome: a fair death. In this way the pilgrim's scale of values changes dramatically. By using a pair of words which have a proverbial ring Herbert brings home the Christian message in a pithy, economical way.

---

63. Kenneth Muir, ed., *Macbeth* (London: Methuen, 1964), p. 4. The note refers to the *Faerie Queene*, IV, viii. 32: "Then faire grew foule, and foule grew faire in sight."
64. See *Works*, pp. 568-573 on the connection between Herbert and the *Outlandish Proverbs*. The *Outlandish Proverbs* are included in *Works*, pp. 321-355.
65. "Conscience," l. 2 (*Works*, p. 105).
66. L.C. Knights, *Some Shakespearean Themes* (London: Chatto & Windus, 1959), p. 122.

182

The question that remains is, what does Herbert mean when he calls death "fair"? For an assessment of the significance of the poem as a whole it is essential to determine the attitude towards death it exhibits. I think that the attitude here is not ironical or bitter but simple and straightforward. The pilgrim accepts death, almost desires it at this stage of his pilgrimage. The final words of the poem are not cynical but express the pilgrim's faith. He has been instructed to do penance, he has renounced his worldly cravings and possessions and all this has been a preparation for the free surrender of life in order to reach a goal that lies, by definition, beyond death.

In "Mortification" Herbert writes:

> Yet Lord, instruct us so to die,
> That all these dyings may be life in death.[67]

Herbert is here writing in a time-honoured tradition, that of the *ars moriendi*. The line from "The Pilgrimage" makes much better sense, both in itself and in its relation to the rest of the poem, if it is viewed against the background of that tradition.

6.2. *Ars moriendi* and *contemptus mundi.*

Ars moriendi, the art of dying, originated in the late Middle Ages and was one of the manifestations of the concept of *memento mori* that was such a predominant element in medieval life, literature and the arts.[68] In

---

67. *Works*, p. 99, ll. 35-6. Cf. Donne, "Song":

> But since that I
> Must dye at last, 'tis best,
> To use my selfe in jest
> Thus by fain'd deaths to dye. (ll. 5-8)

John Donne, *The Elegies and the Songs and Sonnets*, ed. Helen Gardner (Oxford: Oxford Univ. Press, 1965), p. 31.
68. On *ars moriendi* see, for instance, W. Meredith Thompson, *Der Tod in der englischen Lyrik des siebzehnten Jahrhunderts* (Breslau: Priebatsch, 1936); Sister Mary Catherine O'Connor, *The Art of Dying Well: The Development of the Ars Moriendi* (New York: Columbia Univ. Press, 1942); J. Huizinga, *Herfsttij der Middeleeuwen* in *Verzamelde Werken*, III (Haarlem: Tjeenk Willink, 1949), 163-179; Martz, pp. 135-144; Robert G. Collmer, "The Meditation on Death and Its Appearance in Metaphysical Poetry," *Neophil.*, 45 (1961), 323-333; Chew, pp. 250-52; Philippe Ariès, *Attitudes toward Death: From the Middle Ages to the Present*, trans. Patricia M. Ranum (Baltimore: Johns Hopkins Univ. Press, 1975. Several English translations of Latin and French medieval treatises on the subject were collected and edited by Frances M.M. Comper in *The Book of the Craft of Dying and Other Early English Tracts Concerning Death* (London, 1917; rpt. New York: Arno Press, 1977). J.W. Lever mentions several 16th and 17th c. writings in the tradition in his edition of Shakespeare's *Measure for Measure*, rev. ed. (London: Methuen, 1965), p. lxxxvii.

literature and the arts *ars moriendi* coexisted with other offshoots of the *memento mori* philosophy such as the *contemptus mundi,* the *ubi sunt-*theme, the Triumph of Death and the Dance of Death, and the rhetoric of the gruesome physical aspects of death.[69] Frequently, two or more of these themes are found combined.[70] *Ars moriendi* functioned as a source of consolation that could be set off against the grim reality man was daily confronted with in the age of the Black Death. It was given great popularity in the 15th century by the illustrated blockbook editions that were among the earliest books in print.[71]

In its pure form the *ars moriendi* was "meant for the use of the clergy when attending the dying."[72] It described or depicted the temptations with which the devil confronts a dying person. Five temptations are involved: lack of faith, despair caused by sins, impatience and lack of charity, complacence or spiritual pride, and attachment to temporal things and worldly goods. Although the warding off of these five temptations invariably formed part of the *ars moriendi* texts, the main emphasis came to lie on the preparation for death by the dying person himself. The following quotation from *The Book of the Craft of Dying* may be considered characteristic and indicates the general state of mind expected of a man who wished to die well:

> And therefore every good perfect Christian man, and also every other man though he be imperfect and late converted from sin, so he be verily contrite and believe in God, should not be sorry nor troubled, neither dread death of his body, in what manner wise or for what manner cause that he be put thereto; but gladly and wilfully, with reason of his mind that ruleth his sensuality, he should take his death and suffer it patiently, conforming and committing fully his will to God's will and to God's disposition alone, if he will go hence and die well and surely: witnessing the wise man that saith thus: BENE MORI, EST LIBENTER MORI. To die well is to die gladly and wilfully.

The author of the treatise goes on to explain how the true Christian can *learn* to die properly:

> Furthermore, that a Christian man may die well and seemly, him needeth that he con [=learn to] die, and as a wise man saith: SCIRE MORI EST PARATUM COR SUUM HABERE, ET ANIMAM AD SUPERNA: UT QUANDOCUNQUE MORS ADVENERIT, PARATUM CUM INVENIAT UT ABSQUE OMNI RE-TRACTIONE EAM RECIPIAT, QUASI QUI SOCII SUI DILECTI ADVEN-TUM DESIDERATUM EXPECTAT. To con die is to have an heart and a soul

---

69. Huizinga, p. 163.
70. Huizinga discusses Chastellain's *Miroir de Mort* in which the horror of physical death is combined with the *ubi sunt*-theme, the Dance of Death and the *ars moriendi* (p. 175).
71. See A. Hyatt Mayor, *Prints & People: a social history of printed pictures* (Princeton, N.J.: Princeton Univ. Press), 23-25.
72. Hall, p. 32 *s.v.* "Ars moriendi."

ever ready up to Godward, that when-that-ever death come, he may be found all ready; withouten any retraction receive him, as a man would receive his well-beloved and trusty friend and fellow, that he had long abideth and looked after .... And so he should have his life in patience, and his death in desire, as *Saint Paul* had when he said: CUPIO DISSOLVI ET ESSE CUM CHRISTO. I desire and covet to be dead, and be with Christ.[73]

In these treatises the attitude towards death is one of acceptance, an acceptance that has to be learned. The need to acquire such an attitude is often emphasized by a contrast between the promise of life in the hereafter and the misery of life on earth.[74] Such a contrast is made, for instance, in the following passage from *The Art and Craft to Know Well to Die* (1490), chapter I: "Of the Allowing or Praising of the Death: and how one Gladly Ought for to Die":

> ... the bodily death of good people alway is none other thing but the issue, or going out, of prison and of exile, and discharging of a right grievous burden, that is to wit of the body; finishing of all things, and end of all maladies and sicknesses, and also of all other strifes mortal. It is the voiding of this present wretchedness; it is consumption of all evils, and the breaking of all the bonds of this cursed and evil world; it is the payment of the debt of nature, return into the country, and entry into joy and glory. Therefore saith the wise man: That the day of the death is better than the day of the birth. But this word ought to be understood for them that be good only.[75]

Contempt of the world makes death bearable and deflates its horrors.[76]

The *ars moriendi* and its precepts were not only set forth in the medieval treatises referred to. Throughout the sixteenth century books and tracts on the subject were published and in Herbert's century, too, there was a widespread interest in the subject of death and, more specifically, the process of dying.[77] In his *Anatomy of Melancholy* Burton reiterates some of the medieval ideas in his own peculiar idiom:

> *Excessi e vitae aerumnis facilisque lubensque*
> *Ne pejora ipsa morte dehinc videam.*

> I left this irksome life with all mine heart,
> Lest worse than death should happen to my part.

73. Comper, pp. 6-7 (first quotation); pp. 8-9 (second quotation).
74. The contrast between the miseries of the present life and the glory of the hereafter surfaces time and again in various guises. Here we are dealing with it under the colours of *ars moriendi*; in section 4.2. of this chapter it was discussed in relation with *post amara dulcia*.
75. Comper, p. 57. Cf. Donne, "Death be not proud": "And soonest our best men with thee doe goe, / Rest of their bones, and soules deliverie" (*The Divine Poems*, p. 9).
76. The basic text for the philosophy of the contempt of this world is Innocentius III, *De Contemptu Mundi sive de miseria conditionis humanae libri tres*, Migne, CCXVII.
77. The revival — no pun intended — of interest in death can be partly accounted for by the repeated outbreaks of the bubonic plague in the early decades of the 17th c.

Cardinal Brundusinus caused this epitaph in Rome to be inscribed on his tomb, to show his willingness to die, and tax those that were so loath to depart. . . . and so should we rather be glad for such as die well, that they are so happily freed from the miseries of this life. . . . And so for false fears and all other fortuite inconveniences, mischances, calamities, to resist and prepare ourselves, not to faint is best: *Stultum est timere quod vitari non potest*, 'tis a folly to fear that which cannot be avoided, or to be discouraged at all.

> *Nam quisquis trepidus pavet vel optat,*
> *Abjecit clypeum, locoque motus*
> *Nectit qua valeat trahi catenam.*

For he that so faints or fears, and yields to his passion, flings away his own weapons, makes a cord to bind himself, and pulls a beam upon his own head.[78]

As Martz points out in his study of seventeenth century English religious literature, the art of dying, together with the *Imitatio Christi*, were incorporated into the meditative exercises that were characteristic of the spiritual life of the period:

> Among all these instruments to self-knowledge, the most widely and intensely cultivated remains to be considered: the meditation upon death ... ideally, the devout man attempted to keep the thought of death forever in his mind, as the *Imitation of Christ* and the whole great tradition of the *Ars Moriendi* had urged ... it was a mode of meditation which, as Puente says, "is very profitable for all those, that walke in any of the three wayes, Purgative, Illuminative, and Unitive; wherein all men ought often to exercise themselves, though with different endes." For "Principiants," the aim is "to purge themselves of their sinnes"; for "Proficients," "to make hast to store up vertues"; for the Perfect, "to despise all things created, with a desire to unite themselves by love with their Creator."[79]

Ars moriendi was only acceptable within the confines of Christian principles.[80]

78. Robert Burton, *The Anatomy of Melancholy* (1621), ed. Holbrook Jackson (London: Dent, 1972), part 2; section 3; memb. V: "Against Sorrow for Death of Friends or otherwise, vain Fears, etc.," pp. 184-85.

79. Martz, pp. 135-36.

80. These principles are absent, for instance, in *Measure for Measure*, where the beginning of Act III is a subtle distortion of the *ars moriendi* and the *contemptus mundi* connected with it:

> *Cla.* The miserable have no other medicine
> But only hope:
> I have hope to live, and am prepar'd to die.
> *Duke.* Be absolute for death: either death or life
> Shall thereby be the sweeter. Reason thus with life:
> If I do lose thee, I do lose a thing
> That none but fools would keep. (III, i, ll. 2-8)

As Lever explains, the Duke's speech is wanting in spirituality and "is essentially materialist and pagan" (*Measure for Measure*, p. lxxxvii). Claudio's reaction

> Ay, but to die, and go we know not where;
> ... The weariest and most loathed worldly life

One of the best accounts of the influence of the *ars moriendi* on the way some people actually prepared for death in Herbert's day is to be found in Walton's *Lives*. Walton's description of the last few weeks of John Donne's life is probably the best known example of the *ars moriendi* put into practice.[81] Donne personally made the arrangements for his sepulchral monument and had a full-length painting made of his body in its winding-sheet to serve as a *memento mori* while he was still alive and as a model for the marble monument to be erected after his death. When the moment of death arrived, "as his soul ascended, and his last breath departed from him, he closed his own eyes; and then disposed his hands and body into such a posture as required not the least alteration by those that came to shroud him" (pp. 81-2). How much of this is fact and how much fiction it is hard to determine but one part of Donne's step by step preparations for his death has come down to us in his own words: the famous last sermon, preached by him at St. Paul's only a few weeks before his death. Walton describes the occasion with a proper sense of drama:

> And, when to the amazement of some beholders he appeared in the Pulpit, many of them thought he presented himself not to preach mortification by a living voice: but, mortality by a decayed body and a dying face. . . . after some faint pauses in his zealous prayer, his strong desires enabled his weak body to discharge his memory of his preconceived meditations, which were of dying: the Text being, *To God the Lord belong the issues from death*. Many that then saw his tears, and heard his faint and hollow voice, professing they thought the Text prophetically chosen, and that Dr. Donne *had preach't his own Funeral Sermon* (p. 75).

The sermon was entitled "Deaths Duell, or, A Consolation to the Soule, against the dying Life, and living Death of the Body." Excerpts cannot do justice to its magnificent eloquence, but for the purposes of this chapter

---

> That age, ache, penury and imprisonment
> Can lay on nature, is a paradise
> To what we fear of death. (III, i, ll. 117; 128-131)

gains in force when we read it as a parody of the *ars moriendi*. Without the art of dying that derives its significance from Christ's death and resurrection, death can hardly be other than frightening. Claudio has "hope to live" but he suffers from despair which in his case, unlike that of Herbert's pilgrim, is not counteracted by faith. Viewed in this light, Claudio's preparation for death is essentially different from the preparation that is part of the *ars moriendi* proper. The fact that Shakespeare could manipulate the tradition without fear of being misunderstood is proof of its being commonly known. Other instances in the play of the influence of *ars moriendi* are Isabella's entreaty in II, iv, ll. 39-41: "That . . . he may be so fitted / That his soul sicken not"; II, i, ll. 35-6; ". . . let him be prepar'd, / For that's the utmost of his pilgrimage"; II, ii, l. 85: "He's not prepar'd for death"; III, i, ll. 166-67: ". . . prepare your- / self for death"; II, iv, l. 186: "And fit his mind to death, for his soul's rest."

81. Walton, pp. 75-82.

those passages will be quoted that illustrate Donne's awareness of the *ars moriendi*:

> ... in this sense, this *exitus mortis*, this *issue of death*, is *liberatio per mortem*, a *deliverance by death*, by the death of this *God* our *Lord Christ Jesus*. And this is Saint *Augustines* acceptation of the words, and those many and great persons that have adhered to him.... *First*, then, we consider this *exitus mortis*, to bee *liberatio à morte* that with *God*, the *Lord* are the *issues of death*, and therefore in all our deaths, and deadly calamities of this life, wee may justly *hope* of a good *issue* from him; and all our *periods* and *transitions* in this life, are so many passages *from death* to *death*.... for wee come to *seeke a grave* ... Even the *Israel of God* hath no mansions; but journies, pilgrimages in this life. By that measure did *Jacob* measure his life to *Pharaoh*, *The daies of the years of my pilgrimage*. And though the *Apostle* would not say *morimur*, that, whilest wee *are in the body* wee *are dead*, yet hee sayes, *Peregrinamur*, whilest wee are *in the body*, wee are but in *a pilgrimage*, and wee are *absent from the Lord*.... If wee had not sinned in *Adam*, *mortality had not put on immortality*, (as the *Apostle* speakes) nor *corruption had not put on incorruption*, but we had had our *transmigration* from this to the other world, without any *mortality*, any *corruption at all*.... this *issue of death* is *liberatio in morte*, *Gods care* that the *soule* be *safe*, what *agonies* soever the *body suffers* in the *houre* of death.... That *Moses* and *Elias talkt with Christ* in the *transfiguration*, both Saint *Mathew* and Saint *Marke* tel us, but what they talkt of, only S. *Luke*, *Dicebant excessum eius*, says he, *they talkt of his decease*, *of his death*, which *was to be accomplished* at Ierusalem.... *Moses* who in his *Exodus* had *prefigured* this *issue of our Lord*, and in passing *Israel* out of *Egypt* through the *red Sea*, had foretold in that actual *prophesie*, *Christs passing* of *mankind through* the *sea* of his *blood*, and *Elias*, whose Exodus and issue out of this world was a figure of Christs ascension, had no doubt a great satisfaction in talking with our blessed Lord *de excessu eius*, of the full consummation of all this in his death, which was to bee accomplished at Ierusalem.[82]

"... all our *periods* and *transitions* in this life, are so many passages *from death* to *death* ... for wee come to *seeke a grave* ..." Donne writes, and "... whilest wee are *in the body* wee are but in *a pilgrimage*" and "... this *issue of death* is *liberatio in morte*, *Gods care* that the *soule* be *safe*, what *agonies* soever the *body suffers* in the *houre* of death." Words like these help the reader of "The Pilgrimage" understand the pilgrim's attitude at the end of the poem better. The case for the relevance of *ars moriendi* will be even stronger if the poet's own life and writings show signs of its influence.

6.3. Herbert and the *ars moriendi*.

To try and determine the relevance of the brief sketch of the *ars moriendi* and the texts exemplifying that tradition for the interpretation of "The Pilgrimage," the first, although perhaps not entirely reliable step,

82. John Donne, *The Sermons*, ed. Evelyn M. Simpson & George R. Potter, 10 vols. (Berkeley: Univ. of California Press, 1953-1962), X, no. 11 (Lent, 1630), pp. 229-248.

is to turn to Walton's *Life of Herbert*. Though we need not believe that every single word was actually spoken by Herbert, Walton's description clearly reveals his general attitude:

> ... *I do not repine but am pleas'd with my want of health; and tell him,* [Nicholas Ferrar] *my heart is fixed on that place where true joy is only to be found; and that I long to be there, and do wait for my appointed change with* hope *and* patience (Walton, p. 314).

> *I now look back upon the pleasures of my life past, and see the content I have taken in* beauty, *in* wit, *in* musick, *and* pleasant Conversation, *are now all past by me, like a dream, or as a shadow that returns not, and are now all become dead to me, or I to them;* ... *and I praise God I am prepared for it; and I praise him, that I am not to learn patience, now I stand in such need of it; and that I have practised Mortification, and endeavour'd to dye daily, that I might not dye eternally; and my hope is, that I shall shortly leave this valley of tears, and be free from all fevers and pain: and which will be a more happy condition, I shall be free from sin, and all the temptations and anxieties that attend it; and this being past, I shall dwell in the new* Jerusalem, *dwell there with men made perfect;* ... *But I must dye, or not come to that happy place: And this is my content, that I am going daily towards it; and that every day which I have liv'd, hath taken a part of my appointed time from me; and that I shall live the less time, for having liv'd this, and the day past* (Walton, p. 316).

The second passage is an example of the *ars moriendi* in its classic form: it shows the writer's determination to oppose the temptations besieging him. Herbert affirms his faith, expresses hope rather than despair, sets no store by worldly and temporal things, accepts his suffering and has learnt patience. Phrases like "I am prepared " and "I am not to learn ..." should be taken more literally than a modern reader is inclined to do. They refer to the actual practice of the art of dying. Another indication of the way Herbert prepared for death can be found in Barnabas Oley's account of Herbert's life in which he praises Herbert's "mortification of the body, his extemporary exercises thereof, at the sight or visit of a Charnell House ... at the stroke of a passing bell ... and at all occasions he could lay hold of possibly ..."[83]

A still more relevant source of information than these reports of Herbert's life is the poet's own work. We have already referred to one example of the art of dying in "Mortification" where the poet asks God to "instruct us so to die, / That all these dyings may be life in death." At this stage of our investigation it has become clear that the word "instruct" is not only a metaphor expressing God's influence over man but derives from the *ars moriendi* tradition and has a quite literal meaning as well. We also quoted several of the *Outlandish Proverbs* in which the 'fair death' of the *ars moriendi* occurs. In a number of poems the *ars moriendi* plays an important role, "Life," "Mortification," "A Dialogue-

---

83. Barnabas Oley, *Herbert's Remains* (London, 1652); qu. in Martz, p. 141.

Antheme," and "Church-monuments" being the most obvious examples.[84] "Church-monuments" is almost an *ars moriendi* in a nutshell. It is
the poetic counterpart of Donne's elaborate preparations for death:

> While that my soul repairs to her devotion,
> Here I intombe my flesh, that it betimes
> May take acquaintance of this heap of dust; ...
> ... Therefore I gladly trust
>
> My bodie to this school, that it may learn
> To spell his elements ...
>
> ... Mark here below
> How tame these ashes are, how free from lust,
> That thou mayst fit thy self against thy fall. (*Works*, pp. 64-5)

These examples not only substantiate the claim that Herbert was
acquainted with and made use of the *ars moriendi*, they also help us
understand in a general way how the notion 'fair' as used in "The
Pilgrimage" came to be associated with the phenomenon 'death.' A final
and more specific reason to emphasize the relevance of *ars moriendi* for
"The Pilgrimage" is that the "good Angell," who remains faithful to the
pilgrim in Herbert's poem, is reminiscent of the good angel in the
illustrations of the medieval *Ars moriendi*, who rescues the dying man
from each of the five temptations.[85]

It is illuminating to compare Herbert's attitude towards death with
that shown in the passages quoted from Donne's "Deaths Duell."
Donne's attitude towards death, whose grimness he does not deny
elsewhere in the sermon, is made plausible by the example of Christ's
death and the idea of the *Imitatio Christi*.[86] In Herbert's work, too, the
ars moriendi is invigorated by the *Imitatio Christi* but it is expressed in a
vocabulary and tone that are usually quite distinct from Donne's. The
connection between the death of Christ and the art of dying is the theme
of "Death":

84. "A Dialogue-Antheme" is reminiscent of Donne's usual way of writing about
death. See, for instance, "Death be not proud" (*Divine Poems*, p. 9).
85. See Mayor, 23-5: "The illustrations show devils tempting the dying man to
doubt, despair, anger, pride, and greed, from each of which his good angel rescues
him. In the eleventh illustration he has passed his examination and dies in grace." One
could even argue that each of the five temptations specified in the *Ars moriendi* plays a
part in "The Pilgrimage," too: Despair and Pride are overcome in the first stanza,
attachment to worldly goods is tested in the third, impatience or anger is present in the
fourth and fifth and lack of faith or doubt in the fifth stanza.
86. The highly influential treatise *The Imitation of Christ* was known in 16th c.
England by the translation of Richard Whitford (*c.* 1530), which formed the basis of
later, 17th c. translations. See Martz, pp. 285-87. On the connection between the
Imitation of Christ and *ars moriendi* see Martz, p. 136.

> But since our Saviours death did put some bloud
>   Into thy face;
>   Thou art grown fair and full of grace,
> Much in request, much sought for as a good.
>
> For we do now behold thee gay and glad,
>   As at dooms-day;
>   When souls shall wear their new aray,
> And all thy bones with beauty shall be clad.
>
> Therefore we can go die as sleep, and trust
>   Half that we have
>   Unto an honest faithfull grave;
> Making our pillows either down, or dust. (ll. 13-24; *Works*, p. 186)

The picture of death that Herbert draws here is quite different from that suggested in Donne's last sermon. There is an element of acquiescence in the poet's attitude that is absent in Donne. Donne's sermon and Herbert's poem share the idea that death is a liberation from life, but the comely appearance of Death belongs to Herbert's vision rather than to Donne's.

"Thou art grown fair and full of grace," Herbert writes. The meaning of the word "fair" here is different from that discussed before. In proverbial usage it means something like "gentle" or "unobstructed," here it means "beautiful." Once the gruesome aspect is toned down, the way is open for presentations of death as a desirable thing or even, when death is personified, as an attractive young man. Martz defines the difference between Donne's and Herbert's ways of approaching death as follows:

> It is hard to see how meditations on death could be farther apart in mood and tone than are the poetical meditations of Donne and Herbert on this subject. In all Herbert's poems on death there is no trace of fear or horror at the prospect, but a calm, mild acceptance of the inevitable ... But in Donne's "Holy Sonnets" we feel the depravity of the "feeble flesh" — with a consequent fear and horror of judgment, deliberately evoked: even in his "Death be not proud" there is a tone of stridency, almost of truculence — a sense of daring to stand up to the terror. The treatment of death by these two poets is, I think, typical of the way in which, whatever the topic of meditation may be, each poet develops the common tradition along lines suited to his own personality, his own spiritual needs, and also, perhaps, according to the different schools of spirituality in which each poet has been trained or in which he has found his fundamental affinity.[87]

Martz's summary is succinct and convincing. I have added to Martz's analysis an account of the conventions or conventional images that were available to Herbert and that lie behind his definition of the differences

---

87. Martz, pp. 143-44. See also Arnold Stein, *George Herbert's Lyrics* (Baltimore: Johns Hopkins Univ. Press, 1968), pp. 37-43.

between the two poets. The "calm, mild acceptance of the inevitable" that characterizes Herbert's attitude towards death and finds an outlet both in the description of death's appearance in "Death" and in the peculiar structure of the phrase "After so foul a journey death is fair," can be attributed to the *ars moriendi*. When we study the particular way in which this attitude took shape in these two examples two emblematic images, both closely related to the *ars moriendi*, come to mind: *Dulce amarum* and *desiderans dissolvi*.

6.3.1. *Dulce amarum.*

In the course of our discussion of the ascent of the hill we already touched on the motto *dulce amarum*, although in a slightly different form. This 'bitter-sweet,' although it fits in very well with the *ars moriendi* tradition, had its own development and acquired its own characteristics. We have already discussed one of its manifestations in which it is tied up with the pilgrimage of life and presented as a temporal cause and effect relationship: *post amara dulcia*. The image also occurs in a non-temporal, absolute form, as the oxymoron *dulce amarum*. The Greek equivalent of the term, γλυκύπικρον, derives from Sappho and was introduced into the Neoplatonic vocabulary of the Renaissance by Ficino:

> Love is called by Plato bitter (*res amara*), and not unjustly because death is inseparable from love (*quia moritur quisquis amat*). And Orpheus also called Love γλυκύπικρον, that is, *dulce amarum*, because love is a voluntary death. As death it is bitter, but being voluntary it is sweet. *Moritur autem quisquis amat*....[88]

In "Amor as a God of Death," the chapter from Wind's *Pagan Mysteries in the Renaissance* to which I owe the above quotation, Wind argues that the frequent mythological love scenes enacted between gods and human beings on Roman sarcophagi were explained by Neoplatonists as illustrations of the classical equation of Love with Death. In these scenes death appears to be the communion with a god through love. Wind writes:

> Conversant with the idea of Eros as a power that loosens or breaks the chains that bind the soul to the body, the Renaissance antiquarians may also have had a more correct understanding of the *Éros funèbre* than some of the great archaeologists of the recent past who ... thought of Eros in a funerary context as representing only 'life after death,' the 'joys of the blessed.' The Renaissance identified him with Death itself, in its painful no less than its joyous aspect, as is shown so clearly on the Roman sarcophagi which represent the agonies inflicted on Psyche by Eros as a prelude to their ultimate embrace. A god of pain and sadness he remained, but no persistent terror could be attached to Death if he appeared in the image of Amor.[89]

88. From Edgar Wind, *Pagan Mysteries in the Renaissance,* rev. ed.(Harmondsworth: Penguin, 1967), p. 161.
89. Wind, pp. 160-61.

The fact that Love and Death could merge in this way makes the iconography of Death in Herbert's poem "Death" less eccentric than it may appear to be at a first reading. I have not been able to find visual representations that resemble the description of death suggested by the poem. I assume therefore that its background is literary rather than visual and suggest, tentatively, that the description of death as an attractive young courtier fits in very well with the Neoplatonic tradition that equates Death with Love.

Although this brief sketch of *dulce amarum* is specifically useful for "Death," it is applicable to "The Pilgrimage" too, but in a more general way. The line "After so foul a journey death is fair" should be explained in terms of the pilgrimage of life. In such a context *dulce amarum* almost naturally rephrases itself as *post amara dulcia* and assumes the nature of a penitential journey. Jürgen Hahn, writing about *Everyman* in his remarkably lucid study *The Origins of the Baroque Concept of Peregrinatio*, states:

> Everyman may, by performing an ascetic *peregrinatio vitae*, reduce the length of his *peregrinatio mortis*, and mitigate its rigor.... The artistic presentation of the awareness of death preoccupied medieval writers profoundly, and it could take a variety of forms ... one could view it with Christian resignation as a kindly agent, as did Jorge Manrique.... The devout Christian ... should always regard death as imminent and maintain a constant state of preparedness.[90]

Although Hahn does not mention the concept of *post amara dulcia* as such he quotes several examples in which it is clearly present. For example:

> He who has not travelled, what has he seen? He who has not seen, what has he accomplished? He who has accomplished nothing, what has he learned? And what can he call rest, who has never [experienced the vicissitudes of] fortune on sea or on land? For as Ovid says, he who has not tasted bitterness does not deserve the sweet things. Nor has he who never returned into the arms of a friend after a long absence had a truly pleasant day in his homeland.[91]

In this translation of part of *El peregrino en su patria* by Lope de Vega (1562-1635) *dulce amarum* has become an essential aspect of the pilgrimage of life.

Dulce amarum and *post amara dulcia* are to be found, then, in a variety of texts and it would not be easy to pinpoint the exact source of Herbert's use of them in "The Pilgrimage." On the other hand we may safely assume that at least part of the difference in the treatment of death between Donne and Herbert is to be attributed to the fact that the *dulce*

90. Jürgen Hahn, *The Origins of the Baroque Concept of Peregrinatio* (Chapel Hill: Univ. of North Carolina Press, 1973), pp. 128-29.
91. From Lope de Vega Carpio, "El peregrino en su patria," in *Colección de las obras sueltas* (Madrid, 1776), V, 453; qu. in Hahn. pp. 83-4.

amarum tradition must have been more congenial to Herbert than it was to Donne. Herbert even used the phrase "Bitter-sweet" for the title of one of his poems (*Works*, p. 171).

Another interesting observation that can be made when we compare Donne's last sermon with "The Pilgrimage" is the fact that both authors combine the concepts of the pilgrimage of life and the *ars moriendi*. Donne quotes two Bible texts that bring these concepts together, 2 Corinthians 5:6 and Genesis 47:9:

> Even the *Israel of God* hath no mansions; but journies, pilgrimages in this life. By that measure did *Jacob* measure his life to *Pharaoh, The daies of the years of my pilgrimage*. And though the *Apostle* would not say *morimur*, that, whilest wee *are in the body* wee *are dead*, yet hee sayes, *Peregrinamur*, whilest wee are *in the body*, wee are but in *a pilgrimage*, and wee are *absent from the Lord*.[92]

Hahn devotes a chapter of his book to the pilgrimage of life. In a section of the chapter entitled "The Biblical Origin of Peregrinatio Vitae" he quotes 2 Corinthians 5:6-9 and continues:

> For St. Paul, then, the *peregrinatio vitae* is a disagreeable condition, which he would gladly overcome in any way he could.

Then Hahn quotes from the *Confessions* of St. Augustine: "Where were you then [Lord] and how far away? For I strayed far from you ..."[93] After quoting from other parts of the *Confessions* Hahn concludes:

> ...as long as man lives in his earthly *peregrinatio*, distant from God, he remains handicapped, because his senses are inadequate instruments of cognition. His perspective is dulled; everything appears to him as if through a glass darkly (p. 119).

St. Augustine is always to be regarded with special attention when one is dealing with Herbert.[94] The following passage is particularly helpful as background to "The Pilgrimage":

> But as yet we are light *with faith* only, not *with a clear view* (II Cor. 5:7). For *our salvation is founded upon the hope of something. Hope would not be hope at all if its*

---

92. The combination of pilgrimage and *ars moriendi* also occurs, for instance, in *Measure for Measure*, the play quoted from before:

> Ang.   See that Claudio
> Be executed by nine tomorrow morning;
> Bring him his confessor, let him be prepar'd,
> For that's the utmost of his pilgrimage. (II, i, ll. 33-6)

93. St. Augustine, *Confessions*, III, 6; qu. in Hahn, p. 118. Previous quotation. Hahn, p. 117.

94. St. Augustine's works form one of only two book bequests in Herbert's will mentioning the author's name (*Works*, p. 382). About the influence of St. Augustine on Herbert's work see Mark Taylor, *The Soul in Paraphrase: George Herbert's Poetics* (The Hague: Mouton, 1974), p. 4; pp. 21 ff.

object were in view (Rom. 8:24).... Even Paul ... tells us that *he does not claim to have the mastery already but forgetting what he has left behind and intent on what lies before him* (Philipp. 3:13), *he goes sighing and heavy-hearted* (II Cor. 5:4). *His soul thirsts for the living God, as a deer for running water*, and asks *Shall I never again make my pilgrimage into God's presence* (Ps. 41:3,4 (42:2,3). *He longs for the shelter of that home which heaven will give him* (II Cor. 5:2) (from *Confessions*, XIII, 13).

Faith, hope and pilgrimage are the elements these quotations and Herbert's poem have in common. *"Hope would not be hope at all if its object were in view"* could well serve as a motto for the first half of the poem, while the rest of the last quotation helps to understand the kind of attitude adopted by the pilgrim towards the end.

We have seen that the preparation for death that is part of the *ars moriendi* was frequently connected with the pilgrimage of life, and that the impetus of the zealous pilgrim's resolve to overcome his hardships was strengthened by the notion of *post amara dulcia*. When we consider the way the pilgrim surrenders to his impending death another conventional image comes to mind that is likewise interwoven with the art of dying: *desiderans dissolvi*.

6.3.2. Desiderans dissolvi.

Desiderans dissolvi is based on two Bible texts, both Paulinian: Romans 7:24: "O wretched man that I am! who shall deliver me from the body of this death?" and Philippians 1:23: "For I am in a strait betwixt two, having a desire to depart, and to be with Christ." We have encountered this notion in several of the texts quoted to illustrate the tradition of the art of dying. In the three passages quoted last in the previous section it is clearly present and in an earlier quotation from the *Book of the Craft of Dying* St. Paul's words *"Cupio dissolvi et esse cum Christo"* were used (see section 6.2.).

In texts and pictures illustrating the idea that physical death is a desirable thing the role of Death is radically different from that assigned to him in the *triumphus mortis* representations that were so popular in the Middle Ages. Instead of the cruel taskmaster that he had been for so long Death now becomes a helpful servant to man. Chew quotes John More who wrote in *A lively Anatomie of Death* (1596) that Death is "a packhorse to carry [Man] from earth to heaven, from pain to pleasure, from misery, vexation, grief and woe, to endless mirth."[95] In *Emblemes, ou Devises Chrestiennes* (1571) by Georgette de Montenay one emblem

95. *The Pilgrimage of Life*, p. 251. The section of Chew's book in which this quotation occurs is entitled "Death as a Release from Life" (pp. 250-52). It contains several other examples in which Death fulfils a servant's function and presents a "fair" rather than a "foul" aspect.

36

actually bears the motto "Desiderans dissolvi" (see fig. 36).[96] The
emblem's subject is the soul's desire to depart from this life and in it
Death has become a kind helper who assists man on his passage from
earthly life to the life eternal. The text explains that fear of death
disappears when man's desire to join God is sufficiently great and his
heart pure:

> Crainte de mort en son endroit n'a lieu,
> Ainsi qu'elle a au coeur sale & immonde.
> La mort n'est plus au Chrestien sainct & monde
> Qu'un doux passage à conduire à la vie
> Et vray repos, où toute grace abonde.

The picture shows Man in the act of stepping quite literally out of the
world assisted by Death while on the left a steep path leading up the
Heavenly Hill is clearly visible.

Two emblems from Wither's emblem book are relevant here. In the
emblem that bears the circular motto "Mors Vitae Initivm" ("Death is

96. De Montenay, p. 89.

the beginning of life") Wither refers in the following lines to the famous text of I Corinthians 15:55:

> The Venom'd *Sting* of *Death* is tooke away;
> And, now, the *Grave*, that was a Place of *Feare*,
> Is made a *Bed of Rest*, wherein we may
> Lye downe in *Hope*, and bide in safety, there. (p. 21)

We find here several of the ingredients that, though in a different order and with a different emphasis, occur in "The Pilgrimage": the fear, the sting, the 'fair' representation of death, who leads man to a "Bed of Rest" reminding one of Herbert's "chair."

In the other emblem Wither, or rather the excellent engraver, shows the human soul using the skull and the hourglass, death's attributes, as stepping-stones while he keeps his eye fixed devoutly on heaven. The accompanying text explains that faith should nullify our 'human fears' and that the distance between life and death as it is imagined by the human pilgrim is commensurate with the extent of his faith:

> Why, with a trembling faintnesse, should we feare
> The face of *Death*? and, fondly linger here,
> As if we thought the *Voyage* to be gone
> Lay through the shades of *Styx* or *Acheron*?
> Or, that we either were to travell downe
> To uncouth *Deapthes*, or up some heights unknowne? ...
> It is not by one halfe that distance, thither
> Where *Death* lets in, as it is any whither:
> No nor by halfe so farre, as to your bed;
> Or, to that place, where you should rest your head,
> If on the ground you layd your selfe (ev'n there)
> Where at this moment you abiding are. (p. 152)

Death is treated as a servant here, the doorkeeper of Heaven.[97] It is noteworthy that in both of Wither's emblems the attitude towards death is influenced by the promise of a *quieta sedes* afterwards.

The reversal of the roles of man and death that is the consequence of the idea of *desiderans dissolvi* is characteristic of the *ars moriendi*. Montaigne, whose essays were well known to the Elizabethans through the famous English translation by John Florio, wrote an essay entitled

---

97. Wither's emblem is reminiscent of one of Greville's *Caelica* poems (LXXXII):

> You that seek what life is in death,
> Now find it air that once was breath.
> New names unknown, old names gone:
> Till time end bodies, but souls none.
> Reader! then make time while you be,
> But steps to your eternity.

Fulke Greville, *Selected Poems*, ed. Thom Gunn (London: Faber, 1968), p. 113.

"That to Philosophie, is to learne how to die." In this essay he writes about the liberating power of the *ars moriendi*:

> ... the premeditation of death, is a forethinking of libertie. He who hath learned to die, hath unlearned to serve.... To know how to die, doth free us from all subjection and constraint. (I, xix)[98]

Montaigne also analysed extensively the relation between *ars moriendi* and *desiderans dissolvi*. In another essay (II, iii) the idea of death as a good to be sought is defended, not only to stimulate acceptance of death but more particularly the voluntary seeking of death by suicide:

> *Death is a remedy against all evils*: It is a most assured haven, never to be feared, and often to be sought: All comes to one period, whether man make an end of himselfe, or whether he endure it; whether he run before his day, or whether he expect it: whence soever it come, it is ever his owne, where ever the threed be broken, it is all there, it's the end of the web. The voluntariest death, is the fairest. *Life dependeth on the will of others, death on ours.*[99]

"The voluntariest death is the fairest," says Montaigne. "After so foul a journey death is fair," says Herbert. On the surface both the wording and the tone of Herbert's line seem to resemble Montaigne. There is a basic difference between the two, however; from the Christian point of view Herbert's words are based on the religious virtue of Faith, but Montaigne's tend dangerously towards the deadly sin of Despair.[100]

The view of death expressed by Montaigne, stoical rather than Christian in origin, was very much part of the times. In the Elizabethan age the concept of *desiderans dissolvi* frequently led to a somewhat morbid attitude towards death. It was the age of the 'Elizabethan malady' which is described so exhaustively in Robert Burton's *Anatomy of*

---

98. John Florio, trans., *Montaigne's Essays* (1603), 3 vols. (London: Dent, 1910), I, 80.

99. Florio/Montaigne, II, 27. In the same section Montaigne refers to Paul's words: "But a man doth also sometimes desire death, in hope of a greater good. I desire (saith Saint *Paul*) to be out of this world, that I may be with *Jesus Christ*: and who shal release me out of these bonds?" (p. 39).

100. Montaigne was himself aware that this interpretation could be attached to his words: towards the end of his account of suicide, which mainly consists of vivid descriptions from the classics, he writes:

> *Cleombrotus Ambraciota* having read *Platoes Phaeton*, was so possessed with a desire and longing for an after-life, that without other occasion or more adoe, he went and headlong cast himselfe into the sea. Whereby it appeareth how improperly we call this voluntarie dissolution, despaire; unto which the violence of hope doth often transport us, and as often a peacefull and setled inclination of judgement. (Florio/Montaigne, II, 39-40)

Four centuries after they were written Montaigne's words still have a surprisingly fresh ring. But they are un-Herbert-ian. Cf. also the Duke's speech to Claudio in *Measure for Measure*, III, i, mentioned in a previous note (n. 80).

Melancholy (1621).[101] Burton himself committed suicide and Donne wrote the first English defence of suicide, *Biathanatos*. It is most interesting to find identical terms often being used in texts that, as far as their moral intention is concerned, are diametrically opposed. I have juxtaposed Herbert's poem and Montaigne's essay to bring out this phenomenon. Another example is the verbal correspondence between the emblem "Desiderans dissolvi" by Montenay quoted from above and the following passage from *The Faerie Queene*:

> He there does now enioy eternall rest
> And happie ease, which thou doest want and craue,
> And further from it daily wanderest:
> What if some litle paine the passage haue,
> That makes fraile flesh to feare the bitter waue?
> Is not short paine well borne, that brings long ease,
> And layes the soule to sleepe in quiet graue?
> Sleepe after toyle, port after stormie seas,
> Ease after warre, death after life does greatly please. (I, ix, 40)

Spenser repeats Montenay's text almost literally but with a moral intention directly opposed to hers, since the passage is part of the scene in which Despair tries to tempt the Redcross Knight to kill himself. The difference is one between a legitimate desire to die in order to achieve a further, spiritual goal on the one hand and giving in to an illegitimate death-wish on the other. As C.S. Lewis puts it:

> ... in the heavier temptation of Despayre we hear the death-wish itself, which underlies this whole form of evil. He invites St. George to 'enjoy eternall rest And happie ease' (I, ix, 40) — an invitation that is grounded on a subtle perversion of the ideal of resignation.[102]

Elsewhere Lewis distinguishes between a "true" and a "false rest" (p. 95), apropos of the words of Una's father to the Knight:

> But since now safe ye seised haue the shore,
> And well arriued are, (high God be blest)
> Let vs deuize of ease and euerlasting rest. (I, xii, 17)

101. See also Lawrence Babb, *The Elizabethan Malady: A Study of Melancholy in Elizabethan Literature from 1580 to 1642* (East Lansing: Michigan State Univ. Press, 1951); Rudolf and Margot Wittkower, *Born under Saturn* (New York: Norton, 1969); Rosalie L. Colie, *Paradoxia Epidemica* (Princeton, N.J.: Princeton Univ. Press, 1966). These books discuss melancholy and deal with suicide in that context. A useful modern study of suicide is A. Alvarez, *The Savage God* (London: Weidenfeld & Nicolson, 1971). More immediately analogous with "The Pilgrimage" is the 17th c. 'guide' by William Denny, *Pelecanicidium: or the Christian Adviser against Self-Murder. Together with A Guide, and the Pilgrims Passe To the Land of the Living* (London, 1653). The book is also of some interest to our investigation because in the final canto the Holy Hill is described in hill-shaped stanzas (see Chew, p. 224n. 55).
102. C.S. Lewis, *Spenser's Images of Life*, ed. A. Fowler (Cambridge: Cambridge Univ. Press, 1967), pp. 70-1.

The fact that both positive and negative attitudes could be expressed in the same vocabulary shows that the traditions on which these texts are based were expected to be known to the reader. If the reader is not acquainted with an essentially stoic and pagan background on the one hand and a Christian, Paulinian one on the other, it will be much more difficult for him to distinguish the intentions of Montenay, Montaigne, Spenser and Herbert in the texts we have been discussing.

The ideas described in this section had a great influence on the religious poetry of the early 17th century. I have several times referred to Donne's last sermon, in which the poet used all his rhetorical powers to draw a picture of the contrast between the more gruesome aspects of death and the dissolution of the body on the one hand and the hope of the resurrection and recomposition of the new body in Christ on the other. In some of his poems the gruesome aspect is emphasized less and *ars moriendi* and *desiderans dissolvi* are presented more pleasantly:

> From rest and sleepe, which but thy pictures bee,
> Much pleasure, then from thee, much more must flow,
> And soonest our best men with thee doe goe,
> Rest of their bones, and soules deliverie.
> ("Death be not proud," ll. 5-8)

> As virtuous men passe mildly away,
> And whisper to their soules, to goe,
> Whilst some of their sad friends doe say,
> The breath goes now, and some say, no:

> So let us melt, and make no noise ...
> ("A Valediction: forbidding Mourning," ll. 1-5)

In the former of these quotations the central idea is that of death as a release from life. In the latter matters are slightly more complicated. The situation described in this initial comparison of the poem is the exact counterpart of the final stage of the *Ars moriendi* when the dying person, surrounded by his friends, commends his soul into the hands of God. When the comparison is resolved at the beginning of the second stanza in the phrase "So let us melt...," the focus subtly shifts from the religious implications of the first stanza to the profaner implications of the poem as a whole. The subtlety resides in the word "melt" — the literal translation of the Latin 'dissolvere' — , an appropriate metaphor both for death and love.[103] *Ars moriendi* and *ars amandi* meet in these lines and *desiderans dissolvi* is the mediating agent between the two.

---

103. The comparison between death and love in "A Valediction: forbidding Mourning" is reminiscent of the equation of love and death in the *dulce amarum* motif in the Neoplatonic philosophy that was discussed in section 6.3.1. of this chapter.

6.3.3. St. Michael.

One final loose strand of our investigation remains to be picked up: that of the function within the poem as a whole of the good angel that had been tied to the pilgrim's side by "a friend." At this stage we are better equipped to determine that function than when we first discussed the line in which the "good Angell" is mentioned (see section 1.2.). One of the functions traditionally attributed to St. Michael, the archangel depicted on the coin called 'angel' was to accompany and conduct the soul to the other world. He was also often associated with pilgrimages, which is shown iconographically by his sometimes wearing a shell, a common pilgrim's attribute.[104] The phrase "ti'd / Close to my side" that Herbert uses in connection with the angel is perhaps reminiscent of the pilgrim's custom of carrying a scallop shell. At any rate St. Michael is associated with pilgrimages and with the *peregrinatio mortis* in particular.[105] St. Michael is also the appropriate guardian for the pilgrim who travels up hills.[106] One of the prayers in *The Book of the Craft of Dying*, to be said by those attending the dying person, is about the role of St. Michael:

SAINT MICHAEL, the ARCHANGEL of our Lord Jesu Christ, help us at our high Judge. O thou most worthy giant and protector, that mayst never be

104. Cf. Réau, *Iconographie de l'Art Chrétien*, II, i, 47: "Comme saint Jacques, il a pour attribut des *coquilles* à cause du pèlerinage maritime du *Mont-Saint-Michel*. Le plastron de sa cuirasse affecte parfois la forme d'une coquille; see also E. Droulers, *Dictionnaire des Attributs, Allegories, Emblèmes et Symboles, s.v.* "Michel."

105. Hahn points out that the term *peregrinatio mortis* is problematical because "life" and "death" are ambiguous notions in Christian thought (Hahn, p. 126n.).

106. St. Michael is in fact associated with three phenomena that are constituent elements of Herbert's poem: hills, pilgrimage and death. Emile Mâle summed up the various tasks and functions of St. Michael thus:

Throughout the Middle Ages he was held to be the conductor of souls to the other world, the saintly psychagogue. Anxious to divert to St. Michael the worship which the still pagan inhabitants of Roman Gaul paid to Mercury, the Church early endowed the archangel with almost all the attributes of the god. On the ruins of ancient temples of Mercury, built generally on a hill, rose chapels dedicated to St. Michael .... St. Michael, already the messenger of heaven, became like Mercury the guide of the dead. The funeral rôle of St. Michael is attested by ancient custom. Cemetery chapels were dedicated to him and the confraternities instituted to bury the dead recognised him as patron. He is sometimes found carved on sepulchral monuments, sometimes on the tombs. Finally, from mediaeval times the offertory in the Mass for the Dead expressly says: "Signifer sanctus Michael repraesentet eas (animas) in lucem sanctam." St. Michael, as we see, is the angel of death, and it is in virtue of this that he presides at the Last Judgment.

Emile Mâle, *The Gothic Image: Religious Art in France of the Thirteenth Century*, trans. Dora Nussey, from the 3rd French ed. (1913; rpt. New York: Harper, 1972), pp. 377-78.

overcome, be nigh to our brother, thy servant, labouring now sore in his end; and defend him mightily from the dragon of hell, and from all manner guile of wicked spirit. Furthermore we pray thee, that art so clear and so worthy a minister of God, that in the last hour of the life of our brother thou wilt receive the soul of him easily and benignly into thine holy bosom; and bring her into (the) place of refreshing and of peace, and of rest. AMEN[107]

The fact that Herbert's pilgrim is guarded by such a mighty agent is one more justification for his confident attitude towards death; if he is aided by St. Michael himself no mysterious voice can scare him away at this stage of his pilgrimage.[108] The "good Angell" should not merely be regarded as a pun; the words point forward to the end of the poem. The fact that St. Michael is sometimes associated with Moses makes his presence even more apposite in a poem that hinges on the relation between Mount Sinai and Mount Zion.

6.4. Conclusion.

The line "After so foul a journey, death is fair" should be understood both in the context of Herbert's own work and in the wider context of the culture of his time.[109] If our argument is correct the main concepts relevant here are *ars moriendi, dulce amarum* and *desiderans dissolvi*. A recognition of the notion *dulce amarum* is equally essential for the interpretation of the ascent of the hill. This is not surprising since Herbert refers explicitly to that part of his pilgrimage at the end of the poem. After all, he does not just say that "death is fair," but he calls death fair "after so foul a journey." The poem is closely knit indeed; the metaphors and the tone may change but, although this may not be apparent at first sight, the underlying concepts remain the same.

7. Death's chair.

The final words of "The Pilgrimage" have caused some critical and etymological confusion. Death is called "but a chair." But how are we to understand "chair"? Three possible interpretations have been offered. The first is Hutchinson's. In a note to another Herbert poem, "Mortification," l. 29: "A chair or litter shows the biere" he writes:

Cf. *The Pilgrimage*, p. 142, l. 36. The use of the word *chair* has more point when it is

107. Comper, pp. 42-3.
108. Cf. "And I heard a loud voice saying in heaven ..." (Rev. 12:10), part of the Epistle read on the feast of Saint Michael and all Angels (September 29). Michaelmas must have had a special significance for Herbert, since, as Dr. Broeyer tells me, it is the traditional opening day of the academic year at Cambridge.
109. Or, formulated along Panofskian lines, both on the second level of interpretation and on the third.

202

remembered that in Herbert's day it was a symbol of old age: e.g. 'thy chair-days' in Shakespeare, *II Henry VI*, v.ii.48, and *I Henry VI*, iv.v.4-5:

> When saplesse Age, and weake vnable limbes
> Should bring thy Father to his drooping Chaire.

Herbert's thought is anticipated by Southwell, 'Upon the Image of Death,' stanza 5:

> The gowne that I do use to weare,
>   The knife wherewith I cut my meate,
> And eke the old and ancient chaire
>   Which is my onely usuall seate:
> All these do tel me I must die,
> And yet my life amend not I. (*Works*, p. 512)

Hutchinson equates the meaning of the word "chair" in "Mortification" with that in "The Pilgrimage" and concludes that in both cases the chair is related to old age.

Patrides, in his edition of Herbert's poetry, adds the following note to the final line of "The Pilgrimage": "*chair*: literally a sedan-chair, a comfortable mode of transport" (p. 152). Like Hutchinson he compares the chair in "The Pilgrimage" to that in "Mortification," but, unlike Hutchinson, he sees the chair as a vehicle rather than a seat.

Almost simultaneously, but probably independently of Patrides, Morillo wrote a short article in which he rejects the reading of "chair" as a sedan-chair:

> Later, of course, "chair" is the familiar term for "sedan," but the closed chair on poles as a fashionable mode of urban transport was new in 1634 — the year after Herbert's death — when a patent was granted to Sir Sanders Duncombe for a monopoly in supplying the vehicles for use in London streets."[110]

Morillo agrees with Hutchinson and Patrides that the word "chair" has the same meaning in "Mortification" as in "The Pilgrimage," but his way of arriving at this conclusion is different:

> The idea of motion seems to me confirmed in the alternatives of "chair *or* litter." While "chair" alone might be taken as the hearthside seat that "shows" (is emblematic of) the bier, the alternative "litter" directs attention certainly to "conveyance."

And he goes on to show by means of parallels that "chair" should be regarded as a variant of "litter":

> [the] use of the term to mean "a kind of litter" is readily documented by reference to Shakespeare. In *Othello*, V, i. 82-3 and 98-99, Iago twice calls for a chair for the wounded Cassio: "Oh for a Chaire / To beare him easily hence." Similarly in *King*

110. Marvin Morillo, "Herbert's Chairs: Notes to *The Temple*," *ELN*, 11 (June, 1974), 271-75; this qu. p. 274.

Lear, IV, vii. 21, a First Folio stage direction calls for Lear's entrance *"in a Chaire carried by Servants."*

If we sum up these three comments they all agree in their assumption that the words "chair" in "Mortification" and in "The Pilgrimage" refer to the same thing. Hutchinson thinks that the chair is a chair of rest; Patrides and Morillo think it refers to a vehicle; Patrides believes it to be a sedan-chair, whereas Morillo argues that it is a kind of litter.

The first point I wish to call in question is the equivalence of the chairs in the two poems. Hutchinson's interpretation fits "Mortification" better than it does "The Pilgrimage." In "Mortification" and in the other examples given by Hutchinson the chair of old age is seen as a prefiguration of death: "A chair or litter shows the biere, / Which shall convey him to the house of death" ("Mortification," ll. 29-30). In other words, the chair of old age is not identical with the bier that will transport the dead body to the grave but it is a preparation for death. The word "shows" is part of the idiom of the art of dying that comes out most clearly in the final lines of the poem:

> Yet Lord, instruct us so to die,
> That all these dyings may be life in death.

In "The Pilgrimage," on the other hand, the chair is not presented as a preparation for death as it was in "Mortification" and in the passage from Southwell quoted by Hutchinson. In "The Pilgrimage" the chair is a metaphor of death itself. In the examples Hutchinson quotes as analogies Old Age is the subject of the passages in which the image of the chair occurs. This is not the case in "The Pilgrimage." Although the poem contains the pilgrimage of life in a nutshell it is not presented in terms of the Ages of Man. "The Pilgrimage" describes a penitential journey and it is within that context that the word "chair" should be understood. "After so foul a journey, death is fair, / And but a chair," Herbert writes. Not the element of age but that of suffering is decisive here.

The other interpretation, of "chair" as a moveable object, a vehicle, is not very convincing either. Patrides' suggestion of the sedan-chair seems to be ruled out by Morillo's observation that that type of vehicle was not known in Herbert's lifetime. Morillo's defence of his own idea is rather an odd one, however. He argues that the phrase "chair or litter' in "Mortification" indicates that the chair is more or les synonymous with the litter. But the conjunction "or" does not invariably indicate synonymity. Moreover, the line hardly makes sense if "chair" and "litter" are supposed to refer to one and the same thing. Why would Herbert depart from his customary economy of phrase? The word "chair" loses all its power when it refers to just another kind of "litter." I agree with Hutchinson that the chair in "Mortification" is the "hearthside chair."

Although both "chair" and "litter" point forward to the same phenomenon — death — they mean different things. The former implies immobility, the latter movement. The chair refers to the immobility of old age which is a sign of the immobility of the body in the "house of death." "Litter" refers to the infirmity that accompanies old age and points forward to "bier." "Chair" and "litter" together form a perfect *memento mori*: immovable Age is moving towards Death.

Having established that "chair" does not mean "litter" in "Mortification," we still have to consider the possibility that the word has that meaning in "The Pilgrimage." These are Morillo's concluding remarks:

> It seems to me clear, then, that since journeys provide the allegorical terms for both poems and since abundant evidence indicates that "chair" in that context would be readily understood as designating a conveyance for royalty, the sick, wounded, or the feeble aged, Hutchinson's note summons an image of the hearthside chair that is inconsistent with the controlling conceit of both poems.

Unfortunately, Morillo's interpretation is incompatible with one of the basic aspects of "The Pilgrimage." Herbert's pilgrim is not a king, he is not ill or wounded, nor is there any suggestion that he belongs to the "feeble aged." On the contrary, the pilgrim has just "flung away," which hardly suggests infirmity.

Morillo says that the meaning "a kind of litter" is not listed among the possible meanings of "chair" in the *OED*. This is true. There is, however, another meaning of chair, which *is* listed in the *OED*, but which, as far as I know, has never been suggested as a possible meaning for the chair in "The Pilgrimage," namely that of "chariot." This meaning of "chair" was still current in Herbert's day, though it has become obsolete since.[111] The examples listed in the *OED* indicate that the word "chair" with this particular meaning is used often in a religious context indicating a means of transport to Heaven. All this would seem to be relevant to Herbert's poem. I submit that the "chair" in "The Pilgrimage" could be regarded as a chariot that serves to convey the soul to Heaven after the death of the body.

Of the source texts mentioned in the *OED* three refer to 2 Kings, 2:11:

> And it came to pass, as they still went on, and talked, that, behold, there

---

111. This is the relevant lemma in the *OED*:

†*Chair. sb.*[2] *Obs.* or *arch.* [Variant of Char, assimilated in spelling to prec.; perhaps associated with it also in meaning] A chariot or car. *c.*1374 Chaucer *Anel.&Arc.*39 Emelye ... Faire in a chare [*Shirley MS.* chaier] of gold he with him lad. 1480 Caxton *Chron.Eng.*II(1520)14/1 Helyas ... was lyfted up into paradye ... in a chayre .... 1559 T. Bryce in Farr's *S.P. Eliz.* (1845)I.164 When worthy Web and George Roper In Elyes' chayre to heauen were sent .... 1814 Scott *Ld. of Isles* V.xiv, Like a prophet's fiery chair ... travelling the realms of air.

appeared a chariot of fire, and horses of fire, and parted them both asunder; and Elijah went up by a whirlwind into heaven.[112]

In another Bible text, Habakkuk 3:8, God's chariot is called the chariot of salvation:

> Was the Lord displeased against the rivers? was thine anger against the rivers? was thy wrath against the sea, that thou didst ride upon thine horses and thy chariots of salvation?

In Joshua Sylvester's translation of Du Bartas (1605) the chariot is connected with faith:

> Faith sits *Triumphant* on a Carr of gold, ... (Canto I, st. 5)

> Her glorious Charret's rowling wheeles are like
> The holy wheeles the great *Ezechiel* saw; ... (st. 6)

> Next, *Charitie*, that kindly doth prefar
> Her neighbours good before her owne vtilitie:
> *Repentance*, *Hope*, and harty-milde *Humilitie*,
> Doo flanke the wings of *Faiths* triumphant Carr. (st. 15)

> *Elisha's* Faith brought from the lofty Skies,
> Bright fiery Charrets 'gainst the Syrrian hoast; ... (Canto IV, st 14)[113]

Not infrequently the chariot of salvation is found associated with the pilgrimage of life. One of the poems in Sebastian Brant's *Narrenschiff* bears the title "Von dem Weg der Sellikeit."[114] The poem is accompanied by a woodcut showing a dunce pulling a cart. The text makes a distinction between the cart of worldly goods, which is a superfluous obstacle and the chariot of salvation that awaits the pilgrim in Heaven. Whereas the connection between Brant's poem and Herbert's is perhaps rather tenuous, there are other examples which make it more likely that Herbert intended his "chair" to be understood as a chariot. In an emblem book by Benedictus van Haeften, *Regia Via Crucis* (1635), we see a picture of the human soul, called Staurophila ('she who loves the cross'), seated in a chariot drawn by Divine Love on its way to the Heavenly

112. See also 2 Kings 6:17: "And Elisha prayed, and said, Lord, I pray thee, open his eyes, that he may see. And the Lord opened the eyes of the young man; and he saw: and, behold, the mountain was full of horses and chariots of fire round about Elisha." These are the same chariots and horses that appear in Zechariah 6:1-3 and in Psalm 68:17, one of which came down to fetch Elijah.
113. "The Triumph of Faith," in Joshua Sylvester, trans., *Bartas His Devine Weekes and Workes* (1605), pp. 543-577.
114. "On the Road of Salvation." Thus in Zeydel's modern translation from the German original, pp. 170-71. In Barclay's rendering the "cart of syn" is mentioned, not the chariot of salvation (I, 230-33). Both in Brant and Barclay the poem contains passages about the Choice of the Two Paths (see also section 4.1. of this chapter).

Quadrigæ tuæ, faluatio.   *Hab.* 3, 4.

Quam tuleram, tulit hęc me CRVX: CRVCI *et*
   ipsa volucres
Adde rotas; ſi vis currere, currus erit.

37

Jerusalem (see fig. 37).[115] Not only does Staurophila hold a cross in her right hand, the axle and pole of the chariot form a cross as well.

Van Haeften's emblem book is a *vita humana* in the form of a *peregrinatio* and the arrangement of the emblems reflects the progress of the human soul. Both the place of this emblem in the emblem book and the text accompanying the picture — which, by the way, has the text from Habakkuk as a motto — indicate that death is the moment when the soul is transported from earth to Heaven by means of the chariot of salvation. This transition from earth to Heaven is essentially different from the other transitions in human life, since those depend largely on the human will, whereas the final journey to Heaven depends on God's grace. Divine Love is the intermediary between the human soul and God at the moment of transition. The idea of death as a chair/chariot becomes all the more plausible when we consider it in relation to the chariot of salvation, which carries the soul from this earth to the hereafter.

In the second part of *The Pilgrim's Progress* the motif of death combined with the chariots of salvation also occurs, although Christiana's death as Bunyan describes it is a grander affair than that of the pilgrim in Herbert's poem:

> Now the day drew on that Christiana must be gone. So the road was full of people to see her take her journey. But behold all the banks beyond the River were full of horses and chariots, which were come down from above to accompany her to the City Gate.

Some time after Christiana had thus departed from the land of the living, one of her companions, Mr. Ready-to-halt, who goes on crutches, is sent for by God:

> When he came at the brink of the River, he said, 'Now I shall have no more need of these crutches, since yonder are chariots and horses for me to ride on.'[116]

In *The Pilgrimage of Life* Chew mentions another type of chariot that also serves to transport the human pilgrim to Heaven. Chew gives the following description of the 'pilgrim's progress' in *Mundorum Explicatio* (1661):

> Patience is his attendant ... Deceit, "a twy-fac'd Hag," attempts to direct him into the wrong path, but Truth guides him aright and shows him a picture of the heavenly Jerusalem, after which Zeal carries him in his chariot. He is vouchsafed a vision of Sophia, the Holy Wisdom, and at length he meets Death and passes into the "Locus Purgatorius inter Mundus" and thence to Paradise (p. 225).

In this instance the chariot of salvation is associated with the religious zeal of the pilgrim.

115. Benedictus van Haeften, *Regia Via Crucis* (Antwerp: Plantin, 1635), III, xi, 378-79.
116. Bunyan, II, pp. 367-68.

39

38

All these chariots have a common function in "translating" the human soul from its temporary abode to its heavenly destination. All of them, moreover, operate *post mortem*. In both respects the chariots are analogous to the "chair" in Herbert's poem. In other respects, however, they are not quite so similar. The analogue to Herbert's poem we should really like to see is a representation of Death in which Death has a subservient position comparable to that in the emblem by Montenay entitled "Desiderans dissolvi" (see fig. 36) or in the quotation from John More's *A lively Anatomie of Death* where Death is called a "packhorse" (see section 6.3.2. of this chapter). Also, the poem demands a representation in which the human soul is seated in a chair/chariot transporting it to Heaven. Such representations do exist. La Perrière's emblem book *La Morosophie* (Lyon, 1553) contains an emblem showing the Soul in a chariot, laurel-wreathed (see fig. 38).[117] Chew describes the emblem thus:

> The coachman of the chariot is Death and it is drawn by the bees signifying Virtue for "the actions of the just," in Shirley's famous words "smell sweet and blossom in the dust."[118]

The picture is accompanied by a quatrain:

> Voycy (Lecteur) engin victorieux
> Et triumphant, pour la fin de ce liuvre:
> C'est y celuy, qui surpasse les Cieux,
> Et qui nous fait après le trespas viure.

In a quite different context the chariot occurs in Johann Mannich's *Sacra Emblemata* (Nürnberg, 1624). The emblem in question bears the motto "Periculum Vehiculum," paraphrased in German: "Durch Todtes gfahr / Zur Himmels schaar" (see fig. 39).[119] The picture shows a woman with a newly born child in her arms and seated in a chariot drawn by Death. The poem is a consolation for women who die in giving birth. They are holy: "Drumb liebes weib gedulde dich / Stirbst du denn / so stirbst seliglich." The Latin verses underneath the picture affirm the supremacy of faith over death:

> Si tibi mors adstat: noli diffidere. Christo
> Fide modo; & fies, ecce, beata fide.[120]

---

117. Guillaume de la Perrière, *La Morosophie* (Lyon, 1553), sigs. O8ᵛ and P.

118. Chew, p. 251. Has the "sting / Of swarming fears" of Herbert's poem been replaced by the bees of Virtue?

119. Johann Mannich, *Sacra Emblemata LXXVI in quibus summa uniuscuiusque Evangelii rotunda adumbratur* (Nürnberg, 1625), pp. 84-5.

120. Cf. 1 Tim. 2:15, referred to in the emblem's motto: "Notwithstanding she shall be saved in childbearing, if they continue in faith and charity and holiness with sobriety."

The arguments suggested would seem to support quite strongly an interpretation of the "chair" in "The Pilgrimage" as a vehicle or, more precisely, a chariot of salvation. When death is regarded as a release from life, as it is in "The Pilgrimage," it turns out to be a vehicle assisting our passage to salvation rather than the formidable opponent of other contexts.

8. Conclusion.

This analysis has shown that "The Pilgrimage" is a more complex poem than would appear at first sight. The poem forms a unity that is controlled by a few clearly defined, interrelated concepts. The contrasts in the poem are subtly balanced and operate at several levels: the levels of subject-matter, vocabulary, direction and tone. As we have seen, the sources and analogues that serve as a backdrop to the poem are mainly of a verbal nature. References to visual material, however, have helped to elucidate at least two crucial aspects of the poem: the two hills and death's chair. "The Pilgrimage" is a poem written by an erudite poet for an erudite audience. It does not yield its riches easily. But that more is meant than meets the eye is not only implied in the poem but is also true of the poem as a whole.

CHAPTER FIVE

A STUDY OF "LOVE (III)"

Love (III)

Love bade me welcome: yet my soul drew back,
    Guiltie of dust and sinne.
But quick-ey'd Love, observing me grow slack
    From my first entrance in,
Drew nearer to me, sweetly questioning,
    If I lack'd any thing.

A guest, I answer'd, worthy to be here:
    Love said, You shall be he.
I the unkinde, ungratefull? Ah my deare,
    I cannot look on thee.
Love took my hand, and smiling did reply,
    Who made the eyes but I?

Truth Lord, but I have marr'd them: let my shame
    Go where it doth deserve.
And know you not, sayes Love, who bore the blame?
    My deare, then I will serve.
You must sit down, sayes Love, and taste my meat:
    So I did sit and eat.

0. Introductory.

With the exception of "The Collar" no poem of Herbert's has been so widely anthologized and has received so much critical attention in the course of this century as the final poem of *The Church*: "Love (III)."[1] The poem has been analysed much more frequently than the poems whose study formed the core of the preceding chapters. This fact has some obvious consequences for the structure and content of this chapter. For one thing

---

1. In most of the major anthologies since Grierson's the poem was included. In Roberts, *George Herbert: An Annotated Bibliography,* "The Collar" is discussed in 64 items, which is by far the highest score; "Love (III)" comes second with 39 items; then come "The Church-porch" with 35 and "Vertue" with 31 items. The limitation of scope that applies to Roberts' book are, of course, reflected in my arithmetics.

it means it can be considerably shorter, for another that the emphasis will fall more exclusively than in the other chapters on an aspect that, as it happens, has received relatively little scholarly/critical attention: an analysis of the imagery of the senses in "Love (III)." By way of introductory orientation this study of "Love (III)" will begin with a provisional, cursory reading of the poem, a short survey of earlier comments on it and a discussion of a recent interpretative dispute between two major Herbert critics.

0.1. "Love (III)."

The situation described in "Love (III)" is based on Luke 12:37: ". . . verily I say unto you, that he shall gird himself, and make them to sit down to meat, and will come forth and serve them."[2] Ryley, one of the earliest commentators of Herbert's work, pointed out that the subject of the poem is most probably the soul's reception into Heaven rather than a communion on earth.[3] The main basis for this assumption is the place of the poem in both *W* and 1633. "Love (III)" is the last lyric of *The Church* and concludes the sequence of poems that treat of the final stages of the pilgrimage of life: "Death," "Dooms-day," "Judgement," and "Heaven." If one accepts a reading of *The Temple* as the record of the Christian's life, Ryley's interpretation of the significance of the place "Love (III)" occupies in the whole structure certainly seems acceptable.

The poem describes a dramatic moment: the soul's pilgrimage has come to an end, the pilgrim is on the threshold of Heaven. The ensuing dialogue between the weary traveller, covered with the dust of his journey, and the host, welcoming him at Heaven's door, is full of gentle irony. The two play out a debate of hesitation and persuasion, of remorse and consolation. Hesitation is apparent in such phrases as "my soul drew back," "observing me grow slack / From my first entrance in," and "Ah my deare, / I cannot look on thee." The persuasive attitude of Love, the host, shows both in his actions and his speech: "Love bade me welcome," "quick-ey'd Love, observing me ... Drew nearer to me, sweetly questioning," "Love said, You shall be he," "Love took my hand," etc. The hesitation of the soul in pilgrimage arises from feelings of remorse about his "sinne," a sense of being unworthy because of his actions on earth which makes him complain: "I cannot look on thee." The consoling words of Love "Who made the eyes but I?" introduce the decisive

2. See Summers, pp. 88-89.
3. John M. Heissler, "Mr. Herbert's Temple and Church Militant Explained and Improved by a Discourse Upon Each Poem Critical and Practical by George Riley, 1714-15. A Critical Edition," 2 pts. Diss. Univ. of Illinois 1960. Summers rediscovered and reformulated Ryley's criticism in his book on Herbert (1954).

argument: "And know you not, sayes Love, who bore the blame?",
referring to the redeeming function of Christ's Passion. The soul/
traveller finally gives in and expresses his desire to join the banquet to
which he has been invited, but in a humble position: "I will serve." Once
again, however, his request is denied, because Love wants to act as host
and serve his guest, which is in accordance with the prophecy of Luke
12:37. At the end of the poem the soul does the only thing left for him to
do and sits down to eat Love's meat. The resignation of the pilgrim to
Love's will is expressed in the laconic way characteristic of the endings of
many of Herbert's poems: "So I did sit and eat": six short monosyllabic
words.

The debate, as I said, is gently ironic. The atmosphere of mildness is
established by such words as "Drew nearer," "sweetly," "took my hand"
and "smiling." The irony is most noticeable in the two lines: "Love took
my hand, and smiling did reply, / Who made the eyes but I?" and in the
rhetorical question: "And know you not, sayes Love, who bore the
blame?" Apart from these instances of verbal irony, the basic irony, if we
may call it that, is situational and arises from the paradoxical fact that,
precisely because none of the soul's expressed wishes are granted, he
finally receives what he came for: the heavenly repast.

If we follow the poem stanza by stanza, it may be briefly summarized
as follows: In the first stanza the attention is mainly focused on the timid
and hesitant way in which the soul enters Heaven and the host-like
behaviour of Divine Love; the timidity and hesitation are expressed in
terms of movement. In the second stanza the soul's unworthiness is
emphasized and presented dramatically by reference to the senses. When
the soul declares its moral unfitness in "I cannot look on thee," standing,
we imagine, in front of Love with a bowed head Love approaches the
pilgrim and re-encourages him through the sense of touch: "Love took
my hand." The transition from the one point of view to the other is thus
smoothly made and the verbal argument vivified by the concreteness of
the situation. At the end of the stanza the imagery of sight recurs; the
connection between sight and Love is strengthened by the assonance in
"Who made the eyes but I?" The third and final stanza is concerned with
sin, redemption and communion. The soul, having "marr'd" his eyes,
asks for the punishment due to him on that account. Love refers to the
Sacrifice and reminds the soul that He has burdened Himself with the sins
of mankind by His Passion. By the end of the poem the soul is ready and
has adopted the proper attitude for Heavenly Communion.

1. "Love(III)" and criticism.

In the Herbert criticism of this century "Love (III)" occupies a
prominent position. The poem has generally been judged favourably,

although sometimes for incongruous reasons. One critic, for example, calls it "one of the most exquisitely simple poems in English about Holy Communion,"[4] but most commentators have made it their concern to unravel the complex of allusions, traditions and sources that underlie the simple surface structure of the poem. In 1975 Helen Vendler summed up the most important findings of earlier scholars and added a persuasive statement of her own:

> ... even in such a brief poem as *Love* (III), Herbert's originality in transforming his sources, in re-inventing his topic, strikes us forcibly. We know that the poem depends on St. Luke's description of Jesus' making his disciples sit while he served them; and on the words of the centurion transferred to the Anglican communion service, "Lord, I am not worthy that thou shouldst enter under my roof"; and on Southwell's *S. Peter's Complaint*, in which St. Peter knocks on sorrow's door and announces himself as "one, unworthy to be knowne." We also know, as Summers first made clear, that Herbert's actual topic is the entrance of the redeemed soul into Paradise. Now, so far as I know, this entrance has always been thought of as an unhesitating and joyful passage, from "Come, ye blessed of my father" to "The Saints go marching in." The link between St. Peter knocking at a door and a soul knocking at St. Peter's door is clear, but it is Herbert's brilliance to have the soul give St. Peter's abject response, while standing hesitant and guilty on the threshold, just as it is a mark of his genius to have the soul be, instead of the unworthy host at communion, the unworthy guest in heaven.[5]

In addition to Vendler's brief account two critical issues in the various commentaries strike me as particularly relevant to my own investigation; the Petrarchist quality sometimes attributed to the poem and the relation to it of the Catechism.

1.1. Petrarchism,

In 1938 Ford Madox Ford remarked on the "Petrarchist-Christist" note of Herbert's poetry; in 1960 Elizabeth Stambler elaborated the idea of a connection between the tradition of the volumes of courtly love poetry and *The Temple*:

> ... I am led to a discussion of ways in which *The Temple* as a whole resembles a volume of courtly love poetry — the *Vita Nuova*, Petrarch's *Rime*, *Astrophel and Stella* — as individual poems of *The Temple* resemble lyrics of the courtly love tradition. I find these resemblances in several important details and in two fairly large general themes, the theme of loss and the theme of discipline which brings the protagonist at last to a condition of purified desire.[6]

---

4. Elizabeth Jennings, "The Seventeenth Century," in *Christianity and Poetry*, Faith and Fact Books, 122 (London: Burns & Oates, 1965), pp. 48-63; this ref. p. 54. I owe this and several subsequent references to Roberts' *Annotated Bibliography*.
5. Vendler, p. 55.
6. Ford Madox Ford, *The March of Literature: From Confucius' Day to Our Own* (New York: Dial Press, 1938); Elizabeth Stambler, "The Unity of Herbert's 'Temple'," *Cross Currents*, 10 (1960), 251-66, rpt. in *Essential Articles for the Study of George*

215

Stambler continues by comparing the protagonists of these collections with Herbert's *persona* and the title of Herbert's collection with the symbolic titles of the volumes of love poetry. The most interesting part of her essay consists of a comparison between chains of images in the courtly love books and in *The Temple*, particularly those images that have to do with the *cor gentil*. At the end of her essay Stambler writes about "Love (III)":

> *The Temple's* last poem, 'Love (III)' is very close in spirit to the mystical dream of the feast of love in the *Vita Nuova*. It is appropriate that 'Love (III)' should stress the image of purified eye and heart which first appeared in 'Love (I) and (II)'. . . . Desire, not fulfillment, is the emotional sense of the poem; its strength is its delicate, precarious, and tentative intrusion of the human heart and senses into absolute purity. The multitude of meanings in this poem are finally embraced in one: 'Love (III)' completes the protagonist's discipline of the gentle heart. (pp. 349-50)

Before commenting on the analogies suggested by Ford and Stambler I would like to juxtapose them with another, typically twentieth century reaction to the poem. In 1969 Robert Bagg argued that the primary appeal of the poem "is the almost geisha-like care and thoughtfulness of Love; shyness and unworthiness before Christ is felt as unworthiness in an encounter full of sexual ambience."[7] Bagg suggests that Christ's power is expressed metaphorically in the poem by his appearing to the protagonist as a woman in a dream to alleviate his sexual anxiety. This Freudian interpretation, idiosyncratic as it may seem and irritating in its phraseology, does not stand entirely on its own. In a contribution to *The Explicator* (1978) Greg Crossan suggests the possibility of a sexual interpretation in which "drew back" and "growing slack" supposedly refer to sexual impotence on the part of the speaker; "serve" means "to serve in a sexual capacity" and "taste my meat" can be paraphrased as "enjoy my flesh." Crossan's gloss ends:

> The point of the analogy is that both physical and spiritual love require a purgation of guilt-feelings before there can be consummation or atonement (at-one-ment), and it is to my mind one of the most striking and apposite of all metaphysical minglings of love human and love divine.[8]

These sexually oriented interpretations are to a certain extent supported by a piece of more or less contemporary evidence. Herbert's poem was perhaps parodied by Rochester in a poem entitled "Woman's Honor," the first line of which reads: "Love bade me hope, and I obeyed." The rest of the poem does not bear any resemblance to "Love

Herbert's Poetry, ed. John R. Roberts (Hamden, Conn.: Archon Books, 1979), pp. 328-350. This qu. pp. 329-30.
7. Robert Bagg, "The Electromagnet and the Shred of Platinum," *Arion*, 8 (1969), 407-29; this qu. p. 428.
8. Greg Crossan, "Herbert's Love (III)," *Expl.*, 37 (Fall, 1978), 40-41.

(III)."[9] Jeremy Treglown (1973) suggests that Rochester changed the purely Platonic relationship between the protagonists in Herbert's poem into a sexual one.[10] If Treglown is right, this means that Rochester, writing only some forty years later than Herbert, was conscious of Herbert's using an idiom bordering on the erotic. But of course even if Rochester parodied a poem by Herbert in this particular way that does not turn "Love (III)" into a poem "full of sexual ambience." Nor does the resemblance "in spirit" to the poetic cycles of courtly love turn "Love (III)" into a poem about courtly love, or *The Temple* into such a cycle. Stambler, as we saw, relates the imagery of the senses in Herbert's "Love" poems to the 'cor gentil' of the courtly love tradition. In itself the comparison is interesting, but when viewed in the light of literary history and genre one plausible link in Stambler's argument is found to be missing. We must realize that by the time Herbert began to write poetry, the use of profane motifs and a profane vocabulary for sacred purposes had become a stock procedure. Had "Love (III)" been written by a different author, in an earlier age, the relevance of the courtly love poem as a model might have been greater. When Herbert uses these profane elements in the context of the religious lyric of the early seventeenth century, however, the obvious model is no longer the courtly love poem but the sacred emblem book.

There is much more reason to assume a connection, direct or indirect, between the imagery of Herbert's "Love" poems and the sacred emblem books of the *Amor/Anima* and *Schola Cordis* type, than to assume one with a tradition more remote and with connections more oblique.[11] It seems to me that neither the connection with the courtly love cycles assumed by Stambler and Ford nor the ambiguity attributed to the poem by Bagg and Crossan is likely to have been part of Herbert's intention in "Love (III)."

Erskine, the only literary critic who has made an extensive study of the imagery of the senses in Herbert's work, also comments on the relationship between courtly and divine love:

> ... the courtly love tradition as a whole is related to the loving relation between God and the Soul, in which God is the wooer. Just as the various "Laura's" were at

9. John Wilmot, Earl of Rochester, *The Complete Poems*, ed. David M. Vieth (New Haven: Yale Univ. Press, 1968), p. 14.
10. Jeremy Treglown, "The Satirical Inversions of Some English Sources in Rochester's Poetry," *RES*, 24 (1973), 42-48.
11. On the relation between Herbert and the School of the Heart tradition see Colie, *The Resources of Kind* (1973), pp. 48-67. In *English Emblem Books* Freeman suggested the possibility of a connection between "Love (III)" and the Amor/Anima emblem-type (p. 164). Cf. Chapter Three, 3.3. and section 3.2.2. of this chapter.

times indistinguishable from their sacred counterpart, Mary, the *amour courtois* and divine love blend in many of the Petrarchan poems of the Renaissance.[12]

Like Stambler, Erskine over-emphasizes the role of Petrarchism and neglects the emblematic tradition as a likely source for the love imagery in Herbert's verse. In his concluding chapter Erskine writes:

> A case in point is the use both poets [i.e. Herbert and Vaughan] make of the courtly love tradition. Herbert, as we have seen is perfectly at home with the eyes, hearts, and darts of that tradition; he can effectively transcend the secular convention, as he does in "Artillerie" and "The Glance," using it to describe the sacred love relationship between God and man. Although it is difficult to speculate about the reasons for Herbert's use of the tradition, there are several possible explanations (pp. 184-5).

Erskine's "possible explanations" remain vague, however. He refers loosely to Herbert's indebtedness to Donne "whose poetry mixes the sacred and secular worlds" and to the poet's "high hopes at court" which are supposed to substantiate his claim that Herbert was "familiar with the secular love lyric and would have known the lyricists" (p. 185). Herbert may well have known the lyricists, but the imagery of his divine love poetry probably derived from other sources. Saad El-Gabalawy (1971) in an article entitled "George Herbert and the *Ars Amatoria*" tones down the claim that Herbert's imagery of divine love derives from secular love poetry. He argues that "to lay too much stress on it may lead us to disregard the spiritual and ethical connotations of the poet's tears, sighs and complaints, which are, in fact, an integral part of his religious sensibility."[13] He suggests that amatory elements in the Bible, the work of the Church Fathers and medieval religious verse are more relevant source material than the secular love poems. In "George Herbert and *Caritas*" Rosemond Tuve, too, emphasizes the differences between secular love poetry and Herbert's poetry of divine love.[14] None of these critics, however, mentions the relevance of the religious emblem as a possible source for Herbert's love imagery.

The only critic who does discuss the complex relations between Petrarchism, profane and sacred emblems, the Bible and Herbert at any length is Eleanor James in "The Emblem as an Image-pattern in some metaphysical poets" (1942):

> ... the periods fond of conceits are also periods fond of emblems .... After the Alexandrine epigrams and the erotic poetry of Ovid, perhaps the most fertile other source of the sixteenth and seventeenth century emblems was the highly meta-

12. Thomas Erskine, "Eye and Ear Imagery in the Poetry of George Herbert and Henry Vaughan," Diss. Emory Univ. 1970, p. 26.

13. *Xavier Univ. Studies*, 10 (1971), 28-33; this qu. pp. 32-3.

14. In *Essays by Rosemond Tuve*, ed. Thomas P. Roche, Jr. (Princeton: Princeton Univ. Press, 1970), pp. 167-206.

phoric poetry of Petrarch and his school .... And finally, in images drawn from the poetry of George Herbert ... one can trace figures which began as vivid metaphors, which were given graphic representation in religious emblems, to reappear as arresting poetic conceits. For the writer of religious emblems, no source was more fecund than the Bible with its highly metaphorical expression (pp. 34-36).[15]

James points out that the religious emblem is an important source for Herbert's imagery. From the religious emblem the line of tradition goes back to the Bible and its metaphors. I tend to agree with her. Herbert found the emblem congenial to his poetic method and used the Bible as the main source for his imagery. The confusion probably arose from the fact that the Bible is a source both of the Petrarchan conceit and of the religious emblem. On generic and historical grounds one can argue that it is more likely that Herbert's images came from the Bible, through the channel of the emblem rather than from the Petrarchan conceit. Generically his poetry has more in common with the religious emblem than with the Petrarchan love sonnet; historically Herbert's poetry was written at the time when the religious emblem was most popular in England.[16]

Whereas Stambler and Erskine in their assessment of "Love (III)" neglect to a certain extent the aspects of genre and historical development, the readings of Bagg and Crossan turn the poem into a statement about sexual frustration and disregard them altogether. The main problem in dealing with interpretations such as these is their high degree of irrelevance. It is difficult to disprove the arguments on the basis of the words of the poem alone and they are attractive because they have an air of 'modern'-ness. Only by assuming that the poet's intentions were at least partly formed by the historical context in which he was working and by the literary conventions that were available to him can one establish a valid interpretation of the poem being analysed. We are back once more where we started at the outset of this book. If one's only criterion for presenting a new reading is that it should not radically conflict with other

15. Herbert's imagery of love in a poem like "Love (III)" is directly related to the sacred emblem books, which in their turn were influenced by the Petrarchan school. The Neoplatonic philosophy of love propagated by Ficino and his Florentine academy made it morally appropriate to apply profane images to an elevated context. The interrelation of sacred emblem and Petrarchism is not surprising since one of the important classical models for both emblem and Petrarchan conceit was the epigram. See Hutton, *The Greek Anthology in Italy,* p. 204 and Clements, *Picta Poesis,* p. 189.
16. The picture is slightly more complex than I suggest. Herbert wrote two sonnets, sent to his mother on New Year 1609/1610 (*Works*, p. 206), in which he clearly distinguishes between sacred and profane love and contrasts the passion, idiom and metaphors of these two kinds of love. This does not seriously affect my argument, however, because these were early poems that do not form part of *The Temple.* Moreover, it is not unlikely that the contrasts in these two poems reflect the related contrast between the profane and the sacred emblems.

readings there is no safeguard against the irrelevance of the kind exemplified by Bagg's and Crossan's readings of "Love (III)."

Once more Panofsky's model of interpretation comes to mind and particularly his second level, where the object of interpretation is the "*secondary* or *conventional* subject matter, constituting the world of *images*, *stories* and *allegories*," the controlling principle of which is the "history of *types* (insight into the manner in which, under varying historical conditions, specific *themes* or *concepts* were expressed by *objects* and *events*)."[17] The conclusion of the present survey of interpretations must be that for our study of the imagery of "Love (III)" it will be more relevant to explore possible connections with the Bible, the liturgy of the Church and emblems than the tradition of courtly love poetry. This conclusion will be supported by further evidence in the following section.

1.2. Catechism.

The second critical issue I want to comment on here is a difference of opinion between two leading modern critics of Herbert's work, Vendler and Fish. In his book on Herbert, *The Living Temple: George Herbert and Catechizing* (1978) Fish, in an analysis of "Love (III)," argues that Vendler misreads the poem when she characterizes Love's "You shall be he" as "gentle."[18] He writes: "'You shall be he' is the first instance in the poem of direct speech, and while the words are gracious in an ultimate (that is, theological) sense, they are not gentle, but peremptory." Fish ascribes to Love the function of catechist and interprets His speech and actions as being more commanding and the reactions of the speaker as being more enforced than does Vendler along with most other critics. Fish sees the word "must" in "You must sit down ..." as a "naked command" (p. 134) and provides a new reading of the end of the poem:

> In Vendler's reading, the speaker "in sitting down in silent grateful acquiescence, attains at last the perfect simplicity that Love has displayed throughout" (p. 275), but the silence has been forced (he has spent his verbal resources) and gratitude is what he has been all along reluctant to give .... The speaker's "So" is not triumphant, but exhausted ... Vendler says that "during the actual progress of the poem," the distance between God and the soul "shrinks" (p. 274). In a way this is true, but the process is less comfortably benevolent than she implies because what shrinks or is shrunk is the speaker's self. He has been killed with kindness (pp. 134-5).

17. *Studies in Iconology*, pp. 14-15; see Chapter One, 2.2.
18. Stanley E. Fish, *The Living Temple: George Herbert and Catechizing* (Berkeley: Univ. of California Press, 1978), p. 132. On Herbert and catechizing see also Mulder, *The Temple of the Mind* (1969). Chapter 5 treats of Nowell's Catechism as a source and analogy of religious ideas expressed by writers of the period. In Chapter 6 Mulder suggests that many of Herbert's poems can be understood better when they are viewed against the background of religious works like Nowell's Catechism.

His conclusion is:

> To the extent that this reading of "Love III" differs from most others it is because criticism has given us the poem we expect and, indeed, desire to find at the conclusion of "The Church." The poem, we feel, should be climactic and retrospective, recalling and resolving the conflicts that have previously been introduced and explored. In the reading proposed here, "Love III," rather than resolving conflicts, re-enacts them and confirms their durability.... The exercise of preparing to become worthy does not end in becoming worthy, but in the realization (stumbled upon again and again) that you never can be.... Here it is stopped by the very agent whose original act ("do ye this in remembrance of me") makes its goal unattainable, by a Questionist who does not say, "Congratulations, you've passed," but rather, "You still haven't got it right and never will, but come in and sit down anyway." (p. 136)

Fish's observations are attractively novel and acute. Nevertheless there are several reasons why they do not seem well-grounded. The interpretation relies too heavily on Fish's starting-point that the exchange between Love and the speaker is one between catechist and catechumen. The differences between the Catechism and the poem, however, are too pronounced to make the comparison more than just another interesting observation.

The main feature that distinguishes the Catechism from Herbert's poem is the absence of reluctance on the part of the catechumen. The dramatic development in "Love (III)" reaches its climax at the moment when the speaker yields up his individual will in order to be finally united with Christ at Communion. As Nicholas Sharp (1974) points out this union is both spiritual and physical because the word "host" implicit in the guest/host relationship between the speaker and Love does not only refer to the function of Him who invites but, in this context, may also indicate the Communion wafer.[19] In the Catechism there is no contest of wills comparable to that in "Love (III)," which is not surprising in view of the meaning of the word 'catechism' and its religious function. There is dialogue, of a kind, in the Catechism but its nature is entirely different from that in Herbert's poem:

Question. What meanest thou by this word *Sacrament?*
Answer. I mean an outward and visible sign of an inward and spiritual grace, given unto us, ordained by Christ himself, as a means whereby we receive the same, and a pledge to assure us thereof.
Question. How many parts are there in a Sacrament?
Answer. Two; the outward visible sign; and the inward spiritual grace ....
Question. What is the outward part or sign of the Lord's Supper?
Answer. Bread and Wine, which the Lord hath commanded to be received.
Question. What is the inward part, or thing signified?

19. Nicholas Sharp, "Herbert's 'Love(III)'," *Expl.*, 33 (1974), it. 26.

Answer.   The body and blood of Christ which are verily and indeed taken and received by the faithful in the Lord's Supper.[20]

Tone and nature of the questions and the way they are answered differ radically in Herbert's poem. There the tone is complex and ironically subtle, the questions are psychological rather than factual, and the answers evasive and hesitant rather than confident and direct.

Fish denies that the speaker becomes "worthy," whereas the poem affirms his worthiness: "You shall be he." Fish would probably counterclaim that the worthiness is not attained by the speaker's own doing but is accorded to him by his gracious Host. The point of "Love (III)," however, is not that the speaker should prove himself worthy but that he, in partaking of the heavenly repast, receives God's grace which can never be gained by desert. This theological truism is illustrated in the passage quoted from the Catechism in the Book of Common Prayer. Nor do I find the implications of Fish's conclusion satisfactory when he notes that "The speaker's 'So' is not triumphant, but exhausted" and "what shrinks or is shrunk is the speaker's self. He has been killed with kindness." Judged by twentieth century standards the perspective offered by Fish is unfavourable indeed. But it is, I think, Fish's perspective and not Herbert's. Anyway, quite apart from the question of whether the "shrinking" of the self is such a negative matter if judged by the standard of Herbert's religious convictions, I believe Fish makes an error of interpretation of the *tone* of the poem. After all, the soul itself hesitates and needs to be prevailed upon. It would be nonsense to force somebody to realize that he is not worthy, when that somebody is so deeply convinced of this already.[21]

If the poem has a catechismal function it is not *per se* but within the larger framework of *The Church* as a whole. If the poem "instructs" it does so dramatically, not catechismally; the theological instruction is dramatized in the allegorical situation. The yielding of the individual will in the complete union with Love is thus, in Herbert's vision, not an easy act but it is definitely a gain rather than a loss. Centuries before Herbert, Dante ended his great allegory with these lines:

20. The quoted passage is from the part of the Catechism that deals with the Sacraments.
21. The almost flat tone of the line "So I did sit and eat" is comparable to that of T.S. Eliot's "... it was, you may say, satisfactory" ("Journey of the Magi"). In both poems the gradual increase of tension and heightening of expectation is resolved in a matter-of-fact, down-to-earth phrase (no pun intended), the tone of which suggests that truly great events can only be described in the simplest, most undramatic way possible. Rhetoric and logic fall short in the face of ultimate religious truth.

All' alta fantasia qui mancò possa;
Ma già volgeva il mio disiro e il *velle,*
Sì come ruota ch' egualmente è mossa,

L' amor che muove il sole e l' altre stelle.

(High phantasy lost power and here broke off;
Yet, as a wheel moves smoothly, free from jars,
my will and my desire were turned by love,

The love that moves the sun and the other stars.)[22]

Love removes the jars from the wheel of zeal in *Paradise*; Love mends the
marred eyes of faith in "Love (III)." The main problem of Herbert's
weary pilgrim in "Love (III)" is how to adapt to the paradisial state after
the purgatorial stage of his journey as described in allegorical poems such
as "The Pilgrimage," "Christmas," and "Peace," and indicated in the
poem by the word "dust." The harmonious union which he has sought
for so long is finally achieved in "Love (III)." The dialogue in the poem is
an effective means to present this achievement. It allows Herbert to use
the personal pronouns I/thee and the possessive pronouns mine/thine,
which is his favourite way of exploring and defining the relationship
between the speaker and God throughout *The Church.*[23] This kind of
intimate exploration is absent in the Catechism.

The part of the Book of Common Prayer that is relevant for the
interpretation of "Love (III)" is not the Catechism but the Service of
Holy Communion. As James Thorpe (1965) indicates the poem "is in fact
a dramatization of the central portion of that service, from the Exhortation following the offertory through the Administration of the Elements."[24] The Exhortation to be used by the Priest when he "shall see the
people negligent to come to the holy Communion" in particular contains
so many elements also present in "Love (III)" that it could very well be
regarded as one of the chief sources of the poem. Since the Exhortation
provides a convenient link between the critical problems discussed in this

22. Dante, *Paradise*, trans. Dorothy Sayers, Canto XXXIII, ll. 142-45.
23. "Clasping of hands" is the most striking example of Herbert's way of defining
the relationship between God and man by means of personal and possessive pronouns:
"Lord, thou art mine, and I am thine, / If mine I am: and thine much more, ..."
(*Works*, p. 157). See A.L. Clements, "Theme, Tone, and Tradition in George
Herbert's Poetry," *ELR*, 3 (1973), 264-83.
24. James Thorpe, "Herbert's 'Love (III),'" *Expl.*, 24 (1965), it. 16. A succinct
account of the controversial aspects of the chief Sacrament in the liturgy of the Church
of England is given by Horton Davies, *Worship and Theology in England: From
Andrewes to Baxter and Fox, 1603-1690* (Princeton, N.J.: Princeton Univ. Press, 1975),
pp. 286-325.

section and the investigation that is to follow I shall quote the most
relevant part from it:

> ... in God's behalf, I bid you all that are here present; and beseech you, for the Lord
> Jesus Christ's sake, that ye will not refuse to come thereto, being so lovingly called
> and bidden by God himself. Ye know how grievous and unkind a thing it is, when a
> man hath prepared a rich feast, decked his table with all kind of provision, so that
> there lacketh nothing but the guests to sit down; and yet they who are called
> (without any cause) most unthankfully refuse to come. Which of you in such a case
> would not be moved? Who would not think a great injury and wrong done unto
> him? Wherefore, most dearly beloved in Christ, take ye good heed, lest ye,
> withdrawing yourselves from this holy Supper, provoke God's indignation against
> you. It is an easy matter for a man to say, I will not communicate, because I am
> otherwise hindered with worldly business. But such excuses are not so easily
> accepted and allowed before God. If any man say, I am a grievous sinner, and
> therefore am afraid to come; Wherefore then do ye not repent and amend? When
> God calleth you, are ye not ashamed to say ye will not come? When ye should
> return to God, will ye excuse yourselves, and say ye are not ready? Consider
> earnestly with yourselves, how little such feigned excuses will avail before God....
> And as the Son of God did vouchsafe to yield up his soul by death upon the cross
> for your salvation; so it is your duty to receive the Communion, in remembrance of
> the sacrifice of his death, as he himself hath commanded: which if ye shall neglect
> to do, consider with yourselves how great injury ye do unto God, and how sore
> punishment hangeth over your heads for the same; when ye wilfully abstain from
> the Lord's Table, and separate from your brethren, who come to feed on the
> banquet of that most heavenly food.

The resemblances between the Exhortation and "Love (III)" are manifold. The metaphor of the Communion as a feast and a banquet, the
guest/host relation between communicant and God, phrases like "there
lacketh nothing but the guests to sit down" and "withdrawing yourselves
from this holy Supper," are all elements shared by both the Exhortation
and the poem. Moreover, the "feigned excuses" mentioned in the
Exhortation may well have suggested to the poet the idea of the soul's
part in the dialogue while the attitude of Love, both kind and commanding, may have been prompted by such phrases as "lovingly called
and bidden" and "it is your duty to receive the Communion, ... as he
himself hath commanded." Of course there are differences too. There is
no threat of "God's indignation" or "sore punishment" in the poem.
These do not belong to the behaviour and attitude of a charitable God
who presents Himself as Divine Love.

Not only does the Exhortation from the Communion Service exhibit
marked similarities with Herbert's poem, but comparison between the
two texts once more makes clear why its alleged connection with secular
love poetry discussed above is a doubtful matter. There is no reason to
surmise that Herbert derived his imagery and vocabulary from the
courtly love tradition when he could have found his material just as well
in sources that were closer to him — , closer in time and spirit, and closer

224

to his daily concerns. The Book of Common Prayer is one of the most natural of such sources; Herbert the priest must have resorted to it every day.

One aspect of the poem has not yet received the attention it deserves: that of the role played by images of the senses. In our initial analysis of the poem we mentioned briefly that the second and third stanzas in particular are filled with sense imagery, an element that is conspicuously absent from the sources referred to so far. It is the aim of the remainder of this chapter to investigate this element of the poem and its significance for the interpretation of the poem as a whole. Having analysed the pattern poems, whose shape makes an immediate appeal to the senses, and "The Pilgrimage," the imagery of which works mainly through the same appeal, we have now come to a poem in which some of the senses, the eyes in particular, are the most important metaphors.

2. Images of the senses in "Love (III)."

2.1. Introductory.

Four of the five senses play a more or less dominant role in "Love (III)." They are touch, taste, hearing, and sight. The only sense not present, either explicitly or implicitly, in the poem is that of smell.[25] Taste is mentioned explicitly in the penultimate line, touch is implied in "Love took my hand" and hearing in words like "questioning" and "reply" and in the dialogue-form of the poem. The most important sense is that of sight, which occurs in each of the three stanzas. In the first Love is called "quick-ey'd," "observing" his guest; in the second stanza the guest expresses his feelings by another eye-image: "I cannot look on thee," which elicits the retort from Love: "Who made the eyes but I?" The guest maintains his self-critical attitude and says: "but I have marr'd them."

What is the function of the senses and why does Herbert emphasize the sense of sight in particular? Several aspects of the poem, as we have seen, have their roots in the Bible, the Book of Common Prayer and the sacred emblems. Is the imagery of the senses conventional, too, and based on the same sources? These are some of the questions that come to mind once the possibility of a special role for the senses is considered.

2.2. Textual analysis.

On the level of textual analysis the images of the senses should be interpreted in the way indicated in the introductory paragraphs of this

---

25. Cf. "Life," in which smell is the main sense image: "Here will I smell my remnant out, ..." (1.2; *Works*, p. 94). See also n. 35.

chapter. They support the action and add a dramatic element to the dialogue. The scene can be clearly imagined; it could easily be staged. Read as drama, the greater part of the poem is found to consist of dialogue and stage directions. The one notable exception is the opening stanza which contains only reported speech. The first stanza thus serves as an introducton in which the basic ingredients of the scene are presented; it also enhances, by contrast, the immediacy and directness of the other stanzas. The second line of the first stanza refers to the speaker's past, prior to the poem: "Guiltie of dust and sinne." The line is indispensable because it contains the essential information necessary for the reader to understand the speaker's attitude in the subsequent parts of the poem. The word "dust" is nicely ambiguous. In one sense it refers to the dust of the road, in the other it links up with "sinne" and serves to explain it. Sinning was inevitable in the state of "dust," i.e. of life in the body (fallen life). In this latter sense 'dust and sin' form a hendyadis for 'dusty sin,' referring to the sin typical of fallen man. Whatever meaning is attached to the word "dust" it makes the soul unfit to participate in a banquet. The word, therefore, points back and forward. In its first sense it is related to the Christian soul's pilgrimage through the world; in the latter sense it prepares the ground for the cleansing process that takes place in the course of the poem. In this way the line "Guiltie of dust and sinne" is also connected with the eye imagery in the poem, and particularly with the phrase "I cannot look on thee." The debate about the eyes is resolved in Love's words: "And know you not ... who bore the blame?" This line, too, refers to an event outside and prior to the poem, but in this case it is Love's past — the Sacrifice — that is brought into the picture. Thus the poem moves from one basic principle of Christianity, the sinful state of mankind, to another: the redeeming function of the Crucifixion, token of God's love for mankind. These abstract truths are humanized and concretized by the debate and by the imagery of the senses.

The different senses are 'placed' quite effectively in the poem. There is a subtle progression from one sense to another. The sense of touch is emphasized in the initial part of the poem, hearing is prominent in the first and second stanzas, sight in the second and third, and finally taste, which only plays a role, but a decisive one, in the last two lines in the words "taste my meat" and "eat." That "eat" should be the final word of "Love (III)" and therefore also the final word of *The Church* is quite appropriate. It emphasizes once more that for Herbert the Eucharist was the quintessence of the relation between God and man. The whole collection of poems explores and tries to define that relationship and it ends with a fulfilment in Heaven of what had only been a wish or rather an exhortation in the introductory poem of *The Church,* "Super-

liminare": "... approach, and taste / The churches mysticall
repast." The Eucharist is the visible expression of God's invisible grace.[26]
The imagery of touch works in two directions: on the one hand it helps
to reaffirm the bond between man and the Redeemer, on the other Love's
words emphasize God's role as Creator: "Love took my hand, and
smiling did reply, / Who made the eyes but I?"[27] If read in the former
sense, Love's simple gesture reminds one of similar situations in the
Amor/Anima emblem books; if read in the latter sense, the touch of
Love's hand is almost like God's life-inspiring touch of Adam's hand in
Michelangelo's famous fresco. Thus, whereas the function and background of the senses of touch and taste are fairly straightforward, those
of hearing and sight are much more complex.

3. The eye and the ear.

3.1. "Love (III)" and the imagery of eyes and ears.

In section 1.2. of this chapter I drew attention to the remarkable
resemblance between parts of the Communion Service in the Book of
Common Prayer and "Love (III)." The poem differs from the Communion Service in one important respect, namely in its emphasis on
images of the senses.

Thomas Erskine's unpublished dissertation *Eye and Ear Imagery in the
Poetry of George Herbert and Henry Vaughan* (1970) is the only work to
date in which Herbert's imagery of the senses of hearing and sight is
studied at length and in which an attempt is made to place that imagery in
the tradition. Of course the major critical studies of Herbert's poetry
contain passing remarks on the sensuous quality of his work, but Erskine

---

26. See Patrides' edition of Herbert's poetry, p. 18 and Fish, *The Living Temple*, pp.
131-32. On the relation between the Eucharist and the senses see *The Work of Thomas
Cranmer*, introd. J.I. Packer, ed. G.E. Duffield (Appleford, Berks.: Sutton Courtenay
Press, 1964), pp. 45-231: "A Defence of the True and Catholic Doctrine of the
Sacrament of the Body and Blood of Our Saviour Christ" (1550):

And no less ought we to doubt, that our souls be fed and live by Christ, than that our
bodies be fed and live by meat and drink. Thus our Saviour Christ knowing us to be in
this world, as it were, but babes and weaklings in faith, hath ordained sensible signs and
tokens, whereby to allure and draw us to more strength and more constant faith in him.
So that the eating and drinking of this sacramental bread and wine is, as it were, a
showing of Christ before our eyes, a smelling of him with our noses, a feeling and
groping of him with our hands, and an eating, chewing, digesting, and feeding upon him
to our spiritual strength and perfection (pp. 71-2).

27. Cf. *A Priest to the Temple*: "The thrusting away of his arme makes us onely not
embraced." (*Works*, p. 283).

is the only one so far to devote a systematic study to the subject.[28] Erskine traces the background of eye and ear imagery, referring mainly to the courtly love tradition and Petrarchan conceits. He also uses concepts from Platonic and Neoplatonic philosophy and the Church Fathers to describe the function of the senses of sight and hearing in secular love poetry and in religious and philosophical writings. Touching briefly on the subject of the interrelation between secular love poetry and poetry of spiritual love he illustrates his ideas about their connection in comments on Crashaw's poem "The Hymn of Sainte Thomas in Adoration of the Blessed Sacrament."[29] As was pointed out in section 1.1. of this chapter Erskine takes the influence of the Petrarchan school on religious poetry for granted but strangely enough neglects the connection between the English religious lyric of the early seventeenth century on the one hand and the religious emblem and the Bible on the other. Thus a vital element in the formation of the imagery of poets like Crashaw and Herbert — or Vaughan for that matter — is left out of consideration.[30]

28. See Erskine, pp. 65-73 for a survey of comments on this aspect of Herbert's work.

29. *The Poems*, pp. 291-93. The hymn is called "Adoro Te." Crashaw's poem makes use of the whole gamut of Petrarchan conceits of the senses with all their physical and metaphysical connotations. Erskine concludes: "The darts, eyes and hearts of the courtly love tradition are thus elevated and used as a metaphor for spiritual love" (p. 6). See also n. 35.

30. Erskine's bibliography does not mention Praz. Erskine does discuss Freeman's *English Emblem Books* but does not demonstrate more than a superficial knowledge of the subject as witness the following quotation: "Although Herbert's *The Temple* could not have been influenced by Quarles or Harvey's emblem books, Freeman asserts that the visual and intellectual aspects of Herbert's work are emblematic qualities" (p. 72). Crashaw imitated the emblem method more literally than any of the other major religious lyricists of his time. Crashaw became a Roman Catholic in 1645; perhaps he felt a greater affinity to the Jesuit emblem writers than did Herbert and Vaughan, who, though sometimes called Anglo-Catholics, remained within the Anglican Church. Freeman (1948) defines the distinction between the poets thus:

> Crashaw's religious interests naturally led him towards the themes of the Jesuit emblem books; and the imagery of his devotional poetry, with its bleeding and flaming hearts, its emphasis upon the sensations of the devout soul, and its emblematic pictures, perhaps engraved by himself, does in fact recall that aspect of the convention. But the relations of Vaughan and Herbert to it are less obvious and more interesting. Both owed a little and brought much to it, absorbing more than its merely superficial elements and yet succeeding, on occasion, in transforming it into great poetry (p. 149).

It is even more difficult to bypass the emblematic quality of Crashaw's poetry than that of Herbert's. "The Weeper," for instance, a series of epigrammatic stanzas, was originally printed as an emblem showing Mary Magdalene weeping above a winged, bleeding heart, accompanied by the motto:

One of the main themes in Erskine's book is that of the primacy of the Word (i.e. the Scriptures) over the eye. Erskine concludes that Herbert considers the eye the noblest sense, useful for the "acquisition of earthly knowledge" (Erskine, p. 190). On the other hand the ear ranks higher than the eye in spiritual matters: "... the Word is necessary to complete the meaning of the vision" (Erskine, p. 190). The most interesting observation made by Erskine is about the distinct functions of the senses in Herbert's prose and in his poetry. He finds a preference for the Word in Herbert's prose and an emphasis on the eye in the poetry. This observation helps to support the claim that Herbert's poetry is characteristically visual in its appeal. Although Erskine's study includes a section devoted to analyses of selected poems by Herbert, "Love (III)" is mentioned only in passing.[31]

While I have been unable to find any reference to the function of the ear imagery, the prominence of the eye imagery in the poem has elicited some comment.[32] In *Utmost Art* Mary Ellen Rickey writes:

> Herbert in this final poem celebrates the superiority of Divine Love to blind Cupid in that the greater Love is both seeing and wise, and also creates vision, and consequently, acumen, in His adherents: this Love is not blind, but rather a revealer of light.[33]

Rickey's gloss is in a chapter that bears the title "The Classical

---

> Loe, where a WOUNDED HEART with Bleeding *Eyes* conspire,
> Is she a FLAMING Fountain or a WEEPING Fire! (see *Poems*, p. 79)

Another poem, "To the Countess of Denbigh," shows a picture of a winged and padlocked heart. Its motto is: "Non Vi" (Not by force) and the poem is preceded by this epigram:

> 'Tis not the work of force but skill
> To find the way into man's will.
> 'Tis loue alone can hearts vnlock.
> Who knowes the WORD, he needs not knock. (Poems, p. 236)

In 1646 Crashaw published a volume of poetry entitled *Steps to the Temple*, a title intended as a tribute to George Herbert's collection of poems (*Poems*, pp. 73-145). Crashaw's admiration for Herbert's verse also appears from his dedicatory poem "On Mr. G. Herberts booke intituled the Temple of Sacred Poems, sent to a Gentlewoman" (*Poems*, pp. 130-31). See also Chapter Three, 3.4.

31. The poems studied in detail are "Artillerie," "The Glance," "Vanitie (I)," "Self-condemnation," "Faith," "The H. Scriptures (I)," and "Peace." Erskine compares the phrase "full-ey'd love" in "The Glance" with "quick-ey'd Love" in "Love (III)" (p. 87, p. 103).

32. For clarity's sake, the rhetorical aspect of the debate, which is a prominent feature of the poem, has been left out of consideration here. What I am concerned with is the function of the words spoken by Love and heard by the protagonist.

33. Rickey, p. 37.

229

Materials," where she explores the possible connections between pagan themes and images and their sacred counterparts in Herbert's verse. In the *Oxford Anthology of English Literature* the editors give the following note to the phrase "quick-ey'd Love":

> As opposed to the blind or blindfolded Cupid of Renaissance erotic imagery, Caritas or Divine Love is characterized as "quick"- (or "living"-) eyed: the whole poem plays on this contrast.[34]

These comments, one feels, are begging the question; and even if it could be convincingly argued that Herbert intended to emphasize the contrast between Divine and Profane Love in this poem, the separation of the images of the eyes from those of the other senses does not seem warranted.

3.2. Eyes and ears in Herbert's work.

The speaker in "Love(III)" is persuaded by the words of Divine Love. In this way the *ear*, although not mentioned as such, plays a decisive role in determining his attitude at each stage of the poem. On the other hand the cluster of images used to reinforce the verbal argument is centred around the function of the *eye*. Both in the prose writings and in the poetry Herbert's ideas about the various uses of the ear and the eye in the religious life of the Christian are expressed.

In *A Priest to the Temple* Herbert describes how the "Countrey Parson" should convert heretics to "the common Faith":

> The first means he useth is Prayer, beseeching the Father of lights to open their eyes, and to give him power so to fit his discourse to them, that it may effectually pierce their hearts, and convert them. The second means is a very loving, and sweet usage of them, both in going to, and sending for them often, and in finding out Courtesies to place on them... (*Works*, p. 262).

The word of the priest has a twofold function: his prayer is used to intercede on behalf of the apostate and his exhortations are used to convert the sinner. Both the emphasis on God's power to provide perfect vision and on the priest's charitable speech and behaviour that we find in this passage are relevant in connection with our analysis of "Love (III)." "The Authour's Prayer before Sermon" also contains a combination of eye and ear images. The prayer begins:

> O Almighty and ever-living Lord God! Majesty, and Power, and Brightnesse, and Glory! How shall we dare to appear before thy face, who are contrary to thee, in all we call thee? for we are darknesse, and weaknesse, and filthinesse, and shame (p. 288).

The priest here assumes a humble, self-denying attitude that resembles

---

34. Hollander & Kermode, eds., *The Literature of Renaissance England*, p. 678n.

that of the speaker in "Love (III)." Towards the end of the prayer the ear
serves as the channel of faith:

> O make it a word of power and peace, to convert those who are not yet thine, and
> to confirme those that are: particularly, blesse it in this thy own Kingdom, which
> thou hast made a Land of light, a store-house of thy treasures and mercies ... O
> make thy word a swift word, passing from the ear to the heart, from the heart to the
> life and conversation (p. 289).

In *Briefe Notes on Valdesso's Considerations*, which he wrote a few
months before his death as a commentary on the translation of Valdesso's work by his friend Nicholas Ferrar, Herbert defends the importance
of the Scriptures over against visual images. The following two passages
criticize Valdesso's emphasis on the primacy of visual images in matters
of religious faith:

> I much mislike the Comparison of Images, and H. Scripture, as if they were both
> but Alphabets and after a time to be left. The H. Scriptures (as I wrote before) have
> not only an Elementary use, but a use of perfection, neither can they ever be
> exhausted, (as Pictures may be by a plenarie circumspection) ... (*Works*, p. 309)

> Nay it is observeable that in that very place he preferres the Word before the sight
> of the Transfiguration of Christ. So that the Word hath the precedence even of
> Revelations and Visions (p. 318).

In Herbert's verse we find eyes and ears combined, juxtaposed or
opposed. In "The Church-porch" Herbert contrasts the outer and the
inner eyes and advocates a pact between the inner eyes and the outer ears
in prayer:

> In time of service seal up both thine eies,
> And send them to thine heart; that spying sinne,
> They may weep out the stains by them did rise:
> Those doores being shut, all by the eare comes in.
>   Who marks in church-time others symmetrie,
>   Makes all their beautie his deformitie. (ll. 415-20; *Works*, p. 23)

In "The H. Scriptures (I)" the Bible is called "the thankfull glasse, / That
mends the lookers eyes" (ll. 8-9; *Works*, p. 58).

 The Word in "Love (III)" is not presented through the medium of the
Scriptures or of a priest on earth but it is spoken by Divine Love Himself,
the High Priest in Heaven. As Erskine puts it: "When Herbert writes
allegorical poems, the final answer usually comes not in a sight or vision,
but in God's reassurance, His Word" (p. 81). The good tidings of the
Gospel and the prayer of the priest on earth are fulfilled in this final
dialogue between God and man. The Word of God reaches the pilgrim's
ears and confirms his faith. As Crashaw wrote in "The Hymn of Sainte
Thomas in Adoration of the Blessed Sacrament":

Your ports are all superfluous here,
Saue That which lets in faith, the eare.
Faith is my skill. Faith can beleiue
As fast as loue new lawes can giue.
Faith is my force. Faith strength affords
To keep pace with those powrfull words.
And words more sure, more sweet, then they
Loue could not think, truth could not say. (ll. 9-16)[35]

As a consequence of this confirmation of faith, in which the ear plays a decisive role, the eyes are "mended," so that, henceforth, the pilgrim will be able to look at God directly. The significance of the combination of eye and ear images in "Love (III)" does not differ essentially from that in Herbert's other writings. Although there is clearly a greater number of eye images in the poem, they derive a considerable part of their significance from the Word that enters through the ear.

3.2.1. The Bible.

The passages in the Bible in which the eye and the ear are found together, by and large confirm the conclusions reached above (see also section 3.3.3. of this chapter). One text in particular deserves special emphasis, namely the Epistle to the Hebrews. The main subject of Hebrews is the confirmation of faith through the Word and its consequences for the priest's duty on earth.

Paul's Epistle to the Hebrews is an important source for three elements in Herbert's poem: the aspect of hearing and the imagery of the eyes; the relation between Christ as priest and the hesitant communicant; and faith, the religious virtue that, together with charity, dominates the poem. These are the most apposite passages from Hebrews, 4, 5 and 12, respectively:

4:12 For the word of God is quick, and powerful, and sharper than any two-edged sword, piercing even to the dividing asunder of soul and spirit, and of the joints and marrow, and is a discerner of the thoughts and intents of the heart.

35. *Poems*, p. 292. Cf. Guillaume de Deguileville, *The Pilgrimage of the Life of Man*, trans. John Lydgate, ed. F.J. Furnivall, E.E.T.S., 77 (London: Kegan Paul, 1899), pp. 169 ff., where the five senses are likewise compared with gates. Crashaw follows the original hymn in mentioning the same four senses. The lines preceding the passage quoted in the text read:

Down down, proud sense! Discourses dy.
Keep close, my soul's inquiring ey!
Nor touch nor tast must look for more
But each sitt still in his own Dore.
(Cf. Aquinas' own words:
Visus, tactus, gustus in te fallitur,
Sed auditu solo tuto creditur).

13 Neither is there any creature that is not manifest in his sight: but all things are naked and opened unto the eyes of him with whom we have to do.
14 Seeing then that we have a great high priest, that is passed into the heavens, Jesus the Son of God, let us hold fast our profession.
15 For we have not an high priest which cannot be touched with the feeling of our infirmities; but was in all points tempted like as we are, yet without sin.
16 Let us therefore come boldly unto the throne of grace, that we may obtain mercy, and find grace to help in time of need.

5:12 For when for the time ye ought to be teachers, ye have need that one teach you again which be the first principles of the oracles of God; and are become such as have need of milk, and not of strong meat.
13 For every one that useth milk is unskilful in the word of righteousness: for he is a babe.
14 But strong meat belongeth to them that are of full age, even those who by reason of use have their senses exercised to discern both good and evil.

12:22 But ye are come unto mount Sion, and unto the city of the living God, the heavenly Jerusalem, and to an innumerable company of angels,
23 To the general assembly and church of the firstborn, which are written in heaven, and to God the Judge of all, and to the spirits of just men made perfect,
24 And to Jesus the mediator of the new covenant, and to the blood of sprinkling, that speaketh better things than that of Abel.
25 See that ye refuse not him that speaketh. For if they escaped not who refused him that spake on earth, much more shall not we escape, if we turn away from him that speaketh from heaven.
. . . .
28 Wherefore we receiving a kingdom which cannot be moved, let us have grace, whereby we may serve God acceptably with reverence and godly fear.

The two main themes of these verses are priesthood (of Christ in Heaven, "a great high priest," and of his deputies on earth, "teachers"), and faith. Herbert's familiarity with the text is shown by "The Authour's Prayer before Sermon" quoted in the previous section, paraphrasing Hebrews 4:12. The metaphors and vocabulary of Hebrews also bear a remarkable resemblance to "Love (III)." In both, for instance, the same four senses occur. The "quick" word of God in Hebrews and the speech of Love in the poem appeal to the human ear; in Hebrews God's eyes are all-seeing, in the poem Love is called "quick-eyed"; in Hebrews Jesus is a high priest who can be "touched with the feeling of our infirmities," in "Love (III)" Love actually touches the hesitant speaker; in the poem taste is mentioned in the phrase "taste my meat," in Hebrews the same sense is implied in the words "strong meat." Hebrews 5:14 explains unequivocally why the senses deserve this special emphasis: the "strong meat" is appropriate food for those "who by reason of use have their *senses* exercised to discern both good and evil" (emphasis added), in other words, those who have reached perfection. Can "Love (III)," too, be seen as an 'exercise' of the senses? Such an interpretation would certainly add to the coherence of the poem.

One final analogy between the text from Hebrews and the poem is the warning contained in Hebrews 12:25. This verse warns against the kind of attitude maintained by the speaker in the poem until the very last line, when refusal and withrawal are replaced by acceptance.

The differences between the Bible text and the poem are, like the verbal correspondences, significant too. One major difference is that in the poem Love is called "quick-ey'd," in Hebrews God's word is called "quick." If one re-reads the verses 12 and 13 of Hebrews 4 one finds that the string of images in these verses is telescoped into the unified imagery of Herbert's phrase "But quick-ey'd Love, observing me grow slack." In the poem Love acts as a "discerner of the thoughts and intents of the heart" and the true state of affairs of the soul is just as "naked and opened unto the eyes" of Love in the poem as it is to God in the verses from Hebrews.[36] The compound "quick-ey'd" adds to the directness and the personal nature of the contact between Love and the speaker. If Herbert's debt to Hebrews was one that he was conscious of, this change is an apt one.

Hebrews 4:15 and 16 describe a relationship between man and Christ similar to that between the soul and Love in the poem. The concern for the infirmities of the soul that Love shows throughout the poem and the homely nature of the dialogue between the two suggest that Love, by acting on the same level as the speaker, diminishes the distance between them. The use of the sense of touch may well have been suggested to Herbert by Hebrews 4:15, because the touch of Love indicates that he has indeed a "feeling of our infirmities."

Verses 5:12, 13 and 14 are also helpful as a background to "Love (III)." They help clarify two things: the change experienced by the protagonist in the course of the poem and the meaning of the word "meat" in the penultimate line. If we interpret the poem with the help of these verses we see the speaker developing from a state of sin and imperfection at the outset of the poem to a state of spiritual grace and perfection when he sits down to eat meat at the end.

As Summers points out the word "meat" probably derives from Luke 12:37: "Blessed are those servants, whom the lord when he cometh shall find watching: verily I say unto you, that he shall gird himself, and make them to sit down to meat, and will come forth and serve them." As I said at the beginning of this section, the verse corresponds to the concrete situation and the events in the poem: the roles of master and servant are reversed in the poem and the speaker is indeed made "to sit down to meat." Still the comparison leaves one thing unexplained, namely the

36. The emphasis on the word of God in the Bible text also underscores the element of faith. Traditionally, faith was associated with the ear.

precise meaning of the word "meat." After all, the word is used in a context in which we would not really expect it. In the Communion Service and in those passages of the Bible that treat of the Communion, the Communion bread is called Christ's "body" (Matt. 26:26, Mark 14:22, Luke 22:19) or his "flesh" (Book of Common Prayer) but rarely "meat."[37] This, for instance, is how the Communion is described in the priest's prayer that precedes the Communion proper in the Book of Common Prayer:

> We are not worthy so much as to gather up the crumbs under thy Table. But thou art the same Lord, whose property is always to have mercy: Grant us therefore, gracious Lord, so to eat the flesh of thy dear Son Jesus Christ, and to drink his blood, that our sinful bodies may be made clean by his body, and our souls washed through his most precious blood, and that we may evermore dwell in him, and he in us.

Article 28 of the *Articles of Religion*, famous for its refutation of Transsubstantiation, circumscribes the essence of the Communion:

> The Body of Christ is given, taken, and eaten, in the Supper, only after an heavenly and spiritual manner. And the mean whereby the Body of Christ is received and eaten in the Supper is Faith.
>   (Article XXVIII. *Of the Lord's Supper*)

The connotation of the word "meat" is slightly different from that of "body" and "flesh." The meaning of the words in Hebrews 5:14, "strong meat belongeth to them that are of full age" can be better understood with the help of two verses from 1 Corinthians 3:

37. But see John 6:55: "For my flesh is meat indeed..." In J.H. Bernard, *A Critical and Exegetical Commentary on the Gospel According to St. John*, ed. A.H. McNeile (Edinburgh: T & T. Clark, 1928), I, 211 this phrase is explained thus: "... it is really to be eaten, and it nourishes as meat ought to do." See also Cranmer's comment on John 6:55 in "A Defence ... of the Sacrament... ":

> But as touching this meat and drink of the body and blood of Christ, it is true, both he that eateth and drinketh them, hath everlasting life; and also he that eateth and drinketh them not, hath not everlasting life. For to eat that meat and drink that drink, is to dwell in Christ and to have Christ dwelling in him (p. 61).

And:

> For as meat and drink do comfort the hungry body, so doth the death of Christ's body, and the shedding of his blood, comfort the soul, when she is after her sort hungry. What thing is it that comforteth and nourisheth the body? Forsooth, meat and drink. By what names then shall we call the body and blood of our Saviour Christ (which do comfort and nourish the hungry soul) but by the names of meat and drink? And this similitude caused our Saviour to say, *My flesh is very meat, and my blood is very drink* (p. 68).

See also n. 26 *ante*.

1 And I, brethren, could not speak unto you as unto spiritual, but as unto carnal, even as unto babes in Christ.
2 I have fed you with milk, and not with meat: for hitherto ye were not able to bear it, neither yet now are ye able.

The eating of meat is reserved for those who have reached a state of spiritual perfection and who have true faith.[38] This interpretation is in harmony with the context in which the word "meat" occurs in "Love (III)." The pilgrim enters the heavenly inn with the carnal "dust and sinne" still adhering to him, but after the catharsis — through the dialogue — his faith is restored, his vision purified and the meat of the heavenly banquet becomes his proper food.

The word "meat" is very aptly chosen by Herbert. It functions on all levels of the poem's meaning. It does not destroy the literal meaning as the word "flesh" would have done: a visitor is welcomed by the host of an inn and invited to dine with him. It is also in accordance with the allegorical meaning of the Eucharist as a feast. On the anagogical level the word indicates the soul's maturity enabling it to be united with God. Finally, the word also fits in with the tropological system of the poem, because it rounds off the chain of sense images. As Hebrews 5:14 expounds, "strong meat belongeth to ... those who by reason of use have their senses exercised to discern both good and evil." The question raised before can, I think, be answered in the affirmative. "Love (III)" is indeed, in one sense, an exercise of the senses.

The text from Hebrews is an important aid for the interpretation of "Love (III)." It helps particularly in establishing the relation of the final part of the poem and its images of taste to the rest. However, for all the similarities between the two texts there is one important distinction. In Hebrews Christ is presented as a high priest, in "Love (III)" God is called Love. This name opens up a whole set of other connotations that point to a number of different sources and analogies, in the Bible and elsewhere. Some of these have already been mentioned in previous sections of this chapter. In order to complete the picture of the possible backgrounds of the imagery of the eyes and ears in Herbert's poem I shall restrict myself here to pointing out a few parallels in directions not hitherto explored.

3.2.2. Emblems.

Rosemary Freeman was the first to suggest that there might well be a direct relation between the sacred emblem of the Amor/Anima type and

38. Bible texts corroborating the interpretation given in the text are Rom. 14:21-23, 1 Cor. 8:9,10 and 1 Tim. 4:3.

40   **41**

"Love (III)."[39] She does not specify that relation nor does she refer to any particular emblem to substantiate her claim. I think there is both a general and a more specific relationship involved.

The general analogy between the poem and the emblem books is one of method. If we take a look at the pictures in Hugo's *Pia Desideria*, this resemblance can easily be illustrated (see figs. 40 and 41). Amor and Anima move on the same plane; Amor Divinus teaches, warns and comforts Anima, and, like a close friend, he takes her by the hand. I said earlier that Herbert's poem could easily be acted out on a stage. The mise en scène could in that case be provided by the pictures of the Amor/Anima emblem books. The dialogue of "Love (III)" correlates with the fact that there are two protagonists in the Amor/Anima emblems.

The general correspondences are clear. The visual quality of Herbert's poem leads almost naturally to a comparison with the pictures of the emblems rather than their texts. A discussion about specific parallels between emblems and the poem is a different matter. I shall discuss one

39. *English Emblem Books*, p. 164.

emblem extensively in order to illustrate how the comparison between the emblem writer and the poet works out in practice.

The Devout Hart (1634) by Henry Hawkins is a devotional emblem book, consisting of a series of emblems in which the preparation of the heart for Jesus is portrayed. The devotional element manifests itself in the elaborate meditative pattern of the emblems. Each emblem consists of a "Hymne" — a short lyrical poem — that accompanies the picture and four prose passages, called respectively "The Incentive," "Preamble to the Meditation," the "Meditation" proper, and the "Colloquy."

The penultimate emblem of the collection is the one that concerns us here (see fig. 42).[40] The emblem is called: "Iesvs celebrates the Heavenly Nuptials in the Hart"; it elaborates the idea of the marriage of the human soul to Divine Love that goes back to the Song of Solomon and other Bible texts.[41] This is "The Hymne":

> The nuptial supper, now I see,
>   O happy soule! prepar'd for thee;
> The table's couerd: but what seat,
>   Hast thou for thy repose? What meat?
> Except a Lamb, I nothing find,
>   The amourous Spouse is now so kind,
> That what he fed thee with before;
>   From th'eye shalbe conceal'd no more.
> As with a fleece, in species white,
>   He long on earth appear'd in sight.
> As with a fleece, by grace gaue heat:
>   But now behold the Lamb thy meat.
> In him repose, freed from annoy
>   By seeing, comprehend, enioy.

Whereas in Hebrews the word 'meat' had a sacerdotal function, here the meat of the Communion is defined as the meat of the Lamb, offered by Divine Love, the "amourous Spouse." The Lamb traditionally symbolizes Christ in his sacrificial role; the meat of the Lamb is, therefore, a most appropriate dish at the Communion feast in Heaven.[42]

---

40. pp. 254-86. The Devout Hart is a translation of a Latin edition of Etienne Luzvic's Le Coeur Devot (Douai, 1627). See Chapter Three, 3.3.1. On the implications of the meditative structure exemplified in Hawkins' emblem book see Martz, pp. 13-20; pp. 27-36. The "colloquy," which is essential in meditative exercises, is incorporated in "Love (III)" as one of the three degrees of truth (St. Bernard): humble effort, loving sympathy, enraptured vision (Martz, p. 16). After the purification of the soul it can have a "colloquy" with God (Martz, pp. 36-7).

41. Cf. Matt. 22:2-14, 2 Cor. 11:2, Rev. 19:7-9 and Rev. 21:2.

42. Cf. Rev. 5:6: "And I beheld, and, lo, in the midst of the throne and of the four beasts, and in the midst of the elders, stood a Lamb as it had been slain, ..." and Rev. 7:16,17: "They shall hunger no more, neither thirst any more ... For the Lamb which is in the midst of the throne shall feed them, and shall lead them unto living fountains of waters: and God shall wipe away all tears from their eyes."

42

An interesting feature of "The Hymne" in relation to our topic is that both the "meat" and the "fleece" of the Lamb are part of a cluster of eye images. On earth the soul was unable to see the Lamb's meat, because of the fleece, but now, in Heaven, it will be "conceal'd no more" from his eyes. In the final line the function of the eyes is described in terms of a Neoplatonic advancement: "By seeing, comprehend, enioy." The mystical union in the heavenly banquet is achieved through a meditative exercise of the senses and the mind.

In "The Incentive," the second, prose part of the emblem, the details of the picture are explained one by one:

> 1. Iesvs the bloudy Spouse or Spouse of bloud leads his beloued, whom now long since he purchased with the price of his life, vnto the Nuptial supper of the Lamb, into the heauenly Bride-chãber. The hart therefore (who admires not) is the banqueting roome of these Nuptials and the Bed-chamber of the Spouse IESVS himself.
>
> 2. It is a supper truly, because these ioyes are not affoarded til after the toyles of the day and labours past ... *The Lamb himself is the lamp within,* and he the banquet

Host, and Ghest who is the Spouse.
3. Seest thou this royal Table here. These things are al prepared for thee: ... Such as sit downe here are alwayes feeding ... Behold al things are ready. *Come to the wedding, the Spouse cals.*

The "Preamble to the Meditation" that follows the Incentive, begins thus:

Iesvs, receiues the soule, whom he gratiously beheld, though fowly dight with her immundityes before, and now hauing cleansed her with purging waters, and adorned with feminine brauery, takes her I say, not only to his Spouse, but if she keep her holily and chastly to him, casting her out of the most miserable banishment of this life, he leades her vnto the great solemnity of the Nuptials, into the heauenly house of his Father ...

The parallels between the emblem and "Love (III)" are evident. One aspect is worth singling out for comment. "The Incentive" indicates why the banquet is called a supper: "... because these ioyes are not affoarded til after the toyles of the day and labours past" and the "Preamble" likewise refers to the pilgrimage of life, although in a more moralizing vein: "... though fowly dight with her immundityes before, ..." We found the same contrast between present bliss and past misery in "Love (III)," in the line "Guiltie of dust and sinne."

If the parallels between emblem and poem are obvious, the differences between them are equally manifest. The emblem presents a religious truth, Herbert's poem explores it; the emblem tells of the relationship between Divine Love and the human soul, "Love (III)" enacts that relationship in a dramatic dialogue.

The search for relevant background material to clarify Herbert's use of sense imagery in "Love (III)" has yielded a variety of analogical sources, each of which illustrates one or more aspects of that imagery. We have found, among other things, that the word "meat" is often used in conjunction with imagery of the senses. Furthermore it does not seem justified to discuss the function of the senses in isolation from one other. All the senses 'conspire' to bring about the ultimate reunion of God — high priest and spouse — and the soul at the heavenly supper.

The varied nature of the material discussed indicates once more that it is useless to try and pin Herbert down to a particular source. Although "Love (III)" teems with allusions to emblems, the Bible and the liturgy of the Church, its origins cannot be traced back to one exclusive source. The poem is a coherent, self-contained whole in which the conventional and the transformational aspects of Herbert's art are perfectly balanced.

3.3. Imagery of the eyes in "Love (III)."

Bearing in mind the conclusion of the preceding section that the imagery of the senses in "Love (III)" forms a meaningful pattern, I shall here focus on one cluster of images within that pattern and analyse the eye images in the poem. They are central. In commenting on each of the four distinct eye images we shall assume that they are *not* intended by Herbert as a play on the contrast between Divine and profane Love. An interpretation based on such a contrast would be reductive in the same way that the interpretation of the poem as a parody or version of the courtly love tradition is reductive. Such readings are based on a conception of metaphysical images and conceits characteristic of our century rather than Herbert's.

3.3.1. Quick-eyed Love.

The string of eye imagery in "Love (III)" consists of four separate images: "quick-ey'd Love," "I cannot look on thee," "Who made the eyes but I," and "I marr'd them."

I have already indicated the analogy between "quick-ey'd" in the poem and Hebrews 4:12,13, where God's word is called "quick." Some critics have regarded the compound as a pun to bring out the contrast between blind Cupid and "quick-eyed" Divine Love, the word "quick" meaning "living." This is the first meaning of the word in the *OED*: "Living, endowed with life, in contrast to what is naturally inanimate" (*s.v.* Quick, A, I, 1). The *OED* does not, however, list any examples of the compound "quick-eyed" under this meaning. The compound is listed as a separate lemma and the only meaning attributed to the word "quick" in combination with "eyed" is: "Of the eye, ear, etc.: Keen or rapid in its function; capable of ready or swift perception" (*s.v.* Quick, A, I, 20). That is the meaning of the word, for instance, in *The Faerie Queene*, I, ii, 26:

> He in great passion all this while did dwell,
> More busying his quicke eyes, her face to view,
> Then his dull eares, to heare what she did tell;[43]

In none of the examples of "quick-eyed" listed in the *OED* is there a contrast, explicit or implied, between "quick" and "blind." On the basis of these data I conclude that "quick-ey'd," besides pointing forward to "observing," underlines the qualitative difference between the two protagonists in the poem. The speaker is both dull of hearing and dull-eyed, Love is "capable of ready or swift perception" in both respects.

Herbert does not use the compound "quick-eyed" elsewhere in his poetry. The closest he comes to using it is in "Mattens," one of the poems clearly related to the *Schola Cordis* tradition. The third stanza could

---

43. *Spenser's Faerie Queene*, I, 25. These lines are interesting because they exhibit a contrast between the acuteness of the eyes as opposed to the dullness of the ears. In "Love (III)" there is a similar contrast but the "dull eares" are the speaker's, not Love's.

almost serve as a gloss on Love's attitude in "Love (III)":

> My God, what is a heart,
> That thou shouldst it so eye, and wooe,
> Powring upon it all thy art,
> As if that thou hadst nothing els to do? (ll. 9-12; *Works*, p. 62)

"The Glance" shows an even closer verbal resemblance to "Love (III)" than does "Mattens." The whole poem hinges on its central image, "thy first glance":

> If thy first glance so powerfull be,
> A mirth but open'd and seal'd up again;
> What wonders shall we feel, when we shall see
> Thy full-ey'd love!
> When thou shalt look us out of pain,
> And one aspect of thine spend in delight
> More then a thousand sunnes disburse in light,
> In heav'n above. (ll. 17-24; *Works*, p. 172)

Herbert distinguishes God's "first glance" at man on earth from His "full-ey'd love" in Heaven. There is no suggestion of a distinction between a seeing and a blind God of love; the emphasis is on the extent to which man is allowed to be in direct, visual contact with God. Mosaic law forbids him to see God fully while he is alive.[44]

The following passage from Vaughan's poem "Cock-crowing" also mentions God's "full-ey'd love" and, in my opinion, illustrates the transition from Herbert's first eye image in "Love (III)" to the next:

> If joyes, and hopes, and earnest throws,
> And hearts, whose Pulse beats still for light
> Are given to birds; who, but thee, knows
> A love-sick souls exalted flight?
> Can souls be track'd by any eye
> But his, who gave them wings to flie?
>
> Onely this Veyle which thou hast broke,
> And must be broken yet in me,
> This veyle, I say, is all the cloke,
> And cloud which shadows thee from me.
> This veyle thy full-ey'd love denies,
> And onely gleams and fractions spies. (ll. 31-42)[45]

Vaughan, whose debt to Herbert is of course well-known, has "full-ey'd" for Herbert's "quick-ey'd Love."[46] The difference between the two

---

44. Exodus 33:20: "And he said, Thou canst not see my face: for there shall no man see me, and live."
45. From *Silex Scintillans* in *The Works of Henry Vaughan*, p. 489.
46. About the relation Vaughan/Herbert see Herbert's *Works*, pp. xli-xlii. Also Chapter Four, 2 and n. 20.

phrases is that the former emphasizes the completeness of God's love and the latter the acuteness of His vision.

3.3.2. "I cannot look on thee."

The veil in Vaughan's poem is not mentioned in "Love (III)" but is implicit in the second eye image, "I cannot look on thee." Herbert's phrase is much more dramatic than the final two lines of the quotation from Vaughan. Vaughan's image is conventional and strictly emblematic; the veil — the barrier of sin interposing between man and God — is presented more or less statically and in general terms. Herbert's phrase is just as conventional, but it also has a dramatic function. The phrase has been made part of the experience of the speaker and the reader is made to realize and visualize his predicament and all the emphasis falls on the mental struggle of the pilgrim himself, standing before Love with bent head, ashamed to look up and only able to express his feelings of sinfulness and unworthiness: "Guiltie of dust and sinne," "I, the unkinde, ungratefull." On the textual level, therefore, the phrase "I cannot look on thee" has a function similar to that of "quick-ey'd Love." Love is *aware* of the anguish of the pilgrim and, conversely, the pilgrim is *aware* of his unworthiness. This awareness is in both cases expressed by means of imagery of sight.

The phrase "I cannot look on thee" also derives part of its significance from conventional sources, more specifically the Bible. Its source text is God's speech to Moses in Exodus 33:20 (see n. 44). In the corollary of this text the metaphor of the veil is introduced: "And till Moses had done speaking with them, he put a vail on his face" (Exodus, 34:33). The metaphor of the veil returns in the counterpart of these two verses from Exodus in the New Testament, 2 Corinthians 3:

14 But their minds were blinded: for until this day remaineth the same vail untaken away in the reading of the old testament; which vail is done away in Christ.
15 But even unto this day, when Moses is read, the vail is upon their heart.
16 Nevertheless when it shall turn to the Lord, the vail shall be taken away.

The two aspects of the imagery of the eyes in these Bible texts found their way into literature. Sometimes the stress is on man's inability to look directly at God, or at God's ministering agents, because of their unearthly brilliance. Dante, for instance, describes the meeting with an angel in Purgatory as follows:

And near and nearer as he came full sail
The bird of God shone momently more bright,
So that mine eyes endured him not, but fell.[47]

47. *Purgatory*, II, ll. 37-39.

In the courtly context of Chaucer's *Legend of Good Women* the speaker
cannot look at the approaching god of love:

> But of his face I can not seyn the hewe;
> For sikerly his face shon so bryghte
> That with the glem astoned was the syghte;
> A furlong-wey I myhte hym not beholde.[48]

At other times the emphasis is on man's sinful state which prevents him
from directing his eyes at God. This type of imagery controls the final
canto of Dante's *Paradise*. Dante will be allowed to behold the 'Infinite
Good' only after St. Bernard has pleaded with the Holy Virgin to
intercede on his behalf:

> [I pray]
> That of all mortal cloudings which impairs,
>   Thine own prayers may possess the power to clean
>   His sight, till in the highest bliss it shares ...
>
> For now my sight, clear and yet clearer grown,
>   Pierced through the ray of that exalted light,
>   Wherein, as in itself, the truth is known.[49]

Donne's poem "Good Friday, 1613. Riding Westward" is full of eye
images. It contains most of the traditional images that make up the
background of Herbert's line "I cannot look on thee":

> Hence is't, that I am carryed towards the West
> This day, when my Soules forme bends toward the East.
> There I should see a Sunne, by rising set,
> And by that setting endlesse day beget;
> But that Christ on this Crosse, did rise and fall,
> Sinne had eternally benighted all.
> Yet dare I'almost be glad, I do not see
> That spectacle of too much weight for mee.
> Who sees Gods face, that is selfe life, must dye;
> What a death were it then to see God dye? ...
> Though these things, as I ride, be from mine eye,
> They'are present yet unto my memory,
> For that looks towards them; and thou look'st towards mee,
> O Saviour, as thou hang'st upon the tree;
> I turne my backe to thee, but to receive
> Corrections, till thy mercies bid thee leave.
> O thinke mee worth thine anger, punish mee,
> Burne off my rusts, and my deformity,

---

48. *The Works*, p. 487 (G 162-165). The many links between Chaucer and Dante are
of course too well-known to be set forth here. The particular connection between the
passage from Chaucer's *Legend* and Dante's *Purgatory* was made by Mario Praz in
Monthly Criterion, VI, 22 (Robinson, p. 843n.).
49. *Paradise*, XXXIII, ll. 31-33; 52-54.

Restore thine Image, so much, by thy grace,
That thou may'st know mee, and I'll turne my face.[50]

The line "Who sees God's face, that is self life, must die" is a paraphrase of Exodus 33:20. If one regards the respective poems by Donne and Herbert as describing stages of the pilgrimage of life, then Donne's is clearly descriptive of an earlier part of the pilgrim's journey. The corrections which the speaker in "Good Friday" asks for and which are expounded in physical terms, are administered by word of mouth in "Love (III)." The pilgrim's utterance "I cannot look on thee" looks back to his situation before his arrival at Heaven's gate. What he says is true within the context of the previous situation; it is based, after all, on the Mosaic dispensation. Here, however, at the Inn of Heaven, the pilgrim's speech is brushed aside by Love, who reminds him gently but firmly that a different law and a different dispensation now apply: "Who made the eyes but I?"

3.3.3. "Who made the eyes but I?"

What strikes us at first sight, or rather sound, when we read the line "Who made the eyes but I?" is the assonance of "eyes" and "I." It is the corollary of the homophone "Son"/"sun," one of the favourite puns of Renaissance poets, instanced in the line "There I should see a Sunne, by rising set" in the passage quoted from Donne's "Good Friday, 1613." The point of the assonance is that the faculty of vision emanates from God, the centre of light. A similar point is made about the ear in "Longing": "*Shall he that made the eare, / Not heare?*" (ll. 35-6; *Works*, p. 149).

Love's speech, like the pilgrim's remark preceding it, has a counterpart in Exodus: "And the Lord said unto him, Who hath made man's mouth? or who maketh the dumb, or deaf, or the seeing, or the blind? have not I the Lord?" (4:11). The same idea is expressed in Proverbs, 20:12: "The hearing ear, and the seeing eye, the Lord hath made even both of them." By putting the words of God as Creator into the mouth of God as Divine Love, Herbert adds an element of consolation. This consolatory element is strengthened by the context in which the phrase is placed. The pilgrim who, supported by the authority of the Old Testament, has just affirmed his inability to look at the Lord, is reminded by Divine Love that he is not addressing the Old Testament God of the Law but the God of Love of the Christian dispensation.

In the section of this chapter dealing with the poem's relation to emblems I suggested that the intimacy between the soul and God

---

50. *The Divine Poems*, pp. 30-31; ll. 9-18; ll. 33-42.

43   **44**

characteristic of Herbert's poem is equally characteristic of the Amor/
Anima emblems, particularly of their pictures. This relationship is most
clearly expressed in the lines we are considering here:

> Love took my hand, and smiling did reply,
>   Who made the eyes but I?

Although I have not found examples in emblem books that match these
lines exactly, a comparison with one or two Amor/Anima emblems will
demonstrate how closely similar they are. One of the emblems in Hall's
emblem book (1648) shows Divine Love assisting Anima in untying her
blindfold (see fig. 43).[51] The accompanying verses do not fit the picture
at all, but it is not difficult to ascertain its meaning. The blindfold no
doubt refers to the veil of the Old Testament that prevents man from
looking at God directly, and was removed by Christ's Sacrifice.

The other emblem analogous to "Love (III)" is from Hugo's *Pia
Desideria*. It is the first emblem of the second part of the book and bears a
motto from Psalm 119 (see fig. 44). The picture shows Anima in

---

51. *Emblems with Elegant Figures: Sparkles of Divine Love*, p. 20.

the process of making a choice between the two Cupids, Amor Divinus on her right hand and Amor Mundanus on her left. Anima is touching the Tables of the Ten Commandments with one hand and with the other is pushing aside earthly Cupid and his attributes, although the latter tries in vain to deflect Anima's attention from his rival. The scene in the background emphasizes the contrast between the two deities: the un-bridled rearing horse is the symbol of unrestrained passion, whereas the ox signifies the patience and strength of the true Christian and is often used to symbolize Christ's sacrifice. In the verse and prose text that accompanies the emblem the choice of Anima is explained as a conflict between the desire of the flesh and the inclination of the heart. In the following passage from the prose text the metaphor of the eye of the senses and the eye of the heart illustrates these conflicting wishes:

> Petitio cordis quae est? sicut petitio carnis est, velle sibi praeparari oculos, utique ad videndam istam lucem (quae talibus oculis videri potest) ita petitio cordis, ad illam lucem pertinet; *Beati mundi cordes, quoniam ipsi Deum videbunt.*[52]

The italicized line is a quotation of Matthew 5:8: "Blessed are the pure in heart: for they shall see God."[53] The emblem thus contrasts not only the two kinds of love but also distinguishes the Old dispensation from the New. These are not only present in the text but also suggested by the fact that, in the picture, Divine Love is holding the Tables of the Law.

One more emblem is worth mentioning here. It does not belong to the Amor/Anima tradition and is more abstract and philosophical (see fig. 45). The emblem, no. XLIII of Book I in Wither's emblem book, bears the motto:

> *The* Minde *should have a fixed Eye*
> *On Objects, that are plac'd on High.*

The picture shows a rural landscape in which the sun, with kindly countenance, is shooting its rays at a heart with an eye at its centre. The

---

52. "What is the desire of the heart? As the flesh desires for its eyes to be enabled to see the one light (that is visible to such eyes), so the desire of the heart is directed toward the other light." *Pia Desideria*, p. 131. The Latin word *iste* frequently implies scorn or contempt; see Lewis & Short, *A Latin Dictionary* (Oxford: Oxford Univ. Press, 1879), *s.v.* "iste," II, B.

53. St. Augustine remarks about Matt. 5:8: "To the pure of heart — as to those who possess an eye purified for understanding eternal things — the power to see God [is given]" (*De Sermone Domini in monte*, I, 4, 12). In the same commentary on the sermon on the mount he writes, "just as that light [which is around us] cannot be seen except through eyes that are clear, so neither is God seen unless that through which he can be seen is pure" (*ibid.*, I, 2, 8). Hence the Christian should "cleanse the medium through which God can be seen," and this medium is the heart. I owe these quotations to John Edward Sullivan, O.P., *The Image of God: The Doctrine of St. Augustine and its Influence* (Dubuque, Iowa: The Priory Press, 1963), p. 66; see also p. 68.

The Minde *should have a fixed Eye*
On Objects, that are plac'd on High.

ILLVSTR. XLIII.   *Book.* I.

45

text is about sight and the eye of contemplation as the human faculty that
was especially created by God for its capacity to achieve direct contact
with Him. The vocabulary and ideas are Neoplatonic and remind one
occasionally of the final passage of Dante's *Paradise*, which we quoted
before:

> A *Heart*, which bore the figure of an *Eye*
> Wide open to the *Sunne*; by some, was us'd,
> When in an *Emblem*, they would signifie
> A *Minde*, which on Celestiall Matters mus'd:
> Implying, by the same, that there is nought
> Which in this lower *Orbe*, our Eyes can see,
> So fit an Object for a manly thought,
> As those things, which in Heav'n above us be.
>   *God*, gave *Mankinde* (above all other Creatures)
> A lovely *Forme*, and upward-looking *Eye*,
> (Among the rest of his peculiar *Features*)
> That he might lift his *Countenance* on high:
> And (having view'd the Beauty, which appeares

Within the outward *Sights* circumference)
That he might elevate above the Sphaeres,
The piercing Eye, of his *Intelligence*.
Then, higher, and still higer strive to raise
His *Contemplations* Eyes, till they ascend
To gaine a glimpse of those eternall *Rayes*,
To which all undepraved *Spirits* tend.
For, 'tis the proper nature of the *Minde*
(Till fleshly *Thoughts* corrupt it) to despise
Those Lusts whereto the *Body* stands inclin'd;
And labour alwayes, *upward* to arise.

The analogical examples discussed here not only illustrate the significance of the phrase "Who made the eyes but I?" but illuminate the whole
series of eye images in the poem, from the despondent "I cannot look on
thee" to the final self-accusatory image: "Truth Lord, but I have marr'd
them ..."

3.3.4. "I have marr'd them."

On the first level of interpretation this line explains why the pilgrim
cannot look at Love: he has forfeited his right to look because of his
sinful past; "dust and sinne" have ruined his capacity to use the eye of
contemplation properly. The connection of this with the lines preceding
and following it is further strengthened by an underlying idiomatic
structure. Herbert is playing here with the expression ' to make or mar.'
The *OED* defines the meaning of the expression as follows: "to cause
either the complete success or the ruin of (a person or thing)."[54] Herbert
uses the expression in this sense in "The Church-porch":

> ... in service, care or coldnesse
> Doth ratably thy fortunes marre or make. (ll. 255-6; *Works*, p. 16)

Sidney uses it in *The Old Arcadia*:

> Such force hath Love above poore Nature's power,
> That I growe like a shade,
> Which being nought seems somewhat to the eyen,
> While that one body shine.
> Oh he is mard that is for others made.[55]

Sidney is writing about earthly love, Herbert about its divine counterpart.
To Love's "Who made the eyes but I" the speaker reacts "... but I have

---

54. *OED, s.v.* to make v.[1] 46 b.
55. *The Poems of Sir Philip Sidney*, p. 19: "The First Eclogues," 7, ll. 162-166. Cf.
also *Romeo and Juliet*, I, ii, 13: "And too soon marr'd are those so early made" (Brian
Gibbons, ed. (London: Methuen, 1980), p. 95), and Fulke Greville, from *Mustapha*,
"Chorus Tertius, Of Time: Eternity," l. 145: "Cross your own steps; hasten to make,
and mar" (*Selected Poems*, p. 148).

marr'd them," thus ostensibly refuting Love's remark, because his "mar" seems to undermine the force of Love's "make." In the lines that follow, however, Love adroitly counters the pilgrim's argument.

The idiomatic structure I am referring to is completed in Love's words: "And know you not ... who bore the blame?" On the surface level this rhetorical question resolves the conflict between Love and the pilgrim, because the sinful behaviour of the latter can be forgiven through the mediation of the Redeemer. Bearing in mind the expression "make or mar" echoed in the preceding lines, one may detect a hint of another stock phrase, to wit, "make or mend." This phrase also occurs several times in Herbert's work. In "Love (II)," for instance, the expression is used in connection with the eyes:

> Our eies shall see thee, which before saw dust;
> Dust blown by wit, till that they both were blinde:
> ... All knees shall bow to thee; all wits shall rise,
> And praise him who did make and mend our eies. (ll. 9-10; ll. 13-4; Works, p. 54)[56]

In "Love (III)" Love, by bearing "the blame," mends what man has "marr'd." In religious terms this is the ultimate triumph of the New dispensation over the Old. The New dispensation of grace in which Christ figures as Redeemer, as a 'mender' of eyes, solves a conflict that was insoluble under Mosaic law. Vaughan formulated this idea in his "Easter Hymn":

> Death, and darkness get you packing,
> Nothing now to man is lacking,
> All your triumphs now are ended,
> And what *Adam* marr'd, is mended.[57]

---

56. The other two instances in Herbert's work are these:

> Lord, mend or rather make us: one creation
>   Will not suffice our turn:
> Except thou make us dayly, we shall spurn
>   Our own salvation. ("Giddinesse," ll. 25-28; Works, p. 127)

> Come, my Light, my Feast, my Strength:
> Such a Light, as shows a feast:
> Such a Feast, as mends in length:
> Such a Strength, as makes his guest. ("The Call," ll. 5-8; Works, p. 156)

57. Vaughan, Works, p. 457, ll. 1-4. Cf. also Donne, "Thou hast made me ...":

> Thou hast made me, And shall thy worke decay?
> Repaire me now, for now mine end doth haste ...
> I dare not move my dimme eyes any way,
> Despaire behind, and death before doth cast
> Such terrour, and my feebled flesh doth waste

4. Conclusion.

The sense imagery in "Love (III)" does not, as some critics think, imply a contrast between a Christian and a mythological god of love, but suggests a contrast between the two Testaments, between the Mosaic and the Christian dispensations. This contrast is resolved by the redeeming role of Christ. The opposition between a blind Cupid and a seeing God of love is final; the opposition between the sinful human being who has "marr'd" his eyes and the soul joyfully received in Heaven can be bridged and is effectively bridged by the God of Love, who has not only "made" the eyes of man but has, through Christ's Sacrifice, also mended them. The poem describes the progress of the soul from its sinful stage towards a state of bliss. The healing of the eyes is part of the process.

Herbert's religious poetry is closer in spirit to the Platonism of the humanists than to the moralizing mythography of the Middle Ages in which blind Cupid came into being.[58] In "Love (III)" Divine Love 'gives eyes' to his guest as a token of his having made the final step in the Platonic-Christian advancement towards the ultimate good where no veil need any longer separate man from his God.[59]

By sinne in it, which it t'wards hell doth weigh;
Onely thou art above, and when towards thee
By thy leave I can looke, I rise againe; (ll. 1-2; 5-10 from *Divine Meditations*, 1 in *Divine Poems*, p. 12)

58. See Panofsky's seminal essay "Blind Cupid," in *Studies in Iconology*, pp. 95-128.

59. See C.S. Lewis, *English Literature in the Sixteenth Century* (Oxford: Oxford Univ. Press, 1954), p. 339. The case of Neoplatonism has often been overstated or misapplied; for a sensible analysis of the movement see Lewis, *English Literature in the Sixteenth Century*, pp. 8 ff. Also E.H. Gombrich, *Symbolic Images*, pp. 1-22; E. Panofsky, *Studies in Iconology*, pp. 129 ff.; E. Wind, *Pagan Mysteries in the Renaissance*, pp. 36 ff. On the place of the Neoplatonic philosophy in the culture of the 15th and 16th centuries Panofsky writes aptly that it "played a role in Cinquecento society not unlike that of semi-popular books on psychoanalysis in our day. What had been an esoteric philosophy became a kind of social game so that 'finally the courtiers thought it an indispensable part of their job to know how many and what kinds of love there were,' to quote the caustic remark of a sixteenth-century philologist" (p. 146).

251

A FINAL WORD

In this study I have attempted to elucidate a few aspects of Herbert's poetic art by presenting a careful reading of four of his poems within a contextual and comparative framework. The investigation has concentrated on imagery and on the emblematic aspect of the imagery in particular, although it has not been restricted to emblems alone. The poems themselves, written within a particular environment and in a particular period, have determined by and large the direction of the inquiry. Emblematic literature has, however, proved especially useful.

The comparison between Herbert's poems and specific emblems or emblem types has exemplified the extent and nature of the poet's debt to his sources but it has likewise illustrated the measure in which he transcended them, managing to transform them into something new. The poetic imagery that is the result of this transformation process, through its combination of immediacy and intricacy, calls on all the faculties of the reader: the senses and the mind, the feelings and the imagination. The altar in the poem by that name, and the wings in "Easter-wings" are two such images, the two hills of "The Pilgrimage" and the eye in "Love (III)" are two more. Each of these images in its own way gives concrete form to complex ideas, each of them is connected in subtle ways with other images in the poem and each determines to a large extent the structure and coherence of the poem it is part of. Moreover, the images are related to a number of traditions and conventions, literary and other. Finally, they are expressive of the mental state ("The Altar" and "Easter-wings") or the mental development ("The Pilgrimage" and "Love (III)") of the speaker and are therefore determinants of tone.

The investigation may also have enabled the reader to mark certain differences between the poems concerned. The pattern poems are exceptional in Herbert's work because they constitute the emblematic picture that in the other poems can be visualized in the imagination only. "The Altar" and "Easter-wings" are prayers and are static in that they describe a state of mind or an emotional condition. "The Pilgrimage" and "Love (III)" are allegories and are dynamic in that they describe stages of the pilgrimage of life and involve a dramatic confrontation between the speaker and another force or person. To formulate it in another way, the two pattern poems are imploratory, "The Pilgrimage" and "Love (III)" exploratory. In both types the emblematic aspect serves its purpose; in the pattern poems as a means of concentration, perhaps also with a mnemonic function, in the other two poems as a starting-point for the exploration of mysteries that are far more fundamental than the emblematic puzzle.

All this goes to show that Herbert's poems are different from emblems not in degree but in kind. The comparison with emblems has brought out the essential difference between Herbert and the emblem writer. Herbert works by implication, the emblem writer by equation. The poet whose poetry can only be understood by the reader's resorting to the sources is a pedant rather than a poet, but this does not mean that the study of those sources is a useless undertaking. Herbert was, as we have seen, a transformer, who had the ability to reshape and remake any material or subject-matter available to him. He used the resources of his cultural and religious environment as so many stepping-stones towards an end that virtually defies formulation; the ultimate definition of the relation between a human being and his God. A true appreciation of the finished products of that transformation process, the poems, should take account of what fed them. The 'simplicity' of Herbert's verse is a poetic result, not a starting-point; it is a mark of the poet's genius.

There is nothing essentially novel in the way I went about the investigation. Well-established concepts and well-tested procedures were used. Genre, authorial intention, source and analogy, cultural and religious heritage are some of the variegated notions that played a part in this study's progress. I would like to introduce the term 'applied scholarship' as a useful one to define my approach to the relation between the literary text and its background. Applied scholarship avoids the Scylla of a heuristic approach that is purely idiosyncratic and the Charybdis of source hunting as the be-all and end-all of hermeneutic activities.

A term alone can never take the place of intelligent and sensitive reading, however. Critical acumen can be promoted, but is not guaranteed by 'method,' by the tools of literary analysis and by literary theory. Nor can myriads of footnotes by their quantity ensure a truer and fuller understanding of a particular literary text, either by the zealous applied scholar or by his reader.[1] "Accuracy is a matter of relevance," Leavis wrote, "and how in the literary field, in any delicate issue, can one hope

1. In her recently published book *In Defence of the Imagination* (Oxford: Oxford Univ. Press, 1982) Helen Gardner, one of the great authorities in the field of 17th century and religious poetry, deplores the pretence of literary studies that, on the basis of fancy terminology, purport to be critically active: "... there were words which the critic had made up for his own pleasure in a mood of high spirits or 'playfulness,' a word which for some appeared to be a synonym for critical activity" (p. 2).

to be duly relevant — can one hope to achieve the due pointedness and precision of relevance — without being intelligent about literature?"[2]

Trying to be an applied scholar in the full sense of the word I have used my critical judgement as intelligently as lay within my power in selecting, weighing and discussing the materials considered relevant for increasing the understanding of the poems. In this way applied scholarship is a useful and, possibly, an indispensable aid for the validation of literary interpretation. In his book *Milton's Imagery and the Visual Arts* (1978) Mushat Frye writes: "No one has a perfect dictionary to assist in understanding a great poet or a great painter, but it is incumbent upon us continually to improve and expand the dictionaries we do have" (p. 7). I hope I have expanded the Herbert dictionary, albeit in a modest way. The road atlas of Herbert's work having been drawn by other cartographers, the present study has added, I hope, a few quarter inch maps for the pilgrim who prefers to travel slowly, "from virtue to virtue, with exalted steps."[3]

2. F.R. Leavis, "The Responsible Critic: or the Function of Criticism at any Time," *Scrutiny*, 19 (1953), 162-183.

3. I have adapted a metaphor of C.S. Lewis, who writes in *The Discarded Image*:

To be always looking at the map when there is a fine prospect before you shatters the 'wise passiveness' in which landscape ought to be enjoyed. But to consult a map before we set out has no such ill effect. Indeed it will lead us to many prospects; including some we might never have found by following our noses (p. vii).

BIBLIOGRAPHY

Addison, Joseph and Richard Steele. *The Spectator.* Ed. G. Smith. 4 vols. London: Dent, 1945.

Ainsworth, Henry. *Annotations upon the Pentateuch.* Amsterdam, 1617-21.

Alciati, Andrea. *Emblematum Liber.* Augsburg, 1531.

Alger, W.R. *The Poetry of the East.* Boston, 1856.

Allen, Don Cameron. *Image and Meaning: Metaphoric Traditions in Renaissance Poetry.* Baltimore: Johns Hopkins Univ. Press, 1960.

Alvarez, A. *The Savage God: A Study of Suicide.* London: Weidenfeld & Nicolson, 1971.

Anglicus, Bartholomaeus. *De Proprietatibus Rerum.* Trans. John Trevisa (1398). Ed. M.C. Seymour. 2 vols. Oxford: Oxford Univ. Press, 1975.

Apel, Willi. *The Notation of Polyphonic Music, 900-1600.* Cambridge, Mass.: Harvard Univ. Press, 1953.

Ariès, Philippe. *Attitudes toward Death: From the Middle Ages to the Present.* Trans. Patricia M. Ranum. Baltimore: Johns Hopkins Univ. Press, 1975.

Aristotle. *The "Art" of Rhetoric.* Ed. & trans. John Henry Freese. London: Heinemann, 1967.

Augustine, St. *Confessions.* Trans. R.S. Pine-Coffin. Harmondsworth: Penguin, 1961.

Babb, Lawrence. *The Elizabethan Malady: A Study of Melancholy in Elizabethan Literature from 1580 to 1642.* East Lansing: Michigan State Univ. Press, 1951.

Babbitt, Irving. The New Laokoon. Boston: Houghton Mifflin, 1910.

Bagg, Robert. "The Electromagnet and the Shred of Platinum." *Arion,* 8 (1969), 407-429.

Barb, Alfons A. "St. Zacharias the prophet and martyr. A study in charms and incantations." *JWCI,* 11 (1948), 35-67.

Barclay, Alexander, trans. *The Ship of Fools.* Ed. T.H. Jamieson. 2 vols. Edinburgh, 1874; rpt. New York: AMS Press, 1966.

Beachcroft, T.O. "Nicholas Ferrar and George Herbert." *The Criterion,* 12 (1933), 40.

Bennett, H.S. *Chaucer and the Fifteenth Century.* Oxford: Oxford Univ. Press, 1947.

Bennett, Joan. *Five Metaphysical Poets.* 3rd ed. Cambridge: Cambridge Univ. Press, 1963.

Bernard, J.H. *A Critical and Exegetical Commentary on the Gospel According to St. John.* Ed. A.H. McNeile. Vol. I. Edinburgh: T & T. Clark, 1928.

Białostocki, Jan. "Iconography." *Dictionary of the History of Ideas,* 1973, II, 524-541.

Blount, Thomas, trans. *The Art of Making Devises.* London, 1646.

Blunt, Anthony. "An Echo of the Paragone in Shakespeare." *JWI,* 2 (1938-39), 260-62.

Bombaugh, Charles C. *Oddities and Curiosities of Words and Literature: Gleanings for the Curious.* 1890. Ed. Martin Gardner. Rpt. New York: Dover, 1961.

Bornitius, Jacob. *Emblematum Ethico-Politicorum sylloge prior (-posterior).* Heidelberg, 1664.

Bottrall, Margaret. *George Herbert.* London: John Murray, 1954.

255

Boultenhouse, Charles. "Poems in the Shapes of Things." *Art News Annual* (1959), 65-83.
Bowers, Fredson. "Herbert's Sequential Imagery: 'The Temper'." *MP*, 59 (1962), 202-213.
Bowler, Berjouhi. *The Word as Image*. London: Studio Vista, 1970.
Brant, Sebastian. *The Ship of Fools*. Trans. Edwin H. Zeydel. New York: Dover, 1962.
Brown, C.C. & W.P. Ingoldsby. "George Herbert's 'Easter-Wings'." *HLQ*, 35 (1971-72), 131-142.
Bruck, Jacobus â. *Emblemata Politica*. Köln, 1618.
Bunyan, John. *The Pilgrim's Progress*. Harmondsworth: Penguin, 1965.
Burton, Robert. *The Anatomy of Melancholy*. Ed. Holbrook Jackson. London: Dent, 1972.
Bush, Douglas. *English Literature in the Earlier Seventeenth Century: 1600-1660*. 2nd ed. Oxford: Oxford Univ. Press, 1962.
Carmody, Francis J., ed. *Physiologus Latinus*. Paris: Librairie E. Droz, 1939.
Cassirer, Ernst, *et al*. *The Renaissance Philosophy of Man*. Chicago: Univ. of Chicago Press, 1948.
Chambers, R.W. *Thomas More*. 1935; rpt. Harmondsworth: Penguin, 1963.
Charles, Amy M. *A Life of George Herbert*. Ithaca: Cornell Univ. Press, 1977.
————. "The Williams Manuscript and *The Temple*." *RenP* (1972), 59-77.
Charlton, Kenneth. *Education in Renaissance England*. London: Routledge & Kegan Paul, 1965.
Chaucer, Geoffrey. *The Works*. Ed. F.N. Robinson. 2nd ed. London: Oxford Univ. Press, 1957.
Chew, Samuel C. *The Pilgrimage of Life*. New Haven: Yale Univ. Press, 1962.
Chossonery, Paul. "Les 'Poèmes figurés' de George Herbert et ses prétendues fantaisies poétiques." *EA*, 26 (1973), 1-11.
Chub, William. *Two fruitfull and godly Sermons ... the one touching the building of Gods Temple, the other what the Temple is*. London, 1585.
Church, Margaret. "The First English Pattern Poems." *PMLA*, 61 (1946), 636-650.
————. "The Pattern Poem." Diss. Radcliffe College 1944.
Clements, A.L. "Theme, Tone, and Tradition in George Herbert's Poetry." *ELR*, 3 (1973), 264-83.
Clements, Robert J. *Picta Poesis: Literary and Humanistic Theory in Renaissance Emblem Books*. Temi e testi, 6. Roma: Edizioni di Storia e Letteratura, 1960.
Cody, Richard. *The Landscape of the Mind*. Oxford: Oxford Univ. Press, 1969.
Colie, Rosalie L. *Paradoxia Epidemica*. Princeton: Princeton Univ. Press, 1966.
————. *The Resources of Kind: Genre-Theory in the Renaissance*. Ed. Barbara K. Lewalski. Berkeley: Univ. of California Press, 1973.
Collmer, Robert G. "The Meditation on Death and its Appearance in Metaphysical Poetry." *Neophil*, 45 (1961), 323-333.
Comper, Frances M.M., ed. *The Book of the Craft of Dying and Other Early English Tracts Concerning Death*. London, 1917; rpt. New York: Arno Press, 1977.

Concordances:
Eva C. Hangen. *A Concordance to the Complete Poetical Works of Sir Thomas Wyatt*. Chicago: Univ. of Chicago Press, 1941.
Charles G. Osgood. *A Concordance to the Poems of Edmund Spenser*. Gloucester, Mass.: Peter Smith, 1963.
Herbert S. Donow. *A Concordance to the Poems of Sir Philip Sidney*. Ithaca: Cornell Univ. Press, 1975.

Marvin Spevack. *A Complete and Systematic Concordance to the Works of Shakespeare.* Vol. IV. Hildesheim: Georg Olms, 1969.

Homer C. Combs & Zay R. Sullens. *A Concordance to the English Poems of John Donne.* 1940; rpt. New York: Haskell House, 1969.

Malcolm MacLeod. *A Concordance to the Poems of Robert Herrick.* 1936; rpt. New York: Haskell House, 1971.

Cameron Mann. *A Concordance to the English Poems of George Herbert.* Boston: Houghton Mifflin, 1927.

Mario A. di Cesare & Rigo Mignani. *A Concordance to the Complete Writings of George Herbert.* Ithaca: Cornell Univ. Press, 1977.

William Ingram & Kathleen Swain. *A Concordance to Milton's English Poetry.* Oxford: Oxford Univ. Press, 1972.

George R. Guffey. *A Concordance to the English Poems of Andrew Marvell.* Chapel Hill: Univ. of North Carolina Press, 1974.

Imilda Tuttle. *Concordance to Vaughan's Silex Scintillans.* University Park & London: Pennsylvania State Univ. Press, 1969.

Concrete Poetry. Exhibition Catalogue. Stedelijk Museum, Amsterdam, 1970.

Cook, A.S., ed. *The Old English Elene, Phoenix and Physiologus.* New Haven: Yale Univ. Press, 1919.

Cranmer, Thomas. *The Work.* Ed. G.E.Duffield. Appleford, Berks.: Sutton Courtenay Press, 1964.

Crashaw, Richard. *The Poems.* Ed. L.C. Martin. 2nd ed. Oxford: Oxford Univ. Press, 1957.

Crossan, Greg. "Herbert's Love (III)." *Expl,* 37 (Fall, 1978), 40-41.

Curiosités Littéraires. Bibliothèque de Poche par une société de gens de lettres et d' érudits. Paris, 1845.

Curley, Michael J., trans. & introd. *Physiologus.* Austin: Univ. of Texas Press, 1979.

Dante Alighieri. *The Divine Comedy.* Trans. Dorothy L. Sayers. 3 vols. Harmondsworth: Penguin, 1949, 1955, 1962.

Davies, Cicely. "Ut Pictura Poesis." *MLR,* 30 (1935), 159-169.

Davies, Horton. *Worship and Theology in England: From Andrewes to Baxter and Fox, 1603-1690.* Princeton, N.J.: Princeton Univ. Press, 1975.

Denny, William. *Pelecanicidium: Or the Christian Adviser against Self-Murder. Together with a Guide, and the Pilgrims Passe to the Land of the Living.* London, 1653.

D' Israeli, Isaac. *Curiosities of Literature.* London: Routledge, 1867.

Donne, John. *The Divine Poems.* Ed. Helen Gardner. 2nd ed. Oxford: Oxford Univ. Press, 1978.

—————. *The Elegies and the Songs and Sonnets.* Ed. Helen Gardner. Oxford: Oxford Univ. Press, 1965.

—————. *The Satires, Epigrams and Verse Letters.* Ed. W. Milgate. Oxford: Oxford Univ. Press, 1967.

—————. *The Sermons.* Ed. Evelyn M. Simpson & George R. Potter. 10 vols. Berkeley: Univ. of California Press, 1953-1962.

Dorsch, T.S., trans. *Classical Literary Criticism.* Harmondsworth: Penguin, 1965.

Droulers, E. *Dictionnaire des Attributs, Allégories, Emblèmes et Symboles.* Turnhout: Brepols, n.d.

Dryden, John. *Essays.* Ed. W.P. Ker. 2 vols. New York: Russell & Russell, 1900.

Drummond, William. *The Poetical Works.* Ed. L.E. Kastner. 2 vols. Manchester, 1913; rpt. New York: Haskell, 1968.

257

Edmonds, J.M., ed. *The Greek Bucolic Poets*. The Loeb Classical Library, 28. London: Heinemann, 1938.

Einstein, Alfred. "Augenmusik im Madrigal." *Zeitschrift der Internationalen Musikgesellschaft*, 14 (1912-13), 18.

Eliot, T.S. *Collected Poems, 1909-1962*. London: Faber & Faber, 1963.

————. *George Herbert*. London: Longmans, Green & Co., 1962.

————. *Selected Essays*. 3rd ed. London: Faber & Faber, 1951.

Empson, William. *Seven Types of Ambiguity*. Rev. ed. New York: New Directions, 1947.

Erskine, Thomas. "Eye and Ear Imagery in the Poetry of George Herbert and Henry Vaughan." Diss. Emory Univ. 1970.

Estienne, Henry. *L'Art de Faire les Devises, où il est traicté des Hieroglyphyques, Symboles, Emblemes, Aenygmes, Sentences, Paraboles, Revers de Medailles, Armes, Blasons, Cimiers, Chiffres & Rebus*. Paris, 1645.

————. *Exposition et explication des devises, emblèmes et figures énigmatiques du feu construit devant l'hostel de ville ... sur l'heureuse naissance et retour du Roy*. Paris, 1649.

Ferguson, George. *Signs & Symbols in Christian Art*. London: Oxford Univ. Press, 1954.

Fish, Stanley E. *The Living Temple: George Herbert and Catechizing*. Berkeley: Univ. of California Press, 1978.

————. *Self-Consuming Artifacts: The Experience of Seventeenth-Century Literature*. Berkeley: Univ. of California Press, 1972.

Florio, John., trans. *Montaigne's Essays*. 3 vols. London: Dent, 1910.

Ford, Ford Madox. *The March of Literature: From Confucius' Day to Our Own*. New York: Dial Press, 1938.

Fowler, A.D.S., trans. & ed. *De Re Poetica by Richard Wills*. Oxford: Blackwell, 1958.

Freeman, Rosemary. *English Emblem Books*. London: Chatto & Windus, 1948.

————. "George Herbert and the Emblem Books." *RES*, 17 (1941), 150-165.

Freer, Coburn. *Music for a King: George Herbert's Style and the Metrical Psalms*. Baltimore: Johns Hopkins Univ. Press, 1972.

Frye, Northrop. *Anatomy of Criticism: Four Essays*. Princeton: Princeton Univ. Press, 1957.

Frye, Roland Mushat. *Milton's Imagery and the Visual Arts*. Princeton: Princeton Univ. Press, 1978.

Fuller, Thomas. *A Pisgah-Sight of Palestine*. London, 1650.

Gabalawy, Saad El-. "George Herbert and the *Ars Amatoria*." *Xavier Univ. Studies*, 10 (1971), 28-33.

————. "The Pilgrimage: George Herbert's Favourite Allegorical Technique." *College Language Association Bulletin*, 13 (1970), 408-419.

Gardner, Helen. *In Defence of the Imagination*. Oxford: Oxford Univ. Press, 1982.

Sir Gawain and the Green Knight. Trans. Marie Borroff. New York: W.W. Norton, 1967.

"George Herbert's 'Easter-Wings'." *N&Q*, 8th Ser., 7 (26 Jan., 1895), 66.

Giovannini, G. "Method in the Study of Literature in its Relation to the Other Fine Arts." *JAAC*, 8 (1950), 185-195.

Gombrich, Ernst H. "Icones Symbolicae: The Visual Image in Neo-Platonic Thought." *JWCI*, 11 (1948), 163-188.

————. *Symbolic Images: Studies in the Art of the Renaissance*. London: Phaidon, 1972.

Green, Henry, ed. *Andreae Alciati Emblematum Flumen abundans, or, Alciat's Emblems in their Full Stream*. Manchester: Brothers, 1871.

—————. *Andreae Alciati, Emblematum Fontes Quatuor*. Manchester: Brothers, 1870.

Greville, Fulke. *Selected Poems*. Ed. Thom Gunn. London: Faber, 1968.

Grierson, Herbert J.C., ed. *Metaphysical Lyrics & Poems of the Seventeenth Century: Donne to Butler*. Oxford: Oxford Univ. Press, 1921.

Grout, Donald J. *A History of Western Music*. 3rd ed. New York: W.W. Norton, 1980.

Haeften, Benedictus van. *Regia Via Crucis*. Antwerp: Plantin, 1635.

—————. *Schola Cordis*. Antwerp, 1629.

Hagstrum, Jean H. *The Sister Arts: The Tradition of Literary Pictorialism and English Poetry from Dryden to Gray*. Chicago: Univ. of Chicago Press, 1958.

Hahn, Jürgen. *The Origins of the Baroque Concept of Peregrinatio*. Chapel Hill: Univ. of North Carolina Press, 1973.

Hall, James. *Dictionary of Subjects and Symbols in Art*. Rev. ed. New York: Harper & Row, 1979.

Hall, John. *Emblems with Elegant Figures: Sparkles of Divine Love*. London, 1648. Rpt. ed. John Horden. Menston: Scolar Press, 1970.

Harvey, Christopher. *The Complete Poems ... being a Supplementary volume to the Complete Works ... of George Herbert*. Ed. Alexander B. Grosart. Fuller Worthies' Library. London, 1874.

—————. *Schola Cordis: or The Heart of it Selfe, gone away from God ...* London, 1647.

Hastings, Robert. "Easter Wings as a Model of Herbert's Method." *Thoth*, 4 (1963), 15-23.

Hatzfeld, Helmut A. "Literary Criticism through Art and Art Criticism through Literature." *JAAC*, 6 (1947), 1-21.

Hawes, Stephen. *The Minor Poems*. Eds. Florence W. Gluck & Alice B. Morgan. E.E.T.S., 271. London: Oxford Univ. Press, 1974.

—————. *The Works*. Introd. Frank J. Spang. Delmar, N.Y.: Scholars' Facsimiles and Reprints, 1975.

Hawkins, Henry. *The Devout Hart, or Royal Throne of the Pacifical Salomon*. Rouen, 1634. Rpt. ed. John Horden. Menston: Scolar Press, 1975.

Heissler, John M. "Mr. Herbert's Temple and Church Militant Explained and Improved by a Discourse upon Each Poem Critical and Practical by George Riley, 1714-15. A Critical Edition." 2 pts. Diss. Univ. of Illinois 1960.

Henkel, Arthur & Albrecht Schöne. *Emblemata: Handbuch zur Sinnbildkunst des XVI und XVII Jahrhunderts*. Stuttgart: Metzlersche Verlagsbuchhandlung, 1967.

Herbert, George. *The Complete Works in Verse and Prose*. Ed. Alexander B. Grosart. The Fuller Worthies' Library. 3 vols. London, 1874.

—————. *The English Poems*. Ed. C.A. Patrides. London: Dent, 1974.

—————. *The English Works, newly arranged and annotated and considered in relation to his life*. Ed. George Herbert Palmer. 3rd ed. 3 vols. Boston: Houghton Mifflin, 1915.

—————. *The Temple: Sacred Poems and Private Ejaculations*. Ed. William Pickering. 2nd ed. London, 1838.

—————. *The Works*. Ed. F.E. Hutchinson. Oxford: Oxford Univ. Press, 1941.

Herrick, Robert. *The Poetical Works*. Ed. L.C. Martin. Oxford: Oxford Univ. Press, 1956.

Higgins, Dick. *George Herbert's Pattern Poems: In their Tradition*. West Glover: Unpublished Editions, 1977.

Hirsch, E.D. *Validity in Interpretation*. New Haven: Yale Univ. Press, 1967.

Hollander, John. "Talkies." *New York Review of Books*, Dec. 8, 1977, pp. 50-54.
————. *Types of Shape*. New York: Atheneum, 1969.
————& Frank Kermode. *The Literature of Renaissance England*. Vol. II of *The Oxford Anthology of English Literature*. New York: Oxford Univ. Press, 1973.
Horace. *Satires, Epistles, Ars Poetica*. Ed. & trans. H. Rushton Fairclough. London: Heinemann, 1970.
Hugo, Hermannus. *Pia Desideria Emblematis Elegiis et affectibus SS. Patrum illustrata*. Antwerp, 1624; rpt. Menston: Scolar Press, 1971.
Huizinga, Johan. *Herfsttij der Middeleeuwen.* In *Verzamelde Werken.* III. Haarlem: Tjeenk Willink, 1949.
Hutton, James. *The Greek Anthology in Italy to the year 1800*. Ithaca, N.Y.: Cornell Univ. Press, 1935.
James, Eleanor. "The Emblem as an Image-pattern in some metaphysical Poets." Diss. Univ. of Wisconsin 1942.
Jennings, Elizabeth. "The Seventeenth Century." In *Christianity and Poetry*. Faith and Fact Books, 122. London: Burns & Oates, 1965, pp. 48-63.
Johnson, Samuel. *Selected Poetry and Prose*. Eds. Frank Brady & W.K. Wimsatt. Berkeley: Univ. of California Press, 1977.
Jongh, Eddy de. "The Spur of Wit: Rembrandt's Response to an Italian Challenge." *Delta*, 12 (Summer, 1969), 49-67.
Joyce, James. *Ulysses*. London: Bodley Head, 1960.
Kaemmerling, Ekkehard, ed. *Ikonographie und Ikonologie*. Köln: Dumont, 1979.
Keeling, William, ed. *Liturgiae Britannicae: or the Several Editions of the Book of Common Prayer of the Church of England, from its Compilation to the last Revision*. London, 1842.
Kittel, Gerhard & Gerhard Friedrich. *Theologisches Wörterbuch zum Neuen Testament*. Vol. VII. Stuttgart: W. Kohlhammer Verlag, 1964.
Klingender, Francis. *Animals in art and thought: to the end of the Middle Ages*. London: Routledge & Kegan Paul, 1972.
Klonsky, Milton, ed. *Speaking Pictures: A Gallery of Pictorial Poetry from the Sixteenth Century to the Present*. New York: Harmony Books, 1975.
Knights, L.C. *Some Shakespearean Themes*. London: Chatto & Windus, 1959.
Korn, A.L. "Puttenham and the Oriental Pattern-Poem." *CL*, 6 (Fall, 1954), 289-303.
Kostelanetz, Richard, ed. *Visual Literature Criticism: A New Collection*. Carbondale: Southern Illinois Univ. Press, 1979.
Kristeller, Paul Oskar. *Renaissance Thought II: Papers on Humanism & the Arts*. New York: Harper & Row, 1965.
Kuhn, S.M., ed. *Middle English Dictionary*. Ann Arbor: Univ. of Michigan Press, 1952- .
Langland, William. *Piers Plowman: The B Version: Will's Visions of Piers Plowman, Do-Well, Do-Better and Do-Best*. Eds. George Kane & E. Talbot. London: Univ. of London, The Athlone Press, 1975.
Leavis, F.R. "The Responsible Critic: Or the Function of Criticism at any Time." *Scrutiny*, 19 (1953), 162-183.
Lee, Rensselaer W. *Ut Pictura Poesis: The Humanistic Theory of Painting*. New York: Norton, 1967.
Levin, Harry, ed. *The Essential James Joyce*. Harmondsworth: Penguin, 1963.
Lewis, C.S. *The Discarded Image*. Cambridge: Cambridge Univ. Press, 1964.
————. *English Literature in the Sixteenth Century*. Oxford: Oxford Univ. Press, 1954.

260

————. *Spenser's Images of Life*. Ed. A. Fowler. Cambridge: Cambridge Univ. Press, 1967.

Lewis, Charlton & Charles Short. *A Latin Dictionary*. Oxford: Oxford Univ. Press, 1879.

Licetus, Fortunius. *Ad Epei Securim* .... Bononiae, 1637.

————. *Ad Syringam* .... Utini, 1655.

Lydgate, John, trans. *The Pilgrimage of the Life of Man by Guillaume de Deguileville*. Vol. I. Ed. F.J. Furnivall. E.E.T.S. Extra Series, 77. London: Kegan Paul, 1899.

Mâle, Emile. *The Gothic Image: Religious Art in France of the Thirteenth Century*. Trans. Dora Nussey, from the 3rd French ed. 1913; rpt. New York: Harper, 1972.

Mannich, Johann. *Sacra Emblemata LXXVI in quibus summa uniuscuiusque Evangelii rotunda adumbratur*. Nürnberg, 1624.

Mannings, David. "Panofsky and the Interpretation of Images." *BJA*, 13 (1973), 146-162.

Martz, Louis L. *The Poetry of Meditation: A Study in English Religious Literature of the Seventeenth Century*. Rev. ed. New Haven: Yale Univ. Press, 1962.

Marvell, Andrew. *The Poems and Letters*. Ed. H.M. Margoliouth. Oxford: Oxford Univ. Press, 1971.

Maser, Edward A., ed. *Baroque and Rococo Pictorial Imagery: The 1758-60 Hertel edition of Ripa's 'Iconologia'*. New York: Dover, 1971.

Mason, H.A. *Humanism and Poetry in the Early Tudor Period*. London: Routledge & Kegan Paul, 1959.

Massin. *Letter and Image*. Trans. C. Hillier & V. Menkes. London: Studio Vista, 1970.

Maurus, Magnentius Hrabanus. *De Laudibus Sanctae Crucis*. Facs. ed. Graz: Akademischen Druck- u. Verlagsanstalt, 1972.

Mayor, A. Hyatt. *Prints & People: a social history of printed pictures*. Princeton, N.J.: Princeton Univ. Press, 1971.

McCloskey, M. & P.R. Murphy, eds. & trans. *The Latin Poetry of George Herbert: A Bilingual Edition*. Athens, Ohio: Ohio Univ. Press, 1965.

Milton, John. *The Poetical Works*. Ed. Helen Darbishire. 2 vols. Oxford: Oxford Univ. Press, 1952, 1955.

Miner, Earl, ed. *Illustrious Evidence: Approaches to English Literature of the Early Seventeenth Century*. Berkeley: Univ. of California Press, 1975.

Montenay, Georgette du. *Emblemes, ou Devises Chrestiennes*. Lyon, 1571.

Montgomery, Jr., Robert L. "The Province of Allegory in George Herbert's Verse." *Texas Studies in Literature and Language*, 1 (1960), 457-472.

Mooij, J.J.A. *Tekst en Lezer*. Amsterdam: Polak & van Gennep, 1979.

Morillo, Marvin. "Herbert's Chairs: Notes to *The Temple*." *ELN*, 11 (June, 1974), 271-275.

Mulder, John R. *The Temple of the Mind: Education and Literary Taste in Seventeenth-Century England*. New York: Pegasus, 1969.

Munro, Thomas. *The Arts and Their Interrelations*. New York: Liberal Arts Press, 1949; rev. ed. 1967.

Nicolson, Marjorie Hope. *Mountain Gloom and Mountain Glory*. Ithaca: Cornell Univ. Press, 1959.

O'Connor, Sister Mary Catherine. *The Art of Dying Well: The Development of the Ars Moriendi*. New York: Columbia Univ. Press, 1942.

Oley, Barnabas. "Life of Herbert." In *Herbert's Remains*. London, 1652.

Owst, G.R. *Literature and Pulpit in Medieval England*. 2nd ed. Oxford: Blackwell, 1961.

Panofsky, Erwin. *Hercules am Scheidewege und andere antike Bildstoffe in der neueren Kunst*. Studien der Bibliothek Warburg. Leipzig, 1930.

————. *Meaning in the Visual Arts.* New York, 1955; rpt. Harmondsworth: Penguin, 1970.

————. *Studies in Iconology.* Oxford, 1939; rpt. New York: Harper & Row, 1962.

Paton, W.R., ed. & trans. *The Greek Anthology.* The Loeb Classical Library. 5 vols. London: Heinemann, 1918.

Peacham, Henry. *Minerva Britanna.* London, 1612; facs. rpt. Menston: Scolar Press, 1966.

Pennel, Charles A. & William P. Williams. "The Unity of *The Temple.*" *Xavier Univ. Studies,* 5 (1966), 37-45.

Perrière, Guillaume de la. *La Morosophie.* Lyon, 1553.

Plato. *The Symposium.* Trans. W. Hamilton. Harmondsworth: Penguin, 1951.

————. *The Works.* Trans. Benjamin Jowett. Ed. Irwin Edman. New York: Random House, 1956.

Pope, Alexander. *The Poems.* Ed. John Butt. London: Methuen, 1965.

Porfirius, Publius Optatianus. *Carmina.* Ed. Elsa Kluge. Leipzig: B.G. Teubner, 1926.

Praz, Mario. *Mnemosyne: The Parallel between Literature and the Visual Arts.* Princeton: Princeton Univ. Press, 1970.

————. *Studies in Seventeenth-Century Imagery.* 2nd ed. Roma: Edizioni di Storia e Letteratura, 1964.

Puttenham, George. *The Arte of English Poesie.* Eds. G.D. Willcock & A. Walker. Cambridge: Cambridge Univ. Press, 1936.

Quarles, Francis. *The Complete Works in Prose and Verse.* Ed. Alexander B. Grosart. 3 vols. Edinburgh: Edinburgh Univ. Press, 1880.

————. *Emblemes.* London, 1635.

Réau, Louis. *Iconographie de l'Art Chrétien.* Vols. I & II, 1. Paris: Presses Universitaires de France, 1955, 1956.

Reynolds, E.E. *The Life and Death of St. Thomas More.* London: Burns & Oates, 1968.

Richter, Irma, introd. & trans. *Paragone, A Comparison of the Arts by Leonardo da Vinci.* London: Oxford Univ. Press, 1949.

Richter, Jean Paul, trans. & ed. *The Literary Works of Leonardo da Vinci.* 2nd ed. 2 vols. London: Oxford Univ. Press, 1939.

Rickey, Mary Ellen. *Utmost Art: Complexity in the Verse of George Herbert.* Lexington: Univ. of Kentucky Press, 1966.

Ripa, Cesare. *Iconologia: overo descrittione di diverse imagini cavate dall' antichità, e di propria inventione.* Roma, 1603; facs. ed., introd. E. Mandowsky. Hildesheim, N.Y.: Georg Olms, 1970.

————. *Iconologie.* Trans. Jean Baudouin. Paris, 1644; facs. ed., introd. Stephen Orgel. New York: Garland Publ., 1976.

Rivers, Isabel. *Classical and Christian Ideas in English Renaissance Poetry.* London: George Allen & Unwin, 1979.

Roberts, John R., ed. *Essential Articles for the Study of George Herbert's Poetry.* Hamden, Conn.: Archon Books, 1979.

————. *George Herbert: An Annotated Bibliography of Modern Criticism, 1905-1974.* Columbia: Univ. of Missouri Press, 1978.

Robin, P.A. *Animal Lore in English Literature.* London: John Murray, 1932.

Rochester, John Wilmot, Earl of. *The Complete Poems.* Ed. David M. Vieth. New Haven: Yale Univ. Press, 1968.

Rollenhagen, Gabriel. *Nucleus Emblematum Selectissimorum.* 2 vols. Arnhem, 1611-1613.

Seifertová, Hana. "Paupertate Premor, sublevor ingenio." *Umění,* 25 (1977), 224-41.

Sélincourt, E. de. "George Herbert." *The Hibbert Journal,* 39 (1940-41), 389-397.

262

Seznec, Jean. *The Survival of the Pagan Gods: The Mythological Tradition and its Place in Renaissance Humanism and Art*. Trans. B. Sessions. London, 1940; rpt. Princeton: Princeton Univ. Press, 1972.

Shakespeare, William. *Hamlet*. Ed. Harold Jenkins. London: Methuen, 1982.

————. *King Lear*. Ed. Kenneth Muir. 8th ed. London: Methuen, 1952.

————. *Macbeth*. Ed. Kenneth Muir. London: Methuen, 1964.

————. *Measure for Measure*. Ed. J.W. Lever. Rev. ed. London: Methuen, 1965.

————. *Richard II*. Ed. Peter Ure. 4th ed. London: Methuen, 1966.

————. *Romeo and Juliet*. Ed. B. Gibbons. London: Methuen, 1980.

————. *Timon of Athens*. Ed. H.J. Oliver. London: Methuen, 1959.

Sharp, Nicholas. "Herbert's 'Love (III)'." *Expl*, 33 (1974), it. 26.

Sidney, Sir Philip. *Miscellaneous Prose*. Eds. K. Duncan-Jones & J. van Dorsten. Oxford: Oxford Univ. Press, 1973.

————. *The Poems*. Ed. William A. Ringler, Jr. Oxford: Oxford Univ. Press, 1962.

Spencer, John R. "Ut rhetorica pictura." *JWCI*, 20 (1957), 26-44.

Spenser, Edmund. *The Faerie Queene*. Ed. J.C. Smith. 2 vols. Oxford: Oxford Univ. Press, 1909.

————. *Minor Poems*. Ed. E. de Sélincourt. Oxford: Oxford Univ. Press, 1910.

Spingarn, J.E., ed. *Critical Essays of the Seventeenth Century*. 3 vols. Oxford: Oxford Univ. Press, 1908.

Stambler, Elizabeth. "The Unity of Herbert's 'Temple'." *Cross Currents*, 10 (1960), 251-266.

Stanford, W. Bedell. *Greek Metaphor: Studies in Theory and Practice*. Oxford: Blackwell, 1936.

Stein, Arnold. *George Herbert's Lyrics*. Baltimore: Johns Hopkins Univ. Press, 1968.

Stengel, Georg. *Ova Paschalia*. Ingolstadium, 1678.

Stephanus, Henricus (= Henry Estienne), ed. *Theocriti Aliorumque Poetarum Idyllia ... Simmiae Rhodii Ovum, Alae, Securis, Fistula, Dosiadis Ara*. N.p., 1579.

Stroup, Thomas B. "'A Reasonable, Holy, and Living Sacrifice': Herbert's 'The Altar'." In *Essays in Literature*, 2 (1975), 149-163.

Sullivan, John Edward. *The Image of God: The Doctrine of St. Augustine and its Influence*. Dubuque, Iowa: The Priory Press, 1963.

Summers, Joseph H. *George Herbert: His Religion and Art*. London: Chatto & Windus, 1954.

Sylvester, Joshua, trans. *Bartas: His Devine Weekes and Works*. 1605; facs. rpt. Delmar, N.Y.: Scholars' Facsimiles & Reprints, 1965.

Taylor, Mark. *The Soul in Paraphrase: George Herbert's Poetics*. The Hague: Mouton, 1974.

Teyssèdre, Bernard. "Iconologie: réflexion sur un concept d'Erwin Panofsky." *Revue philosophiques de la France et de l'étranger*, 89 (1964), 321-340.

Thompson, W. Meredith. *Der Tod in der Englischen Lyrik des Siebzehnten Jahrhunderts*. Breslau: Priebatsch, 1936.

Thorpe, James. "Herbert's 'Love (III)'." *Expl*, 24 (1965), it. 16.

Tillyard, E.M.W. *The Elizabethan World Picture*. 1943; rpt. Harmondsworth: Penguin, 1963.

Treglown, Jeremy. "The Satirical Inversions of Some English Sources in Rochester." *RES*, 24 (1973), 42-48.

Tuve, Rosemond. *Allegorical Imagery: Some medieval books and their posterity*. Princeton: Princeton Univ. Press, 1966.

————. *Elizabethan and Metaphysical Imagery*. Chicago: Univ. of Chicago Press, 1947.

263

————. *Essays.* Ed. Thomas P. Roche, Jr. Princeton: Princeton Univ. Press, 1970.

————. *A Reading of George Herbert.* Chicago: Univ. of Chicago Press, 1952.

Typus Mundi. Antwerp, 1627.

Vaenius, Otho. *Amoris Divini Emblemata.* Antwerp, 1615.

————. *Amorum Emblemata.* Antwerp, 1608.

Valeriano, Giovanni Pierio. *Hieroglyphica.* Köln, 1631.

————. *Hieroglyphicorum Collectanea, ex Veteribus et Neotericis Descripta.* Lugduni, 1626.

————. *Hieroglyphicorum Collectanea, ex Veteribus et Neotericis Descripta.* Köln, 1631.

Vaughan, Henry. *The Works.* Ed. L.C. Martin. 2nd ed. Oxford: Oxford Univ. Press, 1957.

Vendler, Helen. *The Poetry of George Herbert.* Cambridge, Mass.: Harvard Univ. Press, 1975.

Volkmann, Ludwig. "Bild und Schrift." *Buch und Schrift,* 4 (1930), 9-18.

Walker, John David. "The Architectonics of George Herbert's *The Temple.*" *ELH,* 29 (1962), 289-306.

Walsh, William S. *Handy-Book of Literary Curiosities.* London, 1894.

Walton, Izaak. *The Lives of John Donne, Sir Henry Wotton, Richard Hooker, George Herbert and Robert Sanderson.* Introd. George Saintsbury. London: Oxford Univ. Press, 1927.

Warners, J.D.P. "Translatio - Imitatio - Aemulatio." *De Nieuwe Taalgids,* 49 (1956), 289-95; 50 (1957), 82-88, 193-201.

Warren, Austin. *Rage for Order: Essays in Criticism.* Chicago: Univ. of Chicago Press, 1948.

Weigle, Luther A., ed. *The New Testament Octapla: Eight English Versions of the New Testament in the Tyndale - King James Tradition.* New York: Thomas Nelson & Sons, n.d.

Wellek, René & Austin Warren. *Theory of Literature.* 3rd ed. Harmondsworth: Penguin, 1963.

Wells, Carolyn. *A Whimsey Anthology.* New York: Scribner, 1906.

White, Beatrice. "Medieval Animal Lore." *Anglia,* 72 (1954), 21-30.

Whitney, Geoffrey. *A Choice of Emblemes.* Ed. and introd. Henry Green. London, 1866; rpt. New York: Benjamin Blom, 1967.

Willey, Basil. *Seventeenth Century Background.* London: Chatto & Windus, 1934.

Williams, Emmett, ed. *An Anthology of Concrete Poetry.* New York: Something Else Press, 1967.

Willis, Richard. *Poematum Liber.* London, 1573.

Wimsatt, William K. & Cleanth Brooks. *Literary Criticism: A Short History.* New York: Alfred A. Knopf, 1957.

Wind, Edgar. *Pagan Mysteries in the Renaissance.* Rev. ed. Harmondsworth: Penguin, 1967.

Wither, George. *A Collection of Emblemes: Ancient and Moderne.* London, 1635. Facs. rpt. Ed. John Horden. Menston: Scolar Press, 1968.

Wittkower, Rudolf & Margot Wittkower. *Born under Saturn.* New York: Norton, 1969.

Zesmer, David M. *Guide to English Literature.* New York: Barnes & Noble, 1961.

Zingarelli, Nicola. *Vocabulario della lingua italiana.* 10th ed. Bologna: Zanichelli, 1970.

INDEX

Figures in italics refer to the illustrations.

267

SAMENVATTING

Zoals de titel al aangeeft, staan vier gedichten van de 17e eeuwse Engelse dichter George Herbert in dit boek centraal. Deze gedichten, "The Altar," "Easter-wings," "The Pilgrimage," en "Love(III)" worden bestudeerd vanuit een besef dat een lezer van nu, die poëzie uit een tamelijk ver verleden leest en die tot zo valide mogelijke interpretaties van die poëzie wil komen, een aantal vragen zal hebben die hij met behulp van zijn 20e eeuwse intellectuele en emotionele bagage alléén niet zo maar kan beantwoorden. Hij zal in zekere mate zijn verwachtingen en vooroordelen moeten aanpassen en trachten zich een beeld te vormen van de wereld van conventies en traditles die de achtergrond vormen van de te interpreteren teksten. Zo wordt interpretatie, in Gombrich's woorden (1972), "reconstruction of a lost piece of evidence."

Herbert is, naar algemeen wordt erkend, een van de belangrijkste dichters van religieuze Engelse lyriek vóór G.M. Hopkins en T.S. Eliot voor wie hij als voorbeeld heeft gediend. Er is dan ook wel het een en ander over Herbert geschreven in de decennia na de verschijning van Eliot's geruchtmakende essay over de 'metaphysical poets' van 1921. Grofweg ingedeeld zijn er enerzijds studies geschreven die zich vooral richten op literair-historische aspecten zoals Hutchinson's standaard-editie van Herbert's werk (1941), Freeman's studie over de invloed van embleemboeken (1948), Tuve (1952) over vooral liturgische en kerk-historische achtergronden, Summers (1954) die de nadruk legt op biografie, religie en formele aspecten, en Martz (1962) die de meditatieve kant van Herbert's werk beschouwt. Anderzijds zijn er studies verschenen die een grotere nadruk leggen op de analyse van de gedichten zelf en de rol die de lezer daarbij speelt. Fish (1972) en Vendler (1975) zijn voorbeelden van deze benadering.

Men kan zich afvragen waarom er naast de talrijke publicaties die in het recente verleden over Herbert zijn verschenen zo nodig nog een boek bij moet. Er zijn tweeërlei redenen die de voorliggende studie rechtvaardigen, respectievelijk methodologisch en inhoudelijk van aard.

Ten eerste poogt dit boek een brug te slaan tussen beide, zojuist genoemde benaderingswijzen met behulp van wat het best met 'applied scholarship' kan worden aangeduid. Bij deze aanpak is de literaire tekst steeds vertrekpunt én eindstation van het onderzoek, terwijl onderweg verschillende aspecten van de tekst in hun cultuurhistorische context

270

worden geplaatst. De achtergrond wordt dus voortdurend op relevantie getoetst aan de hand van de tekst zelf. Met de gehanteerde aanpak van 'applied scholarship' heb ik gestreefd naar een verantwoorde tussenweg tussen impressionistische literatuurkritiek en bronnenonderzoek als een doel op zich. Een zekere subjectiviteit valt bij het selecteren en wegen van het materiaal niet uit te sluiten, maar wordt wel beperkt door literair-historische constricties zoals regels van genre, decorum en de retorica en door religieuze gegevenheden als bijbel-exegese en de liturgie van de Anglicaanse kerk die voor Herbert als priester/dichter natuurlijk van bijzondere betekenis waren. Bovendien zijn de conclusies van het onderzoek controleerbaar doordat een zo groot mogelijke explicietheid met betrekking tot de gebruikte gegevens is betracht.

De gevolgde werkwijze maakt het mogelijk om bij de interpretatie van de gedichten te onderscheiden in hoeverre Herbert zich conformeerde aan geldende regels, retorische, liturgische e.a., en in welke mate hij de conventies en tradities transformeerde tot iets eigens.

Een tweede reden die dit onderzoek nuttig en nodig maakt, is dat er nog steeds leemtes bestaan in onze kennis van en inzicht in bepaalde aspecten van Herbert's poëzie die de interpretatie er van bemoeilijken. In de volgende alinea's wordt ingegaan op een aantal van deze aspecten.

Wat als een rode draad door het boek loopt, is de rol van de emblematiek in Herbert's poëzie. 'Emblematiek' heeft hier twee betekenissen. Enerzijds verwijst het naar een bepaalde manier van denken en uitdrukken die wel 'hieroglyfisch' is genoemd (Summers, 1954), anderzijds naar de embleemboeken die tot ver in de zeventiende eeuw in heel Europa zo'n enorme populariteit genoten. In beide betekenissen neemt de emblematiek een belangrijke plaats in in Herbert's werk. Vooral de religieuze embleemboeken van het Amor/Anima en Schola Cordis type zijn hierbij belangrijke hulpbronnen. Dit is wel geconstateerd (zie bijv. Freeman, 1948), maar nooit echt uitgewerkt.

De vier bestudeerde gedichten zijn niet alleen gekozen vanwege hun emblematisch karakter. Herbert's *Temple* is een inhoudelijk en structureel samenhangend geheel en de gekozen gedichten hebben daarin zowel inhoudelijk als structureel een significante plaats. *The Temple* bestaat uit drie delen: "The Church-porch," een tamelijk lang, moraliserend gedicht, *The Church,* dat de collectie voornamelijk lyrische gedichten omvat, en "The Church Militant," waarin de missie van de kerk in de wereld wordt beschreven. "The Altar" is het eerste gedicht van *The Church* en vormt het begin van een serie gedichten over de goede week die met "Easter-wings" wordt afgesloten. Beide gedichten verwijzen naar belangrijke liturgische momenten in het leven van de Christen. "The Pilgrimage" is een allegorie over de pelgrimstocht van het leven. "Love(III)" is het laatste gedicht van *The Church* en sluit zowel de liturgische als de

271

allegorische lijn die door *The Temple* loopt, af. Het behandelt de ontvangst van de menselijke ziel in de hemel, aan het eind van zijn pelgrimstocht. Daar wacht hem een laatste avondmaal dat de vereniging van de ziel met God's liefde betekent. "The Altar" en "Easter-wings" zijn figuur-gedichten. Herbert's gebruik van dit genre gaat terug naar de *Griekse Anthologie*, waarvan in zijn tijd verschillende edities in omloop waren. Dat Herbert's figuur-gedichten hun oorsprong vinden in deze klassieke voorbeelden is eerder opgemerkt, o.m. door Church (1944) en Rickey (1966), maar de precieze aard van deze relatie is nauwelijks beschreven. Waarom maakte een serieus, religieus dichter als Herbert gebruik van dit ogenschijnlijk zo gekunstelde en beperkte medium? Op deze vraag kunnen verschillende antwoorden gegeven worden. Christelijke *aemulatio* speelt een rol: Herbert wil door een dichtvorm te kiezen die door zijn lezers onmiddellijk herkend zou worden als klassiek van oorsprong, de superioriteit beklemtonen van de Christelijke God boven de Griekse goden die in de figuurgedichten van de *Griekse Anthologie* bezongen worden. Een ander antwoord is te vinden in de speciale plaats die visuele aspecten in verbale kunst in Herbert's tijd innamen. De vergelijking tussen verbale en beeldende kunst kwam niet alleen tot uiting in het Horatiaanse adagium *ut pictura poesis* maar vond ook in de kunst en de literatuur velerlei toepassingen. Samen met de hieroglyfische kijk op het universum en de emblematiek verklaart *ut pictura poesis* het nauwe verband tussen poëzie en beeldende kunst in Herbert's tijd en de visuele kant van Herbert's werk.

Ook in de retoriek zijn elementen aanwezig die de relatie tussen de 'sister arts' beklemtonen. Met name de Aristotelische notie *opsis* als één van de zes hoofdelementen van de poëzie zou wel eens een meer specifiek visuele betekenis kunnen hebben dan meestal wordt aangenomen (Stanford, 1936). In Engeland nam Puttenham in de *Arte of English Poesie* (1589) figuur-gedichten op in zijn retorische systeem als voorbeelden van 'ocular proportion.'

Ten slotte is er een morele rechtvaardiging te vinden voor deze gemakkelijk aansprekende vormen in het zeker ook bij Herbert aanwezige besef dat de poëzie diende tot lering en vermaak — *utile dulce*.

"The Pilgrimage" is een allegorie, eigenlijk een miniatuur 'Pilgrim's Progress.' Wat onmiddellijk opvalt, is de 'kale' wijze waarop Herbert de traditionele allegorische elementen introduceert en schijnbaar gehaast afhandelt. Naar mijn idee reflecteert dit niet een onvermogen van de dichter om zijn gedachten vorm te geven, maar is het een bewust gekozen retorische strategie. Andere vragen over "The Pilgrimage" waarop tot nog toe geen bevredigend antwoord werd gegeven, betreffen de rol van de "good Angell," een muntje dat de pelgrim als een soort obool bij zich draagt tot het eind van zijn reis, de geheimzinnige stem die hem na de beklimming van een berg waarschuwt dat hij alleen op straffe van de dood z'n reis kan voortzetten en de "chair" die aan het eind van het gedicht als metafoor van de dood wordt genoemd. Een belangrijke vraag die ook aan de orde komt, is wat de functie is van het optische bedrog dat teweeg wordt gebracht door het feit dat de eerste heuvel die de pelgrim beklimt de tweede maskeert en daardoor aanvankelijk het enige obstakel lijkt dat door hem overwonnen moet worden.

Het laatste gedicht dat besproken wordt, is "Love(III)." Hoewel dit een van de meest geanthologiseerde en besproken gedichten van Herbert is, heeft één opvallend aspect nauwelijks de aandacht gekregen die het verdient: de rol van de zintuigen en vooral die van het oog, dat in een reeks beelden genoemd wordt. Maar ook wordt ingegaan op Herbert's gebruik van het woord "meat" aan het eind van het gedicht dat in plaats van het wellicht verwachte woord 'flesh' gebruikt wordt om het commu- nie-brood aan te duiden. In verband met de zintuigelijke beelden in het gedicht komt de relatie tussen de spreker en zijn hemelse gastheer, de goddelijke liefde, ter sprake. Fish (1978) suggereert dat de catechismus een verklaring kan geven voor de aard van deze relatie. Hier wordt betoogd dat de bron van Herbert's gedicht eerder in de liturgie te vinden is, met name in de Anglicaanse communie-dienst zoals die beschreven wordt in het *Book of Common Prayer*. De omgang van de twee protago- nisten in het gedicht lijkt ook meer op die van Amor Divinus en Anima in de religieuze embleemboeken waarin Amor en Anima op een gelijk niveau worden gepresenteerd dan op die tussen catecheet en catechisant.

Het onderzoek beoogt een beter begrip van de gedichten die er het middelpunt van vormen, maar wil daarnaast ook licht werpen op Herbert's dichtkunst als zodanig. De wijze waarop Herbert gebruik heeft gemaakt van het hele repertoire aan teksten en beelden die een *poeta ductus* nu eenmaal ter beschikking stond, is hier beschreven aan de hand van vier gedichten. Omdat deze gedichten op verschillende manieren representatief zijn voor het hele oeuvre, kunnen de resultaten echter ook in wijder verband relevant genoemd worden. Ten slotte is de gehanteerde werkwijze van 'applied scholarship' eveneens bruikbaar voor andere onderzoeksdoelen dan die van de onderhavige studie.

Herbert is een fascinerend dichter. Zijn gedichten zijn van een verra- derlijke eenvoud. De woordkeus is simpel, de boodschap helder. Maar wat C.S. Lewis in ander verband opmerkte, is ook van toepassing op het merendeel van Herbert's gedichten: "... we turn to the helps only when the hard passages are manifestly hard. But there are treacherous passages which will not send us to the notes. They look easy and aren't" (1964). Herbert's poëzie is makkelijk te lezen, maar lang niet altijd makkelijk te begrijpen. De eenvoud die zijn taalgebruik kenmerkt, is het resultaat

van zijn vermogen om bronnen, tradities en conventies te concentreren en
te transformeren in poëzie die heel persoonlijk en toch toegankelijk is,
eenvoudig en rijk tegelijk. Dat eenvoud niet hetzelfde is als simplisme
wordt in dit proefschrift betoogd en bewezen door Herbert's poëzie.

CURRICULUM VITAE

B. Westerweel werd op 10 december 1942 te Rotterdam geboren. Hij volgde de middelbare school aan het Haags Montessori Lyceum waar hij in 1960 eindexamen Gymnasium Alpha deed. In 1960-61 studeerde hij aan de Southern Methodist University te Dallas, Texas. Van 1961 tot 1967 volgde de studie Engelse Taal- en Letterkunde aan de Universiteit van Amsterdam. Het kandidaatsexamen werd in 1964 afgelegd, het doctoraalexamen (*cum laude*) in 1967. Van 1967-1970 was hij leraar aan de Gemeentelijke School voor Havo te Amsterdam. In 1970 werd hij tot wetenschappelijk medewerker benoemd aan het Instituut voor Engelse Taal- en Letterkunde van de Rijksuniversiteit te Utrecht, waaraan hij sedert 1978 als wetenschappelijk hoofdmedewerker verbonden is.